Irene Hanson Frieze
Daniel Bar-Tal
John S. Carroll
Editors

Foreword by June Louin Tapp

New Approaches
to Social Problems

Jossey-Bass Publishers
San Francisco • Washington • London • 1979

NEW APPROACHES TO SOCIAL PROBLEMS
Applications of Attribution Theory
      by Irene Hanson Frieze, Daniel Bar-Tal, and John S. Carroll, Editors

Copyright © 1979 by: Jossey-Bass Inc., Publishers
                433 California Street
                San Francisco, California 94104
                &*
                Jossey-Bass Limited
                28 Banner Street
                London EC1Y 8QE

Library of Congress Cataloging in Publication Data

Main entry under title:

New approaches to social problems.
   (The Jossey-Bass social and behavioral science series)
   "A publication sponsored by the Society for the Psychological Study of Social Issues."
   Bibliography: p.
   Includes index.
   1. Attribution (Social psychology)—Addresses, essays, lectures. 2. Social problems—Addresses, essays, lectures. I. Frieze, Irene H. II. Bar-Tal, Daniel. III. Carroll, John S., 1948– IV. Society for the Psychological Study of Social Issues.
HM291.N45   362'.042   79-88767
ISBN 0-87589-430-5

Manufactured in the United States of America

JACKET DESIGN BY WILLI BAUM

FIRST EDITION

Code 7932

The Jossey-Bass Social and
Behavioral Science Series

*A publication sponsored by the
Society for the Psychological Study
of Social Issues*

Foreword

The Society for the Psychological Study of Social Issues (SPSSI) has had a long-term dedication to ensuring that social psychological theory and research become resources for defining social issues and resolving social problems. This volume on the applicability of attribution theory to the social arena attests to SPSSI's continued desire to demonstrate Lewin's compelling dictum that there is nothing so practical as a good theory. Sponsorship of this book further highlights another SPSSI guideline—asserted most recently by Cartwright that for Lewin there was nothing so theoretical as a good practical problem. SPSSI has also been governed by a hearty recognition that the concerns of the theorist and researcher, practitioner, and everyday citizen are interwoven. By virtue of such dimensions in its mission, SPSSI is simultaneously committed to abstract theory building and concrete problem solving. This book has such a double mission.

Since the 1950s, attribution theory has gained popularity as one of several mini-theories in social psychology (Heider, 1958; Jones and Davis, 1965; Kelley, 1967; Kelley and Michela, in press; Kiesler and Munson, 1975; Weiner, 1974a). Despite its popularity as a model of inquiry, there have been few books and fewer applications of the theory to an analysis of social and individual problems. Attribution theorists, regardless of predilection, probe how ordinary people with naive perceptions understand and explain the causes of a social event. As theorists, they basically are concerned with the process of seeing and causally connecting the characteristics of persons and/or objects to the process of events. Attributionists have been less concerned with translating their theory for purposes of easing social problems or developing tactics to reduce social ills. These authors tackle the necessary task of linking theory to research to usage.

The effort of these authors is an especially apt exercise. Cognizant that the applications suggested are based more on recommendation than on implementation of a program based on attribution theory intended to affect a social problem, the authors put forward criteria for assessing the applicability of attribution theory. Within the context of theory, the authors then describe possible applications to various concerns—alcoholism, battered women, depression, drug use, crime prevention, consumerism, victimization, and vocational training. These problem areas—dealing with everyday life, health, crime, and education—accentuate the social issues of the 1970s. Interestingly, these instances reflect the state of the art as well as the state of the nation.

While many will continue to question the viability of the attribution model for both theoretical and practical reasons, the editors and the authors of this volume have provided both science and society with valuable ways of assessing the amelioration of some real world problems. Their explanations yield new directions for theory and practice—for both the why and how.

In reviewing SPSSI's past and present efforts to use theory and research, to introduce reforms, make policy, remedy social problems, and relieve individual dysfunction, I am again struck by the implicit danger and apparent price of the technological advance over theory. This preference appears not merely in the halls of science (psychology) or the groves of academe, but in the streets of society and the corridors of government. The fear that techniques may overwhelm theories of science and/or theories of human values is not new. What *is* new is that our students and citizens are now technically elegant and statistically sophisticated. What is also new is that both groups may simultaneously lack the ability and interest to construct a considered or grand theory for society or science. For example, students can do a regression analysis on the effects of poverty or of crowding on personality or aggression, but they are unclear about or disinterested in the broader meaning or theoretical fit of that analysis to human behavior.

Is the academic and scientific psychological community a microcosm of the larger society wherein technology has outstripped science? If so, the apparent technological advance over theory mirrors a society where science and theory are second to technological development and technical proficiency and where the love and acquisition of knowledge are being replaced by a love and acquisition of procedural gimmickry. The condition requires renewed attention and rekindled loyalty to Lewin's formula for resolving social conflicts: the coincidence and necessity of good theory to good practice. The editors of this book undertake such an effort in the best tradition of both Lewin and SPSSI.

For all these reasons, as president of SPSSI, I am pleased to welcome this volume into the collection of SPSSI-sponsored books. It is timely; it is theory-based; it is technique-oriented. In the shadow of 1984, this offering reminds us that causal attributions are valuable mediators of a variety of important social problems.

August 1979

JUNE LOUIN TAPP
President, 1978–1979
Society for the Psychological
Study of Social Issues
Professor of child psychology
and criminal justice, adjunct
professor of law, University
of Minnesota

Preface

XXXXXXXXXXXXXXXXXXXXXXXXXXXX

New Approaches to Social Problems is designed to provide social psychologists, as well as scientists and practitioners of other disciplines, with a view of how attribution theory can be applied to the analysis of social problems in different areas of society. As the editors, we have tried to bring together a set of original chapters that present the current thinking about possible applications of this branch of social psychology to important social problems. Because attribution theory has become one of the central areas of social psychology, it is important to show how the theories and empirical findings of attribution research can be applied to various real world settings. Many of us in the field believe that social psychology has become an insulated discipline, cloistered in an ivory tower, and separated from social problems that affect people's daily lives. Recently there has been a growing demand to realize Kurt Lewin's conception of combining theory and practice: to develop a social psychology that can help us to understand and perhaps even solve some of the social problems facing society. Attribution theory, concerned with people's thought processes and with how they view the causes of various events, may well be a particularly relevant type of applied research for social psychology. The chapters in this book further support this notion.

The idea behind this volume originated from the symposium, "Applying Attribution Theory to Social Problems," which we organized at the 1975 American Psychological Association convention in Chicago. The symposium group provided the core group of contributors. Later, others were asked to contribute as we heard about their work. However, the distribution of chapters across various applied areas is more reflective of the field than of a selection strategy on our part to represent specific areas.

Along with an introductory chapter and a concluding chapter, the book consists of four parts. The introduction briefly outlines attribution theory with specific reference to the components of attribution theory upon which the various chapters in the book are based. Part One deals with attributions made by people in their everyday lives as they encounter victims of various sorts, deal with loneliness, experience family violence, or find products that fail to work. Chapter Two by Dan Coates, Camille B. Wortman, and Antonia Abbey describes a theoretical framework for how people react to victims of various tragedies and how victims themselves react. Then Letitia Anne Peplau, Dan Russell, and Margaret Heim analyze reactions of the lonely, using a modified Weiner framework (Weiner and others, 1972). Irene Hanson Frieze looks at another type of victim, the battered woman, whose attributions about why she is battered mediate her reactions. Finally, Valerie A. Valle and Eric J. Johnson turn to a different aspect of daily living—being a consumer with a product that does not perform as expected. Once again, a modified Weiner framework is used to predict the reactions of consumers to products with which they are dissatisfied.

Part Two deals with applications of attribution theory to health issues. In Chapter Six, Louis A. Morris and David E. Kanouse discuss drug taking for various physical symptoms.

Three subsequent chapters deal with mental health concerns: Michael D. Storms, Douglas R. Denney, Kevin D. McCaul, and Carol A. Lowery analyze insomnia; Maureen McHugh, Linda Beckman, and Irene Hanson Frieze look at alcoholism; and Lynn P. Rehm and Michael W. O'Hara discuss various attributional models of depression.

Criminal justice is the focus of Part Three. Louise H. Kidder and Ellen S. Cohn look at the general public's perceptions of the causes of crime to see how crime prevention efforts are influenced by causal attributions. They also draw heavily on Weiner's and Bulman and Wortman's (1977) attribution models; while doing so, they develop their own dimensional model to analyze reactions to crime. Daniel McGillis' chapter analyzes jury decisions, using an attributional framework derived originally from Jones and Davis (1965) and more recently from Jones and McGillis (1976) to study the role of stereotypes in jury decisions. In Chapter Twelve, John S. Carroll discusses another major step in the administration of justice, the parole decision. He uses a Weiner attribution framework to analyze the consequences of various causal judgments made about parole applicants by parole board members.

Part Four is concerned with educational issues. Mark R. Lepper and Janet L. Dafoe look at the question of intrinsic motivation from an attributional perspective. Daniel Bar-Tal uses even more explicit attributional language, based on a Weiner framework, to analyze teacher and student behaviors in the classroom. Finally, a similar perspective is used by Marc W. Gold and Kathryn M. Ryan to aid in our understanding and treatment of the mentally retarded.

The final chapter of the book assesses the contributions of the various chapters to the study of social problems.

We would like to thank Philip Brickman and Jeffrey Rubin for their help with this book as chairs of the Society for the Psychological Study of Social Issues (SPSSI) publication committee and all the SPSSI reviewers whose comments were so helpful: Daphne Bugental, Dan Coates, Christine Dunkel-Schetter, George Goethals, Jacqueline Goodchilds, Anna Kun, Martha Mednick, Stuart Oskamp, Clive Seligman, Mark Snyder, and Thomas Tyler. John Levine also gave helpful suggestions on the introductory chapter. Tina Strafalace has been of invaluable assistance in typing memos and manuscripts as well as helping compile the references. We thank the contributors for providing excellent chapters that should stimulate further research in the direction of applying social psychology to social problems.

September 1979   IRENE HANSON FRIEZE
                                              Pittsburgh, Pennsylvania

                                                   DANIEL BAR-TAL
                                                   Tel Aviv, Israel

                                                   JOHN S. CARROLL
                                                   Chicago, Illinois

Contents

Part Four: Education and Training

Contributors

IRENE HANSON FRIEZE is associate professor of psychology and women's studies at the University of Pittsburgh, where she has taught since 1972, and research associate at the university's Learning Research and Development Center. Frieze received her B.A. degree (1967) in psychology-mathematics and her M.A. degree (1968) and her Ph.D. degree (1973) in personality psychology, all from the University of California, Los Angeles.

She is a member of the American Psychological Association and has been elected to Fellow status in division 35 (Psychology of Women) and has served on the council for division 9 (Society for the Psychological Study of Social Issues). Frieze has participated on the editorial board of the *Applied Social Psychology Annual* and has acted as a consulting editor for the *Journal of Personality and Social Psychology, Psychology of Women Quarterly,* and *Sex Roles.* She is coauthor of *Women and Sex Roles: A Social Psychological Perspective* (with J. Parsons, P. Johnson, D. Ruble, and G. Zellman, 1978) and co-editor of a special issue of the *Journal of Social Issues,* "Sex Roles: Persistence and Change" (with D. Ruble and J. Parsons, 1976). She has also published numerous theoretical and applied articles dealing with attributions of success and failure.

DANIEL BAR-TAL is senior lecturer at the School of Education and Department of Psychology at Tel-Aviv University, where he has taught since 1975. Bar-Tal was awarded the B.A. degree (1970) in psychology and sociology from Tel-Aviv University and the M.S. (1973) and Ph.D. (1975) degrees in social psychology from the University of Pittsburgh. During 1974–75 he was a post-doctoral fellow and research associate at the Learning Research and Development Center of the University of Pittsburgh.

At present, Bar-Tal is an editor of the *Israel Journal of Counseling and Psychology in Education.* He is the author of *Prosocial Behavior: Theory and Research* (1976) and co-editor of *Social Psychology of Education: Theory and Research* (with L. Saxe, 1978). Bar-Tal is now engaged mainly in two directions of research, studying the development of helping behavior and investigating the principles of teacher-pupils classroom interaction.

JOHN S. CARROLL is associate professor of psychology at Loyola University, Chicago, where he is a member of the Applied Social Psychology Program. Previously, he was assistant professor of psychology at Carnegie-Mellon University (1973–78). He received his B.S. degree in physics from the Massachusetts Institute of Technology and was awarded the M.A. (1972) and Ph.D. (1973) degrees in social Psychology from Harvard University.

Carroll is co-editor of *Cognition and Social Behavior* (with J. W. Payne, 1976). The National Science Foundation and the National Institute of Mental Health have funded his research on the parole decision process. Carroll's research reports have appeared in the *Journal of Personality and Social Psychology, Journal of Applied Psychology,* and *Law and Human Behavior,* and in several edited collections. Other published research has focused upon his multidisciplinary interests in social psychology, cognitive psychology, and criminal justice, including the use of base-rate information in predictions, the effect of imagining an event upon expectations, and how people choose whether to commit crimes.

ANTONIA ABBEY is a doctoral candidate in the Department of Psychology, Northwestern University.

LINDA BECKMAN is adjunct associate professor in the Department of Psychiatry, University of California, Los Angeles.

DAN COATES is assistant professor of psychology in the Department of Psychology, University of Wisconsin, Madison.

ELLEN S. COHN is assistant professor of psychology in the Department of Psychology, University of New Hampshire.

JANET L. DAFOE is a doctoral candidate in the Department of Psychology, Stanford University.

DOUGLAS R. DENNEY is associate professor of psychology in the Department of Psychology, University of Kansas.

MARC W. GOLD is president of Marc Gold & Associates, Urbana, Illinois.

MARGARET HEIM is a doctoral candidate in the Department of Psychology, University of California, Los Angeles.

ERIC J. JOHNSON is a doctoral candidate in the Department of Psychology, Carnegie-Mellon University.

DAVID E. KANOUSE is associate social scientist in the Rand Corporation.

LOUISE H. KIDDER is associate professor of psychology in the Department of Psychology, Temple University.

MARK R. LEPPER is associate professor of psychology in the Department of Psychology, Stanford University.

CAROLE A. LOWERY is assistant professor of psychology in the Department of Psychology, University of Kentucky.

KEVIN D. MCCAUL is assistant professor of psychology, Department of Psychology, North Dakota State University.

DANIEL MCGILLIS is a research fellow in the Center for Criminal Justice, Harvard Law School.

MAUREEN MCHUGH is a doctoral candidate in the Department of Psychology, University of Pittsburgh.

LOUIS A. MORRIS is a psychologist in the Food and Drug Administration, Department of Health, Education, and Welfare, Rockville, Maryland.

MICHAEL W. O'HARA is a doctoral candidate in the Department of Psychology, University of Pittsburgh.

LETITIA ANNE PEPLAU is associate professor of psychology in the Department of Psychology, University of California, Los Angeles.

LYNN P. REHM is professor of psychology in the Department of Psychology, University of Houston.

DAN RUSSELL is a doctoral candidate in the Department of Psychology, University of California, Los Angeles.

KATHRYN M. RYAN is a doctoral candidate in the Department of Psychology, University of Pittsburgh.

MICHAEL D. STORMS is associate professor of psychology in the Department of Psychology, University of Kansas.

VALERIE A. VALLE is assistant professor of business administration in the Graduate School of Business, University of Pittsburgh.

CAMILLE B. WORTMAN is associate professor of psychology in the Research Center for Group Dynamics, Institute for Social Research, University of Michigan.

New Approaches to Social Problems

Applications of Attribution Theory

Chapter 1   *Irene Hanson Frieze*

Daniel Bar-Tal

Attribution Theory: Past and Present

In recent years, the study of causal attributions has become one of the most active and expanding areas of social psychology. Not only has a great deal of attention been given to the development of the formal theory of causal attributions, but increasing emphasis has been placed on applying these theoretical ideas in a variety of areas. As the chapters in this book demonstrate, the application of attribution theory to a number of important social problems has enabled us to understand these problems better and to develop more effective programs for alleviating these problems.

     This chapter will attempt to review some of the theoretical work done in attribution theory, so that the reader will have a better background for the following chapters. However, at present, it is difficult to describe one unified and coherent attribution theory, in the same way we describe the balance theory of Heider or the social comparison theory of Festinger. There are numerous theories, models, frameworks, and hypotheses, differing in their content but unified by their objective of understanding how people determine the causes of events. Because attribution theory has become so comprehensive and complex, we will not attempt to discuss all the attribution models. Rather, our focus will be on the basic theoretical concepts used by most researchers and on the specific approaches to attribution theory reflected in the chapters of this book. For more complete reviews of work in attribution theory, see Harvey, Ickes, and Kidd (1976, 1978), Jones and others (1972), or Shaver (1975).

The attribution theorist is concerned with understanding naive perceptions of the causes of an event. Attribution theory assumes that, by understanding naive or common-sense ideas about why people do the things they do, one can better predict the behavior and emotional reactions of people. Understanding why things happen also aids us in predicting and controlling our environments. Social psychologists have typically conceptualized the attribution process as one in which a naive individual first observes an event and then, on the basis of available information and various background or motivational factors, forms a cognition or attribution about why this event occurred. The event can be an individual's behavior in a social setting or his behavior toward an object. It can also be an outcome, such as success or failure on some task or positive or negative outcomes of some other life-event. Whatever the event, it is assumed that the causal attribution made about the cause of that event will affect the reactions of the individual to that event. Causal attributions have been shown to mediate various emotional reactions, attitudes, and behaviors toward other people as well as toward one's own future behaviors and emotional reactions.

The contributors to attribution theory have focused on three major issues: (1) What are the antecedents of an attribution? (2) What are the contents of the attribution process? and (3) What are the consequences of the attributions? These questions are similar to those addressed by cognitive psychologists looking at more general human judgment processes. However, although attributional processes are hypothetically part of the larger study of human judgment and decision processes, only recently have attribution theorists begun to apply the principles of cognitive psychology to the study of how people formulate causal attributions. Originally, attribution theory had its origins within two other subfields of psychology—social perception and social motivation.

Origins of Attribution Theory

Most of the earliest work done by social psychologists in what was later to be called *attribution theory* grew out of the discipline known as *social perception,* or, more specifically, *person perception.* In an excellent review of this field, Hastorf, Schneider, and Polefka (1970) discuss literature demonstrating that social perceptions are influenced by the immediate context of the stimulus, by the prior experience of the perceiver, and by the personality of the perceiver. Thus, perceptions of people are always subjective. Similar processes are involved in the perception of causality. But, whereas person perception focuses on the description of the stimulus person, attribution theory deals with the loci of causality of the person's behavior. Before a person can make a causal judgment, he or she must first perceive the event. The perceptions of causality in the situation may in turn influence how the event is perceived (Heider, 1958).

Researchers studying human motivation, especially achievement motivation, have also helped to develop attribution theory. Several of these researchers (deCharms, 1968; Feather, 1967; Weiner and others, 1972) independently turned to the study of cognitive variables to help them better understand individuals' varying reactions to achievement situations and success and failure. This work and other research dealing with a concept known as *locus of control* (Crandall, Katkovsky, and Crandall, 1965; Rotter, 1966) have become more integrated with the mainstream of attributional research deriving from the person-perception literature. Although the distinctions have become increasingly blurred, the motivational approach to attributions has focused on self-perceptions rather than on perceptions of the causes of events involving other people or on attributions in achievement situations involving success and failure.

Today, motivational processes are much more central to the mainstream of attribution research. On the one hand, the tendency to ascribe causes to events can be seen as a demonstration of the basic desire to make sense of the world (Kelley, 1967) or what might be called an *epistemic motivation* (Kruglanski and others, 1978). On the other hand, there are various motivations, such as a desire to maintain high self-esteem, that affect the attributional process (Bradley, 1978; Jones and Davis, 1965; Jones and Nisbett, 1971; Ross, 1977). Thus, motivational processes are highly important to an understanding of the formation of causal attributions.

Although not one of the original sources for attribution theory, cognitive psychology is inherently related to the study of cognitions or attributions about events. The attributional process involves categorization of information, judgments, and evaluation, all of which are cognitive processes. Studies of these cognitive events have become increasingly important within attribution theory. In some of the early studies within this general framework, Nisbett and Valins (1971) and Storms and Nisbett (1970) demonstrated that people make attributions about their own feelings and beliefs on the basis of information about their present and past reactions to relevant stimuli. Frieze and Weiner (1971) and McArthur (1972) further showed some of the ways that people utilize various sources of information in formulating causal judgments.

With time, more and more lines of research have been incorporated into the study of causal attributions. Weiner (1972a) discusses some of these converging research areas, and Shaver (1975) provides an excellent discussion of the development of attribution theory from its roots in the person-perception literature.

Other Concerns with the Study of Causality

The study of causality has a long history. Scientists and philosophers have often seen this as a central issue. As discussed in Lana (1969), Aristotle identifies four types of causes:

- *Formal causes:* Ultimate or true causes (which can never be knowable to humanity but which are continually being sought after).
- *Material causes:* Human theories of causality (attempts at identifying formal causes).
- *Final causes:* The ultimate purpose of events.
- *Efficient causes:* Apparent physical causes.

Other philosophers have developed and elaborated on these ideas. Even today, the ideas of Hume and Kant remain as basic underpinnings of modern psychological theorizing about causality (Lana, 1969).

Although most scientists seek formal causes in their research, most early scientific enquiry concerned efficient causes and was of the form A causes B if B appears to result from the presence of A and if B does *not* appear when A is *not* present. Such conceptions of causality are empirically testable. They also represent naive conceptions of causality (Heider, 1958) and therefore form the basis for current attributional theorizing.

In modern social psychology, Fritz Heider is generally acclaimed as the founding father of attribution theory. In an initial paper on phenomenal causality (1944) and in subsequent elaboration of his original notions and their extension to the domain of social perception (1958), Heider laid the basis for the various attributional conceptions that have since appeared. But, of course, psychologists were interested in the study of causality long before attribution theory became a formally labeled research domain. For years, social psychologists have stressed people's need for knowledge, including causal knowledge, and the impetus it may provide for social behavior. Along this line, we find Festinger's theory of social comparison (Festinger, 1954), which assumed the existence of a basic drive within individuals to evaluate their own opinions and to compare their abilities with those of other people, and studies by Thibaut and Riecken (1955) and Jones, Davis, and Gergen (1961), which can be considered among the first investigations of how individuals attribute causes for behavior. In addition, Schachter and Singer's (1962) investigation of the importance of environmental influences in the assigning of labels for one's own feelings became the basis for a good deal of research in the area of self-attributions.

Indeed, the concern with understanding people's causal knowledge has been a primary emphasis of social-psychological research since the 1950s (Steiner, 1970). After a period in the 1950s and 1960s when a major focus became the intraindividual concern of the cognitive consistency theorists, the emphasis on causality in the form of attribution theory has again become a dominant influence. Heider (1958) was one of the first social psychologists to bridge the gap between the earlier concerns with causality and the cognitive consistency theorists. Bem's (1967) reinterpretation of earlier work with cognitive dissonance also served as one of the early bridges.

At present, the assumption that the adequate understanding of people's social behavior, formation of knowledge, or labeling of emotions depends on a description of how they perceive and explain their social world has led to a burgeoning amount of research on attribution. Attribution enquiry has grown within social psychology as a consequence of the influential writings by Heider (1958), Jones and Davis (1965), Kelley (1967, 1972, 1973), and Jones and others (1971). Moreover, the attributional framework has been used to analyze different questions in a variety of social-psychological areas (see Harvey, Ickes, and Kidd, 1976, 1978).

The view that people's conduct in society must be understood through understanding their beliefs about causality is not unique to social psychology. At the same time as social psychologists have begun to enquire about the naive psychology of the average person, sociologists have stated that common-sense knowledge must be the central focus of social enquiry. Alfred Schutz, who laid the basic assumptions and definitions for the sociology of knowledge, suggested that lay knowledge has a particular meaning and relevance structure for people. Their common-sense constructs of the reality of everyday life determine their behavior and help them see themselves within the context of their natural and sociocultural environments. These constructs also define their goals and how they will achieve them (Schutz, 1967). Similarly, Garfinkel, the founder of ethnomethodology, suggested that "the task of professional sociologists in the terms of ethnomethodology thus becomes a matter of not taking for granted what is typically taken for granted at the level of everyday actions. They must make the accomplishments of adequacy in meaning (of sense) in everyday, common-sensical explanations, itself a topic of sociological inquiry" (Garfinkel, 1967, p. 216).

Attribution theory, in comparison with the sociological approach to lay knowledge, is much narrower in scope. It deals only with the lay person's knowledge of the cause and effect. The next section will review the specific attributional models that have been proposed within the domain of attribution theory.

Heider's Naive Psychology

Fritz Heider is considered to be the father of attribution theory. He was born in 1896 in Vienna, Austria. He studied with several of the major Gestalt psychologists in Germany, and this Gestalt influence is evident in his work. He came to the United States in 1930 and spent many years arguing in vain against the prevailing behavioral perspective within American psychology. His work has become widely acclaimed only in the last twenty years (Ickes and Harvey, 1978).

First in a paper on phenomenological causality in 1944 and then in an extensive discussion of the phenomenology of social perception in 1958, Heider laid the foundations for many of the basic concepts in attribution theory. In his work, Heider provides basic principles for how people in everyday life "figure out" what causes what. His analysis is phrased in common-sense language, and Heider calls his psychology *naive*, because it is based on the phenomenology of the lay person.

It is possible to identify three fundamental assumptions that guided Heider's naive psychology of attribution (Hastorf, Schneider, and Polefka, 1970). The first is that an adequate understanding of a person's behavior is contingent on the description of how this person perceives and describes his social world. Second, Heider assumes that people desire to predict and control their environment. People want to be able to anticipate the effects that their own and others' behavior will have on other people, on the environment, and on themselves. This goal can be achieved, if people are able to interpret and infer the causal antecedents of behaviors. Third, Heider believes that there are some basic similarities between object and person perception. Predictability in the social world is achieved by the same processes that are involved in perception of the physical world. In both cases, people look for enduring or dispositional properties in others to explain particular behaviors.

According to Heider, the basic feature of interpersonal perception is an understanding of the dispositional properties inherent in objects and people. This understanding renders the perceiver's world more stable, predictable, and controllable. Central to Heider's theoretical position is the proposition that people perceive events as being caused and that the causal locus can be either in the actor or in the environment. Thus, when a person observes an action of another, he tries to determine whether the action was caused by the actor or by the environment. When a person attributes the action to the actor, then he seeks to understand it by ascribing the action to certain dispositional characteristics of the actor.

In Heider's analysis, an action outcome or effect is perceived to be an additive function of the effective environmental force and the effective personal force. Personal force is seen as a multiplicative function of the other's power and the motivation (referred to as *trying*). Thus, Effect = (Environmental Force + Personal Force) or Effect = [Environmental Force + (Power x Motivation)]. According to Heider, power is determined primarily by ability, although other characteristics (for example, temperament) may affect a person's power. The motivational factor refers to a person's intention (*what* one is trying to do) and exertion (*how hard* one is trying to do something). This factor propels and guides action by giving it a purposive quality. The additive relationship between environmental and personal forces suggests one of three things: an environmental or personal force could produce the action outcome, even if one of these forces was absent; the environmental force could work toward the same end as the personal force and thus supplement it; or the environmental force could work to oppose the personal force and thus reduce its effectiveness. The multiplicative relationship between power and motivation, however, implies that, if either component were absent, the strength of the personal force would be zero. In his analysis, Heider discusses two possible environmental forces that may be perceived as possible causes of an outcome or event: the difficulty of a given task and luck. Tasks are judged in terms of how easy or difficult they are. If a task is extremely easy, then virtually no ability is needed to perform it; if a task is extremely difficult, then much ability is needed to perform it. Outcomes are attributed to luck when a person succeeds only once in many trials or when he fails once and succeeds on the remainder of the trials.

Heider suggests that, to make an attribution to personal causes or to environmental causes, the perceiver must estimate the relative strengths of the environmental and personal forces. One of the most important decisions that the person makes is his estimate of the extent to which the internal rather than the environmental force was responsible for the effects of one's own or the other person's actions. In his analysis, Heider further suggests that individuals go beyond the person-environment distinction to differentiate between personal and impersonal causality. Personal causality refers to those instances of internal causality when a person intentionally produces an outcome. Impersonal causality refers to externally caused effects and to effects that were caused by a person unintentionally. The intentions of the person are important aspects of perceiver's attribution. The perceiver tries to determine whether a given outcome of an act is the result of an intention on the part of the actor. The actor is held responsible only for personally caused effects, and only such personally caused effects are informative about the dispositional characteristics of the actor. The attributional process, according to Heider, is the analysis of the underlying conditions that give rise to perceptual experience. The process of attribution itself is based on observations, which provide information concerning the events and dispositional properties. Heider suggests that, although sometimes the attributions are distorted as a result of personal biases, in principle, the process can be seen as analogous to experimental methods.

Reinterpretations and Extensions of Heider

From Acts to Dispositions: Jones and Davis (1965). In 1965, Jones and Davis published what was to become a highly influential paper in helping to initiate the formal study of causal attributions by social psychologists. Based on Heider, Jones and Davis again attempted to develop a theory that would explain people's naive explanations of human actions. By this time, they were able to support their ideas with a good deal of social-psychological research that was relevant to an attributional framework but that had not yet been interpreted from this perspective.

Jones and Davis felt that people seek to find causes or "sufficient reasons" for the actions of other people. To find out what these sufficient reasons are, Jones and Davis hypothesized that the observer of an action analyzes all the potential effects of any possible action that might have been taken in the situation. Some of the effects are common to many possible actions, and therefore they tell the observer little about why a particular action was chosen by the actor. Other, noncommon effects are more diagnostic. Jones and Davis assume that the actor chooses his course of action on the basis of these noncommon effects that are assumed to follow from his action. They further state that these resulting noncommon effects are the desired effects of the action.

Using these principles, Jones and Davis developed a model for how the observer decides if the behavior of an individual is based on the underlying disposition or intention of the person or if the behavior is more attributable to the situation. They felt that this dispositional inference is more likely if the action has few noncommon effects (and thus seems to be uniquely related to a particular outcome) and if the behavior is not common to many people or has low social desirability. If there are too many noncommon effects, it is impossible to tell which of these represents the intentions of the actor. Such a situation is perceived as an "interesting ambiguity." Similarly, if the behavior is a common one with high social desirability, it tells the observer little about the unique characteristics of the particular individual.

Jones and Davis also discuss the ideas of *hedonic relevance* and *personalism*. Hedonic relevance occurs whenever an act has personal relevance to the perceiver. Acts with hedonic relevance are more likely to be attributed to the disposition of the actor. In addition, the observer is more likely to see himself as the source of events that have relevance for him. If an actor perceives that he is the intended target of another's behavior, he tends to see the action as more purposeful. Such personalism occurs whenever the action has personal relevance for the person—under such conditions, the tendency to perceive correspondence is greater. These hedonic relevance and personalism biases (as they later came to be called) have been of great interest to attribution theorists.

Although the work of Jones and Davis has not generated much research that attempts to apply these concepts directly to a social problem, Chapter Eleven by McGillis on jury decisions is one example of such an application. It is based on an elaborated and extended theory of correspondent inferences and the process of moving from acts to dispositions presented in a paper by Jones and McGillis (1976). Jones and McGillis extend the Jones and Davis framework in a number of ways. One important extension ties this research closer to other attribution research by bringing in the idea of expectancies. Jones and McGillis felt that expected actions tell the observer little about the underlying disposition of the actor. These prior expectancies can be based on the observer's past knowledge about the behavior of the particular actor *(target-based expectancies)*, or they can be assumptions made about the individual based on the knowledge that the actor is a member of a particular group or category of people. Stereotypes about the group in general then form the basis of *category-based expectancies*. McGillis' chapter discusses the importance of these expectations.

Attributions as an Analysis of Variance: Kelley (1967). Along with Jones and Davis (1965), Kelley's 1967 paper served to spark the formal study of naive perceptions of causality. Kelley shared many assumptions with Heider and Jones and Davis (see Shaver, 1975, for more detailed discussion of the similarities and differences among these three theoretical conceptualizations of the attributional process). All were concerned with naive psychology and believed that people act in "rational" ways in attempting to understand the behaviors of others. However, whereas Jones and Davis elaborated on some of the ways that people process information in making judgments about the intentionality of a particular behavior, Kelley attempted to extend this analysis to a general theory of how people process various types of information in arriving at judgments about the locus of causality for an event. Shaver (1975) suggests that Kelley (1967) is presenting a model of the naive observer as more than a simple information-processor; the observer is seen as a social scientist.

Kelley feels that there are three types of information that people utilize in making causal judgments. One type of informa-

tion is consensus of information about how other people have
reacted in the same situation that is being evaluated. Thus, if one is
trying to determine why someone laughs at a joke, one might well
consider if other people also laugh at the joke. A second type of
information is consistency—does the actor react in the same way
on other occasions? Finally, there is distinctiveness information, or
information about how the person reacts in similar situations or to
similar stimuli. For example, does the person laugh at all jokes, or is
his laughter distinctive to this particular joke? Events with high
distinctiveness and high consensus tend to be attributed to the particular stimulus (the joke is funny). Low distinctiveness and high
consistency lead the observer to infer that the behavior is the result
of something about the person (he always laughs at jokes, he is the
type of person who laughs at jokes). Low-consistency, low-con-
sensus, and high-distinctiveness situations are attributed to the
unique circumstances of the situation (the joke happened to strike
him as funny at that particular moment). That people can indeed
use these types of informational cues to form these attributional
judgments has been verified by a number of researchers, including
McArthur (1972) and Orvis, Cunningham, and Kelley (1975).

Kelley (1967) further hypothesized that people combine
these multiple sources of information in a naive analysis of variance, with distinctiveness representing the between-conditions
variance and consistency and consensus representing the within-
condition variance.

Although later theorists, including Kelley's more recent
work, have suggested that this analysis of variance model is probably too complex to represent people's actual information-
processing strategies, Kelley's classification of the relevant sources
of information for attributional judgments has been quite influential on later attribution researchers.

Further Elaborations of Attribution Theory

Simplified Principles of Information Utilization: Kelley. In 1971
and 1972, Kelley published two more classic papers in the attribution literature. The first paper outlines three basic principles by
which people form causal judgments. The first of these, the *covaria-*

tion principle, states that effects covary over time with their causes. This principle resembles the efficient-cause concept of Aristotle and certainly summarizes a basic assumption of Heider's work.

The second principle involves a situation with several possible causes of an event. In such a situation, the role of any one specific cause in producing the effect is seen as lower than if there were no other possible causes. Thus, the *discounting principle* states that "the role of a given cause in producing a given effect is discounted if other plausible causes are also present" (Kelley, 1971, p. 8). As Kelley pointed out, the discounting principle is similar to the case of trying to interpret in-role or socially desirable behavior that Jones and Davis were concerned with in their earlier paper.

Kelley's third principle was the *augmentation principle:* "If, for a given effect, both a plausible inhibitory cause and a plausible facilitative cause are present, the role of the facilitative cause in producing the effect will be judged greater than if it alone were present as a plausible cause for the effect" (p. 12). Again, this parallels the Jones and Davis situation of a socially acceptable effect occurring. In such a case, the internal cause (intent) is seen as greater, since external norms inhibit the behavior. These three principles have since been frequently referenced in the literature, because they so succinctly summarize attributional research.

In his 1972 paper, Kelley went on to summarize how people use causal schemata to organize their basic understanding of how various causes combine to produce effects. Thus, some effects may result if any of several causes is present. Such a situation evokes a *multiple-sufficient schema.* Examples of situations fitting this model are doing well on an easy task or doing something for which there is a strong underlying motivation; the act will thus occur whether or not an inhibitory cause is present. Other situations evoke a *multiple-necessary schema,* if the effect will occur only if several causes are all operating simultaneously. This happens in very difficult tasks when both ability and effort are needed to do well (Orvis, Cunningham, and Kelley, 1975) or when any one of the relevant causes is relatively weak. Kelley felt that these simple schemata could be used to describe a number of situations but that other, more complex schemata might also operate in other situations. Although not as much of the applied attributional research has been based on Kelley's causal-schemata theories as on his other theoretical writings, the schemata work might be seen as one of the early theoretical developments in attribution theory that directed this work toward basic research concerning the underlying cognitive processes in decision making and human judgment. Morris and Kanouse also draw upon this work to some degree in Chapter Six on drug use.

Self-Attributions and Misattributions. Several attribution papers were published in 1972 in *Attribution: Perceiving the Causes of Behavior,* edited by Jones and others, which dealt with the question of how people form attributions about their own behaviors and feelings. One of the most widely cited was the paper by Jones and Nisbett, which described a number of systematic differences in the types of causal attributions made by actors about their own behaviors as opposed to the attributions made about someone else by an observer of this other person. The general finding was that people tend to attribute their own actions to the constraints of the situation and the behaviors of others to their personality. Thus, a student who was studying hard for a test might attribute his own behavior to his needing to get good grades to please his parents, whereas a relative observing this student might feel that he was a very studious person. Jones and Nisbett identified a number of reasons why this observer bias might occur. One reason could be that actors have different information available to them than observers. Actors know about their own past history and therefore have more consistency and distinctiveness data available to them, whereas observers typically have only consensus data. Actors also know more about their own feelings about the situation and their reactions to specific stimuli in the environment. In addition to these information differences, there are also differences in the salience of the various forms of information. The actor views his behavior in the context of his past behavior, and his variations in responses to different situations are highly salient, making the possible environmental cause more salient. However, the observer views the behavior of any particular actor in the context of how his behavior differs from the behavior of other people in that same situation. Therefore, the idiosyncratic factors in the actor are highly salient in explaining his behavior.

A good deal of research has been done to explicate further the differences in actor and observer perceptions of causality (Monson and Snyder, 1977; Storms, 1973; Taylor and Fiske, 1975; and Wyer, Henninger, and Hinkle, 1977), and this work has shown that the situation is far more complex than Jones and Nisbett originally suggested. However, their work is still cited in the attribution literature, and many of the chapters in this book use the distinction between the actor and the observer in discussing causal attributions.

In the same volume as the Jones and Nisbett paper were two other papers that elaborated on the ways people make attributions about themselves. These papers were by Nisbett and Valins and by Valins and Nisbett. Nisbett and Valins described how people use information about their own internal reactions to outside stimuli to infer their own feelings about these stimuli. On the most basic level, people tend to feel that, if they acted in a certain way, they must have wanted to act in that way. For example, when a subject in an experiment was induced to persuade someone else to do something, the subject later reported more agreement with this thing than a group that did not act as if they believed in this thing. Similar results were found when subjects were given false information about their heartbeats as they responded to a series of pictures of nude females. They reported more liking for the nudes that had been associated (falsely) with reportedly faster heartbeats.

The Valins and Nisbett paper applied these ideas about inaccuracies in people's perceptions of their own internal feelings and attitudes to the treatment of emotional disorders. One of the techniques they used was to find ways to get people to attribute their undesirable symptoms to external factors rather than to themselves. They suggested that such a technique might work for phobic patients or for insomniacs. Chapter Seven shows how these ideas have been developed in the treatment of insomnia. Chapter Six also relies on these principles to some degree in discussing people's reactions to drugs.

Attributing the Causes of Success and Failure: Weiner. From an entirely different theoretical framework, Weiner and others' paper in the Jones volume attempted to show how cognitive reactions to success and failure were of great importance in understanding achievement-oriented behavior. Thus, the original focus of the Weiner group was to add a cognitive dimension to the earlier theories of achievement motivation developed by McClelland and Atkinson (McClelland and others, 1953; Atkinson, 1964). The focus of this paper was self-attributions, although later work extended the theory to include both actor and observer attributions in achievement situations.

Weiner postulated that individuals attribute success and failure at an achievement task, such as taking an examination in school, to one of four primary causal factors: ability, effort, task difficulty, and luck. These causal elements may be classified in two different ways. One dimension differentiates causal elements in terms of their internality-externality (locus of control), and the second dimension differentiates them in terms of their relative stability over time (stability). Thus, for example, ability and effort originate within the person (internal locus), whereas task difficulty and luck are external to the person (external locus). Also, ability and task difficulty are relatively stable as a person reattempts the same task, whereas effort and luck are unstable, because they may vary from one trial to another. The dimensions of locus of control and stability have been found to be important in understanding the affective reactions to success or failure (feelings of pride or shame) and changes in perceived probability of success for future outcomes. It is further suggested that these affective and cognitive reactions determine the magnitude, direction, and persistence of achievement-related behavior (Weiner, 1974a, 1974b). More recent work (Elig and Frieze, 1975; Frieze, 1976a) has indicated that other causal factors in addition to these four causes are frequently employed by people in explaining achievement success and failure. These include stable effort, other people, mood, personality, and physical appearance. In fact, Frieze and Snyder (1978) have shown that relevant causal categories depend greatly on the specific achievement situation.

The first question that arises from Weiner's attribution model of achievement-related behavior concerns the identification of antecedent stimuli that arouse particular causal ascriptions. Weiner (1974b) suggested three major determinants of causal perception: the specific information the person has about the task or performance, the individual's predispositions, and the individual's causal schemata. Different specific information, such as immediate outcome of the performance, outcomes of previous performances on the same task, outcomes of other people's performances on the same task, and time spent on the task have specific relationships to particular causal attributions (Frieze, 1976b, Frieze and Bar-Tal, 1977; Frieze and Weiner, 1971). In addition, a number of investigators have contended that certain individual characteristics are associated with the disposition to make particular attributions in situations of success and failure. Some data suggest that there are sex differences in attributions and that locus of control and self-esteem as well as achievement motivation play a major role in influencing the nature of causal perception (Bar-Tal and Frieze, 1977; Kukla, 1972; Murray and Mednick, 1975). Finally, following Kelley (1972), Weiner (1974a) suggests that an individual's causal schemata—abstract ideas pertaining to how certain effects are related to particular causes—determine the individual's causal perceptions of success and failure (Kun and Weiner, 1973).

The second question that arises from Weiner's model concerns the consequences of the particular patterns of attributions in the situations of success and failure. In response to this question, Weiner (1974a, 1974b) suggested that the type of causal ascriptions a person makes determines his affective and cognitive reactions, which in turn affect his achievement behavior. Weiner (1972a, p. 374) postulated that "within achievement-related contexts, affect is determined primarily by attributions to internal versus external factors." Attributions of success or failure to internal factors (ability, effort) cause a person to react more emotionally than when he attributes the outcome to external factors (task difficulty, luck). Further research has shown that specific causal attributions may be related to particular emotional responses (Weiner and others, 1978). Thus, for example, effort was found to be associated with pride, whereas luck was found to be associated with surprise.

Weiner also postulated that ascriptions of an outcome to unstable factors (effort, luck) produce greater shifts in expectancy of achievement to desired outcome than do ascriptions to stable factors. This theoretical conceptualization has been verified by numerous empirical studies (McMahan, 1973; Rest and others,

1973; Valle and Frieze, 1976; Weiner, Nierenberg, and Goldstein, 1976). Thus, the expectancy dimension of causality is highly important in looking at the individual's expectancies for future outcomes. Attribution of failure to stable factors can be quite debilitating. Finally, several experiments have shown that the perception of causes for success and failure is related to achievement-related behavior with respect to free-choice behavior, persistence of performance, and intensity of performance (see Bar-Tal, 1978, for a review).

Several of the chapters in this book rely on the basic Weiner framework in using attribution theory to resolve social problems. Chapter Eight by McHugh and others applies these ideas to understanding alcoholics and the reactions of others to the alcoholic. Frieze (Chapter Four) shows that battered women's reactions are mediated by stable as compared with unstable causes. Rehm and O'Hara (Chapter Nine) use these ideas to look at depression, and Carroll (Chapter Twelve) uses the Weiner framework to help understand parole decisions. As might be expected, since the primary focus of the theory concerns classroom achievement, all the chapters looking at educational applications of attribution rely on the Weiner framework to a greater or lesser degree. In addition, Peplau, Russell, and Heim (Chapter Three) draw upon this theory in looking at loneliness, and Valle and Johnson (Chapter Five) use it to explain consumer reactions to dysfunctional products. Kidder and Cohn (Chapter Ten) also use this theory to look at reactions to crime.

Attributions of Responsibility. Ideas about responsibility for an event involve beliefs about legal accountability and moral accountability as well as perceptions of causality for the event. Research attempting to identify the circumstances in which a person is seen as responsible for an action has been done since the 1920s and has continued to be an interest of social psychologists over the last two decades. Although such attribution theorists as Heider and Jones and Davis have applied attributional concepts to understand this phenomenon, much of the early work was done entirely outside of the attributional framework. During the 1970s, however, researchers on responsibility have increasingly turned to attributional language in elaborating their theories and data (Shaver, 1975). This type of synthesis is seen in Chapter Two on perceptions of victims by Coates, Wortman, and Abbey. Other chapters refer to these ideas as well.

A number of factors have been empirically shown to affect responsibility judgments. First, the actor must be perceived as causing the event and as intending to cause the event. Additionally, as Shaver (1975) points out, people are more willing to attribute responsibility to the actor who causes negative events than the actor who is responsible for positive outcomes. The most typical explanation of this phenomenon is that people are making defensive attributions to the actor to avoid thinking about the possibility that a similar misfortune might befall them. If a negative event is attributed to environmental factors, then presumably it could happen to anyone. The more negative the event, the more likely is this defensive attributional pattern (Lerner and Miller, 1978; Walster, 1966).

Current Developments in Attribution Theory

The formation of a causal attribution is a cognitive process, since it involves categorization, judgment, and the evaluation of various sources of information. Only in the last few years have attribution theorists begun to question seriously the hypothesized thought-processes involved in formulating causal attributions in the light of current research on human judgment and cognition.

One of the first ways these concerns were expressed was in the form of critiques of the assumptions made by Kelley about how people process large amounts of information and critiques of the idea that people are rational in their attributions (Carroll and others, 1976; Fischhoff, 1976). These papers demonstrated that people could not possibly process all the information required by the early informational attribution theories and that information had to be simplified in some way, so that it would not exceed the limits of the human mind. Another set of criticisms has been that people do not systematically process information at all; instead, they seem to react with little thought and make "top of the head" responses in laboratory studies (Langer, 1978; Taylor and Fiske, 1978).

One of the responses to these types of criticism has been to develop models of attributional information-processing that are based on underlying causal schemata or scripts. Kelley's schemata theory was presented earlier; Abelson (1976) has also suggested a model whereby people use scripts or schemata in forming attributional judgments. Schemata influence what information is attended to or recalled from memory; they provide a framework for looking at multiple sources of information at one time, since much information can be integrated into one schema.

Another important recent development is the attempt by Kruglanski to integrate the various attribution theories into a lay epistemological theory (Kruglanski, 1978b; Kruglanski and Bar-Tal, 1978; Kruglanski and others, 1978). The theory distinguishes between the contents of knowledge and the process of knowledge-acquisition. The attributional process corresponds to the process of knowledge-acquisition, and it works in accordance with the validational principle of consistency. According to the theory, the various attribution models speak of the same logic underlying the attributional process, but they differ from each other in the attributional contents they deal with.

Other theoretical developments are also seen in the chapters in this book. Chapter Two is really as much a theoretical development in the area of attribution of responsibility as it is an application; several of the other chapters refer to this theory and the related work by Wortman (for example, Bulman and Wortman, 1977). Several of the chapters deal with the questions of what causal attributions people make and how these can be meaningfully classified. Others deal with the question of how people use information in making causal judgments and the behavioral and affective reactions of people as a function of their causal attributions. All these issues have been central in the various attribution theories discussed in this chapter. It appears as though the process of attempting to apply various attributional concepts has strengthened and added to our theoretical knowledge as well as helping to solve social problems.

Chapter 2

Dan Coates
Camille B. Wortman
Antonia Abbey

Reactions
to Victims

People who are hurt, suffering, or otherwise under severe stress have a special need for close supportive relationships with others. Some time ago, Schachter's (1959) experiments demonstrated that subjects wanted the company of other people when they were anxious about receiving an electric shock. A number of more recent experiments have replicated Schachter's findings (see Cottrell and Epley, 1977, for a review). There is also considerable evidence that close social ties may lessen the destructive impact of undesirable life events (see Cobb, 1976, and Wortman and Silver, in press, for reviews). Wortman and Silver have concluded that perceived social support is an important predictor of good emotional adjustment to a variety of stressful life events, including physical disability (Kel-

Note: Research presented in this chapter was supported in part by National Science Foundation Grant BNS78-04743 to Camille B. Wortman.

man, Lowenthal, and Muller, 1966; Litman, 1962; Smits, 1974), malignant disease (Carey, 1974; Jamison, Wellisch, and Pasnau, 1978), bereavement (Bornstein and others, 1973; Clayton, Halikas , and Maurice, 1972), and rape (Burgess and Holmstrom, 1978). Social interaction has been shown to facilitate recovery from stress or injury in both men and animals (Bovard, 1959; Ellison, 1977; Epley, 1974; Kaufman, 1973; Raphael, 1977). Social isolation and separation, however, increase the likelihood of disease and deterioration among humans as well as other social mammals (Bakan, 1968; Dearaujo and others, 1973; Nuckolls, Cassel, and Kaplan, 1972; Scott and Senay, 1973; Weisman and Worden, 1975).

Unfortunately, there is also evidence suggesting that victims may encounter considerable difficulty in gaining the social support they need. Research by Lerner and his colleagues (Lerner, 1970; Lerner and Simmons, 1966; Simons and Piliavin, 1972) has consistently demonstrated that study participants derogate a fellow subject who has been made to suffer painful shocks. Several authors (Carling, 1962; Davis, 1961; Goffman, 1963) have provided compelling anecdotal evidence indicating that nonvictims feel uncomfortable interacting with people who are maimed, ill, or disfigured and that they usually seek to avoid such interactions. In experiments in which they meet disabled people, normal people typically show more rigid and controlled motor activity, more restricted verbal expression, fewer smiles, greater interpersonal distance, and earlier exits than they demonstrate when interacting with other able-bodied individuals (Kleck, 1968; Kleck, Ono, and Hastorf, 1966; Kleck and others, 1968). Symonds (1975), on the basis of his observations as psychiatric consultant to the New York City Police Department, maintains that people often blame and denigrate victims of violent crime and exclude them from normal social exchange. Several investigators indicate that negative social reactions are commonly experienced by former mental patients (Farina, Allen, and Saul, 1968; Farina and others, 1971; Phillips, 1963; Whatley, 1959). It is also well established that people avoid contact with individuals who are ill or dying, apparently because they find such contact distressing (Wortman and Dunkel-Schetter, in press).

Considered together, these research results delineate a broad and serious problem confronting those who suffer from unfortunate life events. Although victims genuinely need the comfort and company of others, they may often discover that such social support is very difficult to find. It has been proposed by several theorists (Lerner and Miller, 1978; Walster, 1966) that the social rejection of victims is due to the negative attributions that nonvictims form about individuals who are suffering. However, past investigators have not defined the process by which these negative attributions result in interpersonal difficulties for the victim.

We shall discuss in this chapter how previous work has tended to focus exclusively on either the victim or the observer and seldom on the contributions that they both make to their interactions. A detailed consideration of the feelings and behaviors of both the victims and those around them suggests that some of the same actions that enable victims to cope best with their misfortune are also most likely to aggravate the negative attributions of observers. We shall review evidence indicating that victims' coping needs and others' attributional biases sharply conflict and research suggesting some conditions under which this conflict might be minimized. We shall then describe an experiment that examines observers' reactions to a rape victim's coping mechanisms and discuss the implications of our findings for victims' interpersonal relationships and for further research on this issue.

Past Approaches

Researchers and clinicians are increasingly recognizing the value of an interactional approach to human problems (Meir, 1969; Rausch and others, 1974). For example, several authors have proposed compelling theoretical models suggesting that psychological disturbances such as paranoia (Lemert, 1962) and depression (Coyne, 1976) may stem from dysfunctional interactional patterns between the afflicted individuals and members of their social environment. These authors argue that mental illness cannot be adequately understood, unless consideration is given to the roles that both the patients and those around them play in its development and maintenance. Similarly, theorists such as Goffman (1963) have pointed out that it is important to examine the reactions and behaviors of both the victim and the observer in investigating the social predicament of the unfortunate. In victims' relationships and interactions with others, all the participants provide input and influence outcomes. Unfortunately, much of the past work in this area has tended to focus primarily on only one side of the interaction or the other.

Several previous writers have pointed out that psychologists, helping professionals, and social planners often overemphasize victims' responsibility for their problems (Caplan and Nelson, 1974; Maslach, 1976; Ryan, 1971). Because victims are usually powerless and amenable to manipulation, those attempting to solve their problems often find it most expedient to focus on the victim's contribution rather than the impact of more potent but less controllable external factors. Drabeck and Quarantelli (1967) have argued that attributing blame to individuals is counterproductive, because it draws attention away from more fundamental systemic causes and thereby minimizes the likelihood of social change.

This singular focus on the victim as the source of difficulty has often been applied to the problems that afflicted individuals have in their relationships with others. For example, Baker and Smith (1939) have suggested that people with facial disfigurements are responsible for their social difficulties, because they defensively tend to attribute all the negative reactions they elicit from others to their handicap and so fail to change other features of their behavior that may make them unattractive to people. However, there is considerable evidence showing that such stigmatizing physical defects are indeed powerful elicitors of strong social rejection that may be very difficult for the stigmatized to overcome by any means (Davis, 1961; Goffman, 1963; Kleck, 1968; Kleck, Ono, and Hastorf, 1966). Similarly, several theorists have argued that the clinically depressed are isolated and lonely because they lack communication skills or interpersonal skills (Lewinsohn, 1974; Ruesch, 1957). Recent research indicates, however, that the social problems of the depressed may result as much from the way they are treated as from their own inadequacies (Hinchliffe, Hooper, and Roberts, 1978; Schrader, Craighead, and Schrader, 1978). Generally, former mental patients are rehospitalized and treated when serious disruptions develop in their social relationships, whereas the considerable contribution that relatives and others make to such relapses is often ignored by mental health professionals (Gove, 1970; Scheff, 1966, 1974). When scientists and clinicians focus only on the victim's role in interpersonal problems, they may oversimplify the complex difficulties actually confronting the victims by ignoring the important influence of the social environment.

Although there has been some past discussion and criticism of the tendency to focus exclusively on the victim, less attention has been paid to the alternative problem of focusing primarily on the observer's role in rejecting the unfortunate. Examples of this orientation are provided by several attribution theories, which suggest that the judgments and evaluations that people make about unfortunate others are primarily determined by their own needs for security or self-esteem rather than the reactions or behaviors of the victim. Observers' needs presumably motivate them to view victims as responsible for their misfortune and thereby prompt negative social behaviors, such as ignoring or avoiding the victim.

One such theory is Lerner's just-world model, which holds that we want to believe that the world is a fair place where bad things do not happen to good people (Lerner and Miller, 1978; Lerner, Miller, and Holmes, 1976; Lerner and Simmons, 1966). Lerner argues that the need to believe in a just world begins with early socialization. People make implicit contracts, agreeing to give up certain immediate fulfillments and to save, work, and invest in return for greater fulfillment in the future. If we believed that even good people could be stricken by unwarranted tragedy, the value of our implicit contracts would be brought into serious doubt. Consequently, if someone suffers misfortune, we convince ourselves that he or she caused the unhappiness or is the kind of person who deserves such troubles. In this way, we can continue to see the world as a fair place, despite the evident pain and misery around us, and can maintain the conviction that our own sacrifices and efforts will be rewarded. A related position on the attributions that observers are likely to make about victims was presented by Walster (1966). Her theory stipulates that people do not want to believe that severe negative outcomes can happen at random, since such a belief implies that they could encounter some unavoidable and horrible affliction. Rather than face the frightening prospects of their own vulnerability, people will often blame the victim and convince themselves that the victim is a different, less capable kind of person than they are.

Finally, Shaver (1970, 1975) has proposed what he calls a *defensive-attribution model*. Shaver agrees with Walster and Lerner that people do not want to believe that bad things can happen to them and so will often blame the victim rather than attribute the negative outcome to chance. However, Shaver has suggested that people are also biased toward protecting their self-esteem. When people anticipate being in the same situation as the victim, blaming or derogating the victim might imply that they, too, would be at fault, if they encountered a similar misfortune. Consequently, according to Shaver, people will judge the victim more leniently under such conditions, in the hope that similarly lenient standards can be applied to them.

These theories provide a useful description of the processes underlying people's reactions to victims. Concentrating principally on the observer's motivations and biases may seem more kind than blaming the victim, but it is no less one-sided and so may ultimately do those in need a disservice by presenting a rather limited picture of the social predicament they face. To determine whether such biased attributions can lead to interpersonal problems for the unfortunate, it is important to examine not only the observer's reactions but also how these reactions are likely to be influenced by changes in the victim's behavior. In most of the studies designed to test the theories we have described, the behavior of the victim has been held constant, while various features of the victimization, such as the severity of the consequences, are varied (Chaikin and Darley, 1973; Shaver, 1970; Shaw and Skolnick, 1971; Walster, 1966).

Some experiments within this research tradition have examined how the personal characteristics of the victim and even certain features of the victim's behavior influence others' attributions (Feldman-Summers and Lindner, 1976; Godfrey and Lowe, 1975; Jones and Aronson, 1973; Landy and Aronson, 1969; Lerner and Simmons, 1966). Unfortunately, many of these studies have interesting theoretical and practical implications (see Wortman, 1976, and Lerner and Miller, 1978, for reviews) but shed little light on the interpersonal problems that victims are likely to face. One problem in applying these findings to victims' interpersonal difficulties is that researchers have rarely examined observers' reactions to victims of serious misfortune in an involving setting (Lerner and Miller, 1978). Some of these experiments have presented observers with a brief third-person account of a victimizing incident (for example, Jones and Aronson, 1973). This paradigm presents a convenient context for examining observers' reactions to victims, but there may be little relationship between how people respond to a hypothetical victim and how they would react in a more involving situation. Other studies have confronted subjects with a victimizing experience in the laboratory. For example, subjects may witness a fellow subject receiving electric shocks in a "learning experiment" (Lerner and Simmons, 1966) or may watch a fellow subject lose his reward when his partner "accidentally" knocks over a pile of blocks (Chaikin and Darley, 1973). The primary drawback to this approach is that it is limited to exploring reactions to victimizing incidents that could reasonably occur in a laboratory setting. Although this approach may be more involving than reading a written account, it is limited to exploring reactions to victims of comparatively mild outcomes.

Unfortunately, there is an even more serious problem in extending the research on the victim-attribution theories to the interpersonal problems that victims may encounter. Virtually all the past experiments that have studied the relationship between the victim's behavior and the reactions of observers have focused on the impact of the victim's behavior or character before the misfortune. For example, investigators have examined whether observers' reactions to a rape victim are affected by whether the victim had been a prostitute, a divorcee (Feldman-Summers and Lindner, 1976; Jones and Aronson, 1973), a nude dancer, or a nun (Smith and others, 1976) or whether observers judge a shock victim differently when she accepted her fate willingly than when she expressed reluctance about being shocked (Godfrey and Lowe, 1975). No research has investigated how the behaviors that victims exhibit after their victimization affects others' attributions. However, it is after the victimization that interpersonal problems arise, and it is at this point that an assessment of both the victim's and observer's contribution to the problem is most necessary.

The Victim's Dilemma: Personal Versus Social Adjustment

In short, by focusing solely on the victim or on the observer as the source of victim rejection, most past investigators have de-

voted little attention to the joint relationship between specific behaviors of the victim and the rejection and avoidance of others. In
our judgment, consideration of behaviors that victims are likely to
exhibit and how they affect others are of paramount importance.
We have reviewed a considerable amount of evidence to suggest
that victims need, desire, and seek support from others. If they are
so eager for others' support, why are others consistently driven
away? We feel that the most likely explanation of this paradox is
that, in attempting to cope with their difficulties, victims unwittingly exhibit behaviors that are upsetting to others. Perhaps, behaviors that are common for victims, and maybe even helpful for
them in dealing with their discomfort, make others upset, annoyed,
or uncomfortable. Some of the victim's actions may even prompt
rejection, in part because they heighten observers' feelings of vulnerability and thus accentuate their negative attributions about the
victim.

    We shall next discuss two typical victim behaviors, express-
ing negative affect and self-blame, and the role these behaviors
play in facilitating victims' personal adjustment. We shall also consider the impact these behaviors are likely to have on the reactions
and attributions of others. Victims may be trapped in a complicated
dilemma, in which they can maximize their social acceptance only
at the expense of their personal adjustment.

Expressed Affect and Personal Adjustment

    It is common for victims of undesirable life events to report
experiencing considerable negative affect (Wortman and Silver, in
press). In fact, a number of studies suggest that, for many victim
populations, such depression persists with considerable intensity
for long periods of time. More than a fourth of the widows interviewed by Glick, Weiss, and Parkes (1974) agreed with the statement "I would not care if I died tomorrow" a full year after they
had lost their spouses. Burgess and Holmstrom (1978) likewise report that 25 percent of the rape victims they studied said they did
not feel they had recovered from the attack four to six years after it
had occurred.

    Many researchers and therapists take the view that victims
should divulge their sadness and sorrow to others in order to deal

with it most effectively. Professional treatment of widows often takes the form of "regriefing therapy" (Horn, 1974), which is specifically aimed at encouraging the bereaved to express their grief and negative affect. Similarly, several authors have maintained that rape victims will cope better with their misfortune if they can discuss their sadness and fears with others (Burgess and Holmstrom, 1974; Gager and Schurr, 1976; Halleck, 1962; Medea and Thompson, 1974). Rape victims themselves also seem to appreciate the opportunity to express their negative feelings, as this quote from one victim shows (Schultz, 1965, p. 113): "Some people I knew very well never mentioned the attack to me, though they must have heard of it. The ones who called immediately to offer their sympathy and allowed me to 'ventilate' were perhaps more helpful than they realized." Although there have been few systematic investigations of this issue, the available evidence strongly suggests that it is helpful for victims to have the opportunity to express their negative feelings in the presence of knowledgeable and supportive others (see Wortman and Dunkel-Schetter, in press, and Wortman and Silver, in press, for reviews).

Ideally, we might expect others to realize that it is normal for victims to feel depressed, and we might expect others to respond with concern and compassion when victims openly express their misery and need for consolation. Although the available evidence is not conclusive, it suggests that victims who reveal their pain are likely to be judged as poorly adjusted and unattractive by others. For example, a group of widows interviewed by Glick, Weiss, and Parkes (1974) consistently reported being discouraged by physicians, relatives, and friends from discussing their feelings of grief and depression. Victims who reveal negative feelings are also likely to be avoided by others rather than to receive sympathy and offers of help. Marris (1958, p. 84) found that expressions of grief may drive others away, as this quote from a widow's sister-in-law shows: "I've not seen anything of her for six months. I used to go in there a lot, but I can't stand people moaning all the time." (See Wortman and Dunkel-Schetter, in press, for further discussion.)

Experiments by Gergen and Wishnov (1965) and Coyne (1976) also indicate that unhappy comments may elicit negative reactions from those in the social environment. In the experiment by Gergen and Wishnov (1965), subjects who read a partner's self-description that highlighted her unfortunate experiences and present sadness responded more negatively than subjects who read a description that emphasized their partner's pleasant experiences and current good feelings. Unfortunately, it is impossible to determine whether subjects reacted more unfavorably to the formerly described partner because of her victimizing experiences or her negative affect, since these were confounded in the design. Coyne (1976) arranged for college students to speak with either a clinically depressed or nondepressed person. Perhaps because of the dysphoria the depressed people probably expressed, the students found them much less likable. Coyne, however, indicates that the depressed people engaged in inappropriate self-disclosure during their conversations and says that this rather than their expressions of sadness caused their rejection by others. So, although the results from these studies suggest that expressed unhappiness will increase negative reactions toward victims, the social impact of negative affect alone has not been tested.

Just as these experiments offer limited support for the proposition that people will dislike sad victims, there is also some evidence indicating that individuals have special respect and admiration for victims who are able to maintain a positive attitude despite their affliction. Frankl (1969) has suggested that people are more inspired by a victim who bears his cross with courage and grace than by a nonvictim who is extremely successful. In one study reported by Kleck, Ono, and Hastorf (1966), some unusual findings emerged. Some of the data suggested that normals actually enjoyed interacting with an apparently handicapped confederate more than a nonhandicapped one. Among the explanations for this effect was the fact that the confederate was presented in both conditions as a well-adjusted and very successful college student. These accomplishments may have made the handicapped person appear particularly admirable, almost remarkable, whereas the able-bodied person may have seemed more average and common. Later studies that did not introduce the confederate in this way replicated the more typical victim-rejection effects. Although previous investigators have not directly tested the hypothesis, their comments and findings indicate that a victim who expresses positive affect and still finds life worthwhile and enjoyable despite his or her suffering will be especially well liked by others.

To the extent that victims who express negative affect appear to be suffering more severely than victims who are more positive, the attribution theories alone would predict that the unhappy victims are more likely to be rejected by others. According to the just-world theory, the greater the victim's suffering, the greater is the observer's need to blame and derogate the victim to justify the victim's misery. Following from Walster's (1966) model, more serious negative outcomes are more frightening, and observers would need to attribute more responsibility to the victim to restore their sense of security. These predictions, however, take on added significance in light of the findings that successful coping for victims may require them to discuss the dysphoria they feel with others. The victims' problem may not be solely to adjust to their sadness or solely to deal with the negative reactions of others but rather to balance personal and social adjustment. In past experiments, victims' expressions of affect have always been confounded with other factors, so the extent to which victims must choose between discussing their sadness or maintaining positive social regard remains to be demonstrated.

Self-Blame and Personal Adjustment

Several reviews of relevant research (Ross and Ditecco, 1975; Wortman, 1976) have noted that self-blame is a very common reaction among victims of undesirable life events. These articles have suggested that people frequently take personal responsibility for negative outcomes, even outcomes they have had little influence in producing, such as the terminal illness of their child (Chodoff, Friedman, and Hamburg, 1964), the loss of relatives in concentration camps (Rappaport, 1971), or their own unprovoked sexual assault (Halleck, 1962; Janoff-Bulman, 1978; Medea and Thompson, 1974). Although most of the studies that have discussed the effect of self-blame have not been methodologically rigorous (see Wortman and Silver, in press, for a discussion of this literature), the evidence suggests that, at least under some circumstances, self-blame may be adaptive for the victim (Chodoff, Friedman, and Hamburg, 1964; Medea and Thompson, 1974). For example, Bulman and Wortman (1977) found that, among a group of individuals with severe spinal cord injuries, those whom the hospital staff rated as best able to cope with permanent paralysis were also those who rated themselves as having caused their accident. These authors suggested that, by accepting rather than avoiding personal responsibility, the victims may have been able to see their lives as more controllable and their paralysis as more meaningful. In short, self-blame is not only very common among victims, it also appears to be advantageous for at least certain kinds of victims in certain situations.

How do people react to a victim who expresses self-blame? No previous research has directly tested this question, and what indications are available present a rather mixed picture. On the one hand, victims who make personal attributions for their negative outcomes may prompt rather favorable responses from members of the social environment. Both Jones and Wortman (1973) and Forrest and Hokanson (1975) have suggested that people may learn that they can elicit a more sympathetic and helpful reaction from others by blaming themselves. In an experiment by Godfrey and Lowe (1975), an apparent shock victim who actively accepted her fate was rated as more attractive than someone who was coerced into the painful situation. These investigators suggest that, by taking personal responsibility for her negative outcome, the less coerced victim appeared to be an admirable kind of person who was in control of her life rather than a pawn of external forces.

On the other hand, there could be some social costs attached to accepting openly responsibility for a serious tragedy. There is some indication in the literature that professionals view self-blame as a sign of maladjustment and emotional disturbance (Abrams and Finesinger, 1953). Janoff-Bulman (in press) surveyed personnel at a number of rape-crisis centers in an effort to learn more about their perceptions of the rape victim. A large majority of the personnel who responded indicated that they saw self-blame as a sign of poor coping. If people see a self-blaming victim as more maladjusted, they may respond to him or her in the same negative way that subjects typically treat the mentally ill (Farina, Allen, and Saul, 1968; Phillips, 1963). Thus, any increase in liking that self-blame could create by eliciting sympathy or reducing threat may be offset by the observers' view that the victim is pathologically disturbed.

Limits on the Victim's Dilemma: The Role of Threat

To the extent that victims' statements of self-blame and negative affect accentuate the attributions that observers typically make about them, victims are confronted with a difficult dilemma. A question that might be raised is whether there are factors that can mitigate observers' negative reactions. Information about conditions under which others may react less negatively to victims or to their statements of self-blame or negative affect may be quite beneficial for the victims. We have already indicated that negative reactions may occur, because exposure to victims can make one feel vulnerable to a similar fate. This suggests that the magnitude of our negative reaction to a victim may depend on how likely we feel we are to encounter the victim's predicament.

An interesting feature of the variable of increased personal vulnerability is that the major attribution theories make divergent predictions about how it will affect reactions to the victim. It would seem to follow from the theories of Walster (1966) and Lerner (1970) that people who see their own victimization as more likely will be more inclined to derogate and blame the victim. Shaver (1970) has suggested, however, that, when people see their own victimization as highly likely, they may become more lenient in their judgments. Shaver (1970) has asserted that, if people blamed the victim, this would imply that they, too, would be blameworthy, if they were to become victims.

Available research seems to support this latter prediction. In an experiment by Chaikin and Darley (1973), participants were led to believe that they would play the role of a worker or supervisor. They then watched a video tape, in which a supervisor, through a clumsy accident, destroyed the product of a worker and thus deprived him of his pay. Participants who expected to fill the victim's role (that is, who expected to be workers) rated themselves as more similar to the victim and the victim as more likable than did those participants who expected to fill the supervisor's role. Similarly, Sorrentino and Boutillier (1974) found that their subjects derogated a shock victim less when they thought there was some possibility that they could also be shocked. These findings are quite consistent with Shaver's (1970, 1975) reasoning. The observers who saw their own victimization as more likely judged the victim more kindly, presumably so that similarly lenient standards would be applied to them, if they were victimized. Indeed, these researchers have cited Shaver's theory in explaining their results.

Other investigators have suggested, however, that these findings may best be explained by processes other than those described by Shaver (1970). The greater the likelihood of the outcome, for example, the more inclined the observer may be to empathize with the victim (see, for example, Aderman, Brehm, and Katz, 1974). By putting themselves in the victim's place, they can view the situation as the victim does and so may become more sympathetic and positive in their feelings toward the victim. A few studies provide evidence that heightened empathy can ameliorate the observer's reaction to the victim. For example, Clore and Jeffrey (1972) report that participants who role-played the part of a handicapped person by riding around campus in a wheelchair exhibited more positive attitudes toward a disabled experimenter than subjects who simply walked the same route. Similarly, the results from an experiment by Aderman, Brehm, and Katz (1974) showed that participants derogated a shock victim less when they were given instructions to imagine themselves in the place of the victim.

A second process that may account for the relationship between anticipation of the victim's fate and blame and derogation of the victim has been suggested by Ross and Ditecco (1975). When people expect to find themselves in a victim's situation, they probably pay more attention to that situation. As a result, they may be more aware of environmental pressures on the victim and so make more lenient, external attributions for the victim's outcome. Regan and Totten (1975) found that instructing subjects to empathize with another person led them to make more situational and less dispositional explanations of the other person's behavior. Perhaps observers are kinder to victims when they expect to share their fate, because they focus more attention on the victim's situation.

The Experiment

In the foregoing review of past literature, we have pointed out a number of important issues that have not been fully resolved:

(1) Will a victim who displays negative affect be more rejected by observers than a victim who is more positive, even when other features of their victimization and self-presentation are held constant? (2) Will observers respond more favorably to a victim who accepts responsibility for the victimization or to one who attributes the misfortune to chance? (3) Does enhanced likelihood of encountering the victim's fate lead to more negative or more positive reactions to the victim? Although the available research suggests the latter alternative to be more likely in each case, those studies involved negative outcomes that were relatively mild. No past research has investigated the relationships between observers' perceived threat and their reactions to victims of more serious misfortunes. (4) Will increases in the observer's perceived vulnerability affect his or her reactions to the victim's negative affect or statements of self-blame? Statements of negative affect and self-blame may be especially threatening, if one expects to encounter the same outcome. (5) If increased likelihood of sharing the victim's fate affects reactions to the victim, is this due to enhanced feelings of vulnerability, enhanced empathy, or greater attention to the victim's plight? We have conducted an experiment intended to provide further resolution of these issues.

Method. We (Dan Coates, Camille Wortman, Antonia Abbey, and Elizabeth Holland) investigated people's reaction to a victim of rape, a serious negative outcome. To enhance the immediacy of the experience for the subjects, they heard the victim tell her own story rather than simply reading about it or hearing a third person account. An actress did play the part of the victim, but the script she used was written in collaboration with rape victims and was carefully checked for its veracity by other rape victims. To ensure that only the victim's expressed affect and statements of blame would vary across conditions, the victim's account was tape-recorded, and the tapes were spliced together to create the various conditions.

Three variables were manipulated in a 2 X 5 design: how probable or threatening the event of rape was (high or low vulnerability), the victim's attribution of blame for the rape (self-blame, chance-blame, or no information about blame), and the victim's expressed affect (positive, negative, or no information). Because the theories reviewed previously suggest that vulnerability may interact with self-blame and expressed affect, vulnerability was crossed with each of these variables. Because there was no basis for assuming that self-blame and expressed affect would interact, these variables were not crossed. Thus, subjects were assigned to a high- or low-vulnerability condition and were then exposed to one of five victim types: a victim who expressed a positive attitude or a nega- tive attitude, a victim who was either self-blaming or chance- blaming, or to a control victim, who provided no information about her feelings on these issues.

Subjects were recruited from the Northwestern campus and the Chicago area through advertisements in the student news- paper. The advertisement indicated only that subjects could earn $4.50 for one hour of participation in a research program spon- sored by the University Center for Urban Studies. In all, 228 people, 106 women and 122 men, were included in the study. Sub- jects arrived in the laboratory in groups of ten. To avoid problems with demand characteristics that have plagued some earlier studies, this task was not presented to the subjects as a psychological exper- iment. Subjects were told that they would be examining some mate- rials that were being considered for use in a community program on crime awareness. Specifically, they were told that they would be reading short newspaper excerpts dealing with rape and would then hear brief selections from an interview with a rape victim.

Following these introductory comments, each subject was taken to an individual cubicle, so that he or she could examine the materials in privacy and without distractions from others. Half the participants were randomly assigned to the low vulnerability condi- tion and received written materials that were fairly reassuring with respect to the likelihood of rape in the Evanston area. These arti- cles described the effectiveness of past attempts to reduce on- campus assaults. Included in these "low-risk" articles was the statis- tic that one in two thousand women is the victim of rape. The remaining participants were randomly assigned to the high vul- nerability condition. They read articles focusing on sexual attacks that had ostensibly occurred on or near campus some months ear- lier. Included in these "high-risk" articles was the information that one in six women is raped.

After reading the newspaper excerpts, the participants lis- tened to a tape of an interview with a rape victim. They were told that this tape would last about fifteen minutes and that it contained excerpts from a longer interview. The victim described her assault and the circumstances surrounding it. The incident had taken place on another campus about six months earlier, during summer session. The young woman had been in the library until early evening working on a term paper that was due the next day. She decided to take a break before finishing her work at home and went to the student union. There she met a somewhat older man, who said he was planning to attend the university in the fall. He was polite and complimentary, perhaps too complimentary, but a pleasant enough distraction after a long day in the library. Despite the distraction, the student soon remembered her paper and excused herself to go home. The man offered to drive her. Faced with a long walk under a pile of books, fatigue, and several more hours of labor, the woman accepted. When they reached his car in a dark and deserted parking lot, the man raped her. She was found shortly afterward in a stunned condition by campus security personnel.

All the study participants heard this part of the victim's account. In the control condition, no further questions were asked of the victim. In the expressed-affect conditions, the victim was queried as to what her present feelings were about the rape. Half the subjects in these conditions heard the victim say she was doing fairly well, and the other half heard her report difficulties with forgetting the rape and regaining enthusiasm for formerly enjoyable activities. In the expressed-blame conditions, the victim was asked by the interviewer, "Do you feel in any way responsible for what happened?" Half these subjects heard the victim reply that she thought it was largely her own fault, and the other half heard her answer that it was due to chance. (Verbatim transcripts of the victim's statements in each experimental condition are provided in Table 1.)

We were interested in three principal dependent variables. First, we wanted to know how attractive or likable people would find the victim, so we asked whether they had a negative or positive first impression of her, and then we requested them to evaluate the victim on a number of bipolar scales (bad-good, unfriendly-friendly, irritable-good natured, unlikable-likable, unattractive-

Table 1. Victim's Statements

Positive Affect	*Negative Affect*
Well, actually, I was really upset at first, and what happened still affects me. Uh, I'll give you an example, I'm still scared when I go out at night, of men following me and things like that, things that never really bothered me before. But, I think for the most part I have been able to put the rape behind me. I've always been a fairly happy person and an active person, and the rape hasn't changed that. My family and friends have been very understanding, and that's helped me a lot. I'm still interested in the things I used to be interested in, my schoolwork, my hobbies; actually, I feel very fortunate that I have so much to look forward to in my life.	Well, I was really upset at first, and what happened still affects me. Uh, I'll give you an example, I'm still scared when I go out at night, of men following me and things like that, things that never used to bother me. I just can't put the rape behind me. I've always been a fairly happy person and an active person, but the rape has changed that. My friends and family have all been very understanding, but that hasn't seemed to help very much. I used to enjoy my schoolwork, my hobbies, but now I have a hard time getting interested in them, I just can't forget about the rape.
Chance-Blame	*Self-Blame*
OK, that's a tough question to answer, but I have given it a lot of thought, and I think I've worked it through. I do think that it was largely a matter of chance, something that was just unavoidable. I mean, sure, I said I'd take a ride with him. But, I said, sure, I could sit down with me, and sure, I said I'd take a ride with him. But, people go to the union to meet people. Everyone goes there to talk to strangers and make new friends. And I really had	OK, uh, that's a tough question to answer, but I have thought about it a lot, and I think I've worked it through. I really say that it was basically my fault. I was the one who told him he could sit down with me in the union. Everyone talks to people at the union, but he was older, and that should have made me suspicious, because he wasn't the type that you normally see at the union. I was the one that said I'd take a ride with him. I got a funny feeling in the parking lot, and I could have turned around, but I didn't. I know he

no reason to be suspicious. He was a little older, but that's not unusual. Uh, I got a funny feeling in the parking lot, but, by the time I had any idea what was going on, he had already thrown me down in that car seat. Sure, my mother, like everyone else's, had warned me never to take a ride with a stranger. But he was very respectable looking, he wasn't the type that I thought I had to worry about. He just didn't look like a rapist. Oh, and I think it would have been really stupid of me to struggle. He wasn't big or anything, but he could have had a weapon, and I was so scared. If I had tried to struggle or scream more, he could have killed me. He said he would, and he could have. So, I really think I was just in the wrong place at the wrong time, and it was something that I just couldn't have avoided.

looked respectable and didn't look like the rapist type, but I knew he was older, and I should have been more suspicious. This is going to sound corny, but, I mean, my mother has warned me a million times, never, ever take a ride with a stranger. I also think I should have struggled. I know I was very scared, but I didn't struggle at all. Maybe if I had struggled more, he would have been scared off, and I could have avoided the whole thing. He wasn't that big, and I don't think he had a weapon, so who knows? All in all, I just really do feel that it was my fault, and I was to blame.

attractive, worthless-valuable, unpleasant-pleasant). Second, we wanted to determine how much people blamed the victim, specifically for talking to a stranger, accepting a ride with an unknown man, and not struggling or fighting back more. Finally, we wanted to know how well adjusted the victim was perceived as being. To assess this, we asked people how much the victim needed help, whether she was dwelling too much on the rape, how well adjusted she was, how well she was coping, and how optimistic-pessimistic the victim was.

A secondary issue was whether subjects would identify more with the victim or pay more attention to her situation when they felt more vulnerable to being raped. To see how much people empathized with the victim, we asked them how much they felt they were the same sort of person as the victim and how much they identified with the victim. To see how well subjects attended to the victim's account, we asked them to complete a ten-item multiple-choice quiz on rather minor details of the assault. Finally, we also wanted to know how severe subjects thought the victimization was, so we asked them how much the woman had suffered and how good or bad she felt about the incident.

Our questions for the subjects also included some manipulation checks. To see whether the threat variable was effective, participants were asked how likely it was that they could be raped. Related questions asked for the subject's estimates of the probability a female student could be raped, and only women were asked how interested they would be in self-defense classes to be held later in the academic year. As a check on the self-blame manipulation, subjects were asked how much the victim blamed herself. To check the effectiveness of the affect manipulation, they were asked how happy or sad she was.

Finally, we included some additional items that were designed to measure potential perceptions or feelings among the subjects that could reasonably have sabotaged the results. For example, we asked participants how sincere the victim was. If subjects in some conditions felt the victim was somehow lying, this obviously could have influenced how they reacted to her. Fortunately, these check measures did not indicate any unusual or problematic perceptions among the subjects. All ratings were made on scales marked 1 to 15. The combined measures were also converted into fifteen-point scales.

We shall next discuss how the victim's expressions of affect and blame affected observers' reactions. We shall then look at the impact of increased risk on observers' reactions to the victim and her coping mechanisms. Where an independent variable did not interact with the sex of the subject, we shall discuss the findings for the men and women combined. We shall only consider those significant differences that were consistent across most of the individual measures of any dependent variable.

Expressed Affect. The respondents' ratings of the victim in the affect and blame conditions are presented in Table 2. As these results show, the affect manipulation was successful, with the negative-affect victim being scored as more unhappy than either

Table 2. Effects of Expressed Affect and Blame on Victim Ratings

	Control	Positive Affect	Negative Affect	Chance-Blame	Self-Blame
How unhappy is victim?	6.81^*_a	3.32_a	11.24_a	5.70	7.45
				$F_{(4,223)} = 41.39, p < 0.001$	
How much does victim blame self?	6.20_a	5.81	6.43	3.41_a	12.63_a
				$F_{(4,223)} = 45.56, p < 0.0001$	
Combined maladjustment ratings	$4.21_{a,b}$	2.76_a	6.79_a	3.45_c	$5.13_{b,c}$
				$F_{(4,223)} = 32.14, p < 0.0001$	
Combined severity ratings	10.80	10.15_a	11.98_a	10.06	11.16
				$F_{(4,223)} = 4.96, p < 0.0008$	
Combined attraction measures	11.33	11.95_a	10.86_a	11.80	11.36
				$F_{(4,223)} = 3.36, p < 0.01$	
Combined responsibility measures	5.46	6.11	5.19	4.55	5.66
				$F = $ n.s.	

*Means with the same subscript differ significantly by Tukey-test, $p < 0.05$.

the control or positive-affect victim. The more depressed victim was also rated as coping less well, as suffering more severely, and most importantly, as less attractive than the more positive victim. These results are quite consistent with the prediction, derived from the theories of Walster and Lerner, that a victim who expresses negative affect will be seen as more seriously afflicted and more unlikable than a happier victim. Previous research results (Coyne, 1976; Gergen and Wishnov, 1965) also suggest that expressions of dysphoria prompt negative reactions in others. Unlike these past findings, however, our results cannot be explained as due to the unique victimization or inappropriate self-disclosure of the more unhappy individual. They therefore indicate that victims will sometimes encounter heightened rejection when they try to cope with their sadness by discussing it.

Expressed Blame. As the results in Table 2 show, the expressed-blame manipulation was successful. Subjects rated the self-blaming victim as attributing more responsibility to herself than either the control or chance-blaming victim. We expected that people who heard the self-blaming victim might feel that rapes were more avoidable and alter their attributions about the victim as a result. However, there is no indication that this occurred. There were no significant differences among the blame conditions on subjects' ratings of their own likelihood of being raped or on their ratings of the victim's attractiveness and responsibility for the assault.

On the combined adjustment and coping measures, however, the self-blaming victim was rated as more emotionally disturbed than either the chance-blaming or control victim. Even though some research indicates that self-blame is more often associated with better coping among victims (Bulman and Wortman, 1977), observers evidently take such personal attributions as symptoms of maladjustment.

Increased Vulnerability. The vulnerability findings are presented in Table 3. At first, it appeared that the vulnerability manipulation was only partially successful, since there is a significant difference only on subjects' ratings of how likely others are to be raped and not on the ratings of their own rape likelihood. How-

Table 3. Vulnerability Main Effects and Sex Differences

	High Vulnerability	Low Vulnerability	Men	Women
Likelihood another could be raped	8.94	4.74 $F(1,226) =$ 94.95, p <0.0001	5.94	7.92 $F(1,226) =$ 15.73, p <0.0001
Likelihood you could be raped	5.25	3.98 n.s.	1.26	8.46 $F(1,226) =$ 261.58, p <0.0001
Combined attraction ratings	11.51	11.41 n.s.	11.66	11.23 $F(1,226) =$ 3.98, p <0.05
Combined responsibility ratings	5.55	5.24 n.s.	5.06	5.78 n.s.
Combined maladjustment ratings	4.29	4.58 n.s.	4.42	4.45 n.s.
Combined empathy ratings	8.63	8.26 n.s.	7.96	9.02 $F(1,226) =$ 12.26, p <0.0006
Number correct on quiz	6.88	7.03 n.s.	6.92	7.25 $F(1,226) =$ 3.38, p <0.07

ever, there was a significant sex-by-vulnerability interaction on these latter ratings ($F(1,208) = 12.68$, $p<0.001$), indicating that women felt more personally threatened by rape in the high-risk condition, whereas men did not. For males, the mean rape-likelihood rating was 1.03 in the high-vulnerability condition and 1.48 in the low-vulnerability condition. Females rated their chances of being raped at 7.08 in the low-vulnerability condition and at 9.18 in the high-vulnerability condition. Since men are not ordinarily subjected to sexual assault, it might be expected that they would maintain a fairly constant and low perception of rape likelihood. Given that women in the high-risk condition did see their own

chance of rape as significantly greater, we might expect this increased feeling of vulnerability to affect their evaluation of the
victim. Surprisingly, this did not occur. Even when the women's
scores were analyzed separately, there were no vulnerability main
effects on any of the combined victim ratings.

However, when we look at two naturally occurring groups
that differ in how threatened they felt—that is, men and
women—our findings suggest that increased risk may lead to more
negative evaluations of the victim. As Table 3 shows, women felt
much more vulnerable to sexual attack than men did, rating their
own and another woman's chances of rape significantly higher.
Perhaps because they saw their own assault as more likely, women
also empathized more with the victim and tended to recall correctly
more details of the victim's situation at the time of the rape. But,
even with the greater empathy and attention they gave the victim,
the women's feelings of vulnerability did not lead them to more
sympathetic judgments of the victim. Females rated the victim as
significantly less attractive than males did. Whereas females did not
differ from males on the combined responsibility ratings, they did
rate the victim as being more responsible in general $(F(1,226 =
7.53, p<0.01)$, and they tended to rate her as more responsible for
taking a ride with a stranger $(F(1,226) = 3.39, p<0.07)$.

It is clear that the magnitude of the difference in perceived
threat between men and women is much larger than the difference
between women in the two vulnerability conditions. Perhaps
women also blamed and derogated the victim much more, relative
to men, because of the much greater threat they felt as compared
with men; they did not do this when compared with other women
who were somewhat less threatened. Of course, there are numerous other differences between men and women that might account
for their different reactions to rape victims. Nonetheless, our sex-
difference results are quite consistent with the position of Walster
and Lerner that increasing observers' feelings of vulnerability leads
them to more negative evaluations of the victim, especially when
the victim's outcome is rather severe.

The just-world theory may also offer an explanation for the
unexpected impact of increased vulnerability on observers' reac-

tions to the victim's coping mechanisms. We anticipated that people might find a victim's self-blame or negative affect more objectionable when they felt more vulnerable to sharing the victim's fate, but this was not the case. There was no indication that vulnerability influenced observers' responses to the victims' expressed blame. However, there were significant vulnerability-by-expressed-affect interactions on the women's ratings of the victim's responsibility for the rape. These results are presented in Table 4. As can be seen, the pattern of means is quite similar on all the measures. In the low-vulnerability condition, there is little difference between how much the positive-affect and negative-affect victim is blamed. In the high-vulnerability condition, however, subjects attributed more responsibility to the positive-affect victim. The women generally found the positive-affect victim more likable, so it is somewhat surprising that they would also blame her more when they felt more threatened. However, the just-world theory indicates that, when people feel vulnerable to sharing a victim's fate, they can reduce the risk they feel by either blaming or derogating the victim. Perhaps the high-vulnerability women found it difficult to derogate the positive-affect victim, whom they found to be rather likable and admirable, and so chose instead to reduce the threat they felt by blaming her more. One interesting implication of this finding is that people may sometimes blame victims without necessarily rejecting them.

Jones and Aronson (1973) have also noted that, according to the just-world theory, observers may sometimes attribute more responsibility to a more admirable victim. They tested this prediction by examining whether a respectable rape victim would be blamed more for the assault than a less respectable victim. Their results showed that she was. However, Feldman-Summers and Lindner (1976), using very similar stimulus materials and manipulations, found that a more respectable rape victim was blamed less for the rape. Although it is nearly impossible to assess why such different findings should emerge in similar studies, our results suggest that whether or not people will blame a more admirable victim may depend on how personally threatened they feel. If people feel that their own rape is not very likely, they may have little reason to

Table 4. Vulnerability by Expressed-Affect Interactions on Females' Ratings of Responsibility

How responsible is the victim?	In General		For Talking to a Stranger		For Riding with a Stranger	
	Positive Affect	Negative Affect	Positive Affect	Negative Affect	Positive Affect	Negative Affect
Low Vulnerability:	4.11	6.80	3.78	5.30	7.44	9.40
High Vulnerability:	7.18	4.09	8.55	4.18	11.82	8.18
	$F(1,96) = 4.82, p < 0.03$		$F(1,96) = 4.69, p < 0.03$		$F(1,96) = 3.63, p < 0.06$	

blame even a likable victim. But, if rape seems more probable and individuals do not reduce the threat they feel by derogating the victim, they may be inclined to justify her suffering by blaming her.

Conclusions

Our results show that victims may face a complicated dilemma in trying to maximize their personal and social adjustment. Earlier researchers and theorists (Lerner, Miller, and Holmes, 1976; Walster, 1966) have pointed out that, simply because people are victims because they are hurt or suffering, others are often rejecting and negative toward them. Our experiment has shown that such unfavorable social reactions may be heightened by victims' attempts to cope with their emotions and to explain satisfactorily the cause of their misfortune. As such, the findings from our study enable us to identify some of the specific problems that victims may encounter in their interactions with others. These results also have implications for future research on the victim's predicament.

The Interactional Problems. Previous research has demonstrated that people often form rather negative attributions about victims and so suggests that victims may frequently have problems in their interactions with others. Our experiment extends this past work by pinpointing specific difficulties that victims are likely to encounter in their relationships with other people. One such problem is that those around the victims may be inclined to dissuade them from beliefs and behaviors that are actually quite helpful. Our results show that people consider a rape victim to be more maladjusted when she expresses negative affect or self-blame, even though most of the available evidence indicates that these behaviors can be beneficial to victims. Consequently, members of the social environment may discourage victims from discussing their sadness or feelings of responsibility, because they consider such behaviors maladaptive. Unfortunately, what others consider to be helpful for the victim may actually be detrimental.

A second implication of our results is that others may react negatively to victims precisely at the times when they are most vulnerable. It is when victims are most worried and frightened that

they probably most need the company of others (Schachter, 1959).
Fox and Scherl (1972) noted that the rape victims they observed
were most interested in discussing their problems and feelings
when they were particularly upset or depressed. But, in our experiment, when the victim disclosed her unpleasant feelings, she was
rated as more unattractive. Victims may find that, when they are
feeling most disturbed and in need of comfort, others are more
likely to avoid and reject them. In their darkest moments, victims
may find only social isolation and ostracism.

A final problem suggested by our research is that rape victims may find that those who are most capable of helping them are
least inclined to do so. Previous investigators (for example, Burgess
and Holmstrom, 1974) have pointed out that rape victims are often
understandably wary of men for some time after the attack. They
frequently turn to female friends or acquaintances for support,
perhaps reasoning that other women will have a better understanding of what they have been through than most men will. Although
the female subjects in our study empathized more with the victim,
they also blamed and derogated her more. Thus, rape victims may
discover that those people they are most likely to approach for
support and understanding are least likely to provide it.

Sex differences in reactions to rape victims is one issue that
has been studied in earlier research. These experiments have produced rather mixed results. Some investigators (Krulewitz, Nash,
and Payne, 1977; Nash, 1977) have found, as we did, that women
blame rape victims more than men do. Other research, however
(Calhoun, Selby, and Warring, 1976; Calhoun and others, in press;
Cann, Calhoun, and Selby, 1977; Selby, Calhoun, and Brock, 1977),
has indicated that men are more harsh in evaluating rape victims
than women are. It would appear that, under some conditions at
least, rape victims will find that other women are more supportive.
Unfortunately, this past work does not offer any clear indication as
to what factors may prompt women to be kinder to rape victims.
Since rape victims often do seek the company of other females, one
important issue for future research is to delineate the conditions
under which the victim's search for such support will be successful.
One possible explanation for these results is that, if the victim is
presented as sexually enticing or provocative, men may see it as

more likely that they could be involved in such an incident and so blame the victim more. Most women may feel that they would not do anything to entice a rapist and so would feel less threatened and attribute less responsibility to this kind of victim than men would. However, if the rape is presented as the result of an understandable mistake or misjudgment on the part of the victim, as in the present study, women may see it as more likely that they could be caught in such a situation than men would. Consequently, when the rape is presented this way, women may blame the victim more than men do. We are currently planning a study to test this issue empirically.

Several authors have emphasized the importance of counseling members of the social environment in treating rape victims (Burgess and Holmstrom, 1974; Joseph, 1974). Our experiment shows that the victim-attribution theories, as part of an overall interactional approach, can serve as a useful guide in identifying the kinds of social problems that such counseling might address. However, our findings also point to the need for further research on these social issues.

Directions for Future Research. Some of the most perplexing findings in our study concern the impact of vulnerability on reactions to victims. Although our threat manipulation was successful, at least for women, there was no indication that it directly affected subjects' evaluations of the victim. However, increased vulnerability did influence reactions to certain victim behaviors, as the interaction with the expressed-affect variable indicates. Apparently, threat does affect reactions to victims, but in rather complex ways.

An obvious priority for future research, therefore, is to clarify the role that perceived risk plays in influencing observers' reactions to victims of serious outcomes. Shaver (1975) has suggested that there may be a curvilinear relationship between observers' perceived risk and their judgments of victims. When there is very little chance of sharing the victim's fate, others may be normatively sympathetic or simply indifferent. When the risk is more moderate, others may be inclined to avoid the thought of their own victimization by derogating and blaming the victim. And, when the risk is very high, observers may begin to think about what their own experiences as victims would be like and so judge unfortunate others more leniently. An experiment that included several levels of threat, instead of just two levels, as in our study, might be able to clarify the impact of risk on observers' responses to victims.

Another important issue is to establish the limits of the findings attained for the self-blame and expression-of-affect variables. There are clearly different kinds of self-blame, and these may have very different personal and interpersonal consequences. Janoff-Bulman (in press) has recently distinguished between characterological self-blame, in which the victim attributes responsibility to her character or personality traits, and behavioral self-blame, in which the victim blames herself for certain past behaviors. On the basis of questionnaire data from personnel at rape-crisis centers, she has argued that behavioral self-blame is much more common among victims and that such self-blame may facilitate coping by providing women with a sense of control over their environment. It remains to be seen whether observers will find behavioral self-blame to be less indicative of emotional disturbance than characterological self-blame. Of course, interactional and interpersonal consequences of self-blame may depend on the relationship between the victim's statements of blame and her actual blameworthiness as assessed by observers. The victim who attributes a great deal of blame to herself may be regarded as maladjusted only when observers feel she is not really blameworthy.

Similar questions remain to be answered regarding the impact of expressed negative affect. It is important to investigate whether there are any conditions under which victims' negative comments about their affective states are likely to elicit sympathy rather than rejection from others. In interactions between victims and nonvictims, such factors as the availability of resources to help the victim, the amount of choice involved in interacting with the victim, and possible guilt or responsibility for the victim's fate may determine the nature of the nonvictims' reactions. Our guess is that negative responses are likely, if we have little choice about interacting with the victim but feel obligated to do so, if we feel we can do nothing to alleviate the problem he or she is complaining about, or if we feel in some way responsible for the victim's misfortune.

Our experiment has explored how behaviors that are fairly common among victims influence the reactions and feelings of others. An interesting approach for future research would be to examine subsequent stages in the interactional sequence—that is, how the responses of observers are fed back to the victim and affect her subsequent feelings and behavior. There is considerable evidence that people often feel ambivalent while interacting with victims. They may harbor negative feelings about the victimizing incident but also feel some sympathy for the victim's plight (Wortman and Dunkel-Schetter, in press). Or, as our results suggest, they may blame the victim for the incident while simultaneously holding positive attitudes about him or her. This implies that victims may sometimes receive rather mixed messages from others, messages that are both supportive and rejecting. Unfortunately, there is evidence to suggest that the inconsistent feedback that victims receive from others can contribute considerably to their difficulties (Wortman and Dunkel-Schetter, in press) and can play a role in the development of serious and prolonged depression (Coates and Wortman, in press; Coyne, 1976).

Problems in the interactional sequence may also arise, if the observer judges the victim who displays negative affect or self-blame to be disturbed and maladjusted, as occurred in our study. Several authors (Burgess and Holmstrom, 1974; Fox and Scherl, 1972) have argued that making the victim feel that she is responding to the rape in an unusual or inappropriate way could be very detrimental to her self-concept and continued functioning. If people treat the victim as if she is maladjusted for the way she copes with her misfortune, they may initiate a kind of self-fulfilling prophecy, in which the victim also comes to believe that she is disturbed (Goffman, 1963; Snyder, Tanke, and Berscheid, 1977). All these issues regarding the interactional sequence can best be studied by observing actual encounters between victims and others.

This research has focused on some parameters that may affect how victims are evaluated and judged by relative strangers. An important question for future research concerns whether the factors explored in this study will affect the reactions of relatives and friends. We might expect their evaluations of victims to be less colored by their own vulnerabilities and feelings of threat and more· influenced by strong feelings of love and compassion for the victim. For these reasons, one might conclude that family members and friends will be more tolerant of victim's expressions of their sorrows and difficulties. However, family members may find displays of negative affect from the victim even more difficult to deal with than strangers do. Because they must necessarily spend a great deal of time in the victim's company, such displays may be particularly aversive for them. Moreover, their love and concern for the victim may even make it more difficult to tolerate his or her suffering. Although there is a great deal of descriptive data and anecdotal evidence to suggest that family members may be less willing than strangers to tolerate displays of the victim's negative feelings (see Wortman and Dunkel-Schetter, in press), there is a pressing need for more precise research on this topic.

This is not to suggest, however, that additional research on strangers' reactions to rape victims is not needed. Rape victims cannot usually isolate themselves with just their intimates. They will often need to encounter and explain their assault to a wide range of strangers and near strangers who have considerable impact on their lives: police, lawyers, jurists, health professionals, coworkers, employers, classmates, teachers, and so on. In many ways, the reactions of such strangers are much more difficult to control or modify than the reactions of intimates. Victims have the opportunity to spend long hours with those close to them but may have only a few moments to present themselves and their problems to important strangers.

Our experiment has demonstrated the importance of approaching the victim's social predicament from an interactional perspective by pointing out that both the victim and members of the social environment are likely to contribute to this predicament. The study has also shown that the victim-attribution theories can serve as useful guides in identifying some of the vulnerable points in victims' relationships with other people. By further clarifying how these attributional biases can color others' reactions to victims' behaviors, future research may be able to identify not only the interactional problems that are likely to arise but also how these problems can best be managed and overcome.

Chapter 3

Letitia Anne Peplau
Dan Russell
Margaret Heim

The Experience
of Loneliness

The experience of loneliness has been characterized as "a gnawing . . . chronic distress without redeeming features" (Weiss, 1973). Sullivan (1953) depicted loneliness as "so terrible that it practically baffled clear recall." Descriptions of loneliness by college students we have studied are equally unpleasant. "I felt rejected and inadequate," said one young woman; another wrote, "I felt very depressed, and I hated myself." Loneliness has been linked to other serious problems, including depression (Leiderman, 1969; Ortega, 1969), alcoholism (Bell, 1956), suicide (Jacobs, 1971; Wenz, 1977) and physical illness (Lynch, 1976).

Note: The authors express their appreciation for the thoughtful comments made on earlier versions of this chapter by Martin Bragg, Carolyn Cutrona, Steven L. Gordon, Charles T. Hill, John Michela, Daniel Perlman, Zick Rubin, Bernard Weiner and Scott Wimer.

Loneliness is a distressing problem for Americans of all ages. In one national survey (Bradburn, 1969), 26 percent of Americans reported having felt "very lonely or remote from other people" during the past few weeks. Another national study (Maisel, 1969) found that one in nine Americans had felt severely lonely during the past week. In a recent survey conducted by the UCLA Student Health Service, undergraduates ranked loneliness fifth among common health problems faced by college students, ahead of such problems as drinking, smoking, sexual dysfunction, or unwanted pregnancy.

The existing literature on loneliness (see Peplau, Russell, and Heim, 1978) is rich in theoretical speculations, often based on clinical observations. Psychodynamic theorists (Fromm-Reichman, 1959; Sullivan, 1953) propose that loneliness results when a basic human need for intimacy is not met and suggest that childhood experiences may predispose some individuals to loneliness. Sociological theorists (Riesman, Glazer, and Denney, 1961; Slater, 1970) argue that societal factors, such as social mobility or competitiveness, foster loneliness. Most recently, Weiss (1973, 1974) has taken an interactionist approach, emphasizing the importance of both personal and situational factors. In this view, some people are prone to loneliness because of their personality, social skills, or values; and some situations, such as the death of a spouse or moving to a new city, increase the likelihood of loneliness. Current theories provide important insights about loneliness. Unfortunately, however, they have not led to much systematic empirical research.

In this chapter, we present a cognitive approach to understanding loneliness and describe a program of research based on this framework. While not discounting other factors that contribute to loneliness, we suggest that cognitive processes play an important and neglected part. We begin by defining *loneliness* and describing common antecedents of loneliness. In the next section, we suggest that lonely people are motivated to understand the causes of their loneliness and that they attempt to develop an organized account describing the reasons for their problem. Three basic dimensions (internality, stability, and control) underlying causal explanations for loneliness are then discussed. Next, predictions are outlined concerning the consequences of causal attributions for the individual's future expectations, emotional reaction to loneliness, self-esteem, and coping behavior; and empirical support for these predictions is then presented. In a concluding section, some implications of our attributional analysis for helping lonely people are considered.

A Definition of Loneliness

A cognitive analysis of loneliness emphasizes people's desires and preferences concerning social relations (for a more detailed discussion, see Peplau and Perlman, 1979). Loneliness occurs when a person's network of social relationships is smaller or less satisfying than the person desires. Thus, loneliness reflects a discrepancy between the person's *desired* and *achieved* levels of social interaction. The desired level of interaction may reflect, in part, human needs for intimacy (Sullivan, 1953; Weiss, 1973, 1974), but it is also influenced by such other factors as past experience and normative expectations.

Loneliness is not synonymous with social isolation. This is an objective aspect of achieved social contact that does not take into account the individual's desires for social relations. When a low level of social interaction is desired—as when a person craves solitude after a busy day at work—isolation may be experienced positively. Social isolation results in loneliness only when the person's desires for social contact remain high. Weiss (1973, p. 228) suggests that, over time, social isolates may adapt, so that their standards for interaction "shrink to conform more closely to the shape of bleak reality." Support for this possibility is provided by Lowenthal's (1964) finding that old people with a long history of social isolation were less likely to report feeling lonely than were old people with higher levels of social participation.

Based on this definition, loneliness can be precipitated by a change in a person's achieved or desired social relations. At least four major types of events can alter achieved social relations. First, a common cause of loneliness is the ending of a close emotional relationship through widowhood (Lopata, 1969), divorce (Weiss, 1975), or the breakup of a dating relationship (Hill, Rubin, and Peplau, 1976). Second, physical separation from family and friends may put people at risk for loneliness (Weiss, 1973). Third, status changes, such as retirement or unemployment, may promote loneliness. Finally, changes in qualititative aspects of relationships, such as the degree of conflict, communication, or trust, may cause loneliness.

Changes in desired social relations can also precipitate loneliness. The desire for social contact fluctuates, depending on such factors as the person's mood or the nature of the situation (Schachter, 1959). In addition, social norms dictate the sorts of relationships a person should have, and thus influence desires for social relations. "It is clear to the teenager that he or she should have a date, . . . and it is clear to the average man or woman that he or she should have a mate, family, a circle of friends" (Gordon, 1976, p. 15). When a person's achieved social relations fall short of normative standards, the individual is likely to feel lonely. Finally, personal expectations about the sorts of relationships that are possible or probable in a given situation may temper desires for contact.

We have defined *loneliness* as occurring when there is a discrepancy between a person's desired and achieved social relations. In our view, such discrepancies are typically perceived by the individual as unpleasant and are labeled as loneliness. It is possible that some people suffer from a lack of satisfying social relationships without defining themselves as lonely. In our cognitive analysis of loneliness, however, we focus on those individuals who do define themselves as lonely.

Attributional Accounts of Loneliness

We believe that people are typically motivated to understand the causes of their loneliness. Discovering the reasons for one's loneliness helps to make sense of a distressing situation and is a first step toward reestablishing control over one's social relations. Attributions about the causes of loneliness provide important guides for coping with an aversive experience. The desire to understand the causes of loneliness should be strongest among those individuals whose loneliness is severe or long lasting. Consistent with this idea is research on divorce by Harvey, Wells, and Alvarez (1978), which suggests that "the more lonely and depressed the individual, the greater the concern with rehashing the issues" (p. 27).

People attempt to construct an organized account of the causes of their loneliness rather than a simple list of reasons. This point is clearly illustrated in Weiss' (1975, p. 15) discussion of accounts for marital separation: "The account is of major psychological importance to the separated, not only because it settles the issue of who was responsible for what, but also because it imposes on the confused marital events . . . a plot structure with a beginning, middle, and end, and so organizes the events into a conceptually manageable unity. Once understood in this way, the events can be dealt with: They can be seen as outcomes of identifiable causes and eventually can be seen as past, over and external to the individual's present self." In analogous fashion, lonely people attempt to develop an organized explanation of their unsatisfactory social life.

We suggest that personal accounts of loneliness include three distinct elements. First, lonely people can usually point to *precipitating events* that led to the onset of their loneliness. Precipitating events often concern changes in the person's social life, such as ending a love relationship or leaving home to attend college. Changes in desired social relations, such as the increased interest in opposite-sex dating that occurs during adolescence, can also precipitate loneliness. Precipitating events create a discrepancy between the person's desired and achieved social relations. Second, in trying to explain why their loneliness persists over time and why they are unable to form satisfying social relationships, people consider *maintaining causes* of loneliness. These typically concern a different set of causal factors, referring to characteristics of the person (being too shy to initiate a relationship) or of the situation (being in a setting where it is hard to meet new people). Maintaining causes are those factors that prevent the person from achieving a satisfactory social life, and they are the focus of our attributional analysis. Finally, lonely people typically have some idea of the sorts of changes in their achieved or desired social relations that would alleviate their loneliness. These *anticipated solutions* might include such events as finding a congenial group of friends, establishing a new love relationship, or learning to enjoy solitude.

Attributional accounts for loneliness are not necessarily precise. People may be genuinely puzzled or confused about the reasons for their loneliness, or they may consider many possible causal factors. Initial attributions about loneliness may lead people to engage in informal hypothesis-testing behavior (see Wortman and Dintzer, 1978). For example, speculating that loneliness is due to one's appearance might lead a person to try a new hair style or go on a diet. If the person finds that changing his or her appearance makes no difference, then he or she may decide that other causal attributions are more plausible (Kelley, 1971). Partly as a consequence, personal accounts of loneliness may change with the passage of time. An interview we conducted with a sixteen-year-old freshman illustrates such changes. Peter came to UCLA from out of town and knew no one on campus when he started classes. His first months at college were extremely lonely. Initially, Peter attributed his loneliness primarily to the environment. "I thought, it's because of the immense size of the university, as well as the size of classes . . . it is very difficult to form any kind of primary relationship." Over time, however, Peter began to wonder if his explanation was accurate. He noticed that people seemed reluctant to talk to him in classes, and his few attempts at asking women for dates were rebuffed. "I started wondering if there was something about me," he remembered. "I thought maybe because I'm younger than most people here, or because I'm not too good at talking to girls." Accounts may be revised as the person acquires new information and as earlier explanations become less reasonable.

Finally, it is likely that people consider both specific explanations for their loneliness and more general characteristics of their problem. People might consider such specific maintaining causes as being too shy or not trying hard enough to make friends. At the same time, however, people may ask more general questions about the causes of their loneliness, such as "Who is to blame?" or "Can I change my social life?" A central thesis of this chapter is that people's explanations for the causes of their loneliness have important personal consequences. Since attributions are often made while the experience of loneliness is occurring, they can color people's emotional reactions to loneliness and shape their attempts to cope with loneliness. Causal attributions for loneliness may also affect people's feelings of self-esteem and their expectations for future social success or failure. In the next section, we discuss literature on loneliness indicating the relevance of attributional dimensions of internality, stability, and control.

Dimensions of Causal Attributions for Loneliness

Our analysis of loneliness is based largely on the framework developed by Weiner and his colleagues (see reviews in Weiner, 1974a, 1978) to understand attributions for success and failure in achievement settings. Our research on attributions for loneliness extends Weiner's model to the domain of affiliative behavior and construes loneliness as a form of social failure. In this approach, specific causes of loneliness are less important than general underlying dimensional properties of causes, such as whether the cause concerns a characteristic of the person or of the situation. Although those investigating loneliness have not used the language of causal attribution to describe the experience of loneliness, previous discussions can be reinterpreted within an attributional framework. In particular, discussions of loneliness can be seen as suggesting the importance of causal dimensions of internality, stability, and control.

Internality. A major attributional distinction (locus of causality) concerns whether the cause of loneliness is seen as internal or external to the person. Internal causes would include being unattractive, not knowing how to make friends, or lack of effort; external causes would include being rejected by others, being in situations where it is difficult to make friends, or having bad luck. Research (Weiner, 1974a) has indicated that some internal attributions for failure (especially attributions to factors such as effort, which the individual can influence) may lead to blaming a person for failure. This theme of blame has often been discussed in the literature on loneliness. For example, Lowenthal (1964) identified three distinct groups of semiisolated old people. The *alienated* had never developed close relationships and appeared not to desire any. The *defeated* had tried and failed to establish relationships and tended to "blame themselves for their poor adjustment" (p. 65). The consequences of self-blame were sometimes striking. Although none of the alienated ever attempted suicide, several of the defeated had done so. A third group, the *blamers,* had also tried and failed to establish social relationships, but they "tended to blame others or circumstances for their suffering" (p. 66). Lowenthal suggested that self-blame leads to greater social withdrawal than does blaming other people. Other discussions of loneliness (Gordon, 1976; Riesman, 1973) speculate that people have a pervasive tendency to blame themselves for loneliness and that self-blame is related to shame and a reluctance to reveal one's problems to others.

Stability. A second important causal dimension concerns whether the cause of loneliness is perceived as stable or unstable. Stable causes include relatively unchanging features of the situation (being in large classes, living in an isolated area) or of the person (personality, social skills). Unstable causes include relatively changeable factors, such as effort or luck. Closely related to the dimension of stability are the person's expectancies for future outcomes. Research (for example, Weiner, Nierenberg, and Goldstein, 1976) has clearly shown that attributing achievement failures to stable causes leads to the expectation of repeated failure in the future. Similarly, loneliness attributed to stable causes should lead to lower expectancies about future social relationships and more generally to pessimism and hopelessness. In fact, a sense of hopelessness (low future expectancy) has frequently been described as characteristic of lonely people. For instance, Gordon (1976, p. 28) writes that "hopelessness is part of the vicious cycle of loneliness." Fromm-Reichmann (1959, p. 7) suggested that severe loneliness is characterized by "paralyzing hopelessness and unutterable futility."

Control. A final dimension concerns whether or not the person perceives himself as having control over factors causing loneliness. Controllable causes are unstable factors a person could intentionally change, such as degree of effort. Uncontrollable causes are factors the person is unable to influence, which might include internal factors (personality) or external characteristics of the person's social environment. The ability to control one's social relations so as to maintain a satisfactory balance between desired and achieved social relations is central to our conception of loneliness. Loneliness represents a failure to control this balance. As Gordon (1976, p. 41) suggests, "The lonely person does not have a choice. He or she does not choose to be lonely."

But the exercise of personal control is possible in two other ways (Bulman and Wortman, 1977). First, the events that precipitate loneliness may be controlled by the individual. For example, whereas the lonely widow may have had little control over her husband's death, the lonely divorcee may have deliberately separated from her husband. Thus, the divorcee had responsibility for the event that precipitated her loneliness. One study suggests that control over precipitating events may decrease or minimize loneliness. An investigation of break-ups in dating relationships (Hill, Rubin, and Peplau, 1976) found that partners who wanted to end the relationship and perceived themselves as having initiated the break-up reported feeling less lonely and less depressed after the break-up.

Second, and more pertinent to our attributional analysis, is personal control over factors that maintain loneliness. Studies of the elderly suggest that feelings of lack of control over loneliness are quite common (Peplau and Caldwell, in press). For instance, nearly half the lonely old people studied by Tunstall (1967) said there was nothing they could do to alleviate their loneliness. Two experimental field studies provide some support for the idea that increased personal control may reduce loneliness. In a study of institutionalized old people, Schulz (1976) had undergraduates visit residents for a two-month period. Elderly residents who could choose or predict the frequency and duration of visits were significantly more active and rated themselves as higher in hope and happiness and lower in loneliness than residents whose visitor just dropped in, even though actual interaction time was the same. In another experiment conducted in a nursing home for the aged, Langer and Rodin (1976) found that interventions designed to increase personal choice and responsibility improved the social participation and general sense of well-being of residents. Thus, a sense of personal efficacy, both over social relations and life events in general, may minimize feelings of loneliness.

Having suggested at least the potential relevance of causal dimensions of internality, stability, and control to the experience of loneliness, we next turn to a consideration of the consequences of causal attributions.

The Consequences of Causal Attributions for Loneliness

In this section, we outline a set of predictions about the consequences of causal attributions for loneliness. A major contribution of an attributional analysis of loneliness is to clarify the impact that loneliness can have on a person's future expectations, emotional reactions, self-esteem, and coping behavior.

Expectancies. Earlier, we indicated that, for some people, loneliness is accompanied by feelings of pessimism and hopelessness about the future. We predict that hopelessness (low expectancy of social success) will be characteristic only of individuals who ascribe their loneliness to stable causes. Individuals who attribute their loneliness to unstable causes should show greater hope that their loneliness will end. The link between stability and expectancy is supported by extensive evidence from studies of achievement behavior (Weiner, Nierenberg, and Goldstein, 1976) and has recently been extended to affiliative behavior. Folkes (cited in Weiner, 1978) studied instances in which a person had been turned down for a date. She found that a person was more optimistic about having a future date with someone who initially rejected them for an unstable reason (for example, "she had to study that evening") than for a stable reason (for example, "she didn't like my personality").

A further prediction can be made concerning the effects of the duration of loneliness on expectancy. A number of studies (reviewed by Weiner, 1974a) indicate that a consistent pattern of achievement outcomes, such as several failures in succession, leads to stable attributions and to future expectations that the same outcome will recur. Thus, continued loneliness over a long period of time should lead to attributing loneliness to stable causes and to a lower expectancy of the future alleviation of loneliness.

Affect. Loneliness is an unpleasant emotional experience. A study of college students (Russell, Peplau, and Ferguson, 1978) found that high scores on a loneliness scale were significantly correlated with feeling less happy and less satisfied and with more specific feelings, such as *empty, self-enclosed, awkward, bored,* and *restless.* In another study (Berke and Peplau, 1976), college students wrote open-ended descriptions of their feelings and emotions while lonely. Of 196 adjectives given by 136 students, only two could be considered positive (*self-sufficient* and *good*) and a few others as neutral (*quiet, objective*). The most common responses were *depressed, sad, empty,* and *frustrated.* We predict that some affects, such as *unhappy, sad,* or *empty,* are usually experienced by lonely people regardless of their causal attributions; these affects occur independently of attributions (Weiner, Russell, and Lerman, 1978). There are, however, three patterns of affective response to loneliness that may be linked to specific causal attributions.

First, there is some evidence linking loneliness to feelings of hostility (Jones, Freemon, and Goswick, 1978; Moore and Sermat, 1974). We predict that feelings of hostility and anger are characteristic only of lonely people who ascribe their loneliness to external factors, such as being excluded by other people. This prediction is consistent with evidence about affects associated with failure on an achievement task, where the ascription of failure to other people's efforts or motives was associated with such feelings as *revengeful, aggressive, furious, bitter,* and *fuming* (Weiner, Russell, and Lerman, 1978).

Second, there is anecdotal evidence that some people feel shame and embarrassment about their loneliness and are reluctant to admit being lonely to others (Gordon, 1976). We predict that feelings of shame, embarrassment, and guilt will be most common when loneliness is attributed to internal causes, and especially to internal causes that are under the individual's control, such as effort. This prediction is consistent with evidence that achievement failure ascribed to low effort is associated with feelings of shame and guilt (Weiner, Russell, and Lerman, 1978).

Finally, several psychologists have postulated a link between loneliness and depression (Ortega, 1969; Leiderman, 1969). Russell, Peplau, and Ferguson (1978) found that college students' scores on a loneliness scale were significantly correlated with self-reports of feeling depressed and with scores on the Beck Depression Inventory. In fact, the necessity of distinguishing loneliness from depression appears to be an important step in establishing the independent importance of loneliness as a psychological variable. The causal relationships linking loneliness and depression are undoubtedly complex. We believe, however, that causal attributions are one factor that determines when loneliness is associated with depression and when it is not.

We predict that loneliness will be associated with depression or depressed affect only when loneliness is attributed to internal, stable causes. This prediction is consistent with results found for failure in the achievement domain indicating that "depression-related labels of *hopeless, helpless,* and *depressed* and related affects, such as *resigned* and *aimless,* most appear when there is an internal, stable attribution" (Weiner, Russell, and Lerman, 1978, p. 85). The interrelationship of loneliness, attributions for loneliness, and depression is complex. The pattern we predict could occur in at least two ways. First, for some people, ascribing severe loneliness to internal, stable causes (such as being an unattractive and unlovable person) may lead to depression. In this case, attributions for loneliness are postulated to be a cause of depression. This pattern is most likely to occur when loneliness lasts for a long period of time, since prolonged loneliness should lead to increasingly stable, internal attributions and to lowered expectancies of future social success. Second, it is also possible (as suggested by Abramson, Seligman, and Teasdale, 1978; Weiner and Litman-Adizes, in press) that depressed individuals have a general tendency to attribute negative events to internal, stable causes. In this case, depression may influence the type of attributions a person makes for loneliness.

Self-Esteem. Gordon (1976) suggests that loneliness is often accompanied by feelings of worthlessness and failure. Several studies have reported a significant correlation between loneliness and low self-esteem (Eddy, 1961; Jones, Freemon, and Goswick, 1978; Moore and Sermat, 1974). The small size of these correlations suggests, however, that many lonely people maintain high self-esteem. We predict that loneliness is accompanied by low self-esteem only when the loneliness is attributed to internal causes. This prediction is consistent with evidence showing that, when an achievement failure is attributed to ability or personality, it is associated with feeling incompetent and inadequate (Weiner, Russell, and Lerman, 1978, p. 22).

The relationship between causal attributions and self-esteem is probably reciprocal. An individual's level of self-esteem may influence his or her attributions, as indicated in research by Ickes and Layden (1978). Thus, high-self-esteem people may be more likely to attribute loneliness to external (self-exonerating) factors, whereas low-self-esteem people may be more likely to attribute loneliness to internal (self-blaming) factors. At the same time, causal attributions for loneliness may alter a person's self-esteem, especially if social relationships are important to the individual's self-concept (Snyder, Stephan, and Rosenfield, 1978). Many factors other than self-esteem determine a person's attributions for loneliness. For instance, if loneliness persists over a period of months or years, even high-self-esteem people may come to make more internal attributions. A shift toward more internal self-attributions might in turn lead to a lowering of self-esteem.

Coping Behavior. The literature on loneliness suggests two rather distinct motivational and behavioral responses to loneliness. Some writers suggest that the lonely person is highly motivated, attentive to others, and actively seeks out social relationships. Sullivan (1953) believed that loneliness is a "driving" force that motivates individuals to initiate social interaction despite the anxiety such interactions may produce. Weiss (1973, p. 21) observes that the lonely person's "perceptual and motivational energies are likely to become organized in the service of finding remedies for his or her loneliness." However, some authors suggest that loneliness decreases motivation. According to Fromm-Reichman (1959, p. 3), the most severe loneliness "renders people who suffer it emotionally paralyzed and helpless." The association of loneliness with depression (Bragg, 1978; Russell, Peplau, and Ferguson, 1978) would also suggest that lonely persons, like depressed persons, may experience decreased motivation. A detailed discussion of how people cope with loneliness is beyond the scope of this chapter, but we can suggest a few ways in which attributions about the causes of loneliness may influence coping. These suggestions are rather tentative, since, with a few exceptions (for example, Bulman and Wortman, 1977), little evidence exists concerning the impact of attributions on coping.

First, we predict that a pattern of motivated, active coping designed to alleviate loneliness will be most characteristic of individuals who make internal, unstable attributions (Weiner, 1974a). Such attributions suggest that loneliness can be overcome through the individual's own efforts and so encourage active coping. We further predict that a pattern of passivity and social withdrawal results when loneliness is attributed to stable causes (either internal or external). Stability should lead to feelings of hopelessness (low expectancy) and a belief that "there is nothing I can do" (low control). Consequently, stable attributions discourage active coping and may instead lead individuals to attempt to distract themselves from feeling lonely or to attempt to alleviate symptoms by using alcohol or drugs or by losing themselves in work or hobbies.

Second, specific attributions undoubtedly play a part in guiding coping behavior. For example, whereas *shyness* and *physical appearance* are both internal attributions, they suggest distinctly different directions for change: attributing loneliness to shyness might lead a person to try harder to be friendly or to enroll in an assertion-training course, whereas attributing loneliness to one's appearance might lead to a program of exercise or the purchase of a new wardrobe. Some internal attributions, such as "my not trying hard enough to meet people," might lead the person to try to change his or her social environment by joining a club or moving to a more sociable place of residence. We assume that people engage in a hypothesis-testing process. Preliminary attributions lead to coping responses. In some instances, the coping is effective in alleviating loneliness. In other instances, the coping does not reduce loneliness, and so the person's causal explanations may be revised. We predict that a repeated pattern of active but unsuccessful coping may lead people to ascribe loneliness to stable, uncontrollable causes, which in turn may lead to a pattern of passive withdrawal.

In the next section, we discuss research designed to test some of these predictions about consequences of causal attributions for loneliness.

Testing a Model of Causal Attributions for Loneliness

Establishing the relevance of causal attributions for the study of loneliness requires at least two kinds of empirical evidence. First, it is important to demonstrate that dimensions of internality, stability, and control are salient when people think about loneliness. An attributional analysis concerns the subjective world of lay persons, and so showing that postulated causal dimensions are part of everyday conceptions of loneliness would be a major first step. Second, it is also important to demonstrate that causal attributions for loneliness have predictable consequences. Research conducted at UCLA has provided clear support for both of these points.

In an initial study (Michela, Peplau, and Weeks, 1979), college women and men were asked to imagine a person who is lonely. To add generality to the study, the hypothetical person's loneliness was described in several different ways (as lasting a short or long time; as resulting from a lack of "friends to do things with" or a lack of "a boy friend or girl friend"). Each participant read only one description, followed by a list of thirteen possible causes of the student's loneliness. This list was based on free-response attributions for loneliness written by college students (Berke and Peplau, 1976). Included were such causes as "shyness," "being in impersonal settings," or being "physically unattractive."

In the first part of the study, students rated how similar each of the thirteen causes of loneliness was to every other cause. In addition, they rated each cause on a series of bipolar scales assessing internality, stability, and control as well as other distinctions (for example, how frequently it was a cause, whether it excused or showed the lonely person was to blame, and whether it was normal or abnormal). A multidimensional scaling analysis was performed on participants' similarity judgments to reveal the salient underlying dimensions of perceived similarity among causes. Two dimensions emerged, which, as predicted, reflected internality and stability. The labeling of these two dimensions was verified empirically by their correspondence with separate ratings of causes on bipolar scales of internality and stability. Control did not emerge as a third, orthogonal dimension. The data suggested, however, that the controllability of causes was related to both internality and stability— causes were seen as controllable if they were both internal and unstable (for example, effort).

The results of the multidimensional scaling analyses are important for several reasons. First, they provide an empirical basis for applying existing attributional models to the study of loneliness. Second, results support Weiner's (1978) recent contention that his attributional model, originally developed in the context of achievement, is a more general model of motivation that is applicable to a variety of contexts, including affiliative behavior. This finding is all the more striking, since the methods used in the present study differed markedly from those used in previous attributional research. The dimensional model of stability and internality was originally developed by a *deductive* process of reasoning from characteristics of specific causes to postulating general dimensions and then empirically testing predictions dictated by the model (Weiner, 1974a). In contrast, the study of Michela, Peplau, and Weeks (1979) used an empirical process from the outset, namely, multidimensional scaling, to derive perceived dimensions *inductively*. Third, the results bear on current discussions of whether controllability represents a separate third dimension of causality or is subsumed under dimensions of internality and stability. The present results support the view that controllability is not an independent dimension.

Finally, the results of this study help to clarify how students perceive common causes of loneliness. In several instances, students' perceptions did not correspond to our judgments before the fact. For instance, whereas we might have considered a lack of opportunities to meet people as a stable cause (comparable to Weiner's task difficulty), students viewed it as unstable. Students in our sample seem to believe that new opportunities can be found or will eventually occur over time. The causes that corresponded most closely to task difficulty (that is, those that were external and stable) referred to other people in the lonely person's social environment (for example, "other people have their own groups"). Similarly, students viewed shyness as similar to effort—an internal, unstable, and controllable cause rather than a stable personality trait.

A second set of findings from the Michela, Peplau, and Weeks study bears on the consequences of causal attributions. Participants rated the lonely person on a series of scales, including depression and optimism-pessimism. Predictions were made about the relationship of causal attributions to these consequences, and the predictions were tested using path analysis. Clear evidence was found that the affective reaction of *depression* was significantly related to the dimension of internality; the person was seen as more depressed if his or her loneliness was ascribed to internal causes. Evidence was also found linking *expectancy* about future outcomes (optimism-pessimism) to the dimension of stability; the person was seen as more pessimistic when his or her loneliness was ascribed to stable causes. Finally, the path analysis supported the earlier multidimensional scaling finding that controllability is not an independent dimension. In the path analysis, controllability was significantly related to stability but not to internality. Controllable causes were unstable.

In summary, results of the study by Michela, Peplau, and Weeks provide strong support for the relevance of an attributional framework to the study of loneliness. It was shown that participants have a conceptual structure for loneliness in which attributional dimensions proposed by theory are salient. Furthermore, these dimensions were found to have predictable consequences on participants' judgments about a lonely person. These results are, however, based on perceptions of loneliness in another person. They do not provide direct information about self-attributions and their consequences.

Self-Attributions for Loneliness

Empirical evidence concerning the nature and consequences of self-attributions for loneliness comes primarily from a longitudinal study of UCLA undergraduates. In this New Student Study, a sample of over 300 men and women were studied during their first year in college. Students were initially tested in both their second and seventh weeks at UCLA in fall, 1977 (reported in Bragg, 1978), and again during spring, 1978. There is good reason to believe that college students are a high-risk population for loneliness. A large study of individuals from all age groups (cited in Dyer, 1974) found that loneliness was more frequently reported by high school seniors and college freshmen than by any other age group, including the elderly. According to a survey by the UCLA Student Health Service, over 70 percent of undergraduates viewed loneliness as an important problem.

In the New Student sample, 42 percent of students reported feeling moderately or extremely lonely during their second week at school. This pattern is readily understandable, since, for most students, the transition to college brings about major changes in relations with family and childhood friends and requires the establishment of a new social life in an unfamiliar setting. However, even though college students are an appropriate population for studies of loneliness, it is not known if the loneliness experienced by these young adults is qualitatively comparable to the loneliness of such other groups as the divorced or the elderly.

We first sought to identify factors that students perceive as causing their own loneliness. Students' open-ended descriptions of the reasons for their own loneliness (Berke and Peplau, 1976) provided a lengthy list of causal attributions. From these, a shorter list of thirteen causes was created, which included the most commonly cited reasons as well as less frequently mentioned reasons, such as luck, that were of theoretical interest. Those participants in the New Student Study who reported feeling at least moderately lonely ($N = 140$) rated the importance of each of these thirteen causes for their own loneliness on a five-point scale (see Table 1). As has been found in achievement settings, effort was rated as the single most important cause. Other high-importance causes included both internal factors (fear of rejection, not knowing how to make friends) and external explanations (impersonal situations, few opportunities). Among the least important causes were luck, physical appearance, and personality.

Causal Attributions and Depressed Affects. Our research has examined the relationship between attributions for loneliness and depressed affects. Clear empirical support has been found for the

Table 1. Mean Importance Rating of Thirteen Causes of Loneliness

Cause	Mean Importance
My not trying hard enough to meet someone.	2.05
Not enough opportunities to meet people.	1.78
My being too shy.	1.76
My always being in impersonal situations with too many people.	1.74
My not knowing what to do to start a relationship.	1.62
Other people have their own groups and aren't interested in meeting me.	1.62
Other people don't try to make friends.	1.57
My fear of rejection.	1.41
My personality.	1.31
Other people are afraid to make friends.	1.19
My lack of luck in meeting people.	0.99
My physical appearance.	0.96
My belief that there's little chance of finding someone.	0.89

Note: Ratings were made on a 5-point scale (0 to 4) and are based on responses of 140 students who reported being at least moderately lonely during the second week of fall quarter.

prediction that loneliness is most often accompanied by depressed affects when self-attributions for loneliness are internal and stable. In the Berke and Peplau study (1976), students wrote open-ended descriptions of the "feelings and emotions" they experienced when they were lonely. Although *depressed* was the single most frequently mentioned affect (18 percent overall), it was cited twice as often by students giving an ability attribution for their loneliness as by students giving an effort attribution. Of particular interest was the unique occurrence of helplessness/hopelessness in the ability attribution group. Only when the cause of loneliness was perceived as both internal and stable did students report feeling *helpless, hopeless, despair, shut out, inactive, slow,* or *apathy.* Students who perceived the cause of their loneliness as changeable or external did not report such feelings.

Participants in the New Student Study completed the Beck Depression Inventory (1967b), a clinical measure of depression. Evidence was found (see Bragg, 1978) linking depression to internal, stable attributions for loneliness. Analyses comparing moderately lonely students who scored extremely low on the Beck scale (mean = 2.0) with lonely students who scored extremely high on depression (mean = 18.1) found that depressed students were significantly more likely to rate the causes of their loneliness as internal (t (51) = 1.9, p < 0.03) and as stable (t (51) = 1.9, p < 0.03). No differences were found between the depressed and nondepressed groups on perceived controllability of the causes of loneliness. Further analyses compared the depression scores of students whose attributions for their own loneliness were above versus below the median on internality and on stability. A 2 X 2 analysis of variance indicated a significant interaction between these two attributional dimensions (F (1, 43) = 3.7, p < 0.03). Depression scores were highest for students whose attributions for loneliness were both internal and stable.

Three internal causes of loneliness were particularly important for depression in our college sample. Students scoring high on the Beck Depression Inventory were significantly more likely than low scorers to cite as important reasons for their loneliness their physical appearance, personality, and fear of rejection. Further, for all lonely students (regardless of Beck scores), giving importance to any of these three causes was correlated with reports of feeling depressed, hopeless, and helpless.

Taken together, these results support the idea that the relationship between loneliness and depression is mediated by causal attributions for loneliness. The data also support Weiner and Litman-Adizes (in press) and others, who propose that depression is generally associated with stable, internal attributions. This pattern of results might occur because depressed persons have a generalized tendency or "attributional style" to attribute negative outcomes to internal, stable causes. But another possibility deserves consideration. In this study, unlike most research on attributions and depression, individuals made attributions for an important negative life event (loneliness) rather than for their performance on some arbitrary experimental task (see, for example, Rizley,

1978). It is therefore possible that, for some individuals, the experience of severe or enduring loneliness, coupled with internal, stable attributions for their loneliness, is actually a cause of depression.

Causal Attributions and Coping Behavior. We suggested earlier that causal attributions both motivate and direct coping behavior. We predicted that a pattern of active problem-solving behavior would be most characteristic of individuals who make internal, unstable attributions for their loneliness. Partial support for this prediction is provided by data from the New Student Study concerning the social activities that lonely students had recently engaged in. A significant relationship was found between perceiving the causes of loneliness as unstable and reporting both "going somewhere or doing something to meet new people" and "going to a party." Contrary to prediction, however, no relationship was found between these active coping behaviors and internality.

Preliminary evidence that attributions for loneliness guide or direct coping behavior comes from the Berke and Peplau (1976) study. In this study, it was found that students who attributed loneliness primarily to their own low effort were most likely to cite as a main coping strategy "try harder to be friendly," whereas students who attributed loneliness primarily to being in a situation where it was difficult to make friends were most likely to cite "look for activities where I could meet new people." Both these coping strategies are active and involve personal effort, but the effort is directed quite differently in the two cases. Further research on the impact of attributions for loneliness and for other aversive life experiences on coping behavior is clearly needed.

Duration of Loneliness and Causal Attributions. We have proposed that causal attributions for loneliness are often revised as loneliness continues over time. Two processes affecting such changes concern the general *plausibility* of particular attributions for short-term versus long-term loneliness and the results of informal *hypothesis-testing* of preliminary attributions. In general, we predict that, when loneliness persists over time, there is a tendency for attributions to become more internal and more stable. In turn, these changes may lead to lower expectancies for the future and, ultimately, to depression.

Evidence that the plausibility of attributions differs depending on the duration of loneliness comes from a study of ninety-eight UCLA undergraduates (Peplau, Russell, and Heim, 1977). After reading descriptions of a college student who had been lonely for "a short period of time" or for "six months," participants made causal attributions for the person's loneliness. Duration of loneliness had a striking effect on the internality of attributions (χ^2 (1) = 60.2, $p < 0.001$). Only 22 percent of attributions for short-term loneliness were internal, as compared with 85 percent of attributions for long-term loneliness. Duration had no effect, however, on the stability of attributions; in both conditions, about 80 percent of attributions were unstable. It appears that such explanations as being in large classes or having few opportunities to meet people are plausible for short-term loneliness but are less reasonable for enduring loneliness. Over time, the possibility that internal factors, such as shyness, lack of effort, or poor social skills, may contribute to loneliness becomes more plausible. Although we do not have direct evidence on this point, we suspect that similar plausibility considerations affect self-attributions for loneliness.

The New Student Study provides some evidence for shifts toward more internal self-attributions as loneliness persists over time. Among students who remained moderately lonely from their second to seventh week at UCLA, significant decreases occurred in the rated importance of such external causes as "other people don't try to make friends" or "others have their own groups." Further, a significant relationship was found between the length of the student's current loneliness and the importance given to particular attributions; students who had been lonely for longer periods of time were more likely to attribute their loneliness to their physical appearance and personality.

Reactions to Lonely Others

Although people sometimes react toward lonely individuals with warmth and compassion, this is not invariably the case. The opposite tendency, for people to reject and avoid the lonely, has frequently been noted. For example, Fromm-Reichman (1959, p. 6) observed that "the lonely person may be displeasing if not frightening to his hearers, who may erect a psychological wall of ostracism and isolation about him as a means of protecting themselves." Both Fromm-Reichman (1959) and Burnside (1971) suggest that this pattern of avoiding the lonely may characterize health professionals as well as lay persons.

Although the factors that lead people to react negatively to the lonely are complex (see Peplau and Perlman, 1979), we believe that attributions play a part. Weiss (1973) has commented that "Our image of the lonely often casts them as justifiably rejected" (p. 12). "It is easy to see the lonely as out of step, as unwilling to make necessary overtures to others, as lacking in qualities necessary to satisfactory human relations. In this way, we blame as we purport to explain" (p. 75).

The attributions observers make for the causes of another person's loneliness may contribute to a pattern of avoidance and rejection. Undergraduates' open-ended descriptions of why "college students at UCLA" are lonely (Berke and Peplau, 1976) frequently included attributions to the person that had an element of blame. For instance, one student wrote, "The fault, I believe, always lies within the individual who is lonely. If a person is lonely, it is because that person has not taken the initiative in attempting to meet people." Our attributional analysis suggests that sympathy for the lonely should be greatest when they are perceived as lonely through no fault of their own (external or uncontrollable causes). In contrast, rejection and avoidance should be greatest when the lonely individual is perceived as personally responsible for his or her loneliness (attributions are internal and controllable).

Empirical support for these predictions comes from two studies conducted at UCLA. In one study (Wimer and Peplau, 1978), college students read a brief description of a fictional college student who had gone to a university counseling center because he had been feeling lonely. Liking for the lonely person was significantly related to perceiving the causes of loneliness as situational rather than personal (internal), and liking was least when the person's loneliness was attributed to his personality. Results also indicated the importance of the individual's perceived effort to overcome his loneliness. High effort was significantly correlated with greater liking and sympathy for the lonely person and with rating the lonely person as being more friendly and more interesting to talk to. These data are consistent with findings (see Weiner, 1974a) that effort is a major determinant of rewards and punishments for achievement behavior.

A second study (Berke and Peplau, 1976) included questions about more general attitudes toward the lonely. Included in a longer questionnaire were items about the extent to which lonely people are responsible for their loneliness: "People can be lonely through no fault of their own" and "People who are lonely bring it on themselves." Other items assessed reactions toward the lonely, such as "I have little sympathy for a person who is lonely" or "I prefer not to associate with a person who is lonely." As predicted, believing that lonely people are responsible for their problem was significantly correlated with having little sympathy for the lonely and with avoiding the lonely.

Taken together, these results suggest that attributions can influence reactions to lonely others. Certain explanations for loneliness may lead us to blame the lonely person and hence to derogate and reject him or her. The possibility that this tendency may affect the reactions of clinicians and helping professionals is particularly worthy of investigation.

Implications for Helping the Lonely

Lonely people seek to understand their problem in order to alleviate it. Causal attributions for loneliness serve primarily to help individuals control and change their unsatisfactory social life. But, as Kelley (1971, p. 22) has observed, "control of one's environment undoubtedly involves some sort of balance between controlling the *controllable* and controlling the *important*." We believe that it is essential for lonely people to maintain a sense of personal control over their social environment. But, if attempts to alleviate loneliness are misdirected at unimportant or inaccurate causes, they are unlikely to succeed and so may ultimately lead to feelings of lowered control. Thus, a major goal of counseling or of self-help for the lonely should be to identify accurately the important causes of an individual's loneliness and to assess correctly the potential changeability of these causes. To this end, special care should be taken to avoid two common errors affecting causal attributions for loneliness.

Underestimating Situational Causes. There is a tendency to underestimate the importance of situational causes of loneliness and to overestimate the role of personal factors—to commit what Ross (1977, p. 183) has called "the fundamental attributional error." This tendency is especially clear in cases where loneliness is severe or enduring. It is encouraged by the emphasis in both folk wisdom and psychological thinking on a characterological theory of loneliness (Weiss, 1973). It is fostered by an image of the lonely as willful social deviants who fail to live up to normative expectations concerning appropriate social relationships. The tendency to see the lonely as unusual is also affected by a general reluctance among people to reveal feelings of loneliness to others. A situation of pluralistic ignorance about loneliness may commonly exist, in which people assume that their own loneliness is unique or abnormal. Our own view is that loneliness is most often caused by an *interaction* of personal and situational factors. Loneliness typically results from a poor match between the individual's interests, social skills, or personal characteristics and his or her social environment. Thus, careful consideration should be given to both internal and external causes.

Underestimating the Changeability of Causes. Several factors may lead people to underestimate the potential changeability of causes of loneliness. First, lonely people often focus their attention on the precipitating causes of loneliness rather than on the maintaining causes. Precipitating events, such as the death of a spouse or a recent divorce, are stable and irrevocable. In contrast, factors that perpetuate loneliness and impede the development of a satisfactory social life, such as shyness or limited opportunities to meet people, may be more amenable to change. Encouraging the lonely to examine the maintaining causes of loneliness may thus lead to perceptions of greater changeability.

Second, people may inaccurately assess the stability of specific causal factors. For example, students in our research identified physical appearance and personality as stable causes of loneliness. Although it may be more difficult to change these factors than to change one's degree of effort, they are by no means intractable. People can learn new social skills, can improve their appearance, can learn to be more assertive in social settings, and so on. It may be helpful to emphasize that judgments of stability concern the relative changeability of causal factors rather than an absolute stable-versus-unstable dichotomy.

Finally, the common assumption that it is easier to change the person than to change the situation needs to be reexamined. People can often influence and change their social environment by selecting from among alternative social settings, finding other people with similar interests, and influencing their position within various social institutions. For example, the new college student can select a small school or a large university, can join clubs or teams, move on campus, go to social events and dances, sign up for small seminars rather than large lecture classes, and in many ways control the nature of his or her social interactions. In some instances, the new student can even create new social groups, perhaps by starting an ecology club or a consumer-interest group. The notion that people must adjust to a fixed or invariant social environment is false. In fact, it may be easier for individuals to alter their social surroundings than to change long-standing attitudes, interests, social skills, or personality characteristics.

Increasing Personal Control. Several researchers (Abramson, Seligman, and Teasdale, 1978; Dweck and Goetz, 1978) have suggested that a key factor in enhancing perceived control is to attribute failure to low effort. In the case of loneliness, we believe that the crucial issue is not the degree of effort a person exerts but rather where the person's effort is directed. In laboratory studies of attributions and behavior, the nature of the effort required is typically implicit in the task. In an achievement context, for example, effort might mean concentrating more attentively, working faster, or checking one's answers more carefully. In the case of loneliness, in contrast, it is not necessarily clear whether the person's effort should be directed at being more friendly, at improving social skills, at finding new ways to meet people, or at any one of many other possibilities. The key to helping lonely people to develop satisfying social relationships may be to direct the person's effort toward remedying important and potentially changeable causes of loneliness.

Perceptions
of Battered Wives

XXXXXXXXXXXXXXXXXXXXXXXXXX

Wife-battering is not a new phenomenon. Historically, husbands have been expected to use physical force when their wives failed to obey them (Davidson, 1977). In Roman times (753 B.C.), for example, "A wife was obligated to obey her husband and he was given the legal right and the moral obligation to control and punish her for any 'misbehaviour.' . . . Any indication that a wife was not under the complete control of her husband was deemed sufficient grounds for beating her, even to excess" (Dobash and Dobash, 1978, p. 428). "During the Middle Ages women throughout Spain, Italy, France, and England could be flogged through the city streets, exiled for years, or killed if they committed adultery or numerous 'lesser' offenses. . . . Even the French code of chivalry specified that the husband of a scolding wife could knock her to the earth, strike her in the face with his fist, and break her nose so that

Note: Funds for this project were provided by the National Institute of Mental Health (Alcohol, Drug Abuse, and Mental Health Administration), NIMH Grant #1 R01 MH30193.

she would always be blemished and ashamed" (p. 429). And, "Under English Common Law a married woman lost all of her civil rights, had no separate legal status, and became the chattel of her husband. The right of the husband to chastise his wife was considered a natural part of his responsibilities" (p. 429).

Although wife-battering was still accepted in the late nineteenth century in England and the United States, the courts at that time were beginning to punish severe assaults (Davidson, 1977; Tomes, 1978). Both Alabama and Massachusetts officially rescinded the "privilege" of wife-beating in 1871, but most states in their legal codes continued to tolerate abuse until fairly recently. Although our legal system is becoming less and less tolerant of wife-battering, especially of severe cases, assault from one's husband today still carries a lesser punishment than a similar assault from a stranger (Davidson, 1977; 1978). Things are changing though. On a national level, the United States Commission on Civil Rights sponsored a consultation on battered women in 1978, and both federal and state legislatures are adopting laws to aid battered women.

Legal changes are reflected in public attitudes. In 1970, Stark and McEvoy reported that about 25 percent of their male sample and 17 percent of their female sample would approve of a husband slapping his wife under certain circumstances. Today, an even larger majority of men and women report that it is "never" okay for a husband to hit his wife (men's mean response is 1.2, women's is 1.1 on a five-point scale from "never" to "always"; Knoble and Frieze, 1979).

In spite of these changes in the law and in public attitudes, wife-battering continues to be a widespread problem—one so common that it seems more than appropriate to classify it as a problem in everyday life. Studies conducted in Norwalk, Connecticut, and Harlem, New York, suggest that police across the country probably receive a half million calls a year to aid battered wives (Ball and Wyman, 1976). Looking at divorce applicants, O'Brien (1971) reported that 17 percent of his cases spontaneously mentioned overt violent behavior. Levinger (1974) found spontaneous complaints of physical abuse by 37 percent of wives in a study of six hundred couples seeking divorce in the Cleveland area. A study of cases of aggravated assault in St. Louis (Pittman and Handy, 1964) found 11 percent of the victims had been assaulted by their spouses. A similar study in Detroit found that 52 percent of the assaults were between husbands and wives (Boudouris, 1971). In 1974, one fourth of all murders were within the family and, for half of these, one spouse killed the other. In all, nearly 1,300 women were killed by their husbands in 1974. Spouse-homicide rates have been similar over the past several years (U.S. Department of Justice, 1975). A recent national survey suggests that about 1.8 million wives are beaten by their husbands in any given year (Straus, 1978) and that at least 25 percent of American families have at least minimal levels of husband-wife violence (Gelles and Straus, 1979). Our own data from forty-two control women suggest that 32 percent of the wives in the Pittsburgh area have experienced some degree of violence from their husbands. However, only 10 percent have experienced severe violence.

It is clear that many women face the problem of being physically assaulted by their husbands. The simple solution is for the battered woman to leave the marriage. Frequently, people are heard to say, "I'd never stand for it. I'd just leave!" Or, "Why does she stay?" On the surface this viewpoint seems reasonable, but researchers have found that the situation is very complex. Women stay in violent relationships for a variety of reasons; in general, their reactions to the violence, which vary greatly, include denial, passive acceptance, seeking help from others, and leaving.

This chapter uses an attribution theory framework to look more closely at the responses of battered women. Specifically, beliefs these women have about the causes of the violence they have experienced seem to be highly correlated with their reactions to the battering. An attributional model of the women's reactions will be presented, after first looking at attributions made by various people about wife-battering. The discussion will also attempt to answer the commonly asked question of why such abuse occurs.

Perceived Causes of Wife Battering

Attribution theory is a theoretical perspective for understanding people's ideas about why things happen. Some of the most relevant research within this area looks at beliefs about the causes of success and failure or why good or bad events occur (Weiner, 1972a; Weiner and others, 1972). In any situation, there are many potential reasons why one does well or poorly. A person may succeed because of his or her general competence, effort, mood, or good luck; because the situation made it easy to succeed; or because of someone else's help. Similarly, failure may result from incompetence, not trying hard enough, being in a bad frame of mind, bad luck, an impossible situation, or the negative influence of another person (Elig and Frieze, 1975; Frieze, 1976a).

Psychological and sociological researchers either implicitly or explicitly make various assumptions about why wife-battering occurs, and so do others who are directly or indirectly involved in violent situations. Some of the causal factors that have been mentioned are: she allows it, she wants it, she provoked it, he was drunk, he needed to keep her in line, he is a bully, he wants to prove he is a real man, and he is under job pressure.

Locus of Causality. The theoretical attribution model mentioned earlier classifies causal statements about good and bad events in two ways, as shown in Table 1. First, where is the source of the violence, or who is responsible? This dimension, called the *locus* of the cause, can be analyzed in terms of causes associated with the wife, causes associated with the husband, joint causes, and causes in the society as a whole. Laboratory-based attribution research would predict that, if she feels she is the cause of the violence, the wife will experience more shame than if she attributes the cause to her husband or to society (Weiner and others, 1972). Similarly, if others attribute the cause to her, they would be expected to blame her and be unsympathetic. One example of this view is the belief that women who remain in abusive relationships must like them (Waites, 1978). Deutsch (1939), writing in a psychoanalytic tradition, equated femininity with passivity and masochism. Others using this framework have assumed that battered women are masochistic, like being beaten, and therefore deserve little sympathy. Wife blamers might also advise the battered wife to seek psychological help for the personal problems they see her as having.

The idea that the wife is basically at fault is not a new idea.

Table 1. Possible Causal Explanations for Why Women Are Beaten by Their Husbands

	Internal to the Wife		
Stable	Uncertain	Unstable

Stable	Uncertain	Unstable
She allows it.	She provokes him.	She was cheating on him.
She wants to be beaten; she enjoys it.	She cannot leave.	She provoked him.
She is incompetent.		She did not perform her household
She is dependent.		duties properly.
		She yelled at him.
		She embarrassed him.
		She didn't do what he wanted.

Internal to the Husband

Stable	Uncertain	Unstable
His parents were violent with one another.	He is taking out his frustrations on her.	He was drunk.
He has a violent personality.	He cannot cope with pressures.	He was frustrated.
He was beaten as a child.	He wants her to leave him.	He was unhappy.
He is a bully.	He is threatened by her.	He had job pressures.
He needs power.	He wants to prove he is a real man.	
He is insecure.	He wants to keep her in line.	
He is irresponsible.		
He grew up that way.		
He cannot control his emotions.		
He is an alcoholic.		

Joint Responsibility

Stable	Uncertain	Unstable
They both have problems.	They do not get along.	They were frustrated at the time.
They have a pathological relationship.		

Environmental

Cultural acceptance of wife-battering.
Laws are not helpful.
Part of living in a poor family.

Built into many of the legal codes discussed earlier was the idea that wives provoked beatings by disobeying their husbands. Another example of blaming the wife is the common idea of the shrewish wife who needs to be beaten. At a recent performance of Shakespeare's *Taming of the Shrew* in Pittsburgh, the audience cheered as Kate was beaten and subdued. This reaction was probably based on the audience's belief that Kate deserved to be treated violently by her husband.

Current social psychological theory would also suggest a high incidence of placing the blame on the victim (in this case, the wife) for her misfortunes (see Chapter Two in this volume for further discussion of this issue). Such theory assumes that observers blame the victim so that they do not have to see chance as the cause of a severe misfortune (Walster, 1966) or as a protection of their belief that the world is fair (Lerner and Miller, 1978). Shaver (1975) extended these ideas to show that observers blame the victim less if they do not see the possibility of themselves being in the same situation as the victim.

Although both historical evidence and current social psychological theory would predict a high degree of attribution for wife-battering to the wife, empirical data based on women in the Pittsburgh area do not support the idea (Frieze, 1978; Knoble and Frieze, 1979). As shown in Table 2, a very small percentage of battered women, nonbattered women, and men felt that the wife was the cause of her battering when asked to make an attribution about this hypothetical situation: "Karen is a married woman in her late twenties. She has two children, and she and her husband have a moderate income. Yesterday Karen confided to you that her husband beat her up fairly badly last week. Why do you think he might have done this?" As Shaver (1975) predicted, women who had themselves been battered were somewhat less likely to blame the woman than female subjects who had not experienced violence in their marriages.

There are numerous reasons why more blame was associated with the husband than with the wife in these studies. First, many of the results compare blaming the husband or the wife with blaming chance or fate. Since chance is not seen as a reasonable attribution for battering, these studies may not be relevant. Second,

Table 2. Beliefs About the Causes of a Hypothetical Wife-Battering

Subject Group	Husband	Source of Violence Wife	Other	Don't Know
Battered women				
n = 42[a]	81%	5%	7%	7%
n = 30[b]	56%	16%	4%	24%
Nonbattered women				
n = 28[a]	79%	11%	11%	0%
n = 20[b]	65%	20%	10%	5%
Men				
n = 44[a]	75%	14%	5%	7%

[a]Knoble and Frieze (1979).
[b]Frieze (1978).

as discussed earlier, few people today feel it is acceptable for a husband to hit his wife; such unacceptable behavior may thus make him more blameworthy. Third, the locus of an attribution depends on where attention is focused (Monson and Snyder, 1977; Taylor and Fiske, 1975). Since the question asked "Why do you think *he* might have done this?", subjects may have responded with explanations relating to the husband. Further research is needed to fully explore this issue.

Shaver's (1975) defensive blame attribution theory is supported by the Pittsburgh area data and may also provide a clue to understanding the high level of husband blame. When asked if they knew someone who had been battered, most subjects in all groups knew at least one person. They also reported that wife-battering was a fairly frequent phenomenon (Knoble and Frieze, 1979). Thus, even nonbattered women may have felt that the violence could happen to them. However, the frequency of wife-battering would also suggest that the men should have showed a greater tendency to blame the wife or factors other than the husband. This result was not found. All these discrepancies indicate that further attribution research in nonlaboratory settings is needed.

Many researchers share the view that the husband is to be blamed for wife-battering. Examples are the theories that wife-batterers are basically violent people (Pizzey, 1974), that males may learn to be aggressive as part of their male role socialization (Pleck, 1976), that aggression is associated with masculinity in our society (Broverman and others, 1972; Huggins and Straus, 1975), and that males are more violent than females outside the home as well as in it (Johnson, 1972). The expectancy that men will be aggressive toward their wives has traditionally been incorporated into law, and thus many may still see aggressiveness as normal behavior (Calvert, 1974; Straus, 1976). The fact that many husbands do not perceive their violence toward their wives as a problem adds support to the idea that they themselves accept violent behavior as normal (Davidson, 1978; Martin, 1976). Other theories support husband blame—for example, men are socialized to be violent as a part of their male role and also through direct learning as children (Straus, 1977a); and wife-beaters frequently were abused as children or came from homes where they had witnessed their fathers beating their mothers (Roy, 1977; Straus, 1977b).

Other husband-associated causes of wife-battering include his drinking, his being in a bad mood, or his feelings of insecurity about not meeting his own standards of job success (Allen and Straus, 1975; O'Brien, 1971; Prescott and Letko, 1977; Scott, 1974). The last idea might also explain Gelles' (1972) finding that men with lower-level jobs and men with college educations are most often violent, since those two groups might experience the greatest divergencies between their job performance and expectations. Also, unemployed husbands are especially likely to be violent (Prescott and Letko, 1977), as are men whose social status is less than that of their wives' fathers (O'Brien, 1971). Gelles (1972) further suggests that men may compensate for their wives' superior verbal skills by using physical force.

Other researchers see the husband and wife as jointly responsible for wife-battering. The spouses may fail to adapt to each other's needs (Harper, 1978; Scott, 1974), not get along, or not know how to handle anger (Geller and Walsh, 1978).

Finally, there are several societal explanations for violence between husbands and wives. Straus (1977b) suggests that many features of family life tend to increase the probability of violence occurring in the home, including the large amount of time spent together by family members, whose divergent interests may conflict. Also, the high degree of emotional involvement between family members tends to exacerbate any difficulties that do arise. Since outsiders generally consider family life a private concern of the family members themselves, they hesitate to interfere with violent behavior or other disapproved actions unless the behavior becomes quite severe. Finally, family ties can be difficult, if not impossible, to foresake. Straus feels that all these factors, coupled with the generally violent society in which we live, make the family an especially likely candidate for violence.

Another societal explanation is that the stresses of being poor create more violence. Komarovsky (1964) reports more physical violence in blue-collar families. Gelles (1972) finds that abusing men tend to be less educated *or* highly educated. Although police statistics for calls about domestic violence suggest that such requests are more frequent in poorer areas of the city, researchers believe such statistics are the result of middle- and upper-class women being less likely to call for police help (Straus, Gelles, and Steinmetz, 1976). Certainly, the husbands of women who have reported battering are from all social groups (Martin, 1976; Pizzey, 1974). Thus, the exact relationship between the socioeconomic status of the husband and his abuse of his wife is still ambiguous (Straus, Gelles, and Steinmetz, 1976).

Stability of Causality. The second commonly used causal dimension within the Weiner framework is that of the stability or changeability of the causal attribution. Stable causes such as one's personality or family background can be expected to continue as causal factors in the future; thus an attribution to a stable factor such as personality will produce little expectancy for change in the future (McMahan, 1973; Weiner and others, 1972). If a woman attributes a beating to her husband's generally violent personality, she can well expect to be beaten again, since his personality will probably not change—at least in the near future.

Unstable causes, on the other hand, lead to an expectancy for change. If a woman attributes her beating to her husband's temporary unemployment, she will expect such battering to persist only as long as he is unemployed. Examples of stable and unstable causal explanations for violence are shown in Table 1. Other causes listed in this table are considered intermediate between stable and unstable causes since they are not readily codeable into either extreme (see Elig and Frieze, 1975, for further discussion of coding attributional explanations for good and bad events).

Although little research has been done on the stability of the causal explanations people actually use for marital violence, several writers (such as Walker, 1979) suggest that many women see the cause of the violence they have experienced as due to stable or unchangeable elements in their husbands. Our research supports the idea that a problem with the husband's personality is a primary explanation given for a hypothetical case of wife-battering (Frieze, 1978).

An Attributional Model of a Woman's Reactions to Battering

As we just discussed, a woman could potentially make a variety of attributions if she were battered by her husband. In this section, we will show how previous research in attribution theory might predict the attributions and how various attributions might mediate the woman's reaction to being battered. Then, using our own research data as well as those of others, we will examine how much support there is for the various predictions.

Predicting the Causal Attributions of the Battered Wife. A number of predictions could be made about how a woman might perceive the situation in which she were battered by her husband. Given the general tendency to attribute good things to oneself and bad things externally (Heider, 1958; Frieze and Weiner, 1971; Ross, 1977), one might expect that women would be most likely to blame their husbands or societal factors for being battered. Based on an extensive review of the literature, Miller and Ross (1975) outlined a number of explanations for this bias toward attributing negative events to others and positive events to oneself. They suggest that it is reasonable for people to take more responsibility for something good that they intended to make happen than for something bad that they had attempted to avoid. Second, subjects in laboratory studies accept more personal responsibility for an expected than an unexpected event, and they tend to expect success more than failure. Third, subjects experiencing a pattern of increasing success are more likely to see how their own efforts co-vary with these successes than are people experiencing increasing failure. Seeing co-variation between one's outcomes and one's efforts leads to more internal attributions in general (Kelley, 1971).

Most of this research has been done with college students in artificial laboratory situations. A study done by Veroff and Melnick (1977) found similar results when a large random sample of adults were asked about a variety of life problems. They found that women reported somewhat more marital problems than men but that they were somewhat less likely to see these problems as caused by their own behavior. However, both men and women saw the primary causes of their marital problems as due to external cir-cumstances or to joint problems in their relationship.

In spite of this evidence for a prediction of high blaming of external factors by battered women, two areas of research make the opposite prediction—a general tendency for women to blame themselves more for failure and for victims to blame themselves. Once again, the research on sex differences in attributional pat-terns is based largely on college students doing artificial tasks (Frieze and others, in press). These studies indicate that women blame their own lack of ability for failure on achievement tasks more than men do. Of course, as Frieze and her associates (in press) point out in a review of this literature, these results are strongest for "masculine" tasks for which women have lower expec-tancies for success and more doubts about their own abilities to begin with. There is no evidence that we know of to support the idea that most women have high expectancies for failure in their marriages or for being battered. Even studies that find wife-battering is more likely to occur when men were beaten as children or had witnessed their fathers physically abusing their mothers do not find such patterns for women. Many battered women have had little experience with family violence while growing up, do not expect their husbands' violence, and find that violence quite perplexing (Roy, 1977).

Literature dealing specifically with victims of accidents or rape also makes the prediction of high self-blame for battered women (Bulman and Wortman, 1977; Janoff-Bulman, in press). This research suggests that better coping in these victims is associ-ated with self-blame, possibly because this provides the victims with some sense of control over future occurrences of the same negative event (see Chapter Two in this volume for further discussion of this theory). Janoff-Bulman (in press) suggests, though, that not all forms of self-blame are equally beneficial. An attribution of a negative event to a characterological or personality factor in oneself leads to little opportunity to change in the future even though it gives one a sense of control over the past. Depressed individuals tend to make more characterological blame attributions than nondepressed people. Behavioral self-blame, however, suggests that by changing one's behavior in the future, the negative event can be avoided. This distinction is analogous to one postulated earlier by Weiner and his associates (1972)—the dimension of stability. Stability concerns the changeability of the cause. Stable causes tend to persist, whereas unstable causes fluctuate with time. Stable causes also lead to an expectancy that things will not change, whereas unstable causes imply that there could be a change (McMahan, 1973; Weiner and others, 1972). Thus, one would predict that beatings attributed to unusual or changeable circumstances would not be expected to continue but that those attributed to the wife's competence or the violent personality of the husband would be expected to be repeated. A battered wife would have a far greater chance of controlling her behavior in the future to prevent further beatings than changing her personality. Consistent with this view, one would expect many battered women to attribute their beatings to themselves, especially to unstable or behavioral factors. However, here again, the theories of Coates and others (Chapter Two, this volume), Bulman and Wortman (1977), and Janoff-Bulman (in press) generated for rape victims or victims of unforeseen accidents may not be applicable to battered women. The battering situation, unlike many types of accidents, clearly involves an interpersonal situation where either or both parties are potentially at fault. It also involves a long-term, continuing relationship, unlike a rape. Thus, the probability of recurrence of the event is far greater than for accidents or rapes.

All these studies provide clues for various types of attributional "biases" or tendencies to make one type of causal attribution more than another. However, the various theories lead to quite different predictions, and so we cannot confidently state what types of causal explanations will be more commonly used by battered women. We can, perhaps, make some suggestions about causal attributions made as a function of the specific type of battering situation.

Both the severity of the violence and the frequency of similar incidents in the past may affect the causal attributions the woman makes for a particular act of battering. Theoretical attribution theory research has shown us that events consistent with what has happened in the past tend to be more attributed to stable causes and causes within the person (Frieze and Weiner, 1971; McArthur, 1972; Orvis, Cunningham, and Kelley, 1975). Thus, people who have previously done well in school and who do well again will attribute this new success to their own abilities. Or, if they have had a history of failure, they will often attribute another failure to lack of ability. A woman who has been battered in the past will be more likely to attribute the cause to a stable factor within herself, such as her personality, or to stable characteristics of her husband. She may also be more likely to perceive that the cause of the first violent incident was a unique circumstance that might not be repeated. She may feel it was the result of her not doing something that she should have or of her husband's being in a particularly bad mood. If the battering was totally unexpected, as well as having never happened in the past, she might attribute it to unstable circumstantial factors (Feather and Simon, 1971a, 1971b). Such an attribution might consist of her feeling that the battering occurred because she was extraordinarily tired from having had to work overtime and he had just been notified that he was being laid off. Such surprise would be especially high in women who had had no experience with family violence when they were growing up and who were not personally acquainted with other battered women. It may well have been more common a few years ago when there was little discussion of wife-battering in the media. (Just within the past two years, several television and radio shows have discussed wife-battering, as have numerous popular books and newspaper articles.)

Other attribution research would predict that the more severe the violence, the more likely the battered woman would attribute the violence to her husband. More extreme behavior is generally seen as being more likely to have been caused by the actor, and it is seen as being more intended by the actor (Jones and Davis, 1965). Extreme levels of violence are considered unusual within a family setting. People are often shocked by stories of wives who have been permanently injured (total loss of sight in one eye, severe internal injuries requiring lengthy hospital stays, and so forth). Such behavior on the part of these husbands is seen as quite extreme, so much so that even by the late nineteenth century the legal system was acting to attempt to stop such violence. Other researchers using different methodologies, such as Walster (1966), have shown the same results—people are seen as more responsible for their actions when the consequences of these actions are more severe.

To summarize, three major factors might potentially affect the attributions of a battered woman (see Figure 1). Attributional biases may operate in a variety of ways. An egocentric bias in the woman would make her blame her husband or external factors for the battering. At the same time, the general tendency of women to blame themselves for failure and the tendency for victims of various types to blame themselves would suggest that the battered woman would see herself as responsible. We would expect that all these factors or a combination might operate for any given individual and that we would find some women who blame themselves and others who blame their husbands. We would further expect that repeated violence and more severe violence would be more attributed to the husband.

Emotional Reactions to Battering. Since women react in a variety of ways to being battered, an attributional model should account for various emotional and behavioral reactions as a function of different causal attributions. The model in Figure 1 suggests three basic emotional reactions that battered women may have after a violent incident. They may be upset about the experience but hope that things will be better in the future. Or, they may be fearful of future violence being even more severe—perhaps severe enough to threaten their own life or the lives of their children. Finally, the battered woman may feel helpless to change her situation.

Each of these reactions could be predicted to result from a particular causal attribution or pattern of attributions for the vio-

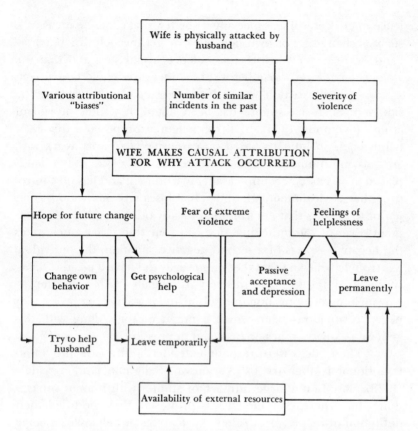

Figure 1. An Attributional Model of Women's Reactions to Battering.

lent incident. Hope for future change is linked to having an unstable attribution. If the cause of the violence is seen as something that could change, there is, by definition, more hope than if the cause is stable. "Hope" in this situation is closely linked to future expectancies in the theoretical, laboratory-based research on attributions for achievement successes and failures. Future expectancies are closely related to attributional stability, as discussed earlier.

A second reaction might be fear of increased violence in the future. Such a reaction should be incompatible with hoping things will get better and, thus, should be related to more stable causal attributions for violence. However, it would be possible for a woman to hope for a nonviolent future and still fear that the violence might get worse, especially if she felt that concrete measures, such as changing her own behaviors or getting help for her husband, were needed before the violence would stop and that the violence might get worse before these measures could take effect.

A third reaction would be to feel helpless to change the situation. Such a response has been noted in victims of violent crimes (Symonds, 1975). In 1975, Seligman proposed a theory of helplessness in humans based on extensive laboratory work with animals and humans. He had observed that when an individual is placed in an extremely unpleasant environment and has no control over that environment, the individual loses any motivation to attempt to change that environment or any other negative environment. Even if the individual does do something that ameliorates the negative aspects of a second negative situation, the individual has trouble believing that the action really did have a positive benefit and may fail to make this response again. With time, the organism loses all motivation to respond and passively accepts further negative situations from which it might escape. Along with this general passivity comes anxiety and depression.

These ideas were recently extended and recast into an attributional framework by Abramson, Seligman, and Teasdale (1978). Based on a large number of studies with human subjects done since the earlier model was proposed, they modified their definition of helplessness. They saw feelings of helplessness being generated when a person attributed a particular failure or negative event to a global rather than a specific cause. Global causes were seen as more encompassing and as more generalizable than specific causal attributions. For example, attributing a failure on a mathematics test to a lack of mathematics ability or to an unfair test is far less debilitating than attributing the failure to an overall lack of intelligence or to a belief that all mathematics tests are unfair. Similarly, a woman could attribute rejection by her lover to the specific causal factors of being unattractive to him or his having problems relating to women, or she could make an attribution to global factors, such as being unattractive to all men or all men having trouble relating to women. In the specific case, a stable attribution is made, but the effects on future expectancies for the relationship apply only to this particular man. There would be no reason to believe that a new relationship might not be successful. A global attribution, however, would imply that any relationship could result in serious problems, and the woman might then feel helpless about establishing a good relationship with any man; these feelings of helplessness would be especially strong if the attribution was stable as well as global. Temporary feelings of helplessness might result if the woman attributed her rejection to an unstable, global cause, such as the idea that men get into rejecting moods sometimes but not always. Abramson, Seligman, and Teasdale (1978) further suggest that feelings of helplessness are even more likely if people are sure of their attributions and if the events are very important to them. Furthermore, attributions to internal causes create somewhat more feelings of helplessness, since they are almost always more global and stable.

Applying these ideas to battered women, we would expect that attributions to internal, stable, global factors would result in the strongest feelings of helplessness. Examples might include the woman feeling that she was justifiably being punished for being a poor wife, especially if she felt that she could not improve in this role. Such an attribution would create little expectancy for change, even if she were to try marriage to another man. External, stable, global attributions might also produce very strong feelings of helplessness, such as the belief that all men are violent toward their wives, no matter what their wives do.

Behavioral Responses to Battering. Along with their affective reaction to being battered, women also change their behaviors in a variety of ways after a violent incident. Many women have had several of the proposed reactions at one time or another, perhaps changing their reactions as their attributions change with repeated battering or as they reassess their situations and reformulate their attributions. Some of the most common behavioral reactions are shown in Figure 1.

If the battered woman makes an unstable attribution for the battering, we would expect her behaviors to be similar to those on the left side of Figure 1, ones associated with hoping for future change. As summarized in Table 3, a woman who sees her own behavior as the cause (an unstable, internal cause) probably would attempt to change her behavior so that the violence does not hap-

Table 3. Wife's Reactions to Physical Attack from Spouse as a Function of Her Causal Attribution

Locus of Cause	Stability of Cause		
	Unstable	Moderately Stable	Highly Stable
Internal: Self Blame	Try to do better next time	Seek psychological help	Helplessness and depression
Joint: Couple Blame	Work on relationship	Leave permanently	Helplessness if cannot leave
External: Husband Blame	Try to help husband; leave temporarily	Leave permanently	Helplessness if cannot leave

pen again. Such a prediction is similar to the idea that attributing failure on an examination to lack of effort leads to greater exertion so that the grade on the next examination will be better (Kukla, 1972). Also, we would expect that attributing the battering to a couple-related, unstable cause would lead to trying to improve the interaction of the couple. Trying to help the husband overcome his difficulties would be the expected response if the blame were associated with relatively impermanent difficulties of the husband. We would also expect that any of these attempts could lead to a reassessment of the situation and its underlying cause if the behavior proved to be unsuccessful in stopping the violence.

Another predicted reaction (based on an unstable cause and associated with some hope for future change) would be for the woman to leave temporarily while there is an immediate threat of violence but to return when she sees it is "safe." The battered woman might be especially likely to leave if she sees the locus of the cause being in her husband, for she would have no way of controlling an immediate outburst of violence. A major consideration, however, is whether she would have someplace to go. Having money, a car, nearby friends or family who could shelter her, a "safe house," or a women's shelter would be essential for the option of leaving. Isolated rural women may have the most difficulty in finding somewhere to go. Leaving on a temporary basis would also be a more likely response if the woman fears that the next incident will be extremely violent.

If the woman blamed herself and saw the problem as some type of psychological difficulty within herself, we would expect her to seek personal psychotherapy in an attempt to end the battering. Although personality is generally considered to be a stable attribution (Elig and Frieze, 1975), we have labeled it as only moderately stable in this context since we would not expect the woman to seek psychotherapy unless she felt there was some hope of overcoming her problems. It is also important to note that the prediction here is that the woman would seek personal therapy in order to end the battering; however, since her perception is that the battering results from her internal problems, she might not even bring up the violence with her therapist. We will discuss this point in more detail later. Presumably, if the woman saw her problems as untreatable and highly stable, she would respond with helplessness and depression rather than trying to seek help for herself.

Other reactions of the wife might result from her attributing the violence to stable, global factors. In such a case, along with feeling helpless, she might respond with passive acceptance of the situation and depression. Such reactions are commonly associated with learned helplessness (Abramson and others, 1978). If this helplessness is further compounded with self-blame for the battering, the woman would probably have very low self-esteem as well (Abramson and others, 1978). This image of the passive, self-deprecating, depressed, battered woman is one of the common images in the media today and one that is being labeled as the sterotypic battered woman profile by researchers in the field (Walker, 1979).

Another response to feeling helpless to change the pattern of violence in the marriage would be to simply leave and break off the relationship—the response so commonly seen as the logical thing to do by the general public. Some women cannot leave because they are economically dependent on their husbands; others lack the resources of their own to simply pack up and drive to a motel, or they have no alternative shelter that would not require money. This situation is further complicated if the woman has children she wants to take with her. Other factors that might make it difficult for her to leave would be loss of social status (especially for women with high social status) and fear of disapproval from family or friends (Pagelow, 1977). By leaving, a woman gives up her identity as a wife, risks social disapproval, loses economic support, and loses any love she feels she is receiving from her husband (Waites, 1978). She may also fear her husband's retaliation (Ridington, 1978).

We would further expect causal attributions for violence to mediate leaving the relationship. The woman who, in addition to seeing the cause as stable, attributes the violence to her husband or to the relationship would be more likely to leave than the woman who blames herself. If she blamed herself, she might well expect that she would have similar problems in any future relationship and thus that it would be useless to leave. This response, once again, would result in the passive acceptance, depression, and helplessness associated with these types of global attributions. It is also possible for a woman to want to leave, and even to attempt to do so, and then find that her husband will not let her go or that she actually has nowhere to go. We would expect these cases to result in anger and, eventually, passive acceptance.

Studies of Women's Responses to Battering

Researchers have been quite interested in what wives do after they have been battered. Most studies report empirical findings and make little, if any, attempt to present a theoretical model to predict their results. The attributional model presented here has only been partially tested. However, other studies yield data that shed light on various predictions of the attribution model, even though they were not done within this framework. We will discuss these studies, along with some of our own research data, to see how well attributions for battering predict the responses to it.

Our data are based on findings from an ongoing study of various psychological factors in battered women. Our design calls for lengthy, structured interviews with women who have identified themselves as battered either by seeking help for battering in a women's shelter, by filing legal action to remove violent husbands from their homes, or by responding to publicly posted notices for women who have experienced violence in their marriages. These women, who have experienced violence levels ranging from moderate violence of a few slaps or shoves to extreme physical injury, are known as our "battered group." As Straus (1977b) points out, even one violent incident can have dramatic effects on a relationship by fixing the balance of power in the relationship for many years or even for a lifetime. Once violence has been used, it is always there as a potential threat even if it is never used again. Data from forty-one of these women have been coded and analyzed.

Along with our battered group, we have also interviewed eighty-two control women—women who have been randomly selected from the same neighborhoods from which our battered group has come. Matching neighborhoods for our battered and control groups allows us rough control over such demographics as age, ethnicity, and socio-economic status so that the two groups can be as comparable as possible. After interviewing our controls, we found that twenty-seven of this group (33 percent) had experienced some level of violence in their marriages. We have labeled this group our control battered group. Their levels of violence tended to be somewhat less than in the battered group, although the control battered group also showed a range from mild to extreme violence. This group differs psychologically, however, since they were solicited as controls in a study of "marriage dynamics"; many of them would probably not consider themselves battered even though they have experienced high levels of violence. Some have never sought help of any sort for the violence, while the battered group by definition *has* sought help, either from a shelter, from the courts, or from being in a research project where they can talk about their experiences.

Removing the twenty-seven control battereds from the control group leaves fifty-five control women who have never experienced any violence from their spouses.

Causal Attributions of Battered Women. In the context of a structured interview asking questions about background information, power relations in the marriage, sexual relations, help-seeking behavior, and alcohol use, as well as requests for specific documentation of the types of violence experienced, women were asked two attribution questions. In reference to the first violent incident, the question the women were asked was: "Did you understand at the time why he was violent?" The second question, asked later, was: "Now, thinking back on *all* the times he was violent, do you notice any general pattern(s) to his violence, and particular times more than others that you might also expect it?" The different responses to each of these questions were coded according to the format shown in Table 1.

As shown in Table 4, a large group of women from both of the violent groups reported that they did not know why the first violent incident occurred. For those who gave an attribution, there was a slight overall tendency for self-blame, especially among the control battered group. The battered group was equally divided between husband and wife blame. The large majority of the attributions were unstable. When asked about the general pattern of violence, there were fewer "Don't know's" and more husband-

**Table 4. Causal Attributions for the
First Violent Incident**

Group	Husband	Joint	Wife	Don't Know	Total
		Locus of Causality			
Battered	10	4	11	16	41
Control battered	7	0	11	9	27
	Unstable	Uncertain	Stable	Don't Know	Total
			Stability		
Battered	22	1	2	16	41
Control battered	16	0	2	9	27

blaming responses. Pattern responses were also more stable, as predicted earlier. These differences might be expected partially because of the more stable, long-term nature of the pattern attribution question. These data also suggest that women may become somewhat less self-blaming over time, especially if they have gone to a women's shelter and gotten social support there for the idea that they are not to blame. Note that the shift to more husband blame for the pattern question was more typical for the battereds than for the control battereds.

As a further perspective to these data on wife blame, less than 10 percent of these same battered women, when asked about a hypothetical instance of wife-battering, put the blame on the woman. For a hypothetical battering situation, 82 percent blamed the husband. Thus, although many of our battered women blamed their husbands for their own beatings, they saw themselves as more responsible than they felt other women were—suggesting a relatively high level of self-blame. Similar findings were reported in an earlier study using the same methodology (Frieze, 1978).

Although these data do not strongly support the idea that most battered women will act like other victims and take primary responsibility for their battering, a relatively high level of self-blame is evident. However, since the attributions are unstable as well, this does not suggest that the women felt hopeless after the first incident. Most of the self-blame attributions were to unstable factors in oneself; in other words, the wife basically did not do what the husband wanted.

A higher degree of self-blame in battered women has been reported in other studies (Ball and Wyman, 1978; Hilberman and Munson, 1978; Walker, 1979), but most of these studies have been based on samples of women seeking psychotherapy, the group we predicted to be highest in self-blame. It is also quite possible that the women who felt highly responsible and guilty for the beatings might not have wanted to participate in a study of battered women or of "marital dynamics." Thus, our sampling technique may underrepresent self-blaming women. All these data, then, indicate that battered women respond to some degree like other victims or that they follow the traditional female pattern of showing high self-blame for failure.

Another attributional prediction made earlier was that more severe cases of violence would be more attributed to the actor (specifically, the husband). Although we did not find strong data in support of this prediction, there was a trend for women who had been more seriously hurt to see their husbands as the cause of their battering (correlation $= 0.21, p < 0.10$) and to see the cause as more stable (correlation $= 0.28, p < 0.05$). However, a regression analysis based on a number of attributional and nonattributional predictors showed that the best predictors of women experiencing severe levels of violence were being unfamiliar with other women who had been battered, seeing the cause of one's own violence as stable factors within oneself, and believing that wife-battering was a relatively frequent occurrence. Women who had more severe injuries were also more likely to attempt to hide their injuries from others (correlation $= 0.38 \ p < 0.05$). Taken together, these data suggest that the more severely injured women lack social supports and have no one with whom they can talk about their battering. The stability of their attributions may also indicate that they feel helpless to change their situations and thus passively accept them as being normal in marriage.

The lack of support for the locus hypothesis may relate to women seeing themselves as the actors rather than their husbands. Our measure of level of violence may also have been too rough to show this predicted difference. Unfortunately, we know of no other studies that have investigated this issue, and we must conclude that this hypothesis has not yet been fully tested.

Emotional Reactions of Battered Women. As discussed earlier, learned helplessness in a battered woman can come from a number of sources. She may feel that she causes the violence but not know how she does it, and so she is helpless to control it (Ball and Wyman, 1978). Other women may have been socialized to depend on others and not to attempt to control their own environment (Walker, 1978). Certainly, many battered women show signs of extreme anxiety and depression (Hilberman and Munson, 1978), which are frequently associated with feelings of helplessness.

Although we have no direct test of the relationship of the causal attributions made and whether the woman feels helpless, there is certainly indirect evidence. Many studies reporting that women tend to blame themselves and see little hope for future change also report that the women feel helpless (for example, Walker, 1979). Women are also described as feeling helpless when they see the violence as a permanent part of their husband's personality (Hilberman and Munson, 1978).

Changing One's Behavior. Attempting to change their behavior was a typical response of the battered women we interviewed, regardless of whether they blamed themselves or not. Other researchers have found similar patterns (Hilberman and Munson, 1978; Walker, 1978). Apparently, even when they felt their husbands were responsible, battered women still felt they could do things to minimize the violence. Of course, since the violence typically continued, they were not successful in these attempts. Perhaps this behavior represented an attempt to gain some control over their environments. They talked about doing things like making sure that they had meals ready on time, keeping the children quiet when their husbands were at home, and giving into their husbands' sexual demands. Some women expressed frustration when even these measures did not help (Walker, 1979).

Walker (1978, 1979) and Hilberman and Munson (1978) both report that battered women often discovered a pattern or cycle of violence. They learned that after a certain period of time, violence was inevitable. Sometimes they would deliberately provoke the violence during these periods so that they would not have to continue to wait for it to happen. Once the violence was over for the cycle, their husbands would once again be warm and loving.

Such behavior represents another example of attempting to gain control over a situation clearly associated with husband blame.

Seeking Help from Therapists and Other Sources. We predicted earlier that women who blamed themselves for the battering would be more likely to seek psychotherapy for their problems than women making other causal attributions. In some ways this is difficult to test since so many research projects draw their samples from therapeutic populations.

Research has shown that help seeking is a common response of battered women. Prescott and Letko (1977) found that 81 percent of their sample had contacted friends and 59 percent had gone to relatives or lawyers for help with the violence. They also found that women who had experienced more severe violence were more likely to contact police, ministers, and women's groups for help. Social service agencies were turned to when the violence extended beyond the couple to the children.

In our study, we asked women if they had ever sought help for marital problems from any of a variety of sources, including therapists and counselors, friends, relatives, and ministers or priests. As shown in Table 5, many of the women did seek help. For battered women, the most popular sources of help were relatives, social service agencies, and therapists. The control battered women most often went to either a friend or a relative for help, but this group was less likely to seek help of any sort. Social service agencies were seen as the most helpful for those in both groups who sought help, whereas relatives were seen as least helpful.

Table 5. Women Seeking Help for Marital Problems

| Source of Help | Battered | | Control Battered | |
	Number	Helpfulness [a]	Number	Helpfulness
Priest or minister	11	3.8	4	4.5
Friend	10	3.9	13	4.2
Relative	20	3.2	11	3.7
Doctor	8	3.9	2	5.0
Therapist	13	3.3	4	4.5
Social service agency	16	4.3	3	5.0
Total Sample	41	—	27	—

[a]Ratings on a 5-point scale from 1 (not at all helpful) to 5 (very helpful).

In our data, as predicted, the women who blamed themselves, especially if the cause was seen as stable, were twice as likely
to have sought psychotherapy for marital problems as were the
women who blamed their husbands for the violence. However, the
small number of women who did go to therapy made these conclusions somewhat tentative. Walker's (1978) data are consistent,
though. She found that battered women who go to therapy often
feel they are provoking the violence. They want help for their
feelings of anger, guilt, and anxiety. Further, other data from our
study indicated that the self-blamers felt that therapy was less successful than did the husband-blaming women. One reason may be
that self-blamers failed to deal with the violence in their therapeutic
sessions. Traditional therapists often fail to be sensitive to some of
the problems women have (Washburn, Frieze, and Knoble, 1979);
furthermore, their training has often taught them that battered
wives are masochistic (Straus, 1977a; Martin, 1976) or that these
women play a major role in provoking the abuse (Lion, 1977).
Thus, even if the therapist attempted to deal with the violence, his
or her approach might further intensify feelings of self-blame. Still,
many therapists would probably fail to discover that violence was a
problem if the woman herself never mentioned it (Washburn,
Frieze, and Knoble, 1979). Therapy may be far more successful for
the woman who already sees her husband as to blame, since her
presenting problem of how to cope with the violence is more obvious and could be dealt with more effectively.

Leaving the Relationship. A final set of reactions predicted by
our attribution model consisted of leaving the relationship, either
temporarily or permanently. We predicted that leaving would be
related to the stability of the causal attribution, among other things,
and that husband-blaming battered wives would be more likely to
leave than self-blamers. In our data, as predicted, women were
more likely to want to leave if they blamed their husbands (correlation = 0.48, $p < .01$) or made more stable attributions for the
violence (correlation = 0.41, $p < .05$). However, there was only a
borderline effect for the stability of the causal attribution to be
related to actually trying to leave (correlation = 0.29, $p < .10$), and
there was no relationship between blaming the husband and trying
to leave.

Although one can always hope for cleaner data, we were quite gratified by these findings. Psychologically, we would expect wanting to leave to be most related to cognitive factors. Acting on these desires and actually trying to leave depends upon many external variables. For example, it was suggested earlier that women who feared more violence might be more likely to leave. Gelles (1972) reported that women who had already experienced more severe violence would be more likely to try to leave. We found similar results. In general, the women who had experienced the most severe violence were more likely to leave, although a small subset of these women never attempted to leave. A regression analysis further indicated that women who had called the police in the past, who had threatened to leave before, who had hidden their injuries, who found the police helpful when they were called, and who saw the violence as the result of stable factors were most likely to leave. Since several demographic variables and resources had been included in the list of potential predictors, this may suggest that a variety of psychological factors may be even more important than the woman's resources in understanding why some leave and others do not.

It was interesting that the stability of the causal attribution for battering was more related to trying to leave than seeing the husband as the source of the violence. Women who blame themselves may still leave, out of desperation or fear of their own lives or their children's lives (Hilberman and Munson, 1978; Pagelow, 1977). Such desperation would be greater when a stable attribution is made, since stable attributions produce expectancies that the future will not bring change.

Leaving temporarily and returning after some period is not uncommon for battered women (Pizzey, 1974). In the model proposed here, this behavior was seen as being related to unstable, husband attributions. As with the original leaving, our data weakly supported the idea that women who made unstable attributions and who did leave would be more likely to return. However, there was no relationship between the locus of causality and returning. Once again, women who did leave for whatever reason were likely to be more hopeful about future improvements, if they saw the cause of the violence as less stable and enduring.

A stepwise regression for returning after successfully leaving indicated that women whose husbands had been abused as children, who found the police helpful, who made less stable attributions for the battering, and who hid their injuries were more likely to return. This set of predictors is less easily explainable than the previous analysis. Some of the variables in the regression equation may be there because they were predictors of leaving in the first place. The husband's being abused as a child may be a predictor because the wife feels she should help her husband more if he has this type of family background.

Assessing the Attribution Model

As we have seen, many of the basic predictions of the attribution model for the wife's reaction to battering were at least partially supported. Overall, these data indicated that in many ways the stability dimension was more important than the perceived locus. Although consistent with other data (Valle and Frieze, 1976), this finding suggests that much attribution research is concentrating on the wrong dimension (Weiner, 1974a). Other areas that seemed weakest were predictions that might be explained better by seeing the battered woman as seeking more control over her violent spouse and only giving up the relationship when she felt change was impossible. Thus, the Bulman and Wortman (1977) and Janoff-Bulman (in press) hypotheses about victims' desires for control were supported by our data on battered women.

One distressing aspect of these data on need for sense of control is that outside researchers often note that, once established, the violent marriage rarely improves; battered women's attempts at gaining control are often futile. Psychotherapy for the wife is often unsuccessful (Hilberman and Munson, 1978; Ball and Wyman, 1978). However, techniques that emphasize learning to gain a more positive sense of self-esteem and coping skills can be beneficial for the battered wife (Ball and Wyman, 1978; Walker, 1978). These techniques are usually most effective if the woman manages to leave the relationship. Unfortunately, the women who probably need this type of help the most (those who blame their own personalities), seem least likely to leave. Therapy programs with men

seem to be far more successful in improving the marital relationship (Boyd, 1978; Klingbeil, 1978), but it is difficult to get men into
treatment. Perhaps men rarely see the violence as their problem
and instead either ignore it or blame their wives. Further research
is clearly needed on these aspects of husbands' attributions and the
psychological dynamics of violence in such marriages.

Wortman and Dintzer (1978) raise the question of the
sequencing of attributions, expectancies, and affective reactions.
Although our attribution model suggests a certain sequence in
these events, we have no way of really testing this hypothesis since
our data are collected at one point in time. It is possible that women
form future expectations about their relationships and then make
attributions consistent with these expectations. There is also the
question of how attributions change over time. Some women in our
sample were relating very recent events while others were describing situations that occurred several years in the past. Are there
systematic changes over time in the ways in which negative events
are viewed? Wortman and Dintzer (1978) also question whether
attributions are indeed related to behaviors. Although the attribution model presented here would certainly suggest that they are, all
we really have is a set of consistencies between self-reported behavior and self-reported beliefs. More field research should help il-
luminate what the real relationship is between these cognitions and
behavior.

In conclusion, attribution theory does appear to be a powerful tool in understanding the differential reactions of battered
women. In some ways, given the multitude of variables affecting
her, the fact that attributions are predictors indicates the importance of these cognitive factors in understanding behavior. With
further testing, our attribution model should help us develop better therapeutic procedures for dealing with both violent husbands
and their wives and to fit treatment to the particular psychological
factors operating in a particular couple.

Chapter 5

Valerie A. Valle
Eric J. Johnson

Consumer Response to Product Quality

An observer of modern American society quickly sees that consumption is an integral part of our culture. People of all backgrounds and social classes expend a large proportion of their time and energy deciding how to spend their money, making purchases, and consuming products and services. It has even been suggested that, in mature societies such as ours, the focus of individuals shifts from their activities as producers to the quality of their lives as consumers (Voorhis, 1977). Individuals' satisfaction as consumers can be an important determinant of their perceived quality of life. Therefore, the existence of widespread and active consumer dissatisfaction, as reflected by the consumer movement,

109

has important implications for evaluating the well-being of society in general.

Consumer dissatisfaction and complaint behavior can be important mechanisms in assuring the delivery of desirable goods and services. Complaints serve as feedback to the producers of goods and services, allowing them to alter their products to meet consumers' needs and tastes. Government agencies designed to protect consumers are also interested in the experiences of dissatisfied customers. The Federal Trade Commission, for example, would be interested in the experiences of consumers who feel victimized by misleading advertising. This information could lead to the design of more effective protection for consumers.

The fact is, however, that dissatisfaction is seldom communicated to the providers of products. The majority of dissatisfied consumers do not complain, and those who do complain seldom go to the agencies designed to help them (Day and Landon, 1976). A number of groups need to know who complains, how complaints are manifested, and why dissatisfied consumers choose not to complain. Businesses need to know if the complainers are representative of the general population and how to satisfy all consumers, those who do complain and those who are dissatisfied yet never complain. Agencies concerned with helping consumers need to know who complains and, more importantly, who does not complain. To be more effective, these agencies need to know why people do not come to them and how they can encourage individuals to register valid complaints. Finally, government decision makers need this information to determine what types of legislation are necessary to protect consumers and how to develop programs for dissatisfied consumers.

The study of consumer satisfaction and complaint behavior is a relatively new (yet growing) area in the consumer behavior literature. Few theoretical models have been developed to describe consumers' reactions to products or to explain consumer complaint behavior (Day and Landon, 1976; Landon, 1977). A major problem with the development of such a model is consumers' use of subjective impressions to evaluate products. In a world of technologically sophisticated products, consumers' satisfaction with a product depends more on their subjective impressions of the product's performance than on its verifiable, measurable aspects. It is often difficult for a consumer to check manufacturers' technical claims. Instead, the consumer feels that his television is defective, that the stereo sounds horrible, or that the car is a lemon.

Previous research efforts have tried to determine some of the variables that affect whether a complaint is registered. These studies have investigated the types of products that elicit complaints or the types of people who are prone to complain. Day and Landon (1976), in an extensive survey of consumer satisfaction and complaint behavior, found that the degree of satisfaction and the number of complaints varied across product types. Several studies have demonstrated that those who complain, especially those who complain to government agencies, tend to be well-educated, affluent, managerial-professional men and women (Handy, 1972; Warland, Hermann, and Willits, 1975). In all these studies, however, the percentage of variance accounted for has been very small.

In contrast, an attributional approach to consumer satisfaction focuses on the consumers' perceptions of product performance (satisfaction or dissatisfaction) and consumers' views of responsibility. Specifically, this chapter will explore the implications of consumers' expectations for product performance within an attributional framework. By exploring the consumer's perceptions of the products rather than the products themselves, it may be possible not only to describe who complains but why complaints are made, and, by examining the consumer's attributions of responsibility for product failure, it should be possible to predict who will be the target of the complaint. We shall develop an attributional model of consumers' responses to product performance, examine each of its components, and discuss the implications of the model for research and public policy.

A Model of Consumer Response to Product Performance

The purchase and repurchase of products is an ongoing process. To simplify the model and bring attributional issues to the forefront, we describe consumer satisfaction as a series of discrete steps. This approach hopefully serves as a heuristic tool, even if it does some injustice to the actual experience of the consumer.

The model (see Figure 1) begins arbitrarily with the consumer's expectations for a product's performance. These ex-

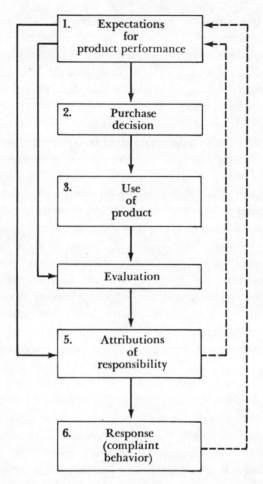

Figure 1. A Model of Consumer Response to Product Performance.

pectations are formed from many information sources, the most important of which is previous experience. Like expectations of achievement (Weiner, 1974b), the effect of past experience is mediated by the attributions people make concerning their experience. These expectations for performance then become the most important of a number of considerations that later affect the purchase decision.

The next step, the process of deciding to buy a product, is complex and varies with the type of product purchased. This process has been the subject of a great deal of research in consumer behavior. Attributions do not influence the choice of products directly; rather, they may be a powerful determinant of buyer behavior through their effect on the purchaser's expectations.

Once a product is purchased, the way in which it is used can influence the consumer's reaction to the product. Direct experience provides an important opportunity to gather information about the product, just as direct experience provides information about people (Frieze, 1976a). The consumer evaluates (explicitly or implicitly) the product both during and after its use. It is this evaluation that is usually referred to as consumer satisfaction or dissatisfaction. These evaluations are usually not simple positive or negative evaluations but can be complex, since some aspects of a product's performance may be satisfying and others disappointing.

After an evaluation, the model suggests that consumers decide who is responsible for the product's performance. These attributions may be complex, since different actors may be responsible for different aspects of product performance. Bad repairs by the local dealer may sour a car owner on the large auto maker, even though the consumer thought that the car was well manufactured. This is especially true if the consumer feels that the manufacturer is ultimately responsible for warranty service.

These attributions about product performance act as a mediator between a person's concrete experience and any behavioral response. Behavioral responses can vary from a complex process of complaint behavior to no overt response at all. Satisfaction with the complaint process and all the preceding steps will influence future product expectations and purchase decisions.

The unique feature of this model is the importance given to attributions as mediators of consumers' responses to product performance. Social psychologists study attributions, because they believe that they help determine behavior. Similarly, students of consumer behavior may turn to the study of attributions in the hope of better understanding consumer complaint behavior. The model is also important, because it applies attributional concepts that have been developed in the laboratory study of people's perceptions of causality to a real-world setting. This application can provide valuable information on the general validity of attribution theory.

Expectations for Product Performance. Any model that attempts to describe a complex process as a series of linear steps must have an arbitrary beginning. Many variables affect a consumer's purchase decision, including situational and psychological variables. Expectations for product performance are the result of combining many inputs (for example, word of mouth from other consumers, advertising, and price) and have particular significance for consumers' choices of reactions to products. Among the most important sources of information that affect a consumer's expectations for product performance is prior experience with the product. These prior experiences are mediated by previous attributions of responsibility and previous responses made by the consumer. This is indicated by the dotted lines in Figure 1.

In more traditional applications of attribution theory, a strong connection between attributions and resulting expectancies has been demonstrated (McMahan, 1973; Valle and Frieze, 1976; Weiner, 1974a). Attributions made to stable causes change expectations more than attributions to unstable causes. Expectations have also been shown to affect subsequent attributions (Feather, 1969; Feather and Simon, 1971a, 1971b). These two effects combine to make initial expectations difficult to change (Valle and Frieze, 1976). We shall discuss these relationships after we have introduced the appropriate attributional framework.

In contrast with expectations of academic success or failure, expectations of product performance have been taken as a nebulous internal state of the consumer. Most consumer researchers have avoided the problem of defining the measurement of expectations by making the assumption that manipulating the mediating variables changes expectations. In contrast, Oliver (1977) used two measures of expectations concerning performance of a car. The first measure was a simple question, with responses rating expectations from very poor to very good. The second measure was fifteen seven-point, bipolar scales, such as "noisy-quiet." This approach acknowledges what may be the fundamental difference between judgments of academic success and failure and the evaluation of products: product evaluations are more complex than simple judgments of success or failure. Subjects in achievement-motivation settings can be expected to describe their performance along a single dimension, but satisfaction with products is seldom described this simply. Products can have many attributes, and the potential purchaser may have very different expectations for each attribute. The buyer of an economy car anticipates good gas mileage and low maintenance costs but may be less enthusiastic about other attributes. Each of these expectations may be weighted in a different way and have different impacts on the subsequent purchase decision. Therefore, combining all expectations about a product could easily lead to misinterpretations.

Our view that product perceptions are based on many attributes is not unique. Much of the research on the formation of consumer attitudes assumes that these perceptions are multiattribute in nature. Models proposed by Fishbein (1963, 1976) suggest that consumers have a significant number of separate evaluations of the attributes of a product. These evaluations can vary independently and are combined to form an attitude toward the product. The individual evaluations are weighted by the subjective beliefs that the product will possess the attributes in question. The combination rules for these beliefs and evaluations are very similar to those suggested by Norman Anderson's information-integrations theory (1971), with both averaging and summation rules proposed (Lutz and Bettman, 1977). These multiattribute models have had significant success in predicting consumers' attitudes, and they demonstrate the value of multiattribute views of product perception.

In summary, we believe that expectations influence and are influenced by attributions and that they have an important role in the purchase decision. These expectations are probably more complex than expectations of success or failure in achievement situations. Let us, therefore, define *expectations* as a subjective estimate of product performance on each of a number of characteristics. No assumptions are made concerning either the weight of these characteristics or the way they are combined. However they are derived, these expectations are important factors in the consumer's purchase decision.

The Purchase Decision. The consumer's method of choosing and purchasing products has been the topic of much theorizing and empirical research. No attempt is made here to review this literature, but the interested reader is referred to Engel, Kollat, and Blackwell (1973). Our model does not see attributions as a direct part of the purchase decision. Instead, expectations for performance (which are influenced by attributions) are seen as an important consideration when a purchase is made. Under optimal conditions, the product with the best expected performance would be bought. However, consumers usually have other constraints, which include the alternatives available, purchase price, convenience of use and maintenance, and the needs of significant others, such as family members. These constraints can lead the consumer to purchase a product that is not expected to perform well, which may mean that consumers buy products for which they have a wide range of prior expectations. The buyer of an inexpensive watch might be quite satisfied with two years of use, whereas the purchaser of an expensive "wrist chronometer" would be dissatisfied with the same performance. The differences in their relative satisfactions lie in their expectations: a cheap watch is not expected to last long, but an expensive watch might be expected to become a family heirloom.

One intriguing line of speculation is that purchase decisions may affect subsequent perceptions of a product. Self-perception theory (Bem, 1972) suggests that people make attributions about their attitudes by observing their own behavior. In Bem's famous example, someone who continually purchases brown bread infers that he must like it, since he buys it so often. Thus, self-perception theory suggests that people's attitudes toward products are determined at least partially by their behavior.

Use of Products. One's reaction to a product is based on the manner in which one interacts with it. Purchase of the product does not assure that the product will be used in the manner it was intended. Instructions may not be followed or may be difficult to comprehend. Consumers' past experiences can lead to differences in how they use products. Furthermore, purchase does not necessarily ensure the eventual use of the product. For example, a person who spontaneously buys a new type of cake mix may never get around to trying it.

The actual use of the product provides the consumer with information about it. For foodstuffs, this includes experiencing the taste, appearance, and texture of the product. For appliances, a consumer gains knowledge of the dependability and effectiveness of the product. In the traditional application of attribution theory—the perception of people—the role of information-search has been somewhat neglected (Frieze, 1976a). It is generally agreed, however, that the experience of interacting with others provides the information that attributions are based on (see Garland, Hardy, and Stephanson, 1976; Newtson, 1976). For products, direct experience allows the consumer to gather additional information that is similarly used in evaluations and attribution of responsibility.

Evaluation. Evaluation, either implicitly or explicitly, occurs throughout the entire purchase process. Evaluation constitutes the heart of consumer satisfaction or dissatisfaction. As with expectations, evaluation is difficult to measure. Overall measures of satisfaction attempt to lump together all aspects of a person's experiences with a product. Attempts to measure consumer satisfaction with a number of different types of products quickly become extraordinarily complicated and difficult to interpret (see Day and Bodur, 1977). A single purchase can have both satisfying and dissatisfying aspects. For example, in an interview in Valle and Koeske (1977), an elderly respondent was dissatisfied with a hearing aid, both in its performance and with the manufacturer's service. Yet, he thought it was the most comfortable hearing aid he ever owned. As with expectations, a product is perceived to have many attributes, many of which are individually evaluated (Johnson and Russo, 1978). Overall evaluations of products are the result of complex combination rules for various aspects. For a discussion of these information-processing strategies as used by consumers, see Bettman (1979).

There is strong evidence that expectations can affect subsequent evaluations. When actual experience with a product disconfirms prior expectations, most researchers find assimilation effects. That is, groups with high expectations of product performance give ratings that fall between ratings of expected performance and ratings given by control groups who had no prior expectations (Anderson, 1973; Oliver, 1977; Olshavrsky and Miller, 1972; Olson and Dover, 1976). This suggests that an advertiser who overexaggerates a product's performance may inadvertently be raising expectations for his product and creating a more favorable evaluation than if the consumer's expectations had not been so high.

   Attributions of Responsibility. If a product fails to perform satisfactorily, a consumer needs to know who is responsible for the failure. These attributions of responsibility are the central mediating variable in the present model. Here is where we deal with the question central to attribution theory: What is the cause? We believe that the way consumers respond to a product's performance will depend on how they answer this question. If a consumer believes that failure was due to incorrectly reading the instructions, he will behave differently than if he believes himself a victim of a purposeful fraud.

   In this section, we shall examine four topics with implications for consumer satisfaction. First, we shall discuss briefly some applications of Harold Kelley's work to the perception of products. We shall then turn to what we believe is a more appropriate method of examining attribution of responsibility, the achievement-attribution framework of Bernard Weiner and his colleagues. Finally, we shall discuss two specific areas of research with applications for consumer satisfaction: actor-observer effects and the role of expectancy in attribution.

   Most research on consumers' attributions has used a framework based on Kelley's (1972) covariance analysis. For example, Settle and Golden (1974) examined consumers' perceptions of product promotions, and Scott and Yatch (in press) have examined their perceptions of product choice. Such work has usually adapted Kelley's (1967) three sources of information (consistency over time, persons, and modality) by considering the product or promotion to be the stimulus object. This leads to manipulations of the variation in the product (distinctiveness) or the reactions of others (consensus). Little work has been done with variation in consumers' reactions with time (consistency).

   Clearly, more work needs to be done before the usefulness of this approach can be evaluated. However, two problems do present themselves. Consumers may not always have enough experience with a product to make a causal attribution using the covariance principle; that is, they may not have interacted with the product enough times, in enough different situations, to know whether their reaction varies with the product, situation, or some other variable (Burnkrant, 1974). Since people can make attributions based on limited data (Orvis, Cunningham, and Kelley, 1975), the notion of a causal schemata (Kelley, 1972) appears to make more sense. Second, most researchers assume that Kelley's framework matches the attributional processes used by consumers. One way of actually observing the naturalistic attributions made by lay people is to observe their responses when they are asked to find the cause of a situation (Frieze, 1976b). However, pilot work using this technique indicates that the open-ended responses of consumers are described well by an achievement-attribution framework (Valle and Wallendorf, 1977). Since the actual attributions are seldom measured (exceptions are Valle and Wallendorf, 1977; Smith and Hunt, 1978), the exact nature of consumers' causal inferences is uncertain. Future work should include appropriate manipulation checks and measures of attributions.

The work dealing with achievement attributions (Weiner, 1974a, chap. 1) also has implications for understanding consumers' reactions to product performance. We define an achievement situation as any event in which a person's actions will lead to an outcome that is perceived as a success or failure. It is quite natural to see purchasing a product as an achievement situation; people often talk about good and bad buys. Americans also tend to define a great number of situations in terms of achievement. For example, a good, sound, happy marriage is often described as a success, whereas a divorce is a failure. Children quickly learn to see their school experiences as successes or failures (Frieze and Snyder, 1978). Even interpersonal relations are seen in achievement terms; a person can feel that he or she was a success or failure at a party (Elig and Frieze, 1975). It is reasonable, then, to see purchases— which are real expenditures of time and money and have real consequences—as achievement situations.

Weiner and his associates have developed a two-dimensional scheme for representing the possible causes of an achievement outcome. Success or failure can be attributed either to something about the actor (an internal attribution) or to something about the environment or situation (an external attribution). Additionally, performance can be attributed to something that does not vary with time (a stable attribution) or to something that does vary (an unstable attribution). Rosenbaum (1972) further elaborated the model by proposing a third causal dimension, intentionality. If performance is attributed to someone who had foresight and control of the outcome, it is considered intentional. For example, both effort (intentional) and fatigue (unintentional) are internal, unstable factors, yet they have difference implications as causal attributions.

Attributions made in response to product performance can be fitted into this three-dimensional scheme. Figure 2 illustrates possible attributions for each of these dimensions. For example, a person who believes that a product has performed poorly because, "if one is always looking for a bargain, one must expect that sometimes the thing won't work" is making a stable, internal, intentional attribution. Someone who feels dissatisfied because she didn't spend enough time shopping would be making an unstable, internal, intentional attribution. Blaming poor service on the lack

Intentional

	Internal	External
Stable	Always looking for bargains	Planned "con" scheme
Unstable	Spending insufficient time shopping	Salesperson saw opportunity for a quick sale

Unintentional

	Internal	External
Stable	Lack of knowledge about product class	Service personnel lack of ability
Unstable	Tired or in a bad mood	Luck, a "lemon"

Figure 2. Examples of Attributions Following Dissatisfaction with a Product.

of ability in service personnel would be a stable, external, unintentional attribution. Finally, perceiving that a product is a lemon (an unusual example of a poor product) is an external, unstable, unintentional attribution.

Evidence supporting this framework is provided by a pilot investigation conducted by Valle and Wallendorf (1977). They administered an open-ended questionnaire about product satisfaction and dissatisfaction to MBA students. Each respondent described a product they were dissatisfied with and a product they were satisfied with. They were then asked what was responsible for the satisfaction or dissatisfaction and who, if anyone, was responsible. The responses did not include sufficient information to make a statement about the relevance of stability or intentionality for product attributions. However, a dimension similar to, but more complex than, the locus of control dimension emerged. Since there are many parties in the manufacture, delivery, and sale of a good, it was felt that a richer classification would be accomplished by enlarging the number of categories on the locus of control dimension. This dimension now represents a continuum, which has, at one end, attributions to oneself (for example, one's shopping ability), corresponding to an internal attribution. The other categories extend, in order of increasing externality, to people known to the consumer, the retailer, sales and service people, the manufacturer, and the larger system (laws, an entire industry). They labeled this dimension the *psychological distance* from the consumer. Psychologically closer entities were those who had personal contact with the consumer; psychologically distant representatives, such as the manufacturer, never had face-to-face contact with the consumer.

Clearly, more work is needed in validating this framework for classifying consumer attributions, but the initial results seem promising. In a later section, we shall discuss work within this framework that examines the implications of these attributions. However, we believe that attributions represent an important mediator for expectancies of future performance, complaint behavior, and affect. We now leave the question of a general framework for consumer attribution and turn to two narrower topics of attribution research: actor-observer effects and the role of expectancies in attribution.

Consumers as Actors, Manufacturers as Observers. The actor-observer effect (Jones and Nisbett, 1972) suggests that observers perceive the behavior of an actor differently than the actor perceives herself. Observers are more likely to make attributions to something internal to the actor, such as a disposition. Actors tend to perceive the same behavior as caused by the situation. For consumer complaint behavior, this implies that a consumer is probably unlikely to make attributions concerning an unsatisfactory purchase to the self, whereas an observer, such as the manufacturer, is more likely to see the consumer as the cause of the product's failure.

The free-response data in the Valle and Wallendorf (1977) study is consistent with this interpretation. More than half (30 of 54) of the respondents mentioned the manufacturer or product construction as the cause of their dissatisfaction. Many fewer attributions of self-responsibility were made, and these appeared to be mostly unstable in nature (effort, for example). It appears that these consumers did not engage in defensive attributions, since there was no tendency to blame others for their dissatisfaction, and they credited themselves for satisfactory purchases.

Empirical work on the perception of complainers by store personnel and manufacturers would provide the other half of the actor-observer effect. Indeed, some difficulties encountered by complaint departments may be due to differences in attributions between the consumer and the store or corporation. Whereas the company representative may see the consumer as at least partially responsible for the product failure, the consumer is likely to blame the product itself. This difference in attributional perspective can lead to bad feelings on the part of the consumer. He may feel unreasonably blamed for something he believes is not his fault. Making company representatives aware of these differences in perspective should enable them to deal with consumers more effectively.

Expectations and Attributions. The most important relationships in the model may be the linkages between expectations and attribution. It has been consistently shown that prior expectations have an important influence on the type of attribution made in response to success or failure. The more consistent actual performance is to prior expectations, the higher is the probability that a stable attribution will be made (Feather, 1969; Feather and Simon, 1971a, 1971b; McMahan, 1973; Valle and Frieze, 1976). Similarly, the farther performance is from expectations, the more likely will an attribution be made to an unstable cause. However, this literature has one limitation—most of the empirical data were gathered during single disconfirmations of prior expectations. It is not clear whether a long series of disconfirming instances would change this picture.

Applying these findings to consumer behavior, one would predict that, the closer a product's performance is to the consumer's expectations, the greater is the probability that the consumer will make a stable attribution about the cause of that performance. The predicted attributions following a satisfactory or unsatisfactory performance of a product are summarized in Figure 3.

This model has some interesting implications. From the seller's point of view, the optimal attribution is for the consumer to be satisfied with a product and attribute that satisfaction to a stable characteristic of the product. From Figure 3, it can be seen that this is the attribution made when a product that was expected to perform well actually does perform well. The attribution made about a product that was expected to perform well but that does not live up to expectations is also reasonably favorable toward the product, because it assumes that this is a rare case. However, the attributions made about a product expected to do poorly are both rather nega-

Expectation

		High	Low
Performance	Good	Stable (excellent product)	Unstable (luck, unusually good performance)
	Bad	Unstable (unlucky, a "lemon")	Stable (poor product)

Figure 3. Attributions Concerning Product Performance as a Function of Expectations.

tive. If the product performs well, it is attributed unstably, implying that this is a rare instance of a good performance by the product. If the product performs poorly, it is seen as due to the nature of the product.

Thus, the model suggests that a marketer who wants satisfied customers should market a product for which high expectations match performance. From the consumer's viewpoint, the most discouraging prediction of this model is for falsely high expectations, such as those encouraged by "puffery" ads that make unsubstantiated claims for product performance. In this case, bad performance will be attributed to unstable causes, and expectations will be unchanged. However, it should be emphasized that these predictions are based on research using one-time disconfirmations and that long periods of poor performance may have different consequences. Still, this lends strength to the argument that consumer satisfaction could be served by regulations ensuring that advertising claims are substantiated.

Expectations are also affected by attribution (McMahan, 1973; Rosenbaum, 1972; Vallé and Frieze, 1976). Usually, in this research, attributions are observed or manipulated, and subsequent expectations are observed. The data strongly support the hypothesis that stable attributions will bring about greater changes in future expectancies. Expectations therefore seem difficult to change: If performance is consistent with expectations, then a stable attribution is made, leading to higher (or lower) expectations. This suggests that supplying consumers with attributions may be a powerful way to change perceptions of products. The advertiser may stress the quality control exercised over the product, thereby leading the consumer to think that good performance is a stable quality and encouraging higher expectations for the product. Consumer activists could try to make people realize that many people are dissatisfied with a given product, thereby leading consumers to believe that the bad performance is a stable quality and encouraging lower expectations for the product. These persuasive messages parallel manipulations used by Valle and Frieze (1976), who argue that changes in performance alone will not change expectations. They argue that it is also necessary to make the performance appear to be due to stable factors to change the perceiver's expectations for the future significantly.

Response. The response of a consumer to a purchase situation can vary widely. People who are satisfied with a product may take no further action (probably the most common occurrence), tell their friends about it, purchase the product again, and even write a letter of praise. Of more interest to government agencies, consumer groups, and producers are the responses of those who are dissatisfied. Past studies of complaint behavior have concentrated on the most easily researched determinants of complaint behavior—demographics. It has been found that those who complain are younger, more highly educated, and have higher incomes than noncomplainers (Warland, Hermann, and Willits, 1975). Other research has been summarized by Landon (1977) in a descriptive model that sees complaint behavior as a function of degree of dissatisfaction, importance of purchase, the perceived benefits of complaint, and personality variables. Although such variables *describe* who complains, they do not *explain* who complains and how they complain.

An important, integral part of the consumer's experience with a product is the attribution made concerning the product's performance. Unless someone other than oneself is perceived to be responsible for a problem, it makes no sense to complain at all. Similarly, one would be unlikely to take action, if the party responsible for the problem is perceived to be one's spouse or a close friend. The attributions permeate the entire perception of the purchase and therefore mediate between the experience and the response of the consumer.

Several studies have been conducted to investigate the mediating effect of attributions. In the pilot study by Valle and Wallendorf (1977), the respondents were asked whether they had taken action in response to their unsatisfactory experience. It was found that actions tended to be consistent with the psychological distance of the attributions (see Figure 4). The action tended to be at a level closer to or equal to the level of the attribution. In other words, those attributing their dissatisfaction to the retailer were likely to channel their postpurchase action toward telling the re-

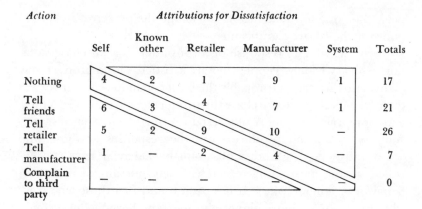

Figure 4. Consumer Action Following Dissatisfaction With a Product.

tailer or someone psychologically closer (such as a friend). Rarely was a complaint registered with someone more psychologically distant than the attribution. If the retailer was seen as responsible, it would be unlikely for the respondent to complain to the manufacturer.

A more systematic study of the relationship between attributions and complaint behavior has been reported by Valle and Koeske (1977). As part of a research project on consumer problems of the elderly, a mail survey was completed by a nationwide sample of 2,849 men and women (62.2 percent were over 65 years of age). The respondents were asked to describe the worst buying experience they had had in the past few years. A number of questions probed the nature of this bad experience, specifically: (1) possible reasons for being dissatisfied, (2) who they blamed for the problem, (3) which actions they took because of the problem, (4) why they might have hesitated or failed to complain, and (5) the monetary and psychological costs incurred.

A discriminant analysis was performed to find which variables distinguished between those who took action after their bad experience and those who did not. A respondent was considered to have taken direct action if he or she reported doing anything more than complaining to friends or deciding not to buy the product again. The variable most strongly associated with taking no direct action was attributing responsibility to oneself. Taking direct action was strongly associated with attributing blame to the company that sold the product. In contrast, traditional demographic variables, such as income, education, and age, were relatively poor predictors of complaint behavior.

Conclusions

The model we have presented stresses the importance of attributions as a mediator within the purchase, evaluation, and re-purchase sequence. Without an understanding of how the consumer perceives the purchase experience, there is little hope of understanding the consumer's response.

The next step in developing this model is an investigation of why certain attributions are made. We have already discussed the possible importance of expectations; more work is needed before we can say that an achievement-attribution framework is entirely accurate for describing consumers' attributions. Other questions also remain: How important are individual differences in determining attributions about product performance? What is the influence of situational variables on attributions about product performance? And, how do people learn to make specific types of attributions?

Understanding attributions and their relationship to perceptions of product performance has important implications for groups interested in consumer satisfaction. To make consumers more effective, consumer groups might want to increase consumers' tendencies to complain by changing their attributions. Both marketers and regulators should be interested in the relationship between expectations, attributions, and product performance. Our model has a number of implications for these groups, and we shall attempt to explore some of them.

Governmental and private agencies concerned with consumer satisfaction need to understand the importance of attributions of responsibility. Any consumer who has been "taken advantage of" or defrauded will suffer because of the experience. The consumer who accurately attributes problems to the producer or seller has at least the potential of receiving restitution, if a complaint is registered. At a minimum, the consumer can learn from the mistake, inform others of it, and avoid similar situations in the future. The consumers who actively respond to an unsatisfactory experience are an important component of the marketing process; by communicating their dissatisfaction to others and the producers, they encourage the improvement of products and services.

The unfortunate consumer who makes an internal attribution and accepts personal responsibility is in a much worse position. This person will not seek restitution and, more importantly, will be more likely to fall prey to the same situation in the future. Those people who make internal attributions about performance are the most victimized yet least visible segment of the consuming public. Obviously, people in this situation do not complain and do not go to consumer agencies for help. It may be desirable for these agencies to become more active in reaching out to consumers with problems. Further research should identify any specific segments of society that are more likely to make internal attributions than others, and such groups could then be the focus for efforts by consumer agencies.

One unintentional side-effect of current consumer education programs may be the promotion of such internal attributions. Consumers may feel that, if they are taken advantage of, they must be responsible and therefore stupid or ill informed. Encouraging consumers to be effective, although a reasonable idea, may lead to more internal attributions by the dissatisfied customer. This may be alleviated by raising the expectations of consumers, so that they expect certain minimum qualities from their purchases. Failure to meet these expectations would result in attributions to unstable causes (Weiner, 1974b), which may be perceived as changeable.

The significance of the consumer movement can also be viewed from an attributional perspective. One of the most important variables for determining attributions is social consensus. When there is a great deal of publicity surrounding a given consumer problem (auto service, for example), the consumer will be more likely to attribute problems to the product or service rather than to himself. The most significant effect of the consumer movement may not be in legislative changes but rather in changes in the way people perceive responsibility for product performance.

Chapter 6

Louis A. Morris
David E. Kanouse

Drug Taking
for Physical
Symptoms

Each year, the average American obtains 5.8 prescription drugs and takes numerous over-the-counter medications. The total annual cost of prescribed medicines is $5.75 billion, a figure that does not include costs for about 950 million prescriptions dispensed to hospital inpatients and another $4 to 8 billion for over-the-counter medicines (Choi, 1977; Fulda, 1976). These drugs are taken to prevent, cure, or alleviate a wide variety of diseases and symptoms, both real and imaginary, mild and serious.

Note: The views expressed in this chapter are solely those of the authors and do not represent the views of the Food and Drug Administration or the Rand Corporation. The authors wish to thank Lloyd Millstein for many valuable suggestions and Marilyn N. Dean for helpful comments on an earlier draft.

Most drugs have the potential for very powerful therapeutic and adverse effects. In view of this potential, it is surprising that so little is known about the psychological factors involved in drug use. Some people conceive of drug taking as a single event that occurs at one point in time. The thesis of this chapter, however, is that drug use is an ongoing process, in which both decisions and outcomes depend heavily on the attributions made by drug users concerning their own behaviors and bodily states.

Drug use poses several questions of interest to attribution theorists. What events lead to decisions to initiate, modify, or discontinue drug therapy? What sources of information about one's state of health are used to judge a drug's success or failure? What causal explanations accompany these judgments? This chapter explores such questions from an attributional perspective, with a special focus on how people interpret physical and behavioral events before, during, and after drug therapy.

The Drug Use Process

It is convenient to divide the drug use process into four stages: (1) noticing symptoms, (2) deciding to medicate, (3) monitoring physical and behavior states for improvement and side-effects, and (4) modifying or discontinuing the therapeutic regimen. The individual may or may not consult a physician or other health professional at any point during this process.

Noticing Symptoms. Sometimes, drugs are taken to prevent illness, and sometimes the decision to medicate depends on the results of medical or laboratory tests. More frequently, however, the initiation of drug therapy follows the onset of symptoms that the individual or the physician assumes can be modified by drugs.

Symptoms may be defined as subjective evidence of a disease or medical or psychological condition. Usually, this evidence takes the form of changes in bodily states. Some signs, such as abnormal bleeding, sneezing, or persistent cough offer clear evidence of injury or disease. The causes and significance of other symptoms, such as headache, ringing in the ears, and blurred vision are more ambiguous. For example, a bodily change may be the result of temporary emotional reactions, the result of natural processes, such as fatigue, or the result of a pathological condition, such as a brain tumor. Identifying a particular reaction as a symptom is easier for some changes in bodily state than for others.

Identifying symptoms requires *attention* to relevant cues and the use of *labels* suggestive of illness. Symptom-like cues may be quite common. Reidenberg and Lowenthal (1968) interrogated 670 health volunteers who were not in treatment, and 81 percent reported that they were currently experiencing what could be described as a symptom. Because the body is constantly reacting to a myriad of stimuli, the number of physical changes that are potential symptoms are enormous. The individual is, however, likely to notice only those reactions that are above a certain "discomfort threshold"; dramatic events or intense activity, for example, may prevent one from noticing even the most obvious physical changes (Beecher, 1962).

Even if a reaction is noticed, it will not be classified as a symptom unless an appropriate label is used. Studies such as Schachter and Singer's (1962) indicate that the same objective bodily state can give rise to different subjective states. If this is true, the experience of symptoms is likely to depend on the availability and salience of labels in the individual's active repertoire (Kanouse, 1972). This, in turn, depends on personality, experience, and situational factors. For example, advertising of drugs purported to treat "the blahs" or "tired blood" a few years ago may have added new labels to our collective repertoire.

Deciding to Medicate. After a potential symptom has been attended to and labeled (correctly or incorrectly) as a condition for which medication may be appropriate, a variety of factors influence whether the individual will begin a medication regimen. These include the severity of symptoms and their expected duration, the availability and cost of medication, belief in its efficacy, the existence of alternative methods for treating the problem, general beliefs about the appropriateness of taking drugs, concern about possible side-effects, and the recommendations of others, including physicians.

When diseases or injuries do occur, the most common response is to self-medicate. Knapp, Oeltjen, and Knapp (1974) report data covering more than 2,600 illness or injury incidents for which patients either took drugs or saw a doctor. For 67 percent of these incidents, patients reported taking over-the-counter drugs without seeing a doctor; for 10 percent, they reported taking prescription drugs without seeing a doctor; for 9 percent, they reported first initiating drug therapy, then seeing a doctor; and for only 14 percent did they report seeing a doctor before beginning drug therapy. Although the majority of patients report getting advice and treatment from a doctor for serious ailments (Knapp, Oeltjen, and Knapp, 1974), other studies (Dunnel and Cartwright, 1972; Morrell and Wale, 1976) support the basic conclusion that patients rather than doctors are more likely to initiate drug therapy.

Monitoring Physical States. Once a drug has been taken, physical states are monitored for signs of change, including improvement or worsening of symptoms and the occurrence of new symptoms or side-effects. The monitoring process is powerfully motivated by the desire to determine whether one is getting better or worse. We believe that this process is a very active one; it involves more than mere passive processing of unambiguous sensory information. An individual who has taken a drug expects physical changes and is likely to be actively looking for them. Both the original symptoms and the action of the drug itself are likely to provide a large number of sensory cues to monitor. Sometimes, these cues may be ambiguous or conflicting, as when improvement of one symptom is accompanied by worsening of another.

In addition to receiving this sensory information, the individual is likely to have knowledge of the nature and course of the disease and the action of the drug. We suspect that the monitoring process largely involves comparing the observed progress of one's own symptoms with the progress one expects, based on that knowledge. Progress that meets or exceeds expectations is viewed as encouraging, whereas progress that falls short of expectations is cause for discouragement or alarm.

When one has a large number of physical cues to monitor, one may be forced to interpret, integrate, and extrapolate a great deal of information to arrive at an assessment of how one is doing. Improvement in symptoms may still leave room for concern when the rate of improvement seems too slow or when the improvement seems largely attributable to transient factors, such as the masking effects of the drug. Conversely, the onset of new symptoms may offer signs of encouragement, if these symptoms are seen as signaling the final stages of the illness or the successful working of the drug. These complexities offer rich material for attributional analysis, and we shall have more to say about them later.

Modifying or Discontinuing the Regimen. As a result of the monitoring process, drug therapy may be modified or discontinued. Although some modification is often necessary even for drugs used in response to acute problems, the modification of drug regimens is apt to be more involved for drugs used on a long-term basis. Chronic drug therapy frequently requires an initial adaptation period, during which the individual becomes accustomed to the treatment. The regimen may be adjusted several times during this period.

The physician is most commonly viewed as the primary decision-maker regarding prescription drug therapy. Utilizing information from patient reports and more objective indices, such as physiological and laboratory parameters, the physician prescribes what he or she considers to be the best course of treatment. Nevertheless, it is the patient who ultimately decides whether this advice is to be followed. The consistent finding that only about half the patients for whom drugs are prescribed follow their regimen (Sackett, 1976) indicates that consumers are not passive partners in the therapeutic alliance. Noncompliance with the regimen may take the form of omitting doses, taking too much of the drug, or prematurely discontinuing drug therapy.

The Role of Attribution in the Drug Use Process

Each stage of the drug use process is either accompanied by or predicated on the formation of attributions that assign meaning to the individual's experience. The first step in the process is attending to physical cues that may indicate the presence of a symptom. Other things being equal, one is less likely to perceive cues that are unexpected, unless they are of sufficient magnitude or duration to force attention. Expectations are derived from the individual's interpretation of current information and from the causal schemata applied to order and interpret the world (Kelley, 1972). When schemata are wrong or are applied inappropriately, they may lead the individual to overlook cues that would otherwise be obvious. For example, pain in the leg could be a sign of too much physical exertion or the first indication of blood clot. The importance of such a reaction may be difficult for the individual to recognize, partly because it is at odds with cultural schemata that suggest that serious illness is accompanied by great pain and disability rather than mere inconvenience.

Before a physical cue is defined as a symptom, it must first be labeled in a way that suggests the presence of a medical condition. Usually, the choice of one label rather than another also narrows the range of potential explanations and appropriate courses of action. In saying that a physical state is one thing rather than another, one may in effect be saying that the observed physical cues are due to one thing rather than to another. For example, one frequently has a choice between somatic and affective labels to describe the same phenomenon. Choosing to describe a set of cues with an affective label like *anger, tension,* or *frustration* rather than a somatic one like *headache* or *indigestion* can have implications both for causal attributions and likely courses of action, including drug use.

This choice between medical and nonmedical labels may often have a strong motivational component. In adopting a label implying illness, the individual can reap the costs and benefits associated with taking on the sick role (Parsons, 1975). We suspect, however, that whether a medical label is more or less attractive than a nonmedical one often depends more on the specific situational factors than on generalized proclivities. Thus, some parents show relief when they discover that their child's learning problems are due to hearing difficulties rather than to lack of intelligence. However, it may be better to be called moody than to be described as a manic depressive.

Adoption of a medical label can have significant affective and behavioral consequences. Recent evidence indicates that hypertensive individuals who have been informed of their illness but not yet treated for it lose more days of work than do hypertensives with equally severe conditions who are unaware of their medical condition (Haynes and others, 1978). Hypertension is frequently an asymptomatic condition whose treatment sometimes produces more symptoms than does the high blood pressure. In line with self-perception theory, it appears not only that people infer that they must be sick from the fact that they are not feeling well but also that they must not be feeling well from the fact that they are labeled as sick.

In selecting a label for a set of physical cues from the available repertoire, the individual is constrained both by the size and sophistication of that repertoire and by causal assumptions suggesting the application of one label rather than another. Advances in medical knowledge involve, among other things, recognition of new syndromes, whose existence was previously ignored, unrecognized, or misdiagnosed. Once knowledge of such syndromes spreads, the incidence of diagnosed cases typically accelerates. In much the same manner as public knowledge of medical syndromes advances (or merely changes), new labels become available to attach to physical cues. For example, in recent years, the public has become acquainted with such syndromes as dyslexia, hypoglycemia, and hyperactivity (minimal brain dysfunction). In these cases, additional knowledge has provided new labels for the cues and behavior associated with reading difficulty, having low blood sugar, or being a difficult child. Thus, new medical labels have become available for phenomena previously ascribed to nonmedical causes and labeled in nonmedical terms, thereby producing widespread changes in the interpretation of physical and behavioral cues.

A different constraint is imposed by the existence of medical conditions whose symptoms violate commonly held beliefs about the nature of disease. For example, hyperthyroidism is characterized by increased basal metabolism and is associated with a high level of energy in the affected individual. High energy may not be labeled as a symptom by the individual, as it violates the common assumption that symptoms do not make one feel invigorated. For the same reason, divers must be explicitly warned that one of the early signs of decompression sickness is euphoria.

Often, attributional errors occur because of the difficulty in distinguishing symptoms of a medical condition from the impact of temporary environmental factors; for example, an individual may attribute a stomachache to overeating rather than to influenza. A more serious example of this type of error involves victims of whiplash, who may consider a recurrent headache to be the emotional aftermath of the accident rather than a potential symptom of spinal injury.

Attributional problems also can arise where symptoms differ from the normal only in degree and are reinforced by custom or fashion. Thus, in the earlier stages of anorexia nervosa, the weight loss and low food intake characterizing the disease are easily attributable to a desire to attain a fashionable state of slenderness.

Deciding to Medicate. The decision to medicate may flow from many of the same considerations and lead to the same consequences as choosing a medical label. First, such a decision validates the medical nature of the condition. Moreover, from a self-perception or attributional standpoint, taking a drug introduces a new cognition about one's own behavior, a fact that can modify later inferences about the severity of one's original symptoms. It is common to hear people say, "My headache was so bad I had to take three aspirin." Self-perception theory would suggest that people gauge the severity of the headache in part by the number of aspirin taken (Bem, 1972). Indeed, taking any drug for symptomatic relief represents pain-avoidance behavior, and knowledge that one has sought to avoid pain can be used as the basis for inferring the severity of the pain (Bandler, Madaras, and Bem, 1968).

The cognition that one has taken a drug may have other implications as well. After taking a drug, for example, it is more difficult to determine the extent to which improvement in symptoms or disease results from the medication rather than one's own recuperative powers. To the extent that individuals wish to retain a sense of causal control over their own recovery, they may resist taking a drug that would aid in the recovery process but rob them of the sense of responsibility for their own improvement.

Monitoring Physical States. If the expected effects occur, the drug is apt to be viewed as efficacious, and the individual will probably judge that recovery is on the way. The monitoring process by which this occurs becomes interesting attributionally only when that judgment is incorrect, when expected effects do not occur, or when unexpected effects occur instead. If an individual takes a presumably effective drug, and expected changes do not ensue, is the failure due to administering an incorrect drug or dosage level, or was the illness worse than originally imagined?

The choice of a drug attribution versus a disease attribution as the cause for a therapy's failure can have important consequences, especially for diseases for which society assigns considerable causal responsibility to the individual. People who suffer from obesity or impotence, for example, may experience extreme self-doubt if drugs that are presumed to be effective are inadequate to treat their condition.

A classic example of how drug administration may lead to an exacerbation of symptoms is the "insomniac cycle"; lack of therapeutic effect causes increased worry about the seriousness of the disorder, and latency of sleep increases. Storms and Nisbett (1970) demonstrated this effect by using placebos to deliver ineffective drugs that were presented as sedatives. Their results suggest that people who do not experience the reported improvement from a drug may attribute this to the disease; rather than judging that the drug is ineffective, they may conclude that the underlying condition is more serious than originally believed. Such a conclusion may exacerbate the original symptoms by adding to the individual's worry and stress. This completes the cycle by which high therapeutic expectations lead to poor therapeutic outcomes, contrary to the usual (positive) placebo effect. Unfortunately, this therapeutic reversal (also known as the *reverse placebo effect* has not been replicated in subsequent attempts (Bootzin, Herman, and Nicassio, 1976; Kellogg and Baron, 1975), suggesting that the conditions necessary to produce this effect are rare and not well understood.

Active medications also can lead to a worsening of symptoms. Mitler and others (1975) suggest that insomniacs build tolerance to sleeping pills, if they are used on a regular basis, so that sedatives used regularly will aggravate the insomnia they are intended to cure.

Although reverse placebo effects may be rare, positive placebo effects are quite common. That the expectations about therapy are apt to be a major determinant of its success has been recognized since the time of Galen (Shapiro and Morris, 1978). The way in which expectations influence outcomes, however, is difficult to specify. Expectations about a drug's effects probably trigger a number of psychological processes that influence drug response; it is difficult, for example, to separate the effects of suggestion, the mobilization of hope, classical conditioning, and the production of internal standards. The choice of which process to define and study depends largely on one's theoretical perspective. For attribution theorists, internal standards, against which observed responses are matched and discrepancies are explained, are a congenial concept for analyzing drug use.

Three features of internal standards help explain how people monitor their treatment and ultimately make decisions to modify or discontinue the drug: *level* (the degree of change expected), *certainty* (the degree of confidence with which the standards are held), and *focus* (the particular symptom or constellation of bodily changes used as data to make judgments about drug effectiveness and course of disease).

Lyerly and others (1964) have shown that, for certain psychotropic drugs in moderate doses, unless people know they have taken a drug and have knowledge of its actions, the drug will not produce its usual effects. Thus, an individual who is unaware that a drug will produce a certain effect will be less likely to recognize that effect. Exaggerated expectations also may reduce the effectiveness of the drug treatment, because the greater the effects that are expected by the individual, the less likely it is that observed changes will match expectations. Valins and others (1971) caution against the overselling of a drug treatment. In their experiment, subjects were given an internal standard by experiencing the effects of nitrous oxide. Oxygen (a placebo) was given in a second experimental session, but half the subjects were told it was the same treatment, and half were told it was a weaker dose. Whereas those expecting the weaker dose attributed the lack of effect to the dosage reduction, subjects expecting the same dose attributed the lack of observed effect to internal factors (fear of electric shock). Valins and Nisbett (1972) interpret this as an indication that, when treatments are described in somewhat less enthusiastic terms, there may be less possibility for a reverse placebo effect.

In addition to using an explicit explanation offered by the physician or relying on direct experiences with the drug or the disease, it appears that patients actively seek information to anticipate levels of change (Valins and others, 1971). For example, the questions most frequently asked of pharmacists by customers purchasing prescription products pertain to the purpose and actions of the medicine (DeSimone, Peterson, and Carlstedt, 1977). Patients also may rely on subtle and indirect communications from the physician to form expectations about their condition and therapy. Uhlenhuth and others (1959) found that different doctors produce different success rates even with identical drugs and dosage schedules.

The certainty of an internal standard refers to how confidently one expects the reaction to be at the expected level rather than at a stronger or weaker level; it influences how easily one is convinced that an expected change did in fact occur. People who are highly familiar with a drug's effects or who have had a great deal of experience with the target symptoms are likely to have stronger internal standards and therefore are better able to judge whether observed drug effects accurately match expectations. Such people, therefore, should be more accurate in attributing changes to their medication.

Several studies indicate that both previous usage of a drug and duration of illness are predictive of drug and placebo response. In cross-over studies in which patients were first treated with active medication but then switched to placebo, subjects who improved on active drugs were less likely to improve on placebo, whereas patients who were unimproved on active drugs were more likely to improve on placebo (Rickels and others, 1965). In three studies comparing active drug to placebo, patients with one or fewer previous psychotropic medications improved more on placebo than patients who had taken psychotropic drugs at least twice previously (Rickels, Lipman, and Raab, 1966). Chronically ill patients (those who had been ill for seven months or longer) were less likely to improve on placebo than the more recently sick.

Although one cannot rule out other explanations, these results are consistent with the notion that the certainty of an internal standard is greater when the individual has prior experience with the symptoms of a disease or the working of a drug; such individuals should be less likely to respond to a placebo whose effects do not match those standards. Since they know with relative certainty what to expect, such individuals are less likely to confuse physical changes unrelated to the drug or disease with those caused by them. In contrast, less experienced patients who expect only to feel different as a result of the drug therapy should be more likely to label any positive change as improvement.

The certainty of an internal standard seems to be more directly based on experience with a drug rather than on what an individual might have heard from others. Morris and O'Neal (1974) manipulated drug name familiarity by administering identical placebos to college students but introducing them by popular, commonly known names to half the subjects (Dexedrine and Vitamin A) and by unfamiliar, fictitious names to the other half (Butyline and Karadin). Although the suggestion of whether the drug was a stimulant or a vitamin caused significant differences in mood and behavior ratings, the familiarity variable did not cause any significant differences or interact with any other variables.

Drug effects and progress in the course of an illness can be assessed in a variety of ways. To the individual receiving drug therapy, expectations help define a particular constellation of changes that would indicate drug efficacy or relief. In addition, the particular method used to assess drug effects may change the focus of assessment. For example, Storms and Nisbett (1970) found a negative placebo effect when they used latency scores based on subjects' report of the time they went to bed as compared with the time they fell asleep. When subjects were asked how much they suffered from insomnia, however, not only was no significant difference found, but there was a tendency in the opposite direction. Thus, although the investigators were using objective data (sleep latencies) to measure insomnia, the subjects themselves may have been focusing on more subjective indices. Several other attribution studies have demonstrated objective behavioral differences caused by arousal manipulations that were unaccompanied by self-rating differences (Davison and Valins, 1969; Nisbett and Schachter, 1966; Valins and Ray, 1967; Zimbardo, 1969).

Although expectations may provide an initial focus for the assessment of drug effects, unexpected drug effects clearly attributable to a drug's action can be taken as evidence of the drug's efficacy. Morris and O'Neal (1975) gave college students two types of false feedback together with the expectation that the drug (actually a placebo) would cause changes in one of the feedback modalities. When subjects experienced the expected change, they rated the drug as more effective. In the absence of expected changes, unexpected changes also led to high ratings of drug efficacy, but only when there were no other clear attributional alternatives.

The attributional pathways through which observed effects are taken as evidence of drug efficacy probably depend on beliefs about physiology and pharmacology. Whereas some beliefs may be quite specific, certain general organizing principles probably underlie many others. People may be more likely, for example, to perceive physiological states as being related when those states share common attributes. Pain, itching, and redness will probably be seen as related when they occur at the site of a single wound or infection, because they share the attribute of location. Identical symptoms occurring in different parts of the body may suggest a shared underlying cause (for example, stiffness in various joints). But the layman may be less likely to form causal connections between disparate symptoms occurring in different parts of the body. There is something intuitively jarring about the fact that, when carbon dioxide is blown into the fallopian tubes during the Rubin test, pain in the shoulders signals that the tubes are clear.

Side-Effects. In addition to producing intended therapeutic effects, both prescription and nonprescription drugs produce side-effects. Although all drugs can have toxic effects, the frequency and severity of these effects range along a continuum, depending on such variables as dosage and individual sensitivity. Of particular interest from a psychological and attribution-theory perspective are the common side-effects associated with virtually all drugs.

With active medication, side-effects are frequently a result of the same pharmacological mechanism that produces the therapeutic effect. Thus, the hair loss, white cell depression, and liver toxicity that are side-effects of some cancer chemotherapies result from the drug's destruction of rapidly multiplying cells, both cancerous and noncancerous. Patients who receive placebos also frequently report side-effects. In a review of sixty-seven publications, Pogge (1963) found that 23 percent of 3,549 patients given placebos reported at least one side-effect.

Misattribution appears to be a likely explanation for the oc-currence of placebo-induced side-effects. Many of the most com-mon drug side-effects, such as headache, nervousness, depression, and stomach upset, occur naturally among people not taking drugs. The knowledge that one has taken a drug, however, is a salient environmental cue. Naturally occurring bodily changes and the disease under treatment are apt to produce any number of effects that may be misattributed to the drug. Busfield, Schneller, and Capra (1962), in reviewing the commonly mentioned side-effects of antidepressant medication, found few side-effects that could not also be considered a symptom of depression. Moreover, several of the apparent side-effects were present prior to treat-ment. Thus, while monitoring physical states, one may mistakenly attribute inadequately treated symptoms to the side-effects of the drug.

The knowledge that one has taken a medicine also influ-ences the choice of labels to describe bodily events. Although it is commonly assumed that the psychological effect of administering a drug actually causes the production of side-effects, evidence indi-cates that *labeling* rather than *production* of side-effects is most in-fluenced by knowledge of drug administration. Glaser and Whit-tow (1954) administered questionnaires asking medical students to report their current symptoms. Each subject filled out a question-naire on five separate occasions. Although placebos were given prior to some of the trials, the proportion of subjects reporting symptoms did not change on the trials on which placebos were given. Glaser and Whittow conclude that, in forcing subjects to observe their own reactions, the questionnaires made them notice or imagine symptoms they would otherwise have ignored.

The type of label used to describe a reaction appears to be influenced by the cognition that one has taken a drug. Linton and Langs (1962) found that, whereas cognitive symptoms were more common prior to administration of an LSD placebo, somatic symptoms predominated in the postplacebo report. Before taking the placebo, subjects responded to a questionnaire probing their physical and mental state. The most common complaints were dif-ficulty in understanding, performing, or concentrating on tasks.

After placebo ingestion, the most common complaints were dizziness, grogginess, weakness, lightheadedness, dry mouth, and ringing in the ears.

Similarly, in an experiment by Shapiro and others (1974), patients applying for outpatient psychiatric treatment were asked to complete a series of psychological tests. In the drug placebo test, subjects were given a placebo but were told it was a test medication. They were asked to sit in a quiet room for one hour following drug administration and then report any new symptoms or side-effects. In the control placebo test, subjects were not given a placebo but were asked to sit in the room for an hour to see how their symptoms varied spontaneously and to report any new symptoms after the hour wait. After the experiment, each reported side-effect or new symptom was rated on a five-point scale, ranging from entirely cognitive-affective to entirely somatic in nature. There was no difference in the proportion of subjects reporting side-effects (about 60 percent in each condition); however, the type of side-effects reported did differ. Seventy-one percent of the drug-placebo test subjects who had side-effects or new symptoms described them in terms that could be categorized as primarily somatic, 19 percent reported primarily cognitive-affective symptoms, and 18 percent reported a mixture of both somatic and cognitive-affective. In the control-placebo test, however, only 24 percent of the subjects who reported new symptoms used terms that were categorized as primarily somatic, 51 percent used words that were rated as primarily cognitive-affective, and 24 percent reported mixed reactions. Thus, the information that one has ingested a drug influences how subsequent events are described. Apparently, an agent that commonly induces physical changes leads the individual to label observed changes with terms that are consistent with physiological reactions.

One might suppose that the occurrence of side-effects would usually be interpreted negatively; however, the data suggest that this need not be the case. Instead, side-effects may be taken as evidence of drug efficacy, as a sign that the drug is powerful enough to do its job. Shapiro and others (1973) examined the relationship between reported changes in original symptoms and the occurrence of side-effects. Their research employed placebos, so that actual pharmacological effects were not an issue. They found that of thirty-eight subjects reporting the occurrence of side-effects, 44 percent stated that the drug had alleviated their original symptoms, 42 percent thought it had made their symptoms worse, and only 14 percent reported no change. In contrast, among the sixty subjects reporting no side-effects, the majority (56 percent) also reported no change in their original symptoms. Thirty-seven percent of these subjects thought the drug had helped them, and only 7 percent felt worse. Thus, the occurrence of side-effects seems to increase the probability that a patient will report a *change* in the original symptoms, but the change may be in a positive direction as well as a negative one.

If labeling of drug effects is subject to environmental manipulation, and if side-effects may sometimes be interpreted as positive rather than negative events, then the way in which potential side-effects are initially described to the individual may have important consequences for drug efficacy. Drug side-effects are often accurately described as "adverse," "toxic," "negative," and "unwanted." However, as Shapiro and others (1973) demonstrate, some drug side-effects may also be described as "evidence that the drug is working." If the individual interprets side-effects positively rather than as evidence of the drug's toxicity, then attitudes, decisions, and behaviors regarding drug use may be quite different. If interpreted as a signal that the drug is doing its job, the occurrence of side-effects may be a sign that improvement is imminent.

There are studies indicating that, under certain conditions, patients may be induced to interpret side-effects as a signal of improvement. For example, in an experiment by Kast and Loesch (1961), psychiatric outpatients were given atropine sulfate, which causes dryness of the mouth. Half the subjects were forewarned that such dryness was a danger signal indicating that the drug should be discontinued. The other half were told that dryness of the mouth was a sign that the medicine was working and that the symptom should be ignored. Subjects who were encouraged to interpret the side-effect as a signal that the drug was working showed more clinical improvement than those who were offered the opposite interpretation. The therapeutic implications of this finding are obvious.

As is often the case, however, seemingly contrary evidence also exists. Lipman, Park, and Rickels (1966) tested the hypothesis that the meaning attributed to side-effects could influence the clinical course. Four drug groups were tested in a double-blind trial; two groups had atropine as a medication (atropine with chlordiazepoxide or atropine alone) and two did not (chlordiazepoxide alone or placebo). Study physicians told half the subjects that, if they experienced a dry mouth, it was a good sign that the medicine was working effectively (positive set condition). The other subjects were told that, if they experienced a dry mouth, it was nothing to worry about (neutral set). Contrary to expectations, the atropine-positive set combination produced the least improvement of any group. The investigators speculated that side-effects may have negative connotations and that preexisting beliefs may have been more influential than the physician's therapeutic interpretation.

It seems likely that the difference in results between these studies could be caused by differences in the instructional sets used as controls. In the Kast and Loesch experiment, the "drug is working" set was compared with "the drug should be discontinued" set (negative), whereas, in the Lipman, Park, and Rickels experiment, it was compared with "there is nothing to worry about," a set that seems more positive than neutral. Neither study provides a comparison of the "drug is working" set with one that is truly neutral, such as "you may get a dry mouth." The possibility of shaping the individual's experience of side-effects by attention to how those effects are labeled remains an intriguing notion that has not yet been sufficiently tested.

Modifying or Discontinuing Drug Therapy. The final stage in the drug use process is the modification or discontinuation of drug therapy. Physicians may need to make numerous modifications of their initially prescribed therapy, such as adjusting dosage or adding new drugs to the regimen. Similarly, patients may appropriately or inappropriately modify drug therapy, either with or without the advice of their doctor. The lack of patient adherence to prescribed regimens is a major cause of therapeutic failures, and an attribution-theory perspective on why patients modify or discontinue drug therapy can offer important clues for improving patient adherence. Examples of drug-taking behavior for three types of drugs—antibiotics, minor tranquilizers, and antihypertensives—will help illustrate some of the issues involved.

For patients with certain types of infections, antibiotics that kill the invading microorganisms are prescribed. If the infection is widespread and progressive, the individual is likely to feel ill. Once drug therapy is initiated, large numbers of microorganisms are killed, and the patient feels better. Although the physician may have prescribed ten days of treatment, the patient may discontinue drug therapy after three or four days. Unknown to the patient, the more virulent bacteria, which survived the first several days of treatment, may start to multiply and eventually cause a full relapse. Thus, the initial relief of symptoms may be incorrectly interpreted as a signal that drug treatment has been successful in eliminating the infection. Since general drug-taking attitudes may incline an individual to take drugs for the shortest time or as infrequently as believed absolutely necessary (Klerman, 1970), drug therapy may be prematurely discontinued.

The attributional pitfall posed in the use of antibiotics for infections arises, because patients are likely to assume that the degree of improvement in symptoms strongly covaries with the degree of recovery. If patients are warned that this is not the case, they may be much more likely to complete the prescribed regimen (Sharpe and Mikeal, 1974).

Misattribution also can cause patients to continue taking drugs that may no longer be needed. Certain minor tranquilizers, for example, when taken in large doses for prolonged periods, produce dependence reactions (Isbell and Chrusciel, 1970). Discontinuing such a drug after long-term treatment can produce withdrawal-induced anxiety reactions. Rather than attributing this anxiety to drug dependence, patients who attempt to stop taking the drug are likely to assume that the anxiety represents a return of their original symptoms, a sign that they still need the drug.

With asymptomatic conditions, the individual has no clear bodily signals on which to base drug use decisions. A case in point is hypertension, which can be measured only by instruments. Nonadherence to antihypertension therapy takes the form of frequently omitting doses or consciously deciding to discontinue the regimen. Sometimes, the drug causes more symptoms than the disease, but, when people who decided to stop their medicine were asked why they did so (Harris, 1975), only 3 percent named the drug's side-effects. In this study, most former patients (61 percent) said their doctor advised them to stop; about one-fifth (21 percent) said they stopped because they felt they did not need the medicine any more. Thus, among the people who discontinued taking the medicine without their doctor's advice, more said that they did so because they felt the medicine was not needed than because of its side-effects.

We can only speculate about why so many hypertensive patients do not closely adhere to the regimen. Certainly, the social science literature is replete with examples of the difficulty of producing long-term changes in behavior, and hypertension therapy usually requires a life-long commitment. People are much less apt to omit doses of certain life-saving drugs, such as cardiac medicines and insulin (Hulka and others, 1975). These cases suggest that, if the benefit of taking antihypertensive medicine were perceived more clearly, compliance might be improved. Moreover, for some diseases, symptoms may reappear when the drug is not taken, but no such signals exist for high blood pressure. Lack of feedback on the medicine's effectiveness might thus contribute to patient noncompliance. Given the many possible reasons for noncompliance with antihypertensive regimens, it is no wonder that nonadherence to the regimen is of epidemic proportions.

Implications for Drug Information

What practical implications can be drawn from attributional analysis of the drug use process? Our primary recommendation is that patients be more fully and intelligently informed about any given drug—what it treats, how it works, and what to expect as a result of taking it. Certainly, one does not need to invoke attribution theory to justify making such a recommendation. In recent years, the consumer movement has generated increasing pressure toward this end, and support for providing more drug information has grown among large segments of the health profession as well.

Attribution theory does suggest the kinds of specific information that are likely to be most useful to the patient. As we have seen, individuals who take medications often experience physical changes that can be difficult to interpret correctly. Moreover, the consequences of making erroneous attributions can be serious—the individual may prematurely discontinue a drug before it has done its job or continue taking a drug that is no longer needed. Because of these serious consequences, we feel it is important that patients have adequate information not only about therapeutic effects of a drug and its proper use but also about potential side-effects. To be sure, presenting advance information about such effects involves potential dangers—that the patient may be frightened into avoiding a drug that would on balance be beneficial or, if the drug is taken, that the expectation of side-effects may tend to produce those effects through suggestion. These dangers, however, are balanced by the drug user's right to know what may happen and by the fact that the drug user can hardly be expected to make appropriate attributions and intelligent decisions without such knowledge. For example, patients who do not know that certain antihypertension medicines may produce impotence are at a great informational disadvantage, if they experience such an effect. If they do not identify the problem as being due to the drug, they may experience much needless worry and suffering. It is not difficult to imagine such an individual undertaking expensive therapy to cure a problem that merely requires an adjustment in the antihypertension regimen. As discussed earlier, the potential drawbacks to warning drug users about side-effects may be ameliorated somewhat by careful attention to how these effects are described. There is still much to learn about introducing patients to the subject of drug side-effects.

In addition to relying on the traditional oral exchange between health provider and patient, some methods have been developed to provide patients with standardized messages regarding illness and therapy. One such method of particular relevance for drug therapy is the use of leaflets describing the drug's risks, benefits, and proper usage. These leaflets, which accompany the product as it is dispensed to the patient, already exist for some commonly used drugs (isoproterenol inhalants, oral contraceptives, estrogens, and progestational drugs), and more are being written. Using principles derived from attribution theory in drafting these leaflets would constitute a direct and potentially fruitful application of the theory to health care.

Developing an accurate conceptual model of how people use drugs can help professionals to identify the type of information that would enable patients to use medications more wisely. If people can make proper causal assignments to drug, disease, or other environmental factors, they can better understand both illness and therapy; and, if they can properly interpret drug and disease effects, they can gain more control over their own health.

Chapter 7

Michael D. Storms
Douglas R. Denney
Kevin D. McCaul
Carol R. Lowery

Treating Insomnia

While attribution theory was being formulated in the 1960s, the idea developed that attributional processes might be implicated in the etiology and treatment of emotional disorders. The research of Stanley Schachter concerning the labeling of emotions served as the template upon which this idea was fashioned. Schachter demonstrated that both the extent and nature of one's emotional experience were influenced by the source to which one attributed physiological arousal. When individuals experienced symptoms of physiological arousal and believed those symptoms to be caused by an emotion-arousing stimulus present in their environment, they were likely to experience the corresponding emotion. However, when a cogent, nonemotional source for the physiological arousal was available, such as a drug, individuals were less likely to interpret their arousal as an emotional experience (Schachter and Singer, 1962). A logical extension of this view is that aberrant emotionality and disorders stemming from such emotionality might be attenuated by assisting individuals to reattribute arousal symptoms to nonemotional sources available or introduced within their environments.

In this chapter, we will examine the relationship between attribution theory and one particular emotional disorder—in fact, the first such disorder to which attribution theory was applied—insomnia. In so doing, we will focus on attributional approaches to the *treatment* of insomnia. It is through such treatment studies that most of the ideas bearing on the association between attribution theory and insomnia have been substantiated. Insomnia serves as a cogent illustration of the value to be gained from the application of theory to the interpretation and treatment of emotional disorders. We begin with a discussion of an attribution model of insomnia. This discussion is followed by an examination of three treatment techniques predicated on the attribution model and the empirical evidence regarding the effectiveness of these techniques in reducing self-reports of sleep onset latency. We conclude with a discussion of some theoretical issues bearing on the attribution model of insomnia and some general recommendations regarding the treatment of this disorder with attribution therapy and with other, more common forms of intervention.

An Attribution Model of Insomnia

Storms and Nisbett (1970) offered the first discussion of insomnia from the standpoint of attribution theory. They began by noting Monroe's (1967) finding that problem sleepers have higher levels of autonomic arousal at bedtime than good sleepers. Insomniacs frequently report being troubled by such common arousal symptoms as accelerated heart rate, racing thoughts, increased body temperature, and sweating when they are trying to fall asleep. Storms and Nisbett suggested that insomniacs may interpret these arousal symptoms in emotionally charged terms, which in turn may serve to maintain and even augment the arousal, thus further delaying sleep onset. From this analysis was borne the notion of *exacerbation cycles* operating in the case of insomnia as well as other stress-related disorders (for example, stuttering and impotence). In each instance, symptoms of the disorder elicit worrisome ruminations, which in turn further aggravate the disorder. In the case of insomnia, the failure to fall asleep immediately, in conjunction with various arousal symptoms heralding another sleepless night, triggers worrisome ruminations that further attenuate the onset of sleep.

A further elaboration of the attribution model addresses the question of what worries in particular the insomniac may entertain when he or she experiences heightened arousal at bedtime. Storms and Nisbett (1970) and more recently Storms and McCaul (1978) have argued that the specific types of attributions that serve to exacerbate insomnia may be pejorative self-inferences drawn from one's sleep difficulties. In considering the attribution therapies that have been formulated to treat insomnia, it is valuable to distinguish further between two principal types of pejorative self-attributions that may be implicated in the maintenance of insomnia, *pejorative causal attributions* and *pejorative control attributions*. Pejorative causal attributions refer to negative inferences insomniacs might make about the causes of their insomnia, such as inferences of mental instability or generalized personal incompetence. Pejorative control attributions refer to negative inferences insomniacs might make about their ability to control their own sleeping behavior, regardless of what insomniacs believe causes their sleeping problems. Even if the cause itself is deemed to be innocuous, the insomniac may be upset about not being able to control such a basic function as falling asleep, compounded perhaps by worries about the ability to perform adequately the next day, given so few hours of sleep. Both pejorative causal attributions and pejorative control attributions may sustain and enhance bedtime arousal and thus further delay the onset of sleep.

Pill-Attribution Treatments of Insomnia

As stated earlier, Schachter and Singer (1962) demonstrated that, when individuals attributed arousal symptoms to an emotionally neutral external agent, they reported experiencing less emotion. Subsequent studies (Nisbett and Schachter, 1966; Ross, Rodin, and Zimbardo, 1969) extended Schachter and Singer's findings and illustrated the possibility of actually reducing individuals' emotionality by leading them to misattribute their true emotional symptoms to some nonemotional source. For example, Nisbett and Schachter (1966) found that subjects tolerated more electric shock and reported the shocks to be less painful when they were led to attribute their fear-produced arousal to a placebo pill rather than to the shocks. These investigators also observed that such misattribution occurs only when ambiguity exists concerning the true source of arousal. When their subjects experienced strong and unambiguous fear of shock, they did not misattribute their arousal to the pill.

In an initial demonstration of attribution theory, Storms and Nisbett (1970) hypothesized that insomniacs might be assisted to fall asleep more quickly, if it were possible for them to attribute their bedtime arousal symptoms to an emotionally neutral source, such as a placebo pill they had ingested before retiring. Given an emotionally neutral source to which to attribute their presleep arousal, insomniacs may worry less about this arousal, drawing fewer pejorative causal and control connotations about their insomnia and thus falling asleep more quickly.

Storms and Nisbett (1970) recruited a college sample of "light sleepers" under the guise of doing a dream research project. Subjects were assigned to three conditions—arousal-pill, relaxation-pill, and no pill. Subjects in the first two groups were told that the study concerned the effects of bodily activity on dreams and were instructed to take a pill prior to going to bed. Those in the arousal-pill group were told that the pill would increase their level of arousal; those in the relaxation-pill group were told that the pill would decrease their level of arousal and relax them.

The investigators predicted that subjects in the arousal-pill group would be able to reattribute presleep arousal to a nonemotional external source, would experience less emotionality, and therefore would fall asleep in less time than was normally required. Those in the relaxation-pill group would experience their presleep arousal *in spite of the pill* as a heightened emotional state, and this would compound the insomnia problem, keeping the subjects awake longer than usual. These predictions were confirmed. Arousal-pill subjects decreased their reported sleep onset latencies by twelve minutes, and relaxation-pill subjects increased their reported latencies by fifteen minutes from preexperimental to experimental nights.

Subsequent attempts to reduce insomnia by pill-attribution treatments have met with far less encouraging results. Both Kellogg and Baron (1975) and Bootzin, Herman, and Nicassio (1976) have reported failures in their attempts to replicate Storms and Nisbett's findings. In the first of these studies, Kellogg and Baron (1975) proposed an alternative explanation for the effects obtained by Storms and Nisbett. They suggested that the placebo-pill manipulation provided subjects with attributions about why they agreed to take the supposedly arousing drug rather than attributions about the causes of their bedtime arousal. Subjects who took the arousal pill may have decided that, since they had agreed to take a drug that would make their insomnia worse, then their insomnia must not be so bad after all. To examine this notion, Kellogg and Baron gave some arousal-pill subjects and some no-pill subjects strong external justification for participating in the study, telling them that it would be a valuable contribution to science. In two other conditions, subjects were given Storms and Nisbett's arousal-pill and no-pill instructions without additional justification.

Kellogg and Baron (1975) expected to replicate Storms and Nisbett's reverse-placebo effect in the no-justification conditions, whereas they predicted just the opposite—direct-suggestion effects—when subjects were provided with a reason for taking the pill. On a measure of self-reported sleep onset latency, both predictions were disconfirmed. In the high-justification conditions, there were no differences between pill and no-pill subjects. The no-justification condition produced a slight reversal of Storms and Nisbett's findings, with pill subjects reporting somewhat longer periods of insomnia than no-pill subjects.

A second failure to replicate the reverse-placebo effect was reported by Bootzin, Herman, and Nicassio (1976). These authors, like Kellogg and Baron, attempted to demonstrate that increased or decreased self-reported sleep onset latency could result from giving arousal pills to insomniacs. Two conditions in their study formed an exact replication of Storms and Nisbett's arousal-pill and no-pill conditions. In an added condition, subjects were given an arousal-pill and told that it would keep them awake (insomnia suggestion). Bootzin, Herman, and Nicassio expected this last condition to increase self-reported sleep onset latency because the manipulation included a direct suggestion about subjects' overt sleeping behavior. In the two replication conditions, wherein subjects received suggestions about their internal states, these authors expected to replicate Storms and Nisbett's effects. Their results failed to support either prediction. They found no differences among the arousal-pill, insomnia-suggestion, and control conditions.

In summary, one study has shown that the arousal-pill manipulation can reduce self-reported insomnia (Storms and Nisbett, 1970), one study has shown that this procedure can increase insomnia (Kellogg and Baron, 1975), and one study has shown that the procedure has no effect (Bootzin, Herman, and Nicassio, 1976). These inconsistent results raise serious questions concerning the reliability of pill-attribution treatments of insomnia. It is important to note, however, that these studies provide no conclusions about the theory underlying this procedure. Although the evidence now suggests that the placebo-pill procedure is unreliable, the attributional model of insomnia, on which this procedure is predicated, is not necessarily disproved by the failure to replicate this one particular manipulation. The placebo-pill procedure may simply be a poor way to manipulate the attributional variables specified in the model.

According to the model, the pill manipulation was intended to provide subjects with an external, nonemotional account for their bedtime arousal, to short-circuit more harmful, pejorative causal and control attributions, and thereby to reduce anxiety and promote the onset of sleep. This hypothesized sequence of events is crucial to the outcome of pill-attribution treatments. If the placebo pill were not successful in reducing pejorative attributions concerning insomnia, it would not be expected to reduce the insomnia itself. All three pill-attribution treatment studies cited here failed to include sufficient manipulation checks to assess whether the hypothesized sequence of events had occurred. There is evidence that subjects believed the arousal pill caused arousal symptoms, but there is no evidence that subjects attributed less arousal to insomnia, held fewer pejorative cognitions, or experienced less anxiety about their condition. In fact, investigators working with other emotional disorders have generally failed to obtain reduced emotionality via misattribution to placebo pills or even to active drugs such as caffeine (Cotton, Baron, and Borkovec, 1977; Singerman, Borkovec, and Baron, 1976).

Placebo pills may constitute a poor means of reducing pejorative attributions concerning one's insomnia and thereby reducing insomnia. First, there is the problem of convincing insomniacs that the pill is actually causing their arousal each night. With chronic insomniacs, who have a high degree of familiarity with their symptoms, convincing them of the pill's effects may be especially difficult. Even if they initially believe in the pill on the first or second night, that belief is likely to be undermined by subsequent experience. Drugs are supposed to have consistent effects from one administration to the next. However, the insomniac who is taking placebo medication will probably experience a great deal of fluctuation in bedtime arousal. This fluctuation might lead individuals to conclude that their arousal is not really under the control of the medication.

Even assuming that the insomniac can be convinced of the pill's effects, the next problem is to assure that the pill attribution has fewer emotional connotations for the individual than the pejorative self-attributions it is supposed to replace. Pills may represent a nonemotional stimulus to many individuals, but some people have strong emotional reactions to taking pills. Some may fear the drug, resent having to take the pills, worry about becoming dependent on them, and even draw additional pejorative inferences about themselves as a result of having to resort to drugs to treat their problems. To the extent that these reactions occur, insomniacs' overall level of emotionality would not be reduced by the pill-attribution procedure, and there would be little reason to expect their insomnia to abate.

In short, we would argue that the pill-attribution procedure operates in a fairly indirect fashion, triggering a rather complex chain of cognitive events that should ultimately lead to a reduction in insomnia. However, any of several problems can sabotage the intended attributional effects of pill manipulations. Given the lack of evidence that placebo pills successfully reduce pejorative self-attributions and associated emotionality and given the abundance of reasons why they might fail, it is unfortunate that the pill procedure has become a focus of so much controversy. The irreplicability of the pill-attribution procedure has distracted researchers from a more important practical and theoretical issue—namely, is the attribution model valid? Is insomnia sustained by pejorative self-attributions, and can reliable treatments be fashioned to change these attributions and to alleviate insomnia?

Nonpejorative Causal-Attribution Treatments of Insomnia

In a recent study, Lowery, Denney, and Storms (1979) argued that pejorative causal attributions of insomnia could be treated in a more direct way than by inducing misattribution to placebo pills. This could be done by persuading insomniacs that their sleeping problem is not caused by any psychological or emotional disorder. Instead, they could be told that insomnia is the simple by-product of higher baseline levels of autonomic activity. If insomniacs could be convinced to abandon their negative self-inferences about sleeplessness, they should worry less about their general condition and become less anxious about delays in the onset of sleep.

As in Storms and Nisbett's (1970) original study, subjects were informed that the purpose of the study was to evaluate the relationship between dreams and autonomic activity and that insomniacs were being used as subjects because they are light sleepers and thus remember their dreams better. Subjects in the nonpejorative self-attribution condition were also told that insomniacs are also more mentally active than most other people and their autonomic activity levels are somewhat higher—within normal limits, but usually higher than average. The experimenter produced some bogus physiological recordings ostensibly collected from the subject that supported the statements concerning insomniacs and reaffirmed that this higher autonomic arousal level did not mean that insomniacs were maladjusted or less able to handle stress and other problems.

In addition to this nonpejorative self-attribution technique,

Lowery, Denney, and Storms' study also contained a replication of Storms and Nisbett's arousal-pill procedure and a control condition, in which subjects received neither the pill nor the nonpejorative self-attribution manipulation. As in Kellogg and Baron's (1975) study, the experimental period was extended to a full week.

To assess the effects of their manipulations, Lowery, Denney, and Storms directly measured subjects' pejorative attributions about insomnia via a dream and sleep attitude survey. Responses on this postexperimental questionnaire indicated that subjects who received the nonpejorative self-attribution treatment held significantly fewer negative attitudes about insomnia than did control subjects or arousal-pill subjects, whereas the latter two groups did not differ. Evidently, the nonpejorative manipulation was successful in reducing negative attributions. By contrast, and surprisingly, the arousal-pill procedure failed to influence this theoretically important mediating variable.

In terms of the primary outcome variables in the study, no differences were found among the groups after the initial two days of the experimental week. However, after the next five days, subjects in the nonpejorative self-attribution condition were reporting significantly greater reductions in the time it took them to fall asleep and significantly less difficulty falling asleep than were control subjects. By contrast, arousal-pill subjects never differed from control subjects throughout the experimental period.

Thus, the nonpejorative self-attribution procedure influenced the crucial theoretical variable — that is, it reduced negative self-inferences concerning insomnia. Furthermore, this procedure reduced insomnia on two self-report measures. By contrast, the arousal-pill procedure failed to influence either the mediating attributional process or the insomnia itself.

The nonpejorative self-attribution procedure provides more direct support for the attributional model of insomnia and promises several practical and clinical advantages. First, these results suggest that it is fairly easy to persuade insomniacs that their sleep disorder is caused by normal fluctuations in basic autonomic arousal levels. As compared with pill-attribution manipulations, such a procedure is ethically more appropriate, since it involves less deception and has a basis in fact (Monroe, 1967).

Second, the nonpejorative self-attribution procedure appears to result in increased improvement with time. The procedure does not depend on the insomniac's continued use of and unfaltering belief in some external agent, such as a pill. Indeed, the newer technique may gain credibility and power as the insomniac continues to identify and reinterpret his arousal symptoms in nonpejorative terms.

Finally, the nonpejorative self-attribution procedure is more likely to reduce overall emotionality than the pill procedure. Whereas the pill-attribution procedure risks replacing one set of emotionally laden cognitions (pejorative self-attributions) with another set of emotionally laden cognitions (emotional reactions to taking a drug), this is unlikely to occur with the nonpejorative self-attribution procedure. The latter technique simply replaces pejorative inferences about oneself with cognitions that insomniacs are normal and that their insomnia implies nothing negative about their emotional stability or adjustment.

Nonpejorative Control-Attribution Treatments of Insomnia

Lowery, Denney, and Storms (1979) successfully demonstrated that changing insomniacs' pejorative attributions about the cause of their sleeplessness could improve their self-reported sleeping behavior. However, insomniacs may also suffer from another type of pejorative attribution, which stems from negative inferences about their inability to control their sleep. Treating this type of pejorative control attribution may require different procedures from those designed to alter pejorative causal attributions.

The notion of using attributional procedures to influence pejorative inferences concerning control originated in research by Davison and Valins (1969), which was a corollary to Nisbett and Schachter's (1966) work on misattribution of emotional arousal. Nisbett and Schachter demonstrated that individuals could be led to tolerate more intense levels of electric shock by attributing their fear of shock to a placebo pill. Davison and Valins advanced this notion a step farther. They reasoned that individuals could first be led to believe they had tolerated greater intensities of electric shock and then led to attribute this change either to a placebo pill or to themselves. Hypothetically, if individuals make internal attributions concerning their tolerance of shock, this experience should enhance their sense of personal control over aversive events, thereby resulting in further gains when confronting such events at a later time.

Davison and Valins (1969) first illustrated control reattribution in an experimental analog study. First, subjects were convinced that they had tolerated higher levels of electric shock over a series of trials and that a drug (actually a placebo) they had taken earlier in the experiment was responsible for their increased tolerance. Then, the control-reattribution manipulation was introduced. Half of the subjects were told that the pill they had received was a placebo (placebo condition). The remaining subjects continued to believe that the pill contained a real drug but were told that its effects had now worn off (drug condition). All subjects then received another series of shocks under the guise of an unrelated experiment. Subjects in the placebo condition, who had been told the truth about the placebo, tolerated significantly more painful shocks than subjects in the drug condition. Presumably, this result occurred, because the placebo subjects had attributed the enhancement in their tolerance of shock to themselves rather than to some external agent.

In a later study, Davison, Tsujimoto, and Glaros (1973) reasoned that control-attribution manipulations may be useful in the treatment of insomnia. Since most cases of insomnia are treated by drugs, insomniacs may attribute any improvements in their sleeping patterns to the external agent. In Davison, Tsujimoto, and Glaros' (1973) experiment, college students who suffered from insomnia were led to attribute the cause of improvements in their condition to their own efforts rather than to a sleeping medication. First, subjects were administered a treatment package, consisting of a hypnotic drug (1,000 mg. of chloral hydrate), a self-induced relaxation procedure, and the scheduling and regularization of their bedtime routine. Eighty percent of the subjects showed a marked improvement in their condition in response to these treatments. At this point, half of the subjects were told that they had received an optimal dosage of a drug that previous research had shown to be very effective in aiding sleep. The remaining subjects were told

they had received a minimal dosage of a drug that previous research had shown to be ineffective. The drug was then discontinued, but all subjects continued to practice relaxation and
scheduling during the next four days.

The results of this study indicate, first, that the manipulation
successfully induced the desired attributions. Subjects in the
minimal-dosage group felt more personally responsible for their
improvement. On the key dependent measure, subjects in the
minimal-dosage group, who attributed their previous improvement to themselves, maintained their shortened period for onset of
sleep over the four-day posttreatment period. Those in the
optimal-dosage group, who attributed their improvement to the
drug, returned to and even exceeded their original baseline sleep
onset latencies.

In summary, Davison, Tsujimoto, and Glaros' (1973) results
support the notion that pejorative control attributions may be involved in insomnia. They demonstrated that insomniacs can be led
to attribute to themselves greater personal control over their sleeping behavior and that this attribution can produce and maintain
improvements in self-reported sleeping behavior.

Theoretical Issues

We have reviewed a series of studies designed to improve
insomniacs' reported sleep onset latency by changing their attributions about the causes of and control over their sleeping problem.
First, we reviewed research concerning the placebo-pill technique,
which was originally designed to reduce pejorative causal attributions by leading insomniacs to attribute their presleep arousal to a
neutral external agent. We suggested a number of reasons why
insomniacs may fail to attribute their arousal to the placebo pills
and, even if they do make that attribution, why it might not reduce
pejorative self-attributions and reported sleep onset latencies. A
series of recent studies have demonstrated empirically the unrelia-
bility of the placebo-pill procedure. We suggest that these negative
results cast considerable doubt on the pill technique but do not
invalidate the underlying attribution model of insomnia.

We have reviewed two lines of research that do support the notion that pejorative attributions contribute to insomnia and that demonstrate the successful reduction of insomnia with attribution-based treatments. One technique is designed to substitute directly nonpejorative causal attributions (that is, insomnia is caused by a normal but high baseline of autonomic arousal) for pejorative causal attributions. The second technique is designed to substitute directly nonpejorative control attributions (that is, self-controlled improvement in the onset of sleep) for pejorative control attributions (drug-controlled improvement). Both treatment procedures have produced the desired positive change in attributions, which the placebo-pill technique has never been shown to accomplish. Furthermore, both treatments have produced or maintained significant reductions in self-reported sleep onset latencies.

Despite our optimism about the positive results obtained with the nonpejorative causal and nonpejorative control treatments of insomnia, we recognize some potential criticisms of this research. For example, Bem (1972), in his eloquent review of the problems associated with research attribution theory, argued for a greater understanding of the behavioral outcomes of hypothesized cognitive processes. He singled out Storms and Nisbett's (1970) research as an example of drawing unwarranted conclusions about important behavioral problems on the basis of self-report data.

Despite Bem's arguments, few researchers have gathered behavioral measures of cognitive treatment outcomes. In a comprehensive review of literature on cognitive and behavioral treatments of insomnia, Ribordy and Denney (1977) noted that virtually every study in this area has relied on self-report data. However, most investigators have taken steps to avoid the more obvious pitfalls of self-reports, such as using deception and experimenter blindness to avoid demand characteristics and using indirect ways of having subjects record their self-reports to avoid intentional distortions. Furthermore, a number of investigators (for example, Steinmark and Borkovec, 1974) have used counterdemand procedures to assure that demand characteristics cannot account for their results. In fact, both the Storms and Nisbett (1970) study and the Lowery, Denney, and Storms (1979) study employed most of these precautions.

The use of self-report measures and the related criticisms concerning such measures raise another, more theoretical question. Is insomnia only a behavioral problem characterized by actual delays in sleep onset and reductions in total sleeping time? There is evidence that people who consider themselves to be insomniacs have real difficulties falling asleep as early as they would like and sleeping as long as they would like (Haynes, Follingstad, and McGowan, 1974; Monroe, 1967). But cognitively oriented clinicians might argue that insomnia represents an emotionally based disorder involving faults in self-labeling and self-perception, regardless of whether true behavioral sleeping problems actually occur. In addition to treating an insomniac's sleeping behavior, it is equally important to treat the *belief* that one is an insomniac and the emotional travail that results from that belief. Furthermore, these conditions about insomnia may mediate actual sleeping behavior, although such a connection has yet to be proved empirically. For now, Bem's (1972) criticism stands unanswered. In the meantime, researchers would be wise to specify clearly whether they are dealing with actual sleeping behavior or with self-reported insomnia and to limit their conclusions to the realm of their data.

Another criticism one might raise is that both the nonpejorative causal and control attribution treatments simply elevate insomniacs' levels of self-esteem. Although it may be true that individuals who draw pejorative self-inferences about their sleep difficulties also suffer from lowered self-esteem, the nonpejorative causal and control attribution treatments are operationally more specific and refined than are simple attempts to bolster self-esteem. Nonpejorative self-attribution procedures are applicable in those instances in which a client's condition is exacerbated by pejorative self-inferences. Under those circumstances, clients are encouraged to substitute nonpejorative self-attributions to the effect that their condition is a normal one and that they can exercise a fair measure of control over this condition. The information provided in these manipulations is tied specifically to the individual's condition and is confined to correcting damaging inferences drawn from this condition. It remains to be seen whether a similar improvement in insomnia can be achieved through an uncritical and nonspecific bolstering of the client's self-esteem.

Practical Implications

Although some theoretical issues are still unresolved, the attribution model of insomnia has proved useful for offering effective treatments of insomnia and for evaluating other treatments of insomnia currently in practice. In particular, the model suggests reasons why some current treatments of insomnia may be hampered by attributional processes and why other treatments may be facilitated.

For example, traditional psychotherapists typically have adopted the view that insomnia is a symptom of some underlying psychological disorder. Accordingly, psychotherapy is frequently directed toward the discovery of the underlying causes of the client's insomnia and resolving these difficulties. Viewed from the perspective of the attribution model, such an approach could easily represent a confirmation of the negative causal inferences that clients already entertain concerning their insomnia. Traditional psychotherapists may unwittingly support pejorative causal attributions—namely, that the client's insomnia results from grave psychological difficulties—and may increase ruminative concerns exacerbating the client's sleep difficulties even further.

Another common approach to the treatment of insomnia, the use of hypnotic drugs, may confirm and advance pejorative control attributions. The damage resulting from such pejorative control attributions is most clearly evident when sleeping medication is withdrawn. Under such circumstances, it is logical for insomniacs to conclude that the drug was responsible for the improvement in their sleep behavior and that their sleep behavior will deteriorate without the drug. Many of these drugs are responsible for physiologically based rebound effects when they are withdrawn. Alternations in the sleep cycle, increases in REM sleep, jitteriness and nervousness, increased frequency and intensity of dreaming, and even nightmares have been observed following the termination of hypnotic drugs (Kales and Kales, 1973). These rebound effects result in a period of drug-withdrawal insomnia and may thereby confirm the insomniac's beliefs that the drug was responsible for any normal sleeping behavior he or she had previously obtained. The combination of rebound effects and adverse external control attributions may account for the marked psychological dependence on sleeping medication frequently encountered among insomniac clients.

If traditional psychotherapies and drug treatments of insomnia may unintentionally induce harmful pejorative attributions, other therapies may unwittingly encourage helpful nonpejorative attributions. Behavioral treatments of insomnia include systematic desensitization and applied relaxation training to assist the client to reduce presleep arousal levels and classical conditioning procedures to bring sleep behavior under tighter stimulus control (see the review by Ribordy and Denney, 1977). Unlike traditional psychotherapeutic approaches, behavioral treatments are more tightly confined to the "symptom" of insomnia and avoid lending support to pejorative causal attributions that might be entertained by the client. Unlike drug treatments, clients appear to attribute successes achieved through behavioral techniques to their own enhanced resources for exercising self-control over their sleep behavior. Thus, pejorative control attributions are effectively reduced by behavioral treatments of insomnia. Furthermore, behavior therapists' increasing attention to their clients' cognitions (self-verbalizations, irrational beliefs, and so forth) and their increasing emphasis on the attainment of self-control procedures, with which the client can manage his or her problem outside the treatment setting, clearly attend to attributional processes underlying insomnia.

In fact, we would suggest that behavioral therapy could be combined with explicit nonpejorative causal and control attribution procedures to provide an integrated program for treating insomnia. The first goal of such a program would be to produce an initial reduction in sleep onset latency. Nonpejorative causal attribution techniques could be used first to alleviate a patient's anxiety about the causes and implications of his or her sleeplessness. This attributional technique could be combined with relaxation training and other behavior therapies (and perhaps even with some active medications) to produce an initial improvement. Once some gains are made in the patient's condition, nonpejorative control treatments could be used to maintain that improvement. Patients could be told that the medication represented a minimal dosage and that their own efforts and improved ability to relax were primarily responsible for the reduced sleep onset latencies. If drugs are used in this treatment, patients should be given additional aides to cope with any rebound effects that may occur following withdrawal of the drug. With this information, the client would be in a position to attribute any temporary return of sleep difficulties to absence of the drug.

Such an attribution-based treatment package should have several advantages over medication-based treatments and perhaps over standard behavior therapies. The attribution package represents a more complete cognitive reeducation of the patient. It should impact positive new attitudes about the client's ability to control his or her sleeping problems. The beneficial effects of this reeducation should extend beyond the treatment procedures themselves. At the very least, attribution treatments give insomniacs lasting internal methods of coping with their insomnia. At best, cognitive reeducation may actually help the insomniac to continue to improve as he becomes better at identifying and interpreting his sleeping behavior in nonpejorative terms.

In this chapter, we have attempted to review research on attributional treatments of insomnia, elaborate an attribution model of insomnia, describe some of the newer treatments for insomnia based on nonpejorative causal and control attributions, and suggest how these treatments could be effectively integrated with current behavioral therapies. If this approach to the treatment of insomnia should prove successful, both in future research and in clinical practice, clinicians should be encouraged to consider the role of pejorative self-attribution in many other emotional disorders. The attributional procedures suggested in this chapter may be applicable to the treatment of a variety of problem behaviors.

Chapter **8**

Maureen McHugh
Linda Beckman
Irene Hanson Frieze

Analyzing
Alcoholism

Alcoholism and alcohol abuse are among the most serious social problems in the United States today. The National Commission on Marihuana and Drug Abuse (1973) has gone on record as stating that "alcohol abuse is without question the most serious drug problem today." Although definitions of *alcoholism* and *alcohol abuse* vary greatly, an alcohol abuser can be broadly defined as an individual whose drinking has created a problem with family, friends, or employer, a problem with the police or criminal justice system, or a health-related problem. Current estimates of the number of alcohol abusers in this country range from six million to ten million persons (National Association of Blue Shield Plans, 1973; National Institute on Alcohol Abuse and Alcoholism, 1974). However, alcoholism not only results in severe health and emotional problems for alcoholics but also causes social and physical problems for the spouses and children of alcohol abusers and for society in general.

The cost to our economy of alcohol misuse has been estimated at $25 billion annually (Berry and others, 1974). Included in such costs are lowered national production because of time lost from employment, hospital costs because of health problems associated with alcohol misuse, traffic accident costs, criminal justice system costs, social welfare system costs, and the costs involved in supporting programs aimed at alleviating alcohol misuse.

Estimates suggest that approximately one third of all male patients in most general hospitals at any time are problem drinkers (Straus, 1973). Although few such persons are hospitalized specifically for treatment of alcoholism, most are believed to be suffering from alcohol-related diseases. Illnesses linked to alcohol misuse include alcoholic hepatitis, cirrhosis, fatty liver, gastritis, beriberi, alcoholic cardiomyopathy, and alcoholic hypoglycemia. In addition, heavy drinking is associated with increased risk of developing cancer in certain organs, particularly the mouth, pharynx, larynx, and esophagus (National Institute on Alcohol Abuse and Alcoholism, 1974). Alcohol abuse lowers life-expectancy by ten to fifteen years, and alcoholics have a much higher mortality rate than nonalcoholics (Creative Sociomedics, 1977).

The impact of alcohol on traffic accidents has been clearly shown by studies of arrest records and drivers' levels of alcohol in the blood. Straus (1973) states that over 800,000 alcohol-related motor vehicle accidents occur annually. Such alcohol-related accidents account for over half of all traffic deaths (U.S. Department of Transportation, 1968). Violent deaths are characteristically associated with alcohol misuse; one-fourth of all suicides and one-half of all homicides are believed committed while the actor is under the influence of alcohol. In addition, it is important to realize that alcohol misuse is associated with other pressing social problems, such as poverty, unemployment, crime, dependence on other drugs, emotional problems in children, violence in the home, and family disruption (Straus, 1973). Thus, the scope of the problem of alcohol abuse is extremely broad in our society, causing misery and despair among problem drinkers and among persons associated with alcohol abusers.

As social drinking has become more prevalent (National Institute on Alcohol Abuse and Alcoholism, 1974) and alcoholism rates for men and women have risen (Gomberg, 1974; Robinson, 1976), concern about alcoholism has been increasing. People concerned about their own or other people's drinking problems have spent considerable time addressing the question of what *causes* alcoholism. This question is obviously complex and has generated a broad range of causal theories subscribed to by scientists, practitioners, and lay persons. The aim of this chapter is not to evaluate the validity of proposed causal theories but rather to examine the implications of various causal models for the treatment of alcoholism and for understanding the way people behave toward alcoholics. The assumption of the authors is that underlying attributions about the causes of alcoholism affect the way individuals react to and attempt to help the alcoholic. Operating from the perspective that individuals' attributions affect treatment of alcoholics, we will discuss causal explanations of alcoholism on several levels. First, formal theories regarding alcoholism that are offered in the scientific professional literature are discussed in terms of stated or implied causal beliefs. We suggest that the efficacy of various treatment approaches may be one index of the validity of the underlying causal model. Second, the causal beliefs of those who professionally handle drinking problems are examined, along with the causal explanations of alcoholism given by alcoholics and nonalcoholics. These attributions are seen as having implications for the counselors' effectiveness, for the alcoholics' reaction to therapeutic interventions and self-perceptions, and for the degree of support alcoholism-treatment efforts and alcoholic individuals receive from the community. Also, issues of congruence of beliefs (between theory and practice, between treatment approach and counselor, between client and counselor, and between alcoholic and nonalcoholic) are raised as potentially important.

In the second part of the chapter, we make another application of attribution theory to alcoholism. We propose that treatment of alcoholism might include the retraining of alcoholics to make healthy attributions for their success and failure outcomes. Our assumption is that alcoholics' self-attributions, particularly those relating to success and failure, can inhibit or facilitate their achievement of sobriety. In this section, data concerning the attributions made by alcoholics for achievement and interpersonal outcomes are presented, and the implications of various attributional patterns are discussed.

Causal Explanations for Alcoholism

Theories of alcoholism or problem drinking attempt to answer the question "Why do some people drink alcohol in a manner that appears to cause or exacerbate some problem for them or for others?" (Robinson, 1976). The work of a number of attribution theorists and researchers would predict a tendency to attribute the cause of alcoholism to the alcoholic himself or herself and would suggest that causal explanations of alcoholism have important implications for reactions to and treatment of alcoholics.

According to several attribution theorists (Jones and Davis, 1965; Kelley, 1971; Orvis, Cunningham, and Kelley, 1975), attributions to the individual are more likely when the outcome is seen as an uncommon occurrence. Thus, since alcoholism is not a common occurrence of drinking (most drinkers do not become alcoholics), most people would tend to see the individual as the causal factor.

Similar predictions can be derived from the attribution of responsibility literature. Walster (1966) suggests that a person's desire to avoid the frightening thought of the possibility of his or her own victimization results in the assignment of blame to an actor who experiences a severe negative outcome. If an outcome like alcoholism is due to chance or situational factors, then any drinker is a potential victim; however, an attribution to the alcoholic person allows other members of society to dismiss the possibility of their own addiction.

Lerner's conceptualization (1971) of a just world also predicts assignment of responsibility to the actor. Here, the basis of such an assignment is that it helps to maintain the belief that there is a correspondence between one's behavior and outcomes. This formulation infers that blame is assigned to the alcoholic, because, in a just world, the victim deserves his or her negative outcome.

These models predict internal attributions, or victim-blame, and imply that such attributions mediate feelings of disdain and dislike toward the actor. This relationship between the internality of the causal attribution for a negative outcome and resultant affect is explicitly stated in Weiner and others' (1972) attribution model. This model predicts that more shame on the part of the actor and more punishment on the part of the observer are experienced when the negative outcome is attributed to a causal factor internal to the actor. Some research on achievement outcomes has demonstrated this predicted relationship (for example, Weiner and Kukla, 1970). However, research has also suggested that affect and reward or punishment are mediated by the intentionality of the causal attribution. Failures attributed to lack of effort result in more shame and more punishment than outcomes attributed to lack of ability (Weiner and Kukla, 1970). Effort and ability are both internal attributions but are viewed as differing in their degree of intentionality; the actor is seen as having more control over his or her effort than over his or her ability. Thus, this perspective suggests that internal attributions for alcoholism would result in more negative affective reactions than external attributions and that internal intentional attributions would result in the most negative reactions to the alcoholic individual.

A contradictory prediction would stem from the analysis of Shaver (1975). In his presentation of the assignment of responsibility perspective, Shaver suggests that derogation of the victim of a negative outcome is especially likely when the observer cannot attribute the outcome to an action produced by the actor—that is, when an internal intentional attribution is unlikely. The reasoning here is that, if the victim is clearly at fault through some action of his or her own, then derogation is unnecessary. However, when an actor experiences some negative outcome that cannot be traced to his or her own actions, then observers justify the negative outcome by derogating the victim—by assigning internal unintentional attributions to the actor and viewing him as deserving of the negative outcome. This model would seem to suggest that internal unintentional attributions for alcoholism result in the most negative affective reactions. Despite the contradictory predictions concerning the role of intentionality, attribution theorists appear to agree that the internality of the causal attribution is related to affective reactions in the form of shame, dislike, derogation, and punishment.

Theorists concerned with the social control of deviance have also suggested that notions of causality serve as a basis for evaluating others (Stoll, 1968) and propose that etiological or causal belief systems mediate preferences for intervention strategies for controlling deviance (Aubert and Messinger, 1958; Glock, 1964). Specifically, these theorists suggest that, to the extent that individuals believe deviance to be *conscious* defiance of rules, then they will prefer to restrict and castigate deviants, but, to the extent that individuals believe deviance to be the result of *external forces,* then they will prefer to treat or cure deviants without reproach. Here again, the suggestion is made that theories of causality mediate reactions to (deviant) individuals and mediate degrees of punishment versus treatment for negative behaviors. Stoll (1968) labels the important dimension differentiating various causal beliefs as one of voluntarism or personal control (intentionality), but some confusion remains in this theoretical perspective between internality-externality and intentionality. (Note that the model contrasts conscious defiance with external forces.)

Applied to alcoholism, this perspective predicts a relationship between causal beliefs about alcoholism and preferred strategies for controlling alcoholism. Empirical studies have tended to support such relationships. Mulford and Miller (1964) found that those who viewed alcoholism in purely medical terms were most likely to acknowledge the alcoholic's need for medical treatment, whereas those who held a moralistic perspective were the least likely to recognize the alcoholic's need for treatment. Linsky (1972) found that different etiological theories of alcoholism have correspondingly different treatment implications. Respondents who explained alcoholism in terms of biological determinants were more likely to see medical treatment as the most effective, those who felt that alcoholism was due to moral weakness of the alcoholic advocated tighter legal control and use of will power, and those who viewed alcoholism as a personality problem or a psychological response were more likely to recommend treatment by psychologists or psychiatrists.

Friedson (1966) has added another dimension to ideologies

of deviance—*imputed prognosis,* or the degree to which individuals believe the deviancy to be curable. According to Stoll (1968), this dimension suggests two additional hypotheses: To the extent that the deviancy is believed to be curable, there will be a preference for intense rehabilitative efforts, and, to the extent that the deviancy is perceived to be incurable, there will be a preference for permanent isolation of the deviant from society. Applied to alcoholism, this theoretical model suggests that intensive rehabilitation efforts will be made when the underlying causal factors are seen as modifiable, but, when modification of the causal factors is seen as impossible or unlikely, rehabilitative efforts are less likely to be undertaken or supported.

This dimension, imputed prognosis, is similar to the stability dimension proposed by Weiner and others (1972). According to Weiner's formulation, the stability of the given causal attributions mediates future expectations. In terms of alcoholism, the theory suggests that attributions to stable causal factors would result in lower expectancies for future recovery or cure, whereas attributions to unstable factors would result in more optimistic prognoses.

In summary, causal beliefs about alcoholism have several important implications. First, the internality (and possibly the intentionality) of the causal attribution is seen as mediating affective reactions to the alcoholic individual, including the degree of derogation, and the willingness to endorse treatment as opposed to punishment. And, based on several attributional perspectives, a tendency to attribute alcoholism to internal factors is predicted. Second, beliefs about the causes of alcoholism are related to the type of treatment an individual advocates or endorses. Third, the stability of the causal attributions given for alcoholism is seen as mediating an individual's expectations concerning the prognosis of the alcoholic. More intensive efforts are directed toward the alcoholic when he is perceived as curable—that is, when the causal factors are perceived as modifiable. In the following sections, we outline the causal beliefs underlying the basic theoretical approaches to alcoholism and explore the implications of these beliefs in terms of victim-blame, advocacy of treatment, and prognosis.

The Moral Model. The hypothesized tendency to blame the victim is probably most clearly demonstrated by the moralistic perspective, which views the alcoholic as morally weak and degenerate. Although this perspective may not be considered a scientific or professional model today, it was widely held in the late 1800s and early 1900s. According to this perspective, alcoholics are weak people who are influenced by the devil (Keller, 1976). Moral persuasion, strong punishment controls, and coercive legislation (prohibition) are the intervention strategies suggested by this approach. Moral weakness is seen as an internal, intentional, and stable causal factor, theoretically resulting in extensive negative affect directed toward the alcoholic, advocacy of punishment as opposed to treatment, and low expectancies concerning the curability of alcoholism.

Psychological Models. Another perspective that stresses internal factors and thus to some extent blames the alcoholic is the psychodynamic approach of traditional psychotherapy. This approach, in emphasizing unconscious conflicts, assumes that alcoholism is the result of underlying personal pathology that must be changed before excessive drinking can cease. Freud (trans., 1955) suggested that alcoholism originated in traumatic early childhood experiences resulting from defects in the parent-child relationship. McCord, McCord, and Gudeman (1960) assign major importance to conflicts surrounding dependency needs resulting from a repressed but unresolved craving for maternal care. Two of the most contemporary theories of alcoholism may also be viewed as essentially psychodynamic: McClelland's (1972) theory that men drink to feel stronger and more powerful and Wilsnack's (1973) proposal that women drink to enhance their feelings of femininity. In treatment based on this approach, the emphasis is on bringing the unconscious conflict into awareness and fully experiencing it. Unconscious conflicts are viewed as relatively stable and resistant to recognition or resolution. Thus, this perspective suggests a relatively poor prospect for cure.

Other psychological theories suggest that alcoholism is a response to certain personality traits or mood variables that are internal to the alcoholic. For example, studies have indicated that alcoholics manifest low stress tolerance (Lisansky, 1960), low self-esteem (Beckman, in press), high anxiety levels (Barry, 1974), and feelings of isolation, insecurity, and depression (Beckman and others, in press; Irwin, 1968). Kissin (1977) suggests that the characterization of the alcoholic as emotionally immature, passive-dependent, and having great difficulties in relating meaningfully to others is generally accepted by clinicians. The assumption of trait theories is that such personality characteristics must change (if indeed they are mutable) before a recovery from alcoholism can be made. Thus, like psychodynamic theories, trait models assume that excessive alcohol consumption is a symptom of underlying pathology, and attempts at ultimate cure focus on altering the patient's basic personality structure. Although this approach does endorse treatment as opposed to punishment, viewing the alcoholic as possessing pathological personality traits does not appear to be conducive to positive feelings. Furthermore, personality traits are viewed as relatively stable dispositions, and attempts to modify personality structures are considered difficult.

The behavioral learning approach subscribes to the belief that alcoholic behavior is caused and maintained by association of alcohol ingestion with positive rewarding experiences. Bandura (1969) outlines a two-stage behavioral learning model, in which the pharmaceutic effects of alcohol relieve stress in the initial stages and terminate withdrawal symptoms in advanced stages of addiction. Dollard and Miller (1950) propose that alcohol is reinforcing, because it results in a reduction of fear, conflict, or anxiety. Fear, conflict, and anxiety are essentially seen as internal factors, and the behavior (drinking) is therefore seen as internal to the individual; however, the rewarding contingencies may be external to the individual, and learning theorists acknowledge that individuals may be repeatedly subjected to environmental stress, which increases the reinforcing effects of alcohol ingestion. This theory suggests treatment aimed at modifying the behavior by pairing the drinking response with aversive stimuli, such as electric shock or anabuse (a drug that produces nausea when alcohol is ingested) or by systematically desensitizing the individual to stressful situations using relaxation techniques, such as yoga, biofeedback, or Transcendental Meditation. Theoretically, associations can be unlearned as well as learned, which suggests a relatively good prognosis for alcoholics, if this causal theory is valid.

Sociocultural Models. The sociocultural models view social forces as the major factors in alcoholism and emphasize the social context in which drinking begins and continues as the primary source of the problem. Thus, the problem is attributed to factors that are external to the alcoholic. Cahalan, Cisin, and Crossley (1969) conclude that whether a person drinks at all is a sociological and anthropological variable rather than a psychological one, and Cahalan and Room (1974) report that problem drinking among males can basically be predicted using the demographic variables of age, socioeconomic status, urbanization, ethnic origin, and religion. Other theorists have suggested that alcoholism rates are highest in cultures that view ingestion of alcohol as a means of reducing tension (Bales, 1946; Horton, 1965). These theories emphasize that one's beliefs, attitudes, and practices concerning alcohol are culturally prescribed and learned within a cultural and subcultural context. A related idea is that the high incidence of familial alcoholism is a result of role modeling within the family structure and subsequently learning to view excessive alcohol consumption as a primary mode of adjustment (MacKay, 1961).

Specific social factors, such as crisis periods that produce significant changes in one's situation or social role, have also been related to alcoholism (Coleman, 1972; Curlee, 1969). These are external, unstable causal explanations. It is suggested that, during periods of heightened stress, the individual's normal coping methods prove inadequate, and he or she resorts to more extreme means of alleviating the stress—in some cases, to heavy consumption of alcohol.

Sociocultural models have stressed the importance of cultural attitudes, family interaction patterns, and socio-economic factors in the development and maintenance of alcoholism. This approach implies that treatment should attempt to change social variables that are thought to be causal or supportive of alcoholism. Treatments based on this model might include family therapy, job counseling, or other attempts at alterations in the alcoholic's social context.

Medical Models. A widely accepted explanation of alcoholism is the attribution to physiological dysfunction. Physiological dysfunction is, in one sense, internal to the individual, but it may be inherited, and thus the individual is not blamed. Many individuals subscribe to the physiological dysfunction theory without pinpointing a specific physiological mechanism, but some researchers have proposed possible biological processes that may be causal factors. Examples of these processes include inherited metabolic defects (Williams, 1959), genetically inherited biochemical or metabolic imbalances (Goodwin and Guze, 1974), and endocrine dysfunction (Gross, 1945). Although treatment based on these theories is not presently available, this approach suggests that effective treatment ultimately should involve pharmaceutical or even surgical techniques.

A closely related approach is the belief that alcoholism is a physical illness or disease. Jellinek (1960), who discusses this approach in depth, reports that the disease model of alcoholism is widely held. Robinson (1976) explores the implications of the disease concept of alcoholism, suggesting that the major advantage of this position is legitimization of social support for rehabilitation of the alcoholic rather than punishment. The traditional concept of disease clearly places causality and responsibility for the disease outside the individual. However, Robinson (1976) also outlines potentially negative effects of adopting the disease model, including the belief that the medical profession is responsible for treatment; many medical professionals are not trained to treat alcoholism. The treatment resulting from this causal ascription involves the administration of drugs, such as tranquilizers and anabuse, for the physical addiction aspects of alcoholism.

The Alcoholics Anonymous Approach. One of the factors contributing to the popularity of the disease model is its partial acceptance by Alcoholics Anonymous (AA). "AA is a world-wide fellowship of more than 100,000 (now 200,000) alcoholic men and women who are banded together to solve their common problems and to help fellow sufferers in recovery from that age-old baffling malady, alcoholism" (AA, 1955, p. 15). Although AA is not viewed as a formal treatment method, it constitutes one of the major treatment systems in the country today (Kissin, 1977) and is an integral part of most inpatient and outpatient treatment programs. Although the organization claims little, if any, knowledge of the causes of alcoholism, their views as presented in their publications suggest acceptance of the disease model. Yet, they do not advocate chemotherapeutic techniques. Further, AA rejects the idea that alcoholics drink to escape, views social factors and conditions cited as causes as excuses, and terms feelings of anxiety, depression, and anger as insufficient justifications. Instead, alcoholism is referred to as a malady, an insanity, an allergy to alcohol; alcoholics are seen as being mentally and physically different from other individuals and as being powerless over alcohol. Thus, alcoholism is viewed as a physical, mental, and spiritual illness requiring a basically spiritual treatment, in which the alcoholic admits his or her own powerlessness and past wrongs and accepts the help of a Higher Power. Like other disease conceptualizations, the AA approach absolves alcoholics from responsibility for their addiction. Interestingly, however, the alcoholic is viewed as responsible for his or her future behaviors, in that abstinence on a daily basis is seen as under the control of the recovered individual. This potential to modify one's behavior in the future without taking responsibility for past outcomes is a unique aspect of the AA approach. Recent work by Bulman and Wortman (1977) indicates that internal attributions for negative outcomes like accidents and rapes may be related to coping and adjustment, and Janoff-Bulman (in press) suggests that this is because behavioral self-blame allows the individual to focus on the future avoidability of the negative outcome. She distinguishes this behavioral self-blame from characterological self-blame, which would be the equivalent of the victim-blame referred to earlier— the attribution of undesirable personality characteristics to the victim of a negative outcome. Thus, AA's emphasis on future control without attributing past blame or character defects may be especially therapeutic.

Overview of Formal Theories

The basic purpose of this review (portions of which were taken from McHugh, 1977) has been to outline the causal beliefs underlying the basic theoretical approaches to alcoholism. The psychodynamic perspective suggests that the alcoholic's personality structure is a predisposing factor. The behavioral learning model cites the association of alcohol with positive experiences as the cause. The sociocultural model views cultural factors and the sociocultural context as primary in importance. The disease models emphasize dysfunctions in physical processes. AA views alcoholism as a physical, mental, and spiritual illness. For each of these perspectives, the treatment model is derived directly from the causal beliefs.

Examining these causal explanations for alcoholism indicates the number and diversity of theories of alcoholism. As yet, no single theory has proven adequate to explain this complex syndrome (Armor, Polich, and Stambul, 1976). Although most theorists emphasize specific causal factors, many would probably agree that the condition reflects a response to an interactive combination of physiological, psychological, and sociological factors in an individual and his or her environment (Plaut, 1967). This is consistent with attribution theory's prediction that people would have complex causal models or schema for understanding alcoholism. A causal schema describes "the way a person thinks about plausible causes in relation to a given effect" (Kelley, 1973); it is a general belief that a person has about how certain causes interact to produce a certain kind of effect. Kelley (1973) asserts that an extremely negative effect, a designation that alcoholism certainly qualifies for, generally evokes a multiple necessary causal schema—that is, several causes must have been present for the effect to have occurred. The multiple necessary causal schema is reflected in the fact that, although specific treatment models are derived from each theoretical perspective, many treatment programs represent combinations or syntheses of several treatment models.

One important implication of attribution theory for alcoholism is that the *development* and *evaluation* of alcoholism treatment programs should be based on and consistent with underlying causal theories. It would be inconsistent, and possibly ineffective, for professionals who subscribe to the disease model to develop a treatment program employing psychological techniques. Similarly, a person who is willing to institute an "anything that might work" treatment program should realize what this implies about his or her underlying causal schema—the person either has no idea what causes alcoholism or believes in a multiple-causal schema.

Conversely, the efficacy of various treatment approaches might be viewed as an indicator of the validity of the underlying causal models. Failure or success of any particular program or agency in treating alcoholics may be partly (or even mostly) due to characteristics of the staff or clients, but documentation of consistent success or failure of a treatment approach would provide valuable information about the validity of the etiological assumptions of the treatment perspective. If the etiological assumption on which a treatment is predicated is wrong, then such a treatment would be expected to have a higher failure rate than treatments derived from more accurate etiological assumptions. However, treatment evaluations are seldom conducted for the purpose of etiological inquiry but rather focus on whether a given therapy works or not (Armor, Polich, and Stambul, 1976).

Using a national data base supplied by the National Institute on Alcohol Abuse and Alcoholism (NIAAA), Armor, Polich, and Stambul (1976) conducted a large-scale evaluation of alcoholism treatment programs that partially addressed this issue of validity of etiological assumptions. Although their evaluation did not provide specific tests for all the etiological models we have discussed, their comparisons of hospitalization, intermediate care units, and outpatient clinics can be viewed as a general test of the medical (hospitalization), sociocultural (intermediate care) and psychodynamic (out-patient) models of alcoholism. However, their findings indicate that one type of treatment is not more effective than others. These results led them to conclude that the validity of these theories for etiology may be unrelated to their utility for treatment, and they suggested that the causes of alcoholism may be unrelated to its remedy. Their conclusions are intriguing and controversial, in that they contradict both the perspective presented here and that held by the scientific community in general—the belief that cause is intimately linked to cure.

Although the Armor, Polich, and Stambul data did not provide support for the hypothesized relationship between treatment success and the causes of alcoholism, their study had several weaknesses. First, there was no direct measure of the etiological model of the treatment facility. Second, although they addressed the issue of different approaches benefitting some subpopulations of alcoholics, they did not have enough information about clients to rule out the possibility that many or all of the proposed models are more valid for some alcoholics. Third, the research of Armor and others only examined the possibility that some alcoholics would benefit more from one treatment approach than would other alcoholics; they did not acknowledge the possibility that any given case may involve several causal factors and benefit most from a certain combination of treatment approaches. Thus, their results do not necessarily lead to the conclusion that treatment is unrelated to cause. Even if additional research supports the proposal that treatment is not directly related to causal factors, etiological models may continue to have important implications for prevention and may continue to mediate societal reactions to alcoholics.

The separation of cause from treatment closely resembles the traditional stance of Alcoholics Anonymous, whose treatment approach claims to know little about the cause of alcoholism. Although AA to some extent advocates the disease model, it does not advocate medical treatment. As noted earlier, endorsement of the disease model in this case serves to absolve the alcoholic of past responsibility, whereas the spiritual aspects of the AA treatment approach emphasize future responsibility and control, not over the addiction but over one's daily drinking behavior. This analysis would suggest that the dimension of intentionality or personal control is an important mediator of past blame and future recovery. AA is generally thought to be a relatively effective treatment organization, and Armor, Polich, and Stambul (1976) found that regular AA attendance (without additional treatment) was almost as effective as the treatment provided by comprehensive treatment centers (which often include AA). The AA approach includes many components, including social support, a religious perspective, and emphasis on abstinence, and it is not clear which components (or combinations) are responsible for its effectiveness.

Beliefs About the Causes of Alcoholism

Research investigating the attitudes of various groups toward alcoholism and alcoholics has generally included questions concerning the causes of alcoholism. Such research is based on the implicit assumption that one's beliefs about the cause of alcoholism influence one's attitudes toward the alcoholic individual. Such studies have been conducted to assess the attitudes of various professional and preprofessional groups, including medical students (Chodorkoff, 1967), physicians (Mendelson and others, 1964), nurses (Moody, 1971), nursing students (Ferneau, 1967), psychiatrists (Hayman, 1956), psychiatric residents (Ferneau and Gertler, 1971), psychiatric hospital personnel (Freed, 1964), and volunteer alcoholism clinic counselors (Ferneau and Paine, 1972). Researchers have also focused empirical attention on the attitudes of the public toward alcoholism (Haberman and Sheinberg, 1969; Linsky, 1972; Mulford and Miller, 1961, 1964; Ries, 1977).

Theory and research about the attitudes of professional groups or the general public have often characterized etiological attitudes toward alcoholism as either moralistic or medical (for example, Haberman and Sheinberg, 1969; Mulford and Miller, 1961, 1964; Orcutt, 1976). As discussed previously, the moralistic model views the alcoholic as morally weak and degenerate, and the medical model views alcoholism as a disease. Movement away from the moralistic model and toward the disease model is viewed as increasing acceptance or tolerance for the alcoholic, and there is evidence that, over the past several decades, the public has become increasingly likely to view the alcoholic as ill (Haberman and Sheinberg, 1969; Linsky, 1972; Mulford and Miller, 1961, 1964).

There are, however, problems with this simplistic medical versus moralistic dichotomy. As discussed earlier, attitudes toward alcoholism do not necessarily fit into such neat categories. One problem is that greater acceptance of the medical model does not necessarily imply increasing rejection of the moralistic model. Mulford and Miller (1961) found an almost equal division between endorsement of the moralistic and medical models in an initial survey of public attitudes; but, in a subsequent study that allowed the respondents to endorse both models, 41 percent of the sample defined the alcoholic as both morally weak and sick, and smaller proportions demonstrated complete acceptance of the medical (24 percent) or moralistic (34 percent) models. Similar overlapping or ambivalent attitudes were found in a study conducted by Orcutt (1976). It is not clear whether this ambivalence is an aspect of public changes in attitude or a stable multivariate view, but the results suggest that a methodology requiring respondents to choose between two (or more) etiological models is inadequate for assessing public attitudes about alcoholism. Not only does this dichotomy exclude the possibility of multivariate views, it also ignores the diversity of etiological models discussed previously.

Some researchers have attempted to address these methodological issues by including items representative of diverse etiological models in their questionnaires, usually having subjects demonstrate their endorsement by completing Likert-type scales (Beckman, in press; Caddy, Goldman, and Huebner, 1976; Ferneau and Mueller, 1973; Kilty, 1975; Robinson, 1976; Tolor and Tamerin, 1975). This approach, however, does not address an additional methodological issue, that of assuming congruence between the formal etiological models offered by the professional community and the causal beliefs of professionals and lay individuals. Stoll (1968) and McHugh (1977) raise the question of congruence, suggesting that the degree of congruence should be empirically examined rather than assumed. In studies employing the rating-scale approach, subjects are free to endorse or not to endorse the various etiological statements included in the questionnaires, but they are still constrained in the expression of their causal beliefs by the items selected for inclusion in the questionnaires. Even though subjects may have used the scales in meaningful ways, this does not necessarily mean that the specified causal factors are the ones that would be freely specified by the subjects to explain alcoholism.

An alternative approach is to have respondents give free responses to open-ended questions concerning the causes of alcoholism. McHugh (1977) suggests that free-response measures allow comparisons between the causal factors cited by respondents and the causal variables implied by the formal models. Frieze (1976a) proposes the use of free-response measures as a means of validating the use of causal factors without cueing by the experimenter, and Elig and Frieze (1979, in press) suggest that the use of free-response measures is especially important in exploratory studies involving the use of new populations to avoid the assumption that previously generated causal factors will be the most important. A final advantage of utilizing free-response measures is the potential for discovering a valid etiological factor previously unrecognized by theoreticians or practitioners.

Congruence Between Naive Concepts and Formal Models

Free-response methods have been employed by a few researchers in their investigations of attitudes about alcoholism. Linsky (1972) asked a probability sample of an adult population what they believed to be the major cause of alcoholism. Responses were coded into five categories, as shown in Table 1. Although supporting the previous research finding that public attitudes are shifting away from the moralistic model toward an acceptance of alcoholism as an illness, these results indicate that the majority of respondents view alcoholism as a psychological or mental illness rather than a physiological disease. The majority of responses fall into psychological categories, when psychological causal factors are separated from the medical model (failure or breakdown of the biological system). In general, these categories generated from open-ended responses are very similar to the categories of causal variables implied by the formal models reviewed earlier.

The categories of causal explanations generated in a study conducted by McHugh (1979) were also similar to the formal models. In this study, alcoholics and nonalcoholics were presented with a stimulus situation describing an alcoholic and were asked to explain why he or she drank. Attributional categories for coding of responses were developed, using a standard coding scheme for open-ended attribution data (Elig and Frieze, 1975) as a starting point, with modifications made to accommodate the data and to allow comparisons with theoretical conceptions of the causes of alcoholism. The resulting nine categories are shown in Table 2.

Table 1. Categories of Causal Explanations of Alcoholism

Category	Percent of Responses
Disorders of the personality system	27
Psychological reactions to situational problems	27
Failure or breakdown of the biological system	19
Social drinking and alcohol itself	18
Moral character of the alcoholic	9

Source: Linsky, 1972.

Table 2. General Beliefs About the
Underlying Causes of Alcoholism

Beliefs	Percent of Responses
External Factors: money, job pressures, children's misbehavior	18.1
Dissatisfaction: general unhappiness, dissatisfaction with life	16.9
Interaction of Personal and External Factors: bad relationship with spouse, poor home life, conflict with boss	14.8
Addiction: habit, addiction, alcoholic	12.3
Personal Characteristics: feels inadequate, bad nerves, insecure, feels like a failure	12.0
Boredom: nothing to do, too much free time, bored	9.3
Escape: hiding from problems, feels trapped, can't cope with reality	7.5
Likes to Drink: likes alcohol, wants to have a good time, enjoys the taste, wants to drink	7.2
Illness: physiological causes, illness, sickness, allergy	1.8
Total	99.9

Source: McHugh, 1979.

In general, results suggested that attributions of alcoholic and nonalcoholic subjects were similar to the causal factors suggested by major theoretical approaches to alcoholism. External Factors, the most frequently cited category, and Interaction of Personal and External Factors may be viewed as corresponding to the sociocultural models of alcoholism etiology. A psychological approach is most clearly represented by the category of Personal Characteristics and to a lesser extent by the category of Dissatisfaction. The psychodynamic approach to alcoholism may be reflected in the Escape category, and Addiction and Likes to Drink may be viewed as the causal responses most compatible with the philosophy of Alcoholics Anonymous. Very few responses referred directly to the medical model or the disease conceptualization, as indicated by the low percentage indicated for the Illness category. There is no category clearly parallel to the moralistic model, since no responses made clear or direct reference to the moral character of the alcoholic individual. Also of interest is the relatively high number of responses citing boredom as a reason for drinking behavior, since this factor has not received attention in the formal models.

A related study using the same etiological categories with a sample of 152 adult women found that women use the same basic categories to explain alcoholism in another woman. However, they made significantly more use of Dissatisfaction (which was the most common response) and Escape. The female alcoholism was attributed less in this study to Addiction and Liking to Drink. There was no use of the Illness category (Frieze, 1979).

Similar results were obtained by Robinson (1976), who asked people in the general population who did not personally know a problem drinker why they thought people drank "in a way that causes them problems." The most common attribution was to depression, anxiety, or worry. Other common responses were as a response to life problems, because of loneliness or boredom, because of "troubles," to escape problems, or out of habit.

The results of these studies suggest that there is some, although not perfect, congruence between naive conceptions of why alcoholics drink and formal models of the etiology of alcoholism. To the extent that there is not perfect correspondence, these studies indicate the usefulness of an open-ended attributional approach and the necessity for considering causal variables other than those implied in formal models in future research on causal beliefs about alcoholism, especially with nonprofessional populations.

Attributions of Professionals

In our preceding discussion, the causal schemas of the scientific professional community were examined as reflected in the published alcoholism literature. However, the attributions of professionals who interact daily with alcoholic individuals are of equal or greater importance in the treatment of alcoholics, and these may not be accurately represented in published articles. One might expect that the perspectives of various professionals would be the same as the dominant perspective within their respective disciplines—that is, that social workers subscribe to the social model, psychologists adopt the alcoholic-personality approach, physicians believe in the disease concept, and so on. However, a study conducted by Robinson (1976) in South London suggests that this assumption is not necessarily valid. General practitioners, social workers, and probation officers were asked questions concerning their causal beliefs in a semistructured interview. Few interviewees endorsed items expressing the hereditary or biochemical perspective; the statement that alcoholics drink to cope with difficult life-situations received the greatest professional support. The social-learning, alcoholic-personality, and childhood-conflict perspectives received moderate support in general, with general practitioners especially endorsing the statement that alcoholics learn their drinking patterns from friends and relatives.

Subjects were also asked to specify free-response causes concerning a particular recent case of problem drinking. Their responses indicated that general practitioners attributed the cause of a particular case of alcoholism most often to social pressures to drink in a harmful way or to anxiety or other emotional problems. Social workers and probation officers were more inclined to tie alcoholism to childhood or social deprivations and to look for individual weaknesses to explain why these particular people resorted to alcohol to cope with stress. Thus, although differences emerged among the groups, they are not necessarily the differences one might have predicted on the basis of training within their respective disciplines. In addition, Robinson (1976) specifically suggests that the causes, as discussed by these professionals, were not pure scientific theories but were more likely to involve interdisciplinary articulation of several levels of analysis.

The causal beliefs of those counseling alcoholics have implications not only for their reactions to and referrals of clients but also for the effectiveness of alcohol treatment programs. The degree of congruence between the attributions of the individual counselor and the causal beliefs underlying the treatment approach implemented at a given center or clinic may influence the overall effectiveness of treatment. For example, a psychologist who believes in the alcoholic personality may be less effective at behavior modification techniques than one who subscribes to the social-learning perspective. One might like to believe that individuals will find their appropriate niches in the treatment network, but this may not necessarily occur without clear explication of causal attributions by both the treatment program and the individual counselor.

Attributions of Alcoholics and the General Population

Actor-Observer Effects. A theoretical notion that must be explicated before looking at alcoholics' attributions involves actor-observer differences. When perceptions of causality for alcoholism are examined, alcoholics (actors) can be asked about their own alcoholism, alcoholics can be questioned about others' alcoholism, or nonalcoholics (observers) can be questioned about the cause of alcoholism. Bem (1972) and Jones and Nisbett (1971) have noted that actors usually know more about their current internal states and the history of their past behavior than do observers. Also, since actors and observers approach a situation from different perspectives, different information may be available to them, and different aspects of the information may be salient to each. In addition, motivational influences may cause the actor to make ego-defensive attributions. These differences have led Jones and Nisbett (1971) to assert that, generally, an observer is more likely to attribute causality to the dispositional characteristics of an actor, whereas the actor is more likely to attribute causality to external environmental influences. Although many empirical studies support predicted actor-observer differences (for example, Jones and Nisbett, 1971; Nisbett and others, 1973; Storms, 1973), conflicting evidence is also available (Monson and Snyder, 1977; Snyder, 1976).

It has been asserted, however, that observers may make dispositional attributions for events that result in severely negative consequences even when there is no information available to suggest such an attribution. This may happen when defensive attribution is necessary to avoid the frightening thought of the possibility of one's victimization by capricious circumstances (Walster, 1966; Wortman, 1976) or to maintain the belief that there is a relationship between one's behavior and outcomes (Lerner, 1971). For example, the observer believes that another person must have caused an observed accident, because, if this attribution is not made, the observer must admit that the same thing could happen to him or her.

The divergence between actors and observers may be especially likely for a negative event such as alcoholism. Harvey, Harris, and Barnes (1975) report that, when an actor's behavior leads to severe negative effects, observers' and actors' conclusions regarding perceived freedom may diverge. The actors are likely to think that they had much less freedom of choice regarding an action than do the observers. However, Wortman (1976) has pointed out that highly negative events, such as accident, illness, and disaster, not only lead to dispositional attributions by observers but also cause actors to exaggerate the extent to which uncontrollable events are caused by their own prior mistakes or misbehaviors. Therefore, it is unclear how greatly alcoholic actors' and nonalcoholic observers' attributions regarding responsibility for alcoholism might be expected to differ.

Based on attribution theory and the bulk of the research evidence, one can predict some differences in the attributions of alcoholics and nonalcoholics. Specifically, nonalcoholics would be expected to make more dispositional attributions, which, in effect, would be blaming the alcoholic individual for his or her drinking problem. Alcoholics might be expected to cite more external environmental factors, such as stress and pressure to drink, or uncontrollable factors, such as heredity and psychological dysfunctions, than nonalcoholics. As discussed previously, these differences, when found, might be due either to informational differences or to motivational influences.

Discrepant Beliefs About the Causes of Alcoholism

The McHugh (1979) study discussed previously, in which subjects responded to a question about why a hypothetical alcoholic drinks, allows a comparison between the causal explanations of alcoholism given by alcoholics and nonalcoholics. Data were collected from fifty-seven male and forty-one female residents at a halfway house for recovering alcoholics, thirty-one male and thirty-three female nonalcoholic adults, and thirty-three male and thirty-one female undergraduates. Responses are shown in Table 3 by subject group and causal category.

Table 3. Group Differences in Beliefs About the Causes of Alcoholism

Causal Category	Population Group		
	Alcoholic	Control	Student
External factors	17.6%	16.3%	20.2%
Dissatisfaction	8.8	20.4	22.9
Interaction[a]	7.2	13.3	24.8
Addiction[b]	27.2	5.1	1.8
Personal characteristics	10.4	18.4	8.3
Boredom	4.8	15.3	9.2
Escape[a]	5.6	5.1	11.9
Likes to drink[c]	14.4	5.1	0.9
Illness	4.0	1.0	0.0
Total	100%	100%	100%

Note: overall χ^2 = 93.67513, $p < 0.0001$.
[a]$p < 0.05$ that there is no difference among groups.
[b]$p < 0.025$ that there is no difference among groups.
[c]$p < 0.005$ that there is no difference among groups.
These significance levels are from one-way ANOVAS.
Source: McHugh, 1979.

The results of this study demonstrate some discrepancies between the causal beliefs of alcoholic and nonalcoholic respondents. However, the differences found in this study are not those predicted by previous attribution theory and research on the actor-observer effect. Although nonalcoholic adults did cite personal characteristics more frequently than alcoholics, this difference was not significant. Thus, the prediction that nonalcoholics would make more dispositional attributions is not clearly supported. The prediction that alcoholics would be more likely to cite external factors is also not supported. Alcoholics were significantly more likely to cite Addiction, however, which may be viewed as somewhat similar to the predicted attribution to hereditary factors and physiological dysfunctions. However, this difference is more likely to be related to the fact that this attribution is espoused by AA—and the alcoholic subjects in this study were residents at a treatment facility based on the AA approach—than to be related to actor-observer research.

The McHugh (1979) study does not literally involve actors and observers, since both alcoholics and nonalcoholics were giving causal explanations for a hypothetical other. Similarly, in a study by

Beckman (in press), alcoholics and nonalcoholics indicated their causal beliefs about alcoholism in most persons. Data were collected from a sample of 120 female alcoholics, 120 male alcoholics, 118 normal nonalcoholic women controls (who were matched on age, education, religion, marital status, and presence of children with the alcoholic women), 60 college women who were heavy drinkers, and 60 college women who were nonalcoholic social drinkers. The alcoholics were selected in approximately equal numbers from patients in four types of alcoholism treatment facilities in the Los Angeles area.

　　　All subjects were asked to rate the importance of several possible causal factors regarding alcoholism in most persons. More specifically, the question was: "People in the health field have suggested a variety of reasons why people have problems with the use of alcohol. Below are some statements people have made about the causes of drinking problems. In general, who or what do you think is responsible for (or causes) most drinking problems?" Ratings were made for how important each of seven possible causes were. The causal statements were designed to include both internal and external factors and to cover most of the major explanations for alcoholism, with particular emphasis placed on the social and disease models of alcoholism. The causes were:

1. Other people (husband or wife, friends, boss) caused the problem.
2. A distressing event (death in the family, divorce, loss of job) is responsible for the problem.
3. Present or past environment (job, marriage, home life when a child) is responsible.
4. Heredity (it's in the family's genes, they inherited the problem).
5. The person himself or herself is responsible.
6. Alcoholism is an illness or disease (one is born with a weakness or has the illness).
7. Don't know—it must be fate.

　　　Mean ratings of the importance of each causal factor by each subsample are presented in Table 4. Results showed that the nonalcoholic women generally attributed responsibility for drinking

Table 4. Ratings of Importance for Factors Influencing Most Persons' Problem Drinking

Causal Attribution	Female Alcoholics	Male Alcoholics	Sample Normal Controls	Heavy Drinkers	Normal College
Other people	2.56	2.51	2.34	2.39	2.64
Distressing event	2.86	2.79	2.81	2.83	3.07
Environment	2.86	2.85	2.81	3.14	3.00
Heredity	1.66	1.56	1.68	1.42	1.33
Person	3.67	3.70	3.61	3.48	3.36
Weakness or illness	1.93	2.20	1.87	1.59	1.40
Don't know—fate	1.36	1.80	1.29	1.21	1.07

Note: Ratings ranged from 1 (unimportant) to 4 (very important).
Source: From Beckman, in press.

problems to the same factors as did the female and male alcoholics. All groups rated the person's own responsibility highest, and a distressing event such as death or divorce and present or past environment received the next highest ratings. No significant differences emerged between the alcoholics' and nonalcoholics' attributions regarding responsibility for problem drinking. Similarly, normal-drinking and heavy-drinking college students showed no significant differences in attributions. This pattern of results suggests a generally accepted set of norms regarding the importance of various causes of drinking problems.

As previously discussed, attribution theorists (for example, Kelley, 1971) suggest that, since alcoholism is an uncommon response to the use of alcohol (consensus does not exist regarding alcohol's effects), the cause of alcoholism should be attributed internally to the person rather than to alcohol itself. In line with theoretical predictions, both alcoholics and nonalcoholics assign major responsibility for alcoholism or a drinking problem to the individual himself or herself; but, at the same time, environmental influences that may have facilitated the drinking problem are implicated.

The studies reviewed here do not demonstrate consistent results with regard to differences between the attributions of alcoholics and nonalcoholics for hypothetical or general drinking problems. It is not clear whether the inconsistencies are related to population differences (the alcoholics in either or both studies may have adopted causal beliefs suggested in a particular treatment program) or methodological differences (ratings versus open-ended questions).

Beliefs About One's Own Alcohol Problems

Perhaps a more interesting question is how people view the causes of actual alcohol problems. In a sample of over 300 adults, Robinson (1976) identified eight self-defined problem drinkers and thirty-six people who knew a problem drinker. He asked these people why this specific drinking problem existed. The majority (75 percent) of the problem drinkers cited social pressure to drink as the primary cause, thus using an external causal attribution as

predicted earlier. Other people saw drinking as a response to problems (31 percent), because of social pressures to drink (22 percent),
childhood deprivation (11 percent), and loneliness or boredom
(8 percent). Thus, their attributions were more internal to the
problem drinker, again corresponding with the general actor-
observer findings.

The Beckman (in press) study previously discussed also reports on the causes alcoholics rated as most responsible for their
own drinking problems. The data presented in Table 5 compare
alcoholics' perceptions of responsibility for their own drinking with
their perceptions of responsibility for others' drinking and alcoholics' ratings of the importance of various factors in their drinking with nonalcoholics' ratings of various factors in most drinking.

These results can be interpreted within the context of prior
theorizing on actor-observer differences. When rating his or her
own drinking, the alcoholic can be thought of as an actor; when
rating others' drinking, the alcoholic can be thought of as adopting
the role of observer (see Table 5). Similarly, the alcoholic actor

**Table 5. Ratings of the Importance of Factors
Responsible for Own Drinking and Differences Scores
(Own Drinking Scores Minus Others' Drinking Scores)**

| | Own Drinking | | Own Drinking Scores Minus Others' Drinking Scores | |
| | Female | Male | Female | Male |
Causal Attribution	Alcoholics	Alcoholics	Alcoholics	Alcoholics
Other people	2.56	2.21	0.01[d]	−0.31[b]
Event	2.46[a]	2.59	−0.40[b]	−0.21[c]
Environment	2.59	2.37	−0.27[b]	−0.48[b]
Heredity	1.47	1.44	−0.19[b]	−0.12
Person	3.73	3.78	0.06	0.08
Illness or weakness	1.99	2.31	0.06	0.11
Don't know—fate	1.37	1.94	0.01	0.14

Note: Ratings ranged from 1 (unimportant) to 4 (very important).
[a]$p < 0.05$, Normal Controls Others' Drinking versus Female Alcoholics' Own
Drinking.
[b]$p < 0.01$.
[c]$p < 0.05$.
[d]High positive scores indicate more importance attached to factor for self than for a
hypothetical other.
Source: Beckman, in press.

rating his own drinking can be contrasted with the nonalcoholic observer rating most drinking (although this comparison is somewhat more tenuous)—(compare Tables 4 and 5). If the actor-observer effect is valid, it can be predicted that alcoholics should rate other people, some distressing event, the environment, and heredity as more important causal sources for their own behavior than for others' drinking behavior. Similarly, they should rate themselves as less responsible for their drinking problem than they rate most persons with drinking problems. In contrast, nonalcoholics should rate most people more responsible for their own drinking problem than alcoholics rate themselves and should rate some distressing event, other people, the environment, and heredity as less important.

When difference scores, (Own Drinking scores minus Others' Drinking scores) were analyzed, results strongly disagreed with predicted actor-observer differences. In general, males and females showed the same pattern of results. Distressing events and environmental influences, such as job, marriage, or home life when a child, were rated as less important in causing one's own drinking problem than in causing most drinking problems. Female alcoholics also rated family heredity as significantly less important regarding their own drinking, whereas male alcoholics perceived other people as less implicated in their own drinking problem than other people were in the drinking problems of others. Although no significant differences existed in attribution to the Person, difference scores were slightly positive, as were those regarding alcoholism as a disease.

Only one significant difference occurred between alcoholics' ratings of their own drinking and nonalcoholics' ratings of most drinking. Alcoholic women perceived a distressing event as a less important causal source than did nonalcoholic women.

In summary, the differences found between alcoholics' ratings of their own and others' drinking and alcoholics' ratings versus nonalcoholics' ratings of responsibility for excessive drinking behavior cannot be explained within the context of actor-observer differences, when rating-scale data are used. These findings also do not show a tendency among alcoholics to displace blame for their own behavior onto external factors. Alcoholics appear to accept a large amount of personal responsibility for their drinking problem. Other research on Locus of Control shows a similar pattern of high internal scores on the Rotter Scale for alcoholics (for example, Costello and Mandus, 1974; Distefano, Pryer, and Garrison, 1972; Gozali and Sloan, 1971).

The present ambiguous data can perhaps be clarified by reference to Kelley's (1971) discussion of moral judgments and Stevenson's (1963) view of ethical judgments. Stevenson (1963) contends that moral judgments look primarily to the future. Even if what is being judged are past and present acts, the purpose of moral judgment is to discourage morally reprehensible outcomes in the future. According to Kelley, such a statement implies that judgments regarding responsibility (an essentially moral judgment) are guided by estimates of *future* responsibility rather than perceptions of past responsibility. In part, when respondents state that the Person is responsible, alcoholics in their evaluation of their own behavior (and nonalcoholics in their evaluation of alcoholic behavior) are stating that the alcoholic should (or can) try harder to avoid this negative behavior in the future.

According to logical attributional rules, a person should not accept blame for an act if physically or mentally incompetent (Kelley, 1971); however, attribution of responsibility in cases of severe negative consequences often does not follow such logical attributional rules. Studies of uncontrollable life-events suggest that people exaggerate their ability to control such outcomes (Drabeck and Quarantelli, 1967; Wortman, 1976). Innocent accident, illness, and natural-disaster victims have been shown to suffer great guilt (Wortman, 1976). They apparently exaggerate the extent to which uncontrollable outcomes are caused by their own prior mistakes and misfortunes. Similarly, self-blame (attribution of responsibility) for being an alcoholic may be quite severe, even though the person obviously did not intend to become an alcoholic.

Implications of Causal Explanations of Alcoholism

Attempts to understand the ways that people behave in relation to people with alcohol problems can be enhanced by considera-

tion of the causal theories those individuals appear to hold (Robinson, 1976). In this chapter, we have applied this consideration to
four groups of causal theories: formal theories, the causal beliefs of
professionals interacting with alcoholics, the attributions of nonalcoholics, and the causal theories of alcoholics themselves. The attributions of each of these groups have implications for the type of
treatment alcoholics receive within treatment programs and within
the community in general.

First, it was suggested that current methods designed to
treat the alcoholic are based on various causal beliefs and that development and evaluation of treatment programs should be based
on an explicit analysis of causal models. Second, it was suggested
that counselors' backgrounds and experiences are often different
from those of theoreticians and that their attributions may not be
identical to those outlined by the formal theories. The issue of
congruence between counselor and treatment program in reference to causal beliefs was raised. Ensuring compatibility between
the counselor's beliefs and the treatment approach of the program
in which she or he works may increase the effectiveness of treatment. Another possible benefit of investigating the attributions of
experienced counselors is the explication of novel concepts about
the etiology of alcoholism, from which new treatment methods
could be developed.

Also of importance to the effectiveness of the treatment
programs are the attributions of the alcoholics themselves. Many of
the treatment philosophies require the alcoholic to make specific
attributions about alcoholism. For example, according to the *Twelve
Steps and Twelve Traditions* (1952) espoused by AA, the first step to
recovery is admission of one's powerlessness over alcohol. This
admission is considered essential to recovery by AA members, and
data reported by McHugh (1979) indicate that individuals participating in an AA program have subscribed to a large extent to an
AA attributional schema. This suggests that research might be
conducted to trace the attributions given by alcoholic subjects as
they progress through various treatment programs to determine if
acceptance of that treatment's underlying beliefs about causality
occurs and to examine the relationship between such acceptance
and treatment outcomes. Other research questions suggested by

attribution theory involve the issue of congruence among the attributions of the alcoholic, the program, and the counselors. Is an *initial* congruence between the alcoholics' attributions and the underlying causal model of the program essential or beneficial for successful treatment? Does the degree of matching between the client's and counselor's attributions about alcoholism affect the client's progress? Is an *eventual* congruence between the clients' attributions and those of the treatment program or counselor essential or beneficial? Answers to these questions may result in more careful referrals, by matching causal beliefs of the client with the program and counselor, and in more effective treatment, by ensuring acceptance of certain causal beliefs.

A related question is whether any of the causal models underlying formal theories or treatment programs are especially beneficial or detrimental to the recovery of the alcoholic. For example, subscription to the disease model may prevent the alcoholic from feeling debilitating shame over his or her drinking problem, but, at the same time, this attribution may undermine an individual's belief that with effort he or she can recover. Another example is the belief that some personality conflict or weakness is a primary cause of alcoholism. When espoused by an alcoholic, this attribution may result in debilitating depression or self-blame and could also result in the feeling that recovery is unlikely. Storms and McCaul (1978) have suggested that self-attributions of pathology result in increased anxiety, which leads to continuing emotionally dysfunctional behavior. According to their model, the person observing an undesirable aspect of his or her own behavior (excessive drinking) makes a self-attribution for this (presumed) unwanted behavior. The self-attribution leads to feelings of inadequacy and a generally negative view of self. In the case of the alcoholic, it is also likely that a negative self-image may precede excessive drinking. In any case, a negative self-concept gives rise to such unpleasant emotions as anxiety. This increased emotionality in turn exacerbates the occurrence of the dysfunctional behavior—the problem drinker drinks more when he or she is anxious. Although past tests (Valins and Nisbett, 1972) of the model have not included alcoholics, this model can be applied to alcoholism, to the extent that alcohol consumption is increased by anxiety.

Finally, there are the implications of the causal theories held by the general population. The amount of community support for alcohol treatment programs may be determined by the belief that recovery is possible and that alcoholics deserve help. Both of these factors are directly related to the causal attributions held (correctly or incorrectly) by lay members of the community. Further, the type of program that communities support may be related to the match between community causal beliefs and the treatment approaches. Perhaps most importantly, the attributions about alcoholism made by members of a community determine how friends, family, and neighbors will react to the alcoholic individual. If the general population demonstrates a tendency to attribute alcoholism to dispositional factors, as is predicted by theory (although results so far do not consistently demonstrate this effect), this would contribute to negative stereotypes of alcoholics. Thus, the causal explanations given by every segment of society for alcoholism can potentially have adverse or beneficial effects on the treatment and subsequent recovery of the alcoholic.

Alcoholics' Self-Attributions for Success and Failure Outcomes

In the preceding sections of this chapter, an attributional perspective was used to analyze and discuss causal explanations for alcoholism and their implications. In this section, an additional way in which attribution theory may contribute to the understanding and treatment of alcoholism is proposed. Hypotheses concerning the ways in which alcoholics' self-attributions for success and failure outcomes may be debilitating are presented, and results from an initial investigation of these hypotheses are reported.

Applicability of Attribution Theory. Several contemporary theories of depression are based on the individual's cognitions concerning the causality of life-events. For example, in Seligman's (1975) theory of learned helplessness, depression results from the individual's belief that outcomes are uncontrollable. And Beck's (1967a) theory of depression suggests that the depressed individual blames himself or herself for negative outcomes.

Some research has suggested a similar relationship between the individual's cognitions about outcomes and alcoholism. For example, Jessor, Carman, and Grossman (1968) found that heavy drinkers in college tended to have low expectations for future success in satisfying various needs. And Barry (1974) indicates that alcoholics have particularly high anxieties over failure while simultaneously wanting to avoid too much success. He felt that alcoholics drink to sedate these strong emotional reactions to positive and negative outcomes. Jones and Berglas (1978) propose a similar model in their theoretical analysis of alcoholism. They hypothesize that alcohol obscures the usual implications of success or failure for the alcoholic by providing an excuse for failure and increasing feelings of self-pride with success. Frieze and McHugh (1977) have proposed that the low self-esteem demonstrated by alcoholics, particularly female alcoholics, may be related to debilitating attributional patterns for experienced successes and failures.

The work of these authors suggests that the cognitions of alcoholics concerning outcomes that they experience may be implicated in the alcoholism syndrome or at least may inhibit achievement of sobriety. To explore this potential application of attribution theory, the attribution model of Weiner and his associates (Weiner, 1974a; Weiner and others, 1972) dealing with attributions for success and failure outcomes is briefly reviewed. Theoretical predictions based on this model are made for the self-attributions of alcoholics, and an initial investigation of these hypotheses is reported.

Causal Attributions for Success and Failure. The work of Weiner and his associates has focused on the attributions that individuals give for success and failure outcomes in achievement settings. Although much of this research has been laboratory oriented and conducted mainly to explain achievement-oriented behavior, the applications of this work have been useful for furthering our understanding of diverse areas of behavior, including alcoholism (Frieze and McHugh, 1977).

This approach analyzes specific causal attributions or beliefs about why things happen within specific situations. As discussed earlier, there are always a variety of causal attributions that can be made for any situation. However, as shown in Table 6, it is theoretically possible to classify any set of causal attributions into three basic dimensions: internality, intentionality, and stability (Elig and

**Table 6. A Three-Dimensional Model for Classifying
Causal Attributions for Success and Failure**

	Internal	
	Stable[a]	Unstable
Intentional	Stable effort (diligence or laziness)	Unstable effort (trying or not trying hard)
Unintentional	Ability, Knowledge, Background, Personality	Fatigue, Mood

	External	
	Stable[b]	Unstable
Intentional	Others always help or interfere	Others help or interfere with this event
Unintentional	Task difficulty or ease; Personality of others	Task difficulty or ease (task changes); Luck or unique circumstances; Others accidentally help or interfere

[a]Temporal and situational stability.
[b]Temporal stability only.
Source: Adapted from Elig and Frieze, 1975.

Frieze, 1975; Frieze, 1976a). According to attribution theory, each of these dimensions has different consequences for expectancy for future success and for feelings of pride and shame in one's outcomes.

The first dimension, internality, has to do with whether the cause of an event is associated with the primary actor in the situation and is thus internal to this person (for example, ability, effort, mood, personality, or knowledge) or whether this cause is external to the person (for example, luck, an easy task, someone else's help or harm). The dimension of intentionality involves the degree to which an individual intended his or her behavior or had the potential to control the causal factor. For example, ability is viewed largely as unintentional, whereas effort is the classic example of an intentional factor. Both internal and external factors can be classified according to intentionality, but this dimension has been particularly important in distinguishing between internal factors, such as the example of ability and effort. The third dimension, stability, usually refers to temporal stability, or to the degree to which factors may change with time. Ability and personality are seen as stable factors, whereas effort, mood, and luck are classified as unstable factors. Another aspect of stability that must sometimes be considered is situational stability, or the degree to which the causal factors vary across situations. Thus, the task or situation, which is stable with time, is unstable when considering situational stability (Valle and Frieze, 1976; Weiner, Russell, and Lerman, 1978).

These dimensions have been outlined to help predict the consequences of particular attributions. Temporal stability has been related, in previous research, to expectancies for the future for the same task (McMahan, 1973; Valle and Frieze, 1976; Weiner, Nierenberg, and Goldstein, 1976). Stable causes, such as ability, produce expectancies that outcomes will continue to be the same, whereas unstable causes, such as lack of effort, produce possible changes in expectancies—that is, the belief in the possibility of future success despite past failure or vice versa. Although the expectancy effects for situational stability have not been tested, they should function in the same way, if one is predicting future outcomes for a similar task.

There is no question that people feel happier after a good outcome than after a bad outcome (Nicholls, 1975; Ruble, Parsons, and Ross, 1976). However, affective reactions are moderated to some degree by the causal attribution. Studies have shown that outcomes attributed to internal factors are experienced with more pride or shame than outcomes seen as caused by external factors (Weiner, 1974a).

Based on the hypothesized relationship between causal attributions and pride and shame, it is possible also to hypothesize a relationship between certain attributional patterns and the maintenance of self-esteem. Maximum self-esteem would theoretically be associated with a tendency to make internal stable attributions for success and external unstable attributions for failure. Fitch (1970), investigating this hypothesized relationship between self-esteem and attributional patterns, reported that subjects low in self-esteem attributed failure to internal causes more than high self-esteem subjects. Rehm (1977) has suggested that depression is related in a similar way to attributional patterns and that making internal attributions for positive outcomes might decrease depression.

Predicted Attributions of Alcoholics. Many of the personality correlates of alcoholism that have been cited in the literature indicate that alcoholics have lower self-esteem than the general population (Beckman, in press (a); Benensohn and Resnick, 1974; Greenwald, Carter, and Stein, 1973; Wood and Duffey, 1966). Data collected by Beckman and others (in press) suggest that, in addition to low self-esteem, male and female alcoholics are more alienated and socially isolated than a comparison group of nonalcoholic women.

Hypotheses concerning the attributions of alcoholics can be made on the basis of this previous research and theory concerning the relationship between self-esteem and attributions and concerning the low levels of self-esteem in alcoholics. Specifically, it might be predicted that alcoholics would make internal and/or stable attributions for failure, resulting in high levels of self-blame and low expectancies for future success, and external and/or unstable attributions for success, resulting in low levels of self-pride and low expectancies for continued success. This attributional pattern is clearly debilitating, resulting in continuing self-devaluation with failure and no improvement in self-evaluation with success. Given that alcoholics also experience alienation and social isolation, this attribution pattern might be predicted as especially important in social situations.

Jones and Berglas (1978) have proposed a relationship between attributions and alcoholism that, although also based on the concept of low self-worth of alcoholics, generates different predictions concerning their attributional patterns. They suggest that the alcoholic generally has problems with feelings of competence. The alcoholic is generally a person who wants to get equivocal or biased information from the environment to protect a fragile sense of self-worth. Such an "externalizing" person is willing to forego success to protect his or her feelings of competence. Use of alcohol imposes a performance barrier and thus leads to partial avoidance of personal responsibility for failure. However, success, as infrequent as it may be for the problem drinker, can readily be attributed to the self that succeeded despite the drinking problem and thus can enhance positive feelings. The phenomenon of feeling happier about unexpected success has been reported by other researchers as well (Bailey, Helm, and Gladstone, 1975; House and Perney, 1974).

Jones and Berglas (1978) further suggest that alcoholics, like underachievers, are likely to have high expectancies for the future in spite of past failures, saying to themselves "When I stop drinking, I'll be able to do all sorts of things." Thus, the role of the self as a cause for failure is discounted, if other plausible causes (such as alcohol) are also present (Kelley, 1973). To avoid responsibility for failure, alcoholics must create a situation where failure can plausibly be attributed to a source external to the self. Excessive use of alcohol is one such ploy that may be partially successful.

This conception suggests that the alcoholic individual makes an attribution to alcohol, an external factor, in failure situations and an attribution to ability, an internal factor, in success situations. Such an attributional pattern is not in itself debilitating in terms of hypothesized consequences of affect and expectancies, but the alcoholic must continue drinking to provide himself with a plausible external reason for failure and to bolster his feelings of pride with success.

Causal Attributions of Alcoholics. These predicted relationships between alcoholism and the attributional patterns of alcoholics have not received extensive empirical attention, but an initial investigative study has been conducted by McHugh and Frieze (1979). Alcoholic and nonalcoholic subjects were asked to explain why they had succeeded or failed in a variety of hypothetical achievement and social situations. The most frequently cited causal explanations are presented in Tables 7 and 8.

These results do suggest that alcoholics and nonalcoholics make somewhat different causal attributions for their achievement and social outcomes. Most notably, alcoholics cited drinking and drinking-related behaviors, including rowdiness and absenteeism, as reasons for failure outcomes while nonalcoholics did not. However, the dimensional analyses conducted by the authors did not indicate any of the predicted attributional patterns. Alcoholics and nonalcoholics did not differ systematically in the intentionality or stability of their causal attributions. A significant difference in the

Table 7. Most Frequent Causal Explanations for
Achievement Situations

Outcome	Causal Explanation	Percentage of Alcoholics Citing Factor	Percentage of Nonalcoholics Citing Factor
Success	Unstable effort	37.0	40.1
	Stable effort, diligence, conscientiousness	9.0	11.9
	Good job or performance	25.6	19.4
	Interest, personal involvement	10.7	8.8
	Ability	7.9	5.4
Failure	Lack of effort	31.2	23.2
	Poor job or performance	19.4	17.8
	Drinking, drinking-related behavior	10.6	0
	Others' jealousy or incorrect evaluation	5.7	12.3
	Inexperience, misinterpretation of instructions	5.2	7.2

Source: McHugh and Frieze, 1979.

internality of the attributions of the groups was found, but it was not the difference predicted by either of the hypotheses reviewed. Alcoholics were more internal in their causal attributions for both success and failure outcomes than were nonalcoholics. Frieze and McHugh (1977) predicted that alcoholics would be more internal for failure, but more external for success, and Jones and Berglas (1978) predicted that alcoholics would be more external for both success and failures. Attributions to alcohol consumption were considered external in the Jones and Berglas model but were coded as internal in the McHugh and Frieze (1979) study because internality was inferred in the wording of the subjects' responses. The fact that subjects seemed to view alcohol consumption and related behaviors as internal is in itself contradictory to the Jones and Berglas model, although this may be true for the recovering alcoholic population (studies by McHugh and Frieze) while the untreated alcoholic indi-

**Table 8. Most Frequent Causal Explanations
for Social Situations**

Outcome	Causal Explanation	Percentage of Alcoholics Citing Factor	Percentage of Nonalcoholics Citing Factor
Success	Mutual interests	27.5	33.8
	Compatibility	24.2	17.5
	Personality	22.1	26.6
	Appropriate behaviors	4.3	1.0
	Good relations	6.1	5.0
Failure	Nonspecific personal responsibility	19.7	15.4
	Drinking, drinking-related behaviors	15.0	0
	Personality	12.4	17.2
	Inappropriate behavior	9.4	4.8
	Others' behavior	12.0	10.7
	Incompatibility	8.3	17.6

Source: McHugh and Frieze, 1979.

vidual may view alcohol as an external causal factor. In any case, neither of the reviewed hypotheses predicted or explained the internality of the alcoholics' attributions for both success and failure. However, the results of this study are consistent with the research on Locus of Control previously mentioned that indicates a similar pattern of high internality of alcoholics as measured by the Rotter scale (Costello and Mandus, 1974; Distefano, Pryer, and Garrison, 1972; Gozali and Sloan, 1971). The internality indicated in this study and previous research may not necessarily reflect a debilitating pattern; although internality for failure is theoretically viewed as debilitating, general internality is generally viewed as an adaptive perspective.

Implications for Treatment

Additional research must be conducted before the general attributional patterns of alcoholics and their implications can be fully understood. However, even if a particular attributional pattern is not demonstrated for alcoholics in general, the attributions of individual alcoholics can be measured and analyzed for debilitating patterns, such as the ones previously outlined. Therapists and counselors who are aware of the hypothesized consequences of certain attributional patterns and who observe these patterns in their clients could then attempt to modify the client's perceptions of causality. For example, an alcoholic in treatment may verbalize the belief that he or she has been rejected by others because of not possessing the ability to relate to others or having a poor personality. In this case, the counselor may help the client to focus on his or her social successes and attribute them to ability, thereby increasing self-confidence. At the same time, the counselor could offer some other less debilitating reasons for the client's social failures, such as his or her not trying to be friendly or the attitudes of others. This example is especially relevant, since some treatment programs are aimed at helping clients with their interpersonal relations. Attribution theory would imply that providing alcoholics with interpersonal successes is not sufficient to bolster their self-images, if they do not attribute their successes internally. According to the theory and some available research (Dweck, 1975), repeated successes do not automatically alter estimates of one's ability but must be mediated by an ability attribution. Thus, an alcoholic who devalues his or her social skills might attribute any number of successes to luck or to other people's friendliness. This example demonstrates the implications of attributions and the potential importance of developing techniques for analyzing and modifying the alcoholic's attributional pattern.

Chapter 9

Lynn P. Rehm
Michael W. O'Hara

Understanding Depression

~~~~~~

According to National Institute of Mental Health (NIMH) estimates (Secunda, 1973), depression is coming to rival schizophrenia as the nation's number one mental health problem. Five to ten percent of the population are estimated to have an episode of clinical depression at least once in their lifetimes. Research studies have found a surprising degree of subclinical depression among the general population (Brown, Bhrolchain, and Harris, 1975; Levitt and Lubin, 1975). Although estimates vary, the NIMH figures suggest that approximately 15 percent of the population show significant depressive features at any one time. Each year, 125,000 people in the U.S. are hospitalized for depression; another 200,000 are treated as outpatients. An estimated 80 percent of the 23,000 annual suicides are committed by significantly depressed persons.

Note: Preparation of this chapter was supported in part by NIMH Grant MH27822, Lynn P. Rehm, Principal Investigator.

Despite its importance as a mental health problem, little is understood about depression.

Symptomatology

Depression is a construct encompassing a heterogeneous set of behaviors. Sad affect, with its accompanying behavioral manifestations, such as crying and dejected facial expression, is assumed to be only a single symptom accompanying many psychiatric and physical disorders. The symptoms of depression can be distinguished from the clinical syndrome of depression, which includes a range of symptoms beyond sad affect. In clinical depression, overt motor behavior is retarded. Measures of behavioral frequency, amplitude, duration, and latency have all been used to assess psychomotor retardation. For example, studies have assessed speech rate, loudness, length of utterance, and latency of response. Central to the concept of the clinical syndrome are the so-called neurovegetative signs of depression. These consist of classes of overt behavior that are decelerated in rate and are accompanied by reports of motivational deficits. They are assumed to have a physiological base. Loss of appetite, loss of libido, fatigue, and sleep disturbances are the primary neurovegetative signs. A variety of other physical complaints commonly accompany the syndrome as well. There is some evidence for disturbances in basic biological processes in depression—for example, changes in biochemistry, endocrine metabolism, and neurophysiology.

The syndrome of depression also encompasses many cognitive symptoms. Beck (1974) describes the attitudes and beliefs associated with depression as a cognitive triad consisting of a negative view of the world, a negative view of the future, and a negative view of the self. In depression, the world is perceived in a pessimistic way. Events are given their most negative interpretations. The future for depressed persons is seen as hopeless, and these individuals feel helpless to avoid aversive events or to obtain gratification. Low self-esteem is typical of depression, and expressions of guilty concern over past behavior and self-depreciation are common.

To summarize the most prominent symptoms of depression, it could be said that depression is characterized by (1) sad affect,

(2) biological changes, (3) behavioral retardation (slowed activity and speech, inertia, lack of initiation), and (4) generalized attitudes of pessimism (negativity, hopelessness, self-depreciation, guilt) and passivity (loss of interest, lack of motivation, helplessness).

Recent efforts to develop models for the understanding of depression have stressed the cognitive aspects of the disorder (Beck, 1974; Eastman, 1976; Rehm, 1977a; Seligman, 1975). Quite recently, the idea has begun to be explored that cognitive aspects of depression may be ammenable to an attributional analysis.

The symptomatology of depression is intimately related to the manner in which depressed individuals make inferences about the world and their role in the world. An obvious intersection between this view of depression and the tenets of attribution theory presents itself to the psychologist familiar with the attributional approach. Such symptoms as pessimism, low self-esteem, and guilt translate easily into the vocabulary of attribution theory. Guilt, for instance, may represent the attribution of failure to intentional lack of effort. The processes that produce and maintain depression may parallel processes that produce and maintain specific modes of making attributions. Similarly, therapy procedures for depression may be clarified or improved, if they are viewed as procedures for modifying attributions.

This chapter will attempt to assess the potential of the contribution of attribution theory to the analysis of depression. It will do so by addressing three broad sets of questions. First, do attributional constructs describe the behavior of depressed persons? That is, do depressed persons demonstrate a different pattern of attributions than other persons? Second, does attribution theory elucidate the etiology of depression? That is, is there an identifiable parallel between the etiology of depression and the antecedents of a depressed pattern of attributions? Third, does attribution theory suggest processes for the alleviation of depression? Are present therapy procedures consistent with methods of modifying attributions, or are there strategies for modifying attributions that have not been taken into account by depression therapy research? Within these broad questions, the actual and potential contribution of attribution theory will be evaluated. The first question will be addressed in a review of the empirical literature, and the last two questions will be evaluated with a focus on contemporary theoretical models of therapy for depression.

Although little depression research has been done from strictly an attributional perspective, several converging lines of research tie attribution theory to depressive symptomatology. *Locus of control* and *learned helplessness,* concepts closely related to attribution theory, have been applied to the analysis of depressive symptoms. We shall discuss both of these concepts along with other dimensions of attribution and attributional reconceptualization of learned helplessness.

Locus of Control

The attitude of passivity in depression has been interpreted in terms of locus of control of reinforcement. Locus of control of reinforcement (Rotter, 1966) is considered to be a generalized expectancy that rewards are either contingent or noncontingent upon one's own behavior. Individuals who believe that important rewards are not related to their behavior hold a belief in external control. People who perceive important rewards as contingent upon their own behavior hold a belief in internal control. There is an assumption that these beliefs represent stable individual differences. Locus of control is functionally similar to the internal-external dimension of causality in attribution theory (Jones and Nisbett, 1971; Nisbitt and Valins, 1971; Weiner and others, 1972).

It is usually assumed that depressed persons are excessively external and are consequently passive with regard to important events in their lives. Generalized belief in an external locus of causality relates easily to the behavioral deficits evident in depression. Individuals characterized by a belief in external control may not be as motivated to engage in the instrumental responses necessary to achieve gratification. This decreased level of activity is important in two respects. First, the behavioral passivity resulting from a belief in external control is mirrored in many of the symptoms of depression, including psychomotor retardation, loss of libido, and loss of appetite. Second, those individuals who emit little instrumental behavior may be vulnerable to an episode of depression.

The availability of Rotter's (1966) Internal-External Locus of Control Scale has led to a number of correlational studies with depression, which unfortunately have produced ambiguous results. As can be seen in Table 1, studies with normal subjects have generally found moderate correlations between Rotter's scale and standard paper-and-pencil measures of depression. However, Murray (1973) reported no significant relationship between locus of control and self-report of depressed feelings or suicidal thoughts among undergraduates.

The relationship between locus of control and depression in clinical populations is even less consistent. Although Rosenbaum and Raz (1977) found a small and nonsignificant positive correlation among physically disabled men, Goss and Morosko (1970) found no relationship among depressed alcoholic women and a negative relationship among alcoholic men. Rotter (1975) has suggested that alcoholics are traditionally told that they are wholly responsible for their drinking problem, which may account for this result. Also, working with a group of male alcoholic inpatients, O'Leary and others (1977) reported that the high externals were not significantly more depressed than the internals. They did find, however, that a measure of experienced control (Tiffany, 1967) did differentiate subjects in terms of level of depression. For a fuller discussion of attributional behavior of alcoholics, see McHugh, Beckman, and Frieze, Chapter Eight.

Harrow and Ferrante (1969) administered the Rotter scale to 128 psychiatric patients at admission and six weeks later. The forty-one depressed patients showed the greatest shift toward internality following six weeks of treatment, which inferred that improvement in depression was reflected in the change toward generalized internal expectancy.

Lamont (1972a,b) suggests a possible confound in these studies. He demonstrated that depressed subjects may be responding more to mood level of items on an I-E scale that he developed than to the content of the items per se. Lamont (1972a) found that depressed subjects were more likely to endorse items with a low mood level, whereas nondepressed subjects were more likely to endorse items with a higher mood level. There was no significant

Table 1. Studies Correlating the Rotter Internal-External Locus of Control Scale with Depression

Author	N	Population	Correlation	Depression Measure
Abramowitz (1969)	69	college students	r = 0.35	Guilford Depression Scale
Calhoun, Cheney, and Dawes (1974)	37	college students (male)	r = 0.58[a] r = 0.50[b]	
	44	college students (female)	r = 0.38[a] r = 0.09[b]	
Emmelkamp and Cohen-Kittenis (1974)	11	college students	r = 0.44	Self-Rating Depression Scale
Murray (1973)	80	college students	n.s.	Self-Report
Naditch, Gargan, and Michael (1975)	547	army recruits	r = 0.19	Cornell Medical Index-Depression Subscale
Prociuk, Breen, and Lussier (1976)	67	college underclassmen	r = 0.22	Beck Depression Inventory
	44	college seniors	r = 0.10	

[a]Based on use of Self-Rating Scale.
[b]Based on use of Depression Adjective Check List.

difference on endorsement of internal items, although depressed subjects did score significantly higher on external items. Despite the fact that mood level of items was equated by an earlier sample, external items were rated lower in mood level by the experimental subjects.

In a later study, Lamont (1972b) constructed items for which mood level and internality-externality were controlled, and he presented them in a forced-choice format. He found a correlation of -0.84 between the Zung (1965) depression scale and endorsement of items as to mood level. Depressed subjects endorsed more depressed items but were not differentiated on internal versus external items. These studies cast doubt on the nature of the studies cited in Table 1 as well as those discussed earlier (O'Leary and others, 1977; Rosenbaum and Raz, 1977; Tiffany, 1967).

Miller and Seligman (1973) found that depressed subjects demonstrated less expectancy change following success on a skill task than did nondepressed subjects. Their interpretation was that depressed subjects behaved as if they had performed on a chance task and thus did not change their expectancy for future success. Externality, as measured by Rotter's scale, did not predict expectancy-shift differences in this study. Miller and Seligman suggested that this may have been due to inadequacies of the scale. However, Hiroto (1974), utilizing more extreme groups on the I-E dimension, found that externality was related to latency of escape behavior and other helplessness measures. Cohen, Rothbart, and Phillips (1976) found significant differences between high and low external subjects on only one of two tasks after exposure to a helplessness manipulation involving a concept-formation task. Unlike Hiroto, they found no main effect for locus of control. These studies seem to indicate that Rotter's (1966) scale may not accurately predict behavior logically related to locus of control.

It must be remembered that all the data collected thus far have been correlational. The correlations have been modest and occasionally in the opposite to the direction predicted. The data do suggest that perception of control may play some role in the development and maintenance of depression; however, the learned helplessness literature has specified those relationships more clearly.

Learned Helplessness

Seligman (1975) has proposed a model of depression based originally on the observation that animals exposed to inescapable shock exhibit deficits in later escape-avoidance learning (Seligman, 1968; Seligman and Maier, 1967). Seligman (1975) argued that the experience of lack of control over aversive events produces a belief that responding is independent of outcome. This belief, termed *learned helplessness,* parallels Rotter's external locus of control of reinforcement in some ways and is also related to the attributional concept of external attribution of causality.

Learned helplessness is held to be the core symptom of depression. It defines the attitude of passivity and leads to the various external manifestations of the disorder. A person who perceives rewards as generally externally determined would presumably behave in a passive, slowed manner and have a negative outlook.

In attempting to link his learned helplessness model to depression, Seligman and his colleagues (see Seligman, Klein, and Miller, 1976) have employed several research strategies. The first strategy has been to induce helplessness experimentally in normal subjects and observe the extent to which they behave in ways that parallel depression as predicted by the helplessness model. In studies of helplessness induction, one group of subjects is exposed to the helplessness training, which may take many forms (for example, uncontrollable aversive stimulation, unsolvable problems, impossible instrumental tasks). Subjects exposed to controllable aversive stimulation serve as a control for exposure to the aversive stimulation. Subjects in a no-aversive-stimulation condition serve as a baseline comparison group. Subjects in the uncontrollable stimulation group receive exactly the same duration and patterning of aversive stimulation as the subjects in the controllable stimulation. A second series of studies (Klein, Fencil-Morse, and Seligman, 1976) has attempted to demonstrate that depressed subjects behave on experimental tasks in a manner similar to subjects exposed to learned helplessness inductions. A third strategy, which will be discussed later, has been to attempt treatment of depression with methods used to alleviate learned helplessness (Klein and Seligman, 1976).

Overt Motor Behavior. Psychomotor retardation, which may be characterized by a reduced efficiency in performance, has been found in learned helplessness and depression (Dweck and Repucci, 1973; Hiroto, 1974; Hiroto and Seligman, 1975; Jones, Nation, and Massad, 1977; Klein and Seligman, 1976; Miller and Seligman, 1975; Roth and Kubal, 1975; Tennen and Eller, 1977). Klein and Seligman (1976) directly compared depressed and helpless subjects on an instrumental response task. They found that nondepressed subjects receiving inescapable noise and depressed subjects receiving no noise showed escape deficits relative to controls on the instrument response. Hiroto and Seligman (1975) had earlier demonstrated that helpless subjects were impaired on both an instrumental and cognitive response task.

Two studies were conducted by Seligman and his colleagues that assessed impairment of helpless and depressed subjects on an anagram-solution task (Klein, Fencil-Morse, and Seligman, 1976; Miller and Seligman, 1975). In both studies, depressed and helpless subjects were inferior to control subjects on several performance measures, including mean response latency and mean trials to criterion.

These studies provide modest evidence regarding a behavioral link between depression and learned helplessness, considering the narrow range of behaviors assessed. However, these studies do provide suggestive evidence that the behavioral passivity characteristic of helplessness is similar to that of depression.

Cognition and Affect. Seligman and his colleagues have tried to make the case that the primary cognitive symptom of depression is the belief in loss of control. In several studies, they have attempted to demonstrate that depressed and helpless subjects are less likely to alter beliefs regarding future success, despite previous success or failure.

Miller and Seligman (1973) found that depressed subjects demonstrated less expectancy shift following success on skill tasks. This finding supported their hypothesis that depression is characterized by a belief in independence of behavior and outcomes. It should be noted, however, that the difference was obtained only following success. Predicted expectancy differences following failure were not significant.

Miller, Seligman, and Kurlander (1975) compared (1) depressed-anxious, (2) nondepressed-anxious, and (3) nondepressed-nonanxious subjects regarding expectancy changes following success and failure on skill and chance tasks. Consistent but nonsignificant differences in the predicted directions were found between the depressed group and other subjects. Miller and Seligman (1976) compared depressed and nondepressed subjects in inescapable, escapable, and no-aversive-stimulations conditions. In this study, expectancy changes following failure differentiated among the nondepressed subjects. The inescapable aversive-stimulation condition again produced less expectancy shift than the other two conditions. Further, the depressed subjects in the no-aversive-stimulation condition performed in the same manner as the nondepressed inescapable aversive-stimulation subjects. Abramson and others (1978) obtained results similar to Miller and Seligman's (1976) using unipolar depressives, depressed schizophrenics, nondepressed schizophrenics, and normal subjects. The expectancy changes of the depressed-schizophrenic group were no different than either the normal control or the nondepressed-schizophrenic group, leading the authors to suggest that the perception of lack of control was specific to depression and not characteristic of psychopathology in general. This study represents an extension of the helplessness research to clinical populations.

In the clearest demonstration to date, Klein and Seligman (1976), using a paradigm similar to Miller and Seligman's (1976), found clear expectancy differences between depressed-helpless subjects and controls following both success and failure. They attributed these differences to the belief by experimental-group subjects that they had no control over their task performance.

These studies may be regarded as crucial in supporting the learned-helplessness model of depression. They attempt to test directly the central tenet of the helplessness model—the belief of independence between response and important outcomes. The results of these studies have been mixed, again providing modest support for the learned-helplessness model.

Only three studies have directly assessed affective changes produced by helplessness manipulations. Gatchel, Paulus, and Maples (1975) found that subjects who experienced an uncontrollable aversive-stimulation condition were significantly more depressed and anxious than control subjects on the Multiple Affect Adjective Checklist (MAACL) (Zuckerman, Lubin, and Robins, 1965). After the test phase, which consisted of solving anagrams, the differences between groups were no longer significant. In a later study, Gatchel, McKinney, and Koebernick (1977) found similar results; however, helplessness subjects reported significantly more hostility as well. Miller and Seligman (1975) obtained mixed results in a study examining MAACL change scores for depressed and nondepressed college students who were exposed to uncontrollable, controllable, and control conditions. It is notable that, in this study, significant main effects were found for anxiety and hostility but not for depression on the MAACL. The depressed subjects on the average reported a more positive mood after uncontrollable aversive noise. Miller and Seligman attributed this paradoxical finding to two depressed subjects who were angered by the experimental procedure.

These three studies, then, do not provide very strong support for Seligman, Klein, and Miller's (1976) assertion that laboratory-produced helplessness produces depressed mood. The effect of learned-helplessness manipulation on cognitive symptoms of depression, such as lowered self-esteem, pessimism, or adhedonia, has not been assessed.

Physiology. Physiological or neurovegetative manifestations of depression have been little studied in the helplessness literature. Hokanson and others (1971) found that subjects who could control time out from a Sidman avoidance task evidenced a lower systolic blood pressure than those subjects who could not. Gatchel and Proctor (1976) demonstrated that subjects in an inescapable aversive-stimulation condition reduced phasic skin conductance, which the authors viewed as an indication of reduced autonomic arousal, suggesting less task involvement (passivity). Krantz, Glass, and Snyder (1974) reported similar findings in one study but not in a second study using a more aversive stimulus.

Gatchel, McKinney, and Koebernick (1977) directly compared depressed and helpless subjects on a skin-conductance measure. Depressed subjects were characterized by greater skin conductance, responding on later trials than helpless subjects. These findings parallel those reported by Lewinsohn, Lobitz, and Wilson (1973) for depression and Gatchel and Proctor (1976) for helplessness.

The literature to date does not clearly support a parallel between physiological responding in depressed and helpless subjects. However, a narrow range of physiological responses has been assessed. Later research may reveal parallels in other physiological responses.

In summary, depression and learned helplessness show an imperfect correlation. Learned-helplessness manipulations have not clearly demonstrated that they produce changes in depressive affect or expectancy change. Parallels between depression and learned helplessness in performance deficits are much better supported. Parallels in psychophysiology are as yet only hinted at in the experimental literature. Thus, although there is some evidence for arguing that externality is a symptom of depression, it has not yet been powerfully demonstrated that helplessness is the appropriate model for externality.

Research on the relationship between helplessness and depression could benefit from attention to three issues. First, a differentiation should be made between success and failure attributions assessed for depressed and nondepressed groups. In helplessness studies, differences attributable to helplessness seem to be obtainable following either success or failure on a given task but rarely on both. Depressive attributions may be very different for success or failure conditions. Second, evaluation of attributions of causality should be made on multiple dimensions, not just externality. Stability and intentionality may also be important. Third, in those studies that attempt to show parallels between depression and experimentally produced phenomena, there is a need for the assessment of a wider range of depressive symptoms, including cognitive, behavioral, and physiological symptoms, in order to verify the parallel.

Etiological Models

At present, there is little theoretical or empirical agreement regarding the etiology of depression (for example, Friedman and Katz, 1974; Mendels, 1970). Models run the gamut from biological, genetic accounts (Davis, 1977) to explicit environmental models (Lewinsohn, Biglan, and Zeiss, 1976). The models described in this section are particularly amenable to an attributional analysis. They either can be interpreted from an attributional perspective or incorporate attribution theory directly. Seligman's (1975) learned-helplessness model will be reviewed first, followed by the cognitive model of Beck (1976) and the self-control model of Rehm (1977a).

Learned Helplessness. Seligman's learned-helplessness model has presented the most direct empirical evidence with regard to etiology. As already noted, it is a basic tenet of Seligman's model that learned helplessness, and thus depression, derives from experiences of uncontrollability. In both animal and human studies, he has demonstrated that experience of aversive stimulation, delivered independently of the organism's behavior, results in behavioral deficits on a later task (Miller and Seligman, 1975; Seligman and Maier, 1967).

Recently, Seligman's basic model has been questioned on a number of empirical and logical grounds (Hanusa and Schulz, 1977; Lewinsohn, 1975; Roth and Kubal, 1975). Among the problems posed is the generalizability of the effect. Why should the effects of uncontrollability transfer across mode of task to contingencies so discriminably different from the original (Douglas and Anisman, 1975; Roth and Kubal, 1975)? Also, there is the problem of the seeming inconsistency between learned helplessness and the symptom of guilt. If depressed persons believe that they have no control over the major events in their lives, why should they feel guilty about past unhappy events? Guilt implies responsibility and thus an internal attribution of causality. In a recent article, Abramson and Sackeim (1977) discussed this paradox and pointed out that it exists in clinical descriptions of depressive symptomatology, in theoretical accounts, and in empirical findings with depressed subjects. They suggest a number of potential solutions to the problem, none of which seem entirely satisfactory.

These problems are of particular interest, since they can be elucidated by an attributional analysis. Abramson, Seligman, and Teasdale (1978) have recently suggested just such an analysis. They argue that attributions of causality can be classified along three dimensions. These dimensions are internal-external, stable-unstable, and global-specific. The former two dimensions have frequently been cited in attributional analyses (Weiner and others, 1972), whereas the latter is the contribution of Abramson, Seligman, and Teasdale.

Abramson, Seligman, and Teasdale (1978) argue that, following the experience of an uncontrollable aversive event, an individual may make a number of depressive attributions. Attributions on the global-specific dimension will influence the degree of generality of the depression. Individuals may thus be depressed with regard to one specific area of their life or experience a more general debility. Attributions on the stable-unstable dimension will lead to a transient depression, whereas a stable attribution will lead to a more chronic depression. Attribution to internal versus external causes would influence self-esteem. Loss of self-esteem would occur only following an internal attribution to an aversive event. In general, depressed persons are seen as attributing failure to global, stable, and internal causes and success to specific, unstable, external causes. According to this analysis, individuals would vary in their susceptibility to depression as a function of differences in attributional style. Individuals who tend to attribute failure to internal, stable, and global factors would be prone to guilt and chronic generalized depression.

From this analysis, Abramson, Seligman, and Teasdale (1978) suggest two forms of helplessness. In the first form, people are helpless because they believe that events are caused externally and are independent of their own behavior. This is termed a belief in *response unavailability*. These depressed people would logically behave in an apathetic, passive manner but would not necessarily exhibit low self-esteem or self-depreciation. The second type of depressed people would believe they were helpless due to their own lack of ability, skill, or capacity for effort. This personal helplessness would result in low self-esteem and self-depreciation.

The Klein, Fencil-Morse, and Seligman (1976) study is consistent with this analysis. When depressed subjects made attributions of failure to their own incompetence (an internal, stable cause), they showed deficits; but, when they attributed failure to task difficulty, subsequent performance on a different task improved markedly. This analysis may also explain why prior studies found inconsistencies in the correlation between depression and externality. Alcoholic depressives, for instance, may indeed show primarily this internal, stable, or personal form of helplessness. This analysis has not entirely resolved the question of the coexistence of helplessness and guilt. The idea of two forms of helplessness is not entirely consistent with the clinical or research literature (Abramson and Sackeim, 1977), which suggests that both forms of attributions are often present in the same individual. Rizley (1978) assessed attributions of depressed and nondepressed college students in response to success and failure on impersonal or interpersonal tasks. Depressed subjects rated internal factors (ability and effort) as more important on a failure task and as less important on a success task as compared with nondepressed subjects. In a second experiment, which included an interpersonal-influence task, depressed subjects were slightly more likely (nonsignificant) than nondepressed subjects to believe that their advice was responsible for both improving and deteriorating performance by a partner. The findings from the first experiment are consistent with Abramson, Seligman, and Teasdale's (1978) reformulation of learned helplessness. The findings from the second study, although equivocal, certainly are not consistent with any model of depression, cognitive or otherwise.

Teasdale (1978) found that both real and recalled success altered attributions of failure by depressed and helpless subjects; however, only real success experience affected mood. This finding suggests that modifications of attributions alone in the absence of feedback from behavior change may not be sufficient to alter depressed mood.

Wortman and Dintzer (1978) have recently provided a critique of Abramson, Seligman, and Teasdale's (1978) attributional analysis of learned helplessness and, by extension, depression. They question the adequacy of the new model on several points, which will only be briefly mentioned here. One important point they raise is whether persons in fact make attributions and whether attributions affect behavior (Nisbett and Wilson, 1977). They further suggest that factors in addition to attributions and expectations of control may influence reactions to uncontrollable outcomes (for example, meaningfulness of outcome).

Overall, the importance of attributions in the learned-helplessness phenomonen has received mixed support from the literature. More research needs to be done in this area, particularly experimental work in which attributions are manipulated experimentally in order to assess the hypothesized causal link between attributions and helplessness or depression.

Cognitive Distortion. Beck's (1967a, 1976) approach to depression has been prominent in focusing on cognitive events. For Beck, depression can be described entirely in cognitive terms (the cognitive triad), with behavioral symptoms representing secondary consequences. Beck conceptualizes the depressed person as filtering his perceptions of the world through schema that have inherent negative biases. He discusses specific forms of cognitive distortion, such as arbitrary inference, selective abstraction, and overgeneralization. Arbitrary inference refers to an unwarranted assumption that one is responsible for some negative event. Selective abstraction refers to selecting a negative detail out of context in what might otherwise be a very positive total situation. Overgeneralization refers to unjustified generalization on the basis of a single incident. Other forms of cognitive distortion proposed by Beck may involve additional mechanisms.

Many of Beck's constructs relate directly to attribution theory. Arbitrary inferences refer to the incorrect attribution of a negative event to an internal cause. Selective abstraction refers to basing an attribution of causality on less than the total relevant information. Overgeneralization is the making of an excessively broad attribution of causality and is a direct parallel to Seligman's discussion of global attributions of failure.

Although distortions in processes other than attributions of causality may be involved in Beck's theory, an attributional analysis would seem to offer some interesting commentary on Beck's general approach. Beck's approach tends to be largely descriptive, a kind of catalogue of the types of distortion he has observed in depressed and other psychotherapy clients. Attribution theory suggests some additional connections between the various forms of distortion. First, as described previously, Beck's terms can be reduced to a potentially more concise set of equivalents in attributional terminology. Second, attribution theory suggests an alternative way of looking at the relationship between the primary triad of symptoms and the specific forms of distortion. From an attributional point of view, the common element in the various forms of cognitive distortion is that they maintain consistency with a negative expectancy. A generalized negative expectancy would appear to be a translation of Beck's cognitive triad of a negative view of self, world, and future. As such, it might be argued that cognitive distortions are forms of attributions that maintain cognitive consistency with a generalized negative expectancy (cognitive triad). This view would make attribution research a laboratory analog for development and modification of depression as viewed from the cognitive perspective.

Self-Control. Recently, our research team at the University of Pittsburgh has developed a self-control model of depression as an attempt to provide a framework and overview for organizing research in depression (Rehm, 1977a). An attributional component is explicitly incorporated. This model of depression uses Kanfer's (1970, 1971) model of self-control as a basic heuristic device. Briefly, Kanfer has proposed that human self-control can be described in terms of a three-stage feedback loop process. When individuals become aware that some behavior is not producing the expected result, they begin the first stage of self-monitoring. In this stage, people observe their own behavior and its antecedents and consequences. These observations serve as the basis for the second phase, self-evaluation. In this phase, an estimate of performance is compared with an internal standard or criterion. At this point, we have amended Kanfer's model to include self-attributional concerns. It has been argued elsewhere (Rehm, 1977a) that self-evaluation presumes an internal attribution of causality. Thus, our self-evaluation phase involves the attribution of self-attributed performance to an internal standard or criterion. The final phase of the self-control feedback loop is self-reinforcement. In this phase, the individual self-administers a reward, if a criterion for success has been met, and self-administers a punishment, if a criterion for failure has been met. It is presumed that this process of self-reward and self-punishment influences behavior in ways that allow the person to resist temptation and persist in difficult endeavors.

There is some research to date to corroborate the addition

of the self-attributional component in the self-control model. First, in one of the studies reported by Weiner and others (1972), they demonstrated a correlation between self-reward and internal attributions of responsibility. Second, some unpublished data from our laboratory studies (Rehm, Roth, and Farmartino, 1976) demonstrated a relationship between internal attribution and self-reward. Subjects in this study were given questionnaires that described situations that varied on three dimensions. Three types of tasks (motor, social, and intellectual) were described as having success, failure, or neutral outcomes under internal, external, or mixed attributional sets. For instance, a situation was described in which a person in a shooting gallery was told that the gun was very inaccurate, and thus success was generally attributable to luck; however, the outcome was ten out of ten target hits. Subjects were then asked how they would evaluate this performance. Self-evaluation was measured on a bipolar scale from commendability to condemnability, and self-reinforcement was based on a bipolar scale from self-reward to self-punishment. Both evaluation and reinforcement increased in magnitude (in a positive direction following success and a negative direction following failure) as a function of internality of attributional set.

As applied to depression, the self-control model suggests that depressed individuals may exert self-control maladaptively at each of the stages of self-control. In summary, depression can be ascribed to: (1) a tendency to monitor aversive events selectively; (2) a tendency selectively to monitor immediate as opposed to delayed consequences of behavior; (3) a stringent self-evaluative criterion setting; (4) inaccurate attributions of responsibility; (5) insufficient self-reward; and (6) excessive self-punishment. Symptoms of depression are presumed to reflect these various deficits. The model posits that the pessimism of depressed persons is a function primarily of selective attention to aversive events. Low self-esteem is a function of self-evaluational processes involving stringent criterion setting and negative self-monitoring. Passivity in outlook and in behavior results from low rates of self-reward and high rates of self-punishment, which are the products of depressive self-monitoring and self-evaluation. The model is seen as an attempt to incorporate conceptions of depression identified in a variety of other theoretical models.

Of particular concern here is the incorporation of attributional concepts into the model. The assumption is that self-attribution acts as a mediating variable in influencing self-evaluation. Self-evaluation in turn influences the manner in which individuals regulate their own behavior through administration of reward and punishment. In a manner parallel to Seligman's recent revision of his model, Rehm (1977a) argued that depressed individuals may make two forms of attributional error. First, they make excessively external attributions of causality and thus become helpless, in Seligman's original sense of a belief in the independence of performance and consequence. Second, depressed individuals may make excessively internal attributions of causality but perceive themselves to be lacking in ability to obtain positive consequences. The former individual would be apathetic but not self-depreciating; the latter individual would have low self-esteem and high self-depreciation. According to the model, either situation would result in low rates of self-reward; the latter form would also result in high rates of self-punishment.

This formulation encounters the same guilt-helplessness paradox that Seligman's model encounters. That is, how is it that the same depressed individual may display both forms of maladaptive attribution at different times? By looking at the problem again from the perspective of attribution theory, an alternative conceptualization is suggested which also permits a greater consistency between the helplessness, cognitive-distortion, and self-control models. If one assumes that a negative expectancy and not the attributions themselves are the cause of depression, then the seeming paradox may be resolved.

Prior expectancies are known to influence attribution (Weiner and others, 1972). Essentially, the idea is that attributions may be influenced in the direction of consistency with prior expectations. For instance, if a person has an expectation of a success outcome based on consistent prior experience with a particular task, then an outcome that is discrepant with this expectation (a failure) will be more likely to be attributed externally than if the task was novel and there was no prior expectation. If we make the assumption that depressed persons have a generalized negative expectancy regarding outcomes in their lives, then their attributional behavior becomes more consistent. If such a negative expec-

tancy exists, then, for depressed persons, failure experiences will
be consistent with this expectancy and will therefore be attributed
to internal, stable, and global factors. Similarly, success experiences, which would be inconsistent with a negative expectancy,
would be attributed to external, unstable, and specific factors.

This formulation would seem to be more parsimonious than
the Abramson, Seligman, and Teasdale (1978) conception of a stable attributional style, which would include different attribution
patterns for success versus failure experiences. It suggests that
negative expectancy is the primary cause of depression and that
one of the results of the negative expectancy would be a belief in
uncontrollability and thus learned helplessness. The negative-
expectancy formulation would be quite consistent with Beck's view
of depression. Beck's cognitive triad is in fact three expressions of
negative expectancy. They are simply statements that a negative
expectancy holds for personal, external, and future outcomes.
Beck's catalogue of mechanisms of cognitive distortion is a list of
mechanisms for maintaining consistency of perception with a negative expectancy. The negative-expectancy formulation is also consistent with the self-control point of view. As a factor influencing
self-attributions, negative expectancy contributes to negative self-
evaluation and thus to low self-reward and high self-punishment.
The self-control model might also hypothesize that a negative expectancy would influence attention to negative versus positive
events. Research on attributions in depression could benefit from a
closer look at expectancy factors and their influence on attributions
and resultant affect.

Psychotherapy

Following the psychoanalytic speculations of the 1930s and
1940s, the 1950s and 1960s were dominated by biological and
chemotherapeutic advances in the therapy of depression. The late
1960s saw a renewed interest in psychological theorizing about the
nature of depression, and reports of psychotherapy case studies
began appearing. The first controlled group-design studies
employing homogenous depressed populations appeared in 1973
(McLean, Ogston, and Grauer, 1973; Robinson and Lewinsohn,

1973; Shipley and Fazio, 1973). Many innovative therapies have been suggested, but for the most part, recent therapies share the qualities of being structured, short-term, operationalized programs with specific goals. Initial evidence suggests that psychotherapy can be a significant adjunct to chemotherapy (Weissman and others, 1976) and may rival or exceed the effectiveness of psychotherapy alone (Rush and others, 1977). Many of the new treatment programs have arisen from the behavioral point of view. For example, Lewinsohn, Biglan, and Zeiss (1976) have described methods for increasing activity level, teaching social skills, and desensitizing anxiety with depressed persons. McLean (1976) describes a similar program of therapy modules, stressing interpersonal interaction and communication. Another major orientation contributing to new developments in psychotherapy for depression is the cognitive approach. Elements deriving directly from attribution theory are included in some of these therapies, and additional refinements based on attributional concepts appear to be emerging.

Helplessness Retraining. Although Seligman's learned-helplessness model has not yet formed the basis for any reported psychotherapies, recent developments are clearly leading in that direction. Abramson, Seligman, and Teasdale (1978) enumerate potential goals for such a therapy. They suggest that efforts should be aimed at changing unrealistic attributions for failure toward external, unstable, specific factors and changing unrealistic attributions for success toward internal, stable, global factors. This is one obvious and direct set of goals. They also suggest that therapy might be directed toward changing depressed persons' expectations from uncontrollability to controllability. This might be accomplished either by training in specific skills or by providing success experiences with skills a person already possesses. As an example of the former strategy, Klein, Fencil-Morse, and Seligman (1976) were able to improve the anagram performance of depressed subjects by instructing them to attribute past failures to task difficulty rather than to their own incompetence. As an example of the latter strategy, Klein and Seligman (1976) demonstrated a reversal of learned helplessness and depression following experience with solvable discrimination problems.

Another implication of the helplessness model is that training with controllability may provide a form of immunization against depression. Such an effect was initially demonstrated in animal studies (Seligman, Rosellini, and Kozak, 1975). Jones, Nation, and Massad (1977) demonstrated an immunization effect with human subjects in a laboratory analog. They found that a 50 percent schedule of success was superior to a zero percent or 100 percent schedule of success in immunizing subjects against the effects of experimental-helplessness training. Seligman (1975) expands on the possibilities of such immunization training for preventing depression on a broad scale.

Dweck (1975) used an explicit attribution-retraining treatment program in an attempt to alleviate learned helplessness in children. The children who were identified as helpless were selected on the basis of school staff ratings of extreme expectation for failure and deterioration of performance in the face of failure. Half of these children received a training program involving mathematical problems, which stressed success only in the manner of a programmed-learning procedure. The other half of the subjects received a training program that taught them to make *internal* attributions of failure but to attribute them to lack of effort rather than to lack of ability. Results indicated that the children in the attribution-retraining treatment maintained or improved their performance following failure, whereas the children in the success-only treatment continued to evidence a severe deterioration following failure. Evidence was also presented that the experimental treatmental condition did produce changes in the children's mode of attributing failure. It is notable that the strategy used in this study was partly in opposition to suggestions of Abramson, Seligman, and Teasdale (1978). Dweck's children were taught to make internal, unstable attributions for failure—that is, attributions to lack of effort. Abramson and his colleagues suggest the general strategy of training in external, stable attributions for failure. The choice of strategy may be dictated by the nature of the task. The solving of mathematical problems is realistically attributable to internal causes, when the individual's repertoire includes the prerequisite skills. Failure to finish an outdoor project on time because of bad weather would be an example of a situation where some depressed individuals might make internal attributions and where an appropriate strategy would be to train realistic, external, unstable attributions.

In a more recent study, Diener and Dweck (1978) found that helpless children attributed failure to lack of ability; however, mastery-oriented children made few attributions; rather, they engaged in self-monitoring and self-instructions that seemed to identify remedies for failure. This finding suggests that, in addition to the importance of altering attributions for success and failure, the development of more effective problem-solving skills, for example, may be very important in altering helpless behavior. There is some evidence that experiences with controllability or explicit training in reattribution may modify helplessness, but, as yet, the precise procedures are only in the initial stages of development.

Cognitive Therapy. Beck's (1976) cognitive model of psychopathology forms the background for a system of cognitive therapy for depression. This therapy system encompasses a wide variety of specific techniques or approaches that Beck finds useful in dealing with specific problem areas. Beck uses both verbal persuasion techniques and behavioral assignments. None of these techniques is explicitly stated in attributional terms, but a number of them may be regarded as such. For instance, Beck talks about graded-task assignments, in which the depressed individuals, who avow that they are unable to perform a certain job, are given a series of graded tasks, starting from very simple and progressing to more complex, which demonstrates to them that they are capable of performing the job. In attributional terms, he is demonstrating to the clients that they do possess the ability or capacity for effort necessary to complete the tasks. Beck's system has been evaluated as a cognitive-therapy approach in a study comparing it with chemotherapy. Rush and others (1977) reported that the cognitive-therapy program proved to be superior to the medication program on a variety of measures. These differences were maintained at follow-up (Hollon and others, 1977). It is difficult to say to what degree this reattribution plays a role in altering depression in Beck's system.

Self-Control Therapy. The self-control model of depression has been used as an organizing heuristic for a psychotherapy program that has been evaluated in two studies (Fuchs and Rehm,

1977; Rehm and others, 1977). This therapy program has been administered in a structured group format. Weekly didactic presentations, discussion of individual applications, and homework assignments were organized around each of the six hypothesized self-control deficits. For example, following a presentation of the idea that depressed persons tend selectively to monitor aversive events and a discussion of the applicability of this concept to each individual, depressed subjects were given the homework assignment of keeping daily self-monitoring logs of positive activities that they engaged in during the week. They were also given a Positive Activities List (Rehm and others, 1977), which consists of categories of rewarding or potentially rewarding activities for use as a guideline and checklist. The assumption was that monitoring positive activities would intervene in the subjects' self-monitoring behavior. These logs were kept throughout the program and became the basis for later steps.

The two completed studies evaluating this program demonstrated that a self-control program was more effective than a nonspecific therapy program or a waiting-list control condition (Fuchs and Rehm, 1977) and more effective than a social-skills training procedure (Rehm and others, 1977). In both studies, greater improvement was shown on both self-report and overt-activity measures. A third study presently in progress is designed to analyze the therapy package and evaluate the relative contributions of the self-monitoring, self-evaluation, and self-reinforcement components.

As this series of studies has progressed, the therapy program and therapist's manual have been revised and refined. The latest revision of the manual (Rehm, 1977b) has incorporated an explicit exercise designed to make the depressed patients aware of the nature of their attributions and to modify the manner in which they attribute causes of events to themselves. The therapist presents the concept of attribution of causality and defines the dimensions of internal-external, stable-unstable, and global-specific attribution. The idea is presented that people who are depressed tend to attribute success to external, unstable, specific causes and to attribute failure to internal, stable, global causes. Relevant examples are given and discussed. Subjects are encouraged to examine the concept in their own experience. To ensure that the concepts are accurately acquired by each patient, a worksheet was devised. Subjects are asked to select four events that have occurred in the last two weeks—two positive events (from their self-monitoring logs) and two negative or aversive events. They are then asked to list ways in which each event might be attributable to general, stable factors or to unusual, specific factors. In the latter case, attributional dimensions of stability and globality were collapsed to simplify the exercise. These exercises are repeated for the unpleasant events, and the results become the topic of additional discussion in the group. The therapists attempt to prompt and reinforce accurate attribution of positive events to internal, global, and stable causes and to reinforce accurate attribution of unpleasant events to external, specific, and unstable causes. Following the exercise, subjects are given the assignment of recording on their self-monitoring logs a percentage figure, reflecting the degree to which the subject attributed the activity to internal causes for each pleasant activity.

Attribution of Responsibility Exercise

The purpose of this exercise is to look closely at assumptions people make in assigning credit, blame, or responsibility for events. The assumption is that people who tend to be depressed often make faulty assumptions about their responsibility for events.

1. List two fairly important events from your Positive Activity Logs for the last two weeks.

Event a. _____

Event b. _____

2. In what ways were other people, chance, or luck responsible for these events?

Event a. _____

Event b. _____

3. In what ways were you (your efforts, skills, abilities, and so on) responsible for these events?

Event a. _____

Event b. _____

4. What percentage of the responsibility for these events was attributable to you?

Event a. _____%

Event b. _____%

In most cases you will probably find that you have considerable responsibility for positive events in your life. While positive events do sometimes occur purely by chance (winning a lottery), usually positive events are things which you have worked for or contributed to. It is nearly always within your power to influence or increase these events. If you did not conclude that you had more than 50% responsibility for these events, go back to items 2 and 3 and reexamine them. Perhaps you can think of other ways in which you were responsible for the events.

5. Look at the reasons you wrote down in item 3. To what extent are these reasons examples of something generally true about yourself? That is, do they represent a stable pattern or characteristic of you which you show in many situations, or do they represent an unusual or limited aspect of your behavior?

	100-0%	75-25%	50-50%	25-75%	0-100%	
Event a. General, Stable	•————	•———	•————	•———	•→	Unusual, Specific
Event b. General, Stable	•————	•———	•————	•———	•→	Unusual, Specific

In most cases you will probably find that the ways that you were responsible for your positive activities were examples of general, stable characteristics that are true of you in many situations. If you did not conclude that general characteristics were involved, go back and reexamine your response to item 3. Perhaps you can think of general traits that were involved.

6. List two unpleasant or unhappy events that occurred during the last two weeks.
Event c. _____
Event d. _____

7. In what ways were other people, chance, or bad luck responsible for these events?
Event c. _____
Event d. _____

8. In what ways were you (your efforts, skills, abilities, or lack of effort, skills, and ability) responsible for these events?
Event c. _____
Event d. _____

9. What percentage of the responsibility for these events was attributable to you?
Event c. _____%
Event d. _____%

In most cases you will probably find that you are not solely responsible for the unpleasant events in your life. In most cases unpleasant events are attributable to others or to chance. There is one exception to this rule. Being passive, and thus being bored or excessively dependent on others, can be an unpleasant event for which you may be responsible. That is, you could have chosen to act more assertively. If you did not conclude that your unpleasant events (other than passivity) were attributable to external causes or to luck, go back over items 7 and 8 and reexamine them. Perhaps you can think of other ways in which others or chance were responsible for these events. It is important to be able to recognize accurately that certain unpleasant events are not under your control while others may be. Only by separating them out can you control and direct yourself and your mood.

10. Assignment for the coming week: Continue record keeping on your self-monitoring logs for the next week. Continue especially recording activities which you have defined as subgoals on your self-evaluation worksheets. For this week, use the extra column on your self-monitoring logs to record the percent to which you were responsible for each of your positive activities.

Our research program to date has not evaluated the effectiveness of the specific exercises. Anecdotal evidence from the comments of the subjects in the groups indicated that the concepts were fairly easily acquired by the subjects. They seemed to agree with the interpretation of the way in which depressed individuals make attributions, and they presented validating examples from their own lives. Anecdotal comments in later sessions suggested that the exercise and homework assignment contributed to a sense of having some control over their lives and moods.

Each of the therapy approaches reviewed here represents an independent mode of thinking about depression and amelioration, yet all seem to share three broad goals. First, each approach attempts to help the depressed individual to make accurate and realistic appraisals of the world. A major element in this appraisal is making accurate and realistic attributions of causality. The second major goal is the modification of self-perception in the positive direction. To a large degree, self-perception may be a function of the kinds of attributions one makes about successes and failures in life. Third, each strategy attempts to provide an appropriate basis for the individual's initiation, prediction, and control of future behavior. Again, the nature of attributional styles and the expectations that in part result from them are presumed to provide the basis for choices of overt behavior. Although these goals appear to be quite disparate, attributional conceptions may provide a common denominator for comparisons between strategies.

Attributions of Therapists. One further issue concerning psychotherapy for depression is worthy of note. Attributions of clinicians regarding the cause of their client's depression may have important treatment implications. A clinician may select one intervention over another, depending on what cause the client's depression is attributed to. Calhoun, Johnson, and Boardman (1975) and Johnson, Calhoun, and Boardman (1975) have investigated the types of information that influence causal attributions regarding a student's depression. They presented college students, clinic clients (Calhoun, Johnson, and Boardman, 1975) and professionals (Johnson, Calhoun, and Boardman, 1975) with descriptions of depressed students varying on three dimensions: severity (mild or severe), consistency (prior occurrence or no prior occurrence), and typicalness (peer typical or peer atypical). They found that clinicians and students made causal attributions to personality factors when the student's depression was atypical of other students. As might be expected, when the depression had occurred before, it was attributed to stable personality or environmental factors. Of interest was the finding that clinicians as opposed to the other subjects tended to attribute severe depression to environmental factors. We suggest that this tendency may represent a bias among clinicians to hold the environment responsible for severe depression in contrast to mild depression.

These studies suggest that a clinician might well consider the basis for his or her judgments regarding the cause of a client's depression. Whether modifying attributions regarding a client's depression will materially affect treatment is a matter for further investigation. As is the case for the description of symptomatology, theories of etiology, and treatment techniques, attributional analyses are emerging as promising strategies for approaching the problem of depression. The fulfillment of this initial promise represents a potentially fruitful area for applications of attribution research.

Chapter 10

Louise H. Kidder
Ellen S. Cohn

Public Views
of Crime and
Crime Prevention

A radio mystery theater poses the problem: Who killed the maid? As the story begins, a maidservant talks to her employer of twenty-five years. The maid asks for a small favor; she would like the next day off, because it is her birthday. The woman refuses, saying it would inconvenience the household, but she makes a counteroffer as a gesture of good will; she tells the maid to take a taxi to work the next day instead of her usual bus and gives her the necessary carfare. The following day, as the maid rides to work in the taxi, two unemployed house painters rob a nearby bank. As the men run from the bank, a bank guard takes aim and shoots, just as the maid's taxi passes the bank, killing the maid. That night, the maid appears in a dream and accuses the mistress of killing her by making her come to work that morning. As the woman wrestles with her conscience, her husband tries to reassure her. He tells her that there are many other causes of the maid's death. The bank guard pulled the trigger. The robbers made him shoot. Unemployment led the men to rob the bank. The maid was not qualified for other work. As the story ends, we are left wondering: Who killed the maid?

This story illustrates the kinds of attributions that may be made as we form personal theories about the causes of crime. The purpose of this chapter is to examine lay theories or personal theories about the causes of crime and lay or personal crime-prevention efforts. Although both experimental-attribution researchers (see reviews by Pepitone, 1975, and Perlman, in press) and public-opinion survey researchers (Erskine, 1974; Hindelang, 1974) have studied people's beliefs about the causes of crime, they have not related these attributions to people's behaviors in dealing with the threat of crime victimization.

Social psychologists (Langer, 1975; Lefcourt, 1973; Wortman, 1976; Wortman and Brehm, 1975) suggest that personal theories about the causes of events reflect a desire to see the world as predictable and controllable. When seemingly innocent persons get hurt, onlookers try to find reasons for the accident—both to make it appear predictable and to reassure themselves that such unforseen events will not happen to them (Lerner, 1970; Lerner and Simmons, 1966; Walster, 1966). Even when faced with evidence that some events are truly random, people look for patterns and reasons, as though looking for an illusion of control (Langer, 1975; Lefcourt, 1973; Wortman, 1976; Wortman and Brehm, 1975). We shall see how people's theories about the causes of crime and their efforts to prevent crimes relate to feelings of helplessness and control.

In the sections that follow, we examine both the personal theories expressed by people when they talk about crime and the personal theories expressed by their actions when they *do* something about crime. We also explore the feelings of control or helplessness that accompany these theories and acts. Finally, we shall see how social policy can be both a cause and a consequence of lay theories about crime.

The Criminal and the Victim: An Attributional Approach

Our approach to examining thoughts and actions about crime is different from that of laboratory attribution researchers. We worked with a team of researchers who went to the field to observe and interview people in a variety of settings. Sociologists are more acquainted with this research technique than psychologists, and they typically use it to generate rather than test hypotheses (Dean, Eichhorn, and Dean, 1967; Glaser and Strauss, 1967).

The field work was conducted in an anthropological style with participant observations and interviews conducted in a variety of settings. The researchers attended community crime-prevention programs, civic association meetings, and city block meetings. They recorded the discussions, much as a court stenographer would. They also talked with police officers, members of citizen's band radio clubs, merchants, civic leaders, housewives, children, and the ever-present "person-on-the-street." These observations and interviews were recorded in more than a dozen communities in three cities, which we shall simply refer to as *Westside, Eastside,* and *Midwestern.* To complement the qualitative data gathered in the field work, we also examined quantitative survey data gathered by other groups.

Experimental studies of personal theories about the causes of success and failure have developed and tested a model that identifies three dimensions of causal attributions: internal versus external, stable versus unstable, and intentional versus unintentional (Frieze and Weiner, 1971; Weiner and others, 1972). The same model has been applied to lay theories about the causes of specific crimes (see reviews by Pepitone, 1975, and Perlman, in press). Before discussing the model we derived from the field notes, we shall review some of the experimental studies of conditions that make victims and offenders seem responsible for their actions.

Experimental Studies of Offenders' and Victims' Causal Roles

Attributional studies of crime (such as Carroll and Payne, 1977b, and Jones and Aronson, 1973) have focused on which factors make victims and offenders seem accountable for their actions. Raters read descriptions of crimes that varied qualities of the victim or offender. Then, they judged how responsible the victim or offender was for the crime and what a suitable punishment should be. Rather than varying the qualities of victims and offenders together, these studies have generally varied qualities of one or the other (with the exception of Landy and Aronson, 1969, which did vary both).

Offenders who are morally unattractive, have a prior record, and seem mentally competent are held more responsible for their actions than offenders who do not have those characteristics (Landy and Aronson, 1969; Lussier, Perlman, and Breen, 1977; Pepitone, 1975). Offenders who intended to commit the crime and who did it for reasons that appear to be internal, stable qualities of the person are held more responsible for their actions than are offenders who did it unintentionally and for external reasons. When lay people, policemen, or parole officers regard offenders as responsible for their actions, they also recommend harsher penalties and expect offenders to be repeat offenders (Carroll and Payne, 1977b; Rosen and Jerdee, 1974; Shaw and Reitan, 1969).

Experimental studies of the victim's role in causing crime have dealt primarily with rape. Several variations in descriptions of a victim's background and appearance make her seem more or less guilty of having encouraged the crime. A woman who refuses to disclose her previous sexual experience seems more responsible than a woman who says she is a virgin; a divorcee seems more responsible than a married woman (Feldman-Summers and Lindner, 1976; Jones and Aronson, 1973). Physically unattractive rape victims seem more responsible than attractive ones (Seligman, Brickman, and Kowak, 1977), perhaps because we assume that the unattractive woman must have behaved seductively. If a woman has been raped previously, she is blamed more than if she was never raped before (Calhoun, Selby, and Warring, 1976). Although blaming the victim may seem to be adding insult to injury, there may be some kinds of blame that point to workable solutions (Gordon and Riger, 1978).

Janoff-Bulman (in press) distinguishes between two kinds of self-blame—behavioral and characterological blame. A rape victim who engages in behavioral self-blame tries to determine whether something she did or failed to do caused her to be raped. She may reason, for instance, "I should not have walked alone," "I should not have hitchhiked," or "I should have locked my windows, and then I would not have been raped." This line of reasoning is quite different from that which looks for a flaw in the woman's character. To say "I was so stupid, I deserved to be raped" or "I'm the kind of woman who attracts rapists" is to blame oneself in a nonremediable way. In a survey of rape-crisis centers, Janoff-Bulman (in press) found that self-blame was quite common (74 percent of the reports included self-blame). Of the two varieties, behavioral blame was more common than characterological blame; fewer than one-fifth of the women reported characterological self-blame. Janoff-Bulman concludes that characterological self-blame is maladaptive but that behavioral self-blame is an adaptive strategy, whereby women look for ways to avoid being raped again.

Rape-prevention programs focus on such behavioral factors. If both men and women believe that rape victims are responsible for their misfortune by virtue of their appearance, their ignorance, their carelessness, or their unwillingness to defend themselves, then they should presumably try to change some or all these behaviors. Many rape-prevention efforts (Goldstein, 1976; Walker and Brodsky, 1976) teach women how and where to walk, what to carry, and how and when to fight to reduce their chances of being raped.

These experimental studies have the advantage of being able to manipulate a limited number of variables at a time. They show that certain variables have effects on people's perceptions of offenders' and victims' responsibility, when other variables are held constant. The field work that we report in the remainder of this chapter does the opposite. It holds no factors constant but shows instead what causal attributions arise in naturally occurring conversations, community meetings, and crime-prevention programs. This method is more sensitive to lay concerns and preoccupations. Rather than ask respondents to choose from a set of multiple-choice categories, the researchers asked the respondents to talk about crime and neighborhood problems in their own terms. As a result, we developed a model of people's personal theories about the causes of crime that differs from the existing experimental models.

Personal Theories About the Causes of Crime

In this section, we shall examine people's beliefs about the causes of crime as a social event. We shall see where people focus their attention and efforts when they talk about crime and when they decide to do something about crime, and we shall look at factors that influence their choice. We shall also introduce some ways of looking at personal theories about the causes of crime and we shall discuss our model, which was inductively derived from field notes.

A large team of researchers collected and wrote the field notes. They attended crime-prevention meetings and interviewed community organizers, community leaders, merchants, and residents in a dozen communities in three cities. After reading the field notes, we extracted portions that referred to several themes we had discerned. The themes dealt with what people felt were the causes of crime, what they felt were the solutions, and how much control they felt they had over crime in their city or neighborhood. The model or scheme that we developed to organize these themes differs from the model used in the experimental studies we have described. It does not make use of the internal-external or stable-unstable dimensions used in much attribution research. Instead, it develops some new dimensions. We do not know whether this is a scheme that laymen use when they talk about or act on crime. The model is useful, however, in organizing what people say and do about crime. The categories represent our way of coding the attributions that appear in people's statements and actions. Whether they also represent a schemata that laymen possess and recognize still remains to be tested. A recent dissertation (Cohn, 1978) supports our inductive analysis.

Attributional categories derived from the field notes seemed best defined by two dimensions. The first is the victim-offender dimension. With the exception of so-called victimless crimes, we can characterize crime as a social event requiring at least two persons—the victim and the offender. In talking about the causes and prevention of crime, people may focus on the role of the victim or the role of the offender. In reality, it may not always be clear who was the victim and who was the offender. As with two children fighting, we may not always know "who started it" and who was innocent. Studies of dispute settlement show that negotiating blame and deciding who was guilty is not always straightforward or based on fact (Gulliver, 1973; Kidder, 1973). Since we are concerned not with facts, however, but with what people *think* the facts are, we can classify their statements as statements about victims or offenders.

The following examples of conversations in the field notes locate the causes of crime in the victim's chain. They suggest that the victim is at fault:

> In a bar, she's asking for it. People are careless, I don't mean to dwell on this sex, but take rape. Girls are asking for it. If you conduct yourself in the right way, you wouldn't be victimized.

> They [victims] don't use discretion in the manner of associations with other people. They get lost in talk. They walk along aimlessly. Criminals are not dummies. They pick on stupid people.

> I think they [victims] are careless as a rule. They leave their lights on. They don't lock their doors.

> It is an unfortunate fact of life that senior citizens are an easy target.

Other people, in talking about the causes of crime, focus on the offender's chain:

> I think it's those drugs that are causing all this . . . That's how I feel about drugs and drinking, you just don't know what they might make a person do.

> You do see more and more younger people getting into stealing, purse snatching, and mugging. It's because they don't have any recreation that they can afford. . . . I mean, they just have lots of time on their hands. Nothing to do.

The projects are the cause of most of our problems. . . . I'm scared.

Clearly, people do speak about both the victim's and the
offender's role in bringing about crime. What is of interest to us,
however, is where people focus their attention, both when they talk
about the causes of crime as a social problem and when they engage
in crime-prevention activity. They may work either on the causes of
offenders' behavior, the causes of victims' availability, or both. Frequently, both of these tactics are referred to as *crime-prevention measures.* We shall distinguish between actions that lessen the likelihood
that someone will become an offender and actions that lessen the
likelihood that someone will become a victim. We call the former
crime prevention and the latter *victimization prevention* (DuBow,
McCabe, and Kaplan, 1977; McCabe and Kaplan, 1976).

To laymen and professionals alike, the distinction between
crime prevention and victimization prevention may not be clear.
No federal programs or community-based programs carry the label
victimization-prevention programs. They are all called *crime-prevention
programs,* even if they focus on home security and keeping people
safe rather than eliminating the presumed causes of crime. Some
people argue that, if we made all neighborhoods and commercial
areas safe from crime, there would be no more crime—none could
be committed. The Kansas City Patrol experiment (Kelling and
others, 1974) demonstrated, however, that doubling the numbers
of police patrols does not reduce crime rates, because police cannot
maintain surveillance in all the homes and back alleys of the city at
all times. Also, community crime-prevention workers acknowledge
that making one neighborhood safe may simply result in displacing
crime to another locale. It is possible to reduce victimization of
some people and some places without reducing the overall level of
crime. We, therefore, find it meaningful to distinguish between
crime prevention and victimization prevention on both practical
and theoretical grounds.

The second dimension of personal theories about crime distinguishes between distal and proximal factors that lead someone
to become either a victim or an offender. This dimension includes
several overlapping factors that could be isolated in further ex-

perimental work but will be combined in our model, since we lack evidence about their separate functioning. Distal factors are those that are farther removed from the crime in one of several ways. They may be farther removed in time: A history of childhood neglect may seem to predispose people to become criminals, but the neglect is something that took place long before the crime. Distal factors may also be farther removed in a presumed chain of social conditions: Bank lending policies that prevent people in some neighborhoods from getting mortgages or home improvement loans may be causes of neighborhood decline, which in turn may lead to abandoned housing, which may lead to drug addicts congregating in abandoned houses, which may lead to a high incidence of muggings.

Proximal causes are close to the event, either in time or space. Inadequate locks, insufficient police patrols, and careless behavior on the part of a victim are all causes that we call *proximal,* because they appear to be close to the occurrence of a crime, much like the last line of defense. Cohn's (1978) research found that laymen shared our coding scheme and located these factors close to the occurrence of crime.

By saying that some causes may be classified as distal and some as proximal, we are not commenting on the presumed strength of the causes. In some people's theories, distal causes may be viewed as powerful root causes of crime. In others, they may seem like remotely connected factors whose influence is weak by the time a crime occurs. We are proposing simply that some causes may seem closer to the event than others.

In an experimental study of the relative impact of prior and immediate causes, Brickman, Ryan, and Wortman (1975, p. 1060) argue that "most accidents stem not from a single cause but from a combination of causal factors. Causes, in turn, also have causes. Furthermore, the prior causes may or may not be of the same type as the immediate cause. If the immediate cause is perceived as a situational force, it may have been brought into play by a prior personal decision, which may in turn have been made under even earlier situational pressures, and so forth. For example, an accident may be caused by steering failure, which is in turn caused by the driver's failure to have the car inspected . . . because he was erroneously led to believe that the previous owner had recently done so."

This describes a causal chain for a single person. The distal and proximal causes we found in the field work are statements not about single persons but about conditions that make it possible or probable that crime will occur. In both instances, we can raise the question, how far back in time or space do people go when they talk about the causes and prevention of an event? And what are some of the factors that lead them to focus on proximal or distal causes?

The classification of causes as either proximal or distal in the remainder of this chapter again reflects our own coding. Careless behavior on the part of a victim, such as walking alone at night, we code as a proximal or precipitating cause, and living in an area that "breeds crime" we call a distal cause. When people talk about offenders, we code their complaints that courts put criminals right back on the streets as an immediate or proximal cause and their talk of unemployment as a prior or distal cause of crime. Whether these are or are not in fact causes of crime is not at issue here; instead, we are concerned with whether people talk about them as causes and which presumed cause they focus on when they engage in crime prevention.

Table 1 gives examples of causal attributions that describe proximal and distal factors in the victim's or offender's chain. The examples show that, when people talk about crime as a social problem, they do acknowledge the roles of both victims and offenders and immediate (or proximal) and prior (or distal) conditions. Within either the victim's or the offender's causal chain, we can also find stable and unstable causes (Weiner and others, 1972). The elderly seem to be easy targets by virtue of their age, and not much can be done to change that. Age is a stable feature that cannot be tampered with. However, some people seem to be victimized by their carelessness, a presumably unstable cause that can be reversed by learning to take greater care. Unstable causes are ones that we have some hope of changing or controlling, and they are the causes we would expect people to focus their actions on. Such unstable or controllable causes appear in both the victim's and offender's chains and in both distal and proximal categories.

Although laymen's theories about the causes of crime do

Table 1. Examples of Proximal and Distal Causes of Crime for Victims and Offenders

	Victims	Offenders
Proximal Causes	"You come in dressed up and looking affluent, and you become a target."	[Why do kids snatch purses?] "To buy their booze and drugs. . . . Actually, I think the booze is more than drugs . . ."
	"It's an unfortunate fact of life that senior citizens are an easy target."	[One cause of crime is that] "the judge lets 'em off too easy."
	"I think they (victims) are careless as a rule. They leave their lights on. They don't lock the doors."	"The problem was not that the community wasn't organized against crime but that the court system put convicted criminals back on the street."
Distal Causes	"This area breeds crime. And it's very hard to organize, because the population is so transient."	"young adults . . . bumming around because they don't have jobs."
	"As soon as I'm able, I want to live in the country. . . . This isn't the kind of place now that I'd like to raise a family."	[One cause of crime is that] "parents don't care enough. . . ."
	"The most important facet of crime prevention is neighborhood awareness. Unfortunately, people don't want to get involved if a crime happens . . ."	[The structure of society causes crime] "It should go more socialistic"
		"I'd say the main reasons for our problems are (1) the projects . . . (2) the lack of employment and (3) welfare."
		"Sociologists say that's the root of crime any-way . . . deteriorated housing and lack of jobs."

cover the entire spectrum that we have identified in our model, we wish to know where they focus their attention. What seem to be the predominant causes? Erskine (1974) summarizes some of the causes of crime that national survey respondents emphasize. Erskine reports that unrest, polarization, student protest, moral decay, drugs, and youth problems are seen as the major causes of crime. Hindelang (1974) cites surveys that focus on the following causes: lenient laws or gentle penalties, drugs or drug addiction, lack of parental supervision, and poverty or unemployment.

More recent surveys (Kennedy and others, 1973; Market Opinion Research Company, 1975) conducted in Michigan and Oregon find similar causes of crime mentioned: unemployment and poverty, drugs and alcohol, insufficient law enforcement, lack of activities for youth, and lack of parental supervision. In our research, the field workers in Eastside City administered structured interviews to 151 respondents in seven communities. The sample included men and women and black and white respondents.

When we compare these surveys, we find a high degree of agreement, although the order of the causes may vary (see Table 2). The causes are all factors that fall in the offender's chain and include more social conditions than personality dispositions. For instance, although laziness, lack of religion, mental disorder, kicks, lack of moral standards, and attitude toward the government were included in the survey lists, these were not endorsed as causes of crime, nor were they mentioned frequently in the free responses obtained in the field work interviews. Drug use and drinking came closest to being personal dispositions or habits, and, in our model, we regard these as proximal causes in the offender's chain. Insufficient law enforcement is also a proximal cause in our scheme, since it is a failure of the last line of defense. In some respects, it spans the distal-proximal continuum, however, because people may regard stricter laws and stricter enforcement as capable of creating an atmosphere of deterrence and not simply as a last line of defense. The economic situation, the lack of activities for kids, and the general designation *environment* are all distal in our scheme and all in the offender's chain. What is interesting about these surveys and interviews, therefore, is the absence of causes in the victim's chain. Apparently, when asked to speak about the causes of crime (which

Table 2. The Most Frequently Mentioned Causes of Crime in Field Work Interviews and Two Sample Surveys

	Michigan Survey	Oregon Survey	Field Work Interviews
First mention	Drugs/dope	Poverty	Economic situation; poverty, unemployment
Second mention	Kids; lack of activities and parental guidance	Environment	Drinking/drugs
Third mention	Unemployment; poverty	Alcohol	Kids; lack of activities, parental neglect
Fourth mention	Insufficient law enforcement; need for stricter laws	Insufficient law and order	Insufficient law enforcement

we define as the conjunction of the offender's and victim's causal chain), the respondents focus on the offender's causal chain. If we take the alleged causes of crime seriously, they prescribe the appropriate solutions for crime. Straightforward logic would dictate that people direct their efforts to reduce unemployment and poverty, provide more activities for children, enforce drug laws (or legalize drugs) and improve law enforcement generally. Cohn (1978) found both causes and solutions aimed at crime prevention were rated as more important than those aimed at victimization prevention.

It is important to distinguish, however, between what people think the solution *should be* and what people *actually do*. We have evidence from our field work data that, when people act as individuals or as participants in crime-prevention programs, they focus most of their actions on the causal chain for victims to reduce the likelihood that they will become victims themselves. They also say victimization prevention is easier to accomplish than crime prevention (Cohn, 1978).

Crime-Prevention Actions

To understand the relationship between people's theories about the causes of crime and their responses to crime, we must first examine the range of responses people are instructed and encouraged to perform. With the exception of ducking to avoid a swinging fist or running when being pursued, there are no natural responses to the threat of crime. They are all taught, acquired, and socially constructed (Berger and Luckmann, 1966).

To facilitate our discussion of crime-prevention efforts, we will describe a variety of activities and classify them according to our typology of causes. A thorough review of the literature on reactions to crime (DuBow, McCabe, and Kaplan, 1977; McCabe and Kaplan, 1976) provides fuller descriptions of the variety of responses to crime.

- *Avoidance:* staying indoors and away from seemingly dangerous areas.
- *Escort services:* citizens escorting children and elderly people.

- *Personal property protection:* purchasing or using locks, dogs, guns, burglar alarms, house lights, engraving tools.
- *Crime reporting:* calling the police about crimes in progress or the appearance of suspicious people or activities.
- *Citizen patrols:* patrolling of neighborhoods, usually at night, by area residents, with or without citizen's band radios.
- *Block organizing:* calling a meeting of residents in a small area to become acquainted, watch one another's homes, and organize some protective activities, such as use of loud whistles or horns.
- *Police-community relations programs:* acquainting residents with their police department.
- *Street lighting programs:* improving street lighting.
- *Victim-witness assistance:* instructing and encouraging witnesses or victims to process their cases through the courts.
- *Youth services:* providing summer jobs and recreation for young people.

This is a partial description of a longer list with many variations on these themes. The list suffices, however, to demonstrate an important point. With the exception of youth services, none of the programs addresses distal causes in the offender's chain—the causes that survey respondents identify as the major causes of crime. We have categorized the list of programs in Table 3 using the same dimensions we used to categorize people's statements about the causes of crime.

Table 3 shows the lopsided emphasis on victimization prevention and reveals the paradox: when people *talk* about the *causes* of crime, they talk about social conditions and distal causes in the offender's chain, but, when they decide to *do* something about crime, they engage in victimization prevention. McCabe and Kaplan (1976, p. 54) comment on the shift from crime prevention to victimization prevention and speculate about the reasons: "During the 1960s, the issue of crime was often discussed as a symptom of some larger social problem, such as poverty, inequality, or racial injustice. It was these broader social problems which captured political interest and program funding. It was felt that such problems contained the determination of crime and that programs should be directed at the solution of the more fundamental problems. More

Table 3. Proximal and Distal Responses to
Crime Directed at Victims and Offenders

	Victims	Offenders
Proximal Responses	*Individual Protection* Avoidance	*Reliance on Police and Courts* Crime reporting
		Police-community relations
	Property protection	Victim-witness assistance
Distal Responses	*Neighborhood Improvement* Escort services	*Social Programs* Youth services
	Citizen patrols	
	Organizing	
	Street lights	

recently, concern about crime has become manifest in a more direct manner, with emphasis shifting from concern about the perceived determinates and their effect on offenders to the consequences of crime for victims and society. Emphasis shifted from curing poverty or social injustice to preventing victimization."

These authors dramatize this shift in focus by reporting the budget allocation for the Law Enforcement Assistance Administration, an agency that sponsors many victimization-prevention programs. In 1969, the appropriation was $63 million, and in 1976 it was $810 million (McCabe and Kaplan, 1976, p. 54). Although they are called *crime-prevention programs,* many of the activities funded by the Law Enforcement Assistance Administration focus on the conditions that lie in the victim's causal chain. They instruct people to organize neighborhood patrols, to install better locks, to mark their valuables, and generally to protect their own persons, property, and neighbors.

The individual protective measures are surely the easiest to carry out. They take little time, money, or coordinated effort. Yet, as the following section of our chapter demonstrates, many of the actions taken to reduce victimization do not produce a sense of efficacy or optimism, primarily because they do nothing to reduce the likelihood of people becoming offenders. Victimization prevention may succeed in altering one's chances of becoming a victim, but it does nothing to change the acknowledged dangerousness of the environment.

We can illustrate this point by analogy with a caged animal. Suppose we place a rat in a shuttle box that has a shock grid with a few safe corners plus a lever that will terminate shock. If the rat learns to escape shock by pressing the lever, running to a safe corner, or staying in the safe corners forever, it has learned victimization prevention. Were we to interview the rat about the causes and prevention of shock, we would expect to hear a theory about the existence of dangerous places and the utility of pressing levers and staying in safe corners (see Campbell, 1966). We would also expect the rat to rate the environment in the cage as a whole as dangerous, since he can do nothing about the fact that his cage is wired to a shock apparatus, except remain vigilant. Alternatively, if the rat could learn to negotiate with the experimenter to disconnect the grid and eliminate the conditions that produce shock in the first place, its behavior would reflect a different theory about the causes and prevention of shock. The theory would focus not on the location of safe and dangerous places but on the external causes of shock. We would also expect to find the animal in a different psychological state—feeling efficacious instead of helpless, and not eternally vigilant.

Feelings Accompanying Various Solutions

In many respects, people who seek security with locks, dogs, guns, or freon horns act like the rats in our example. Victimization prevention is analogous to escape and avoidance learning in psychology laboratories (Hiroto, 1974; Hiroto and Seligman, 1975; Richter, 1957; Seligman, 1975; Seligman and Maier, 1967). Rats caught in such situations are in no position to disconnect the shock grid, argue with the experimenter, protest against aversive conditions, or tear down the walls of the Skinner box. The subjects in most escape and avoidance learning experiments have limited options. If some crime-prevention efforts promote vigilance and limit the options to escape or avoid crime, they may not reduce fear but simply remind the actors of the danger that lurks outside when they leave their safe corners. DuBow (1978) speaks of this as a "fortress mentality" and contrasts it with the more active and possibly less fearful stance that accompanies some community organizing activities and collective crime-prevention efforts.

Whereas both human and animal subjects in experimental studies of learned helplessness actually give up trying and eventually do nothing, people rarely do nothing about crime. They at least lock their doors, stay in at night, and avoid strangers (Biderman, 1967; Ennis, 1967). Although people may gain some sense of control over a limited portion of their environment or their fate by taking such action, they may also experience little sense of control over the larger environment, which remains untouched. In the following sections, we examine the sense of control or helplessness that accompanies the various types of crime-prevention efforts.

Reliance on the Police and Courts. Several studies suggest that fear of crime and a feeling that the police are ineffective are significantly related. Kim (1976) found that people who say that reporting incidents to the police is a waste of time, the police do not respond quickly, and they do not try to do their best also exhibit significantly higher levels of fear of crime than do those who express more faith in the police. O'Neill (1977) found similar patterns and in addition suggests that people who view the police as ineffective are less likely to report incidents to the police. Such little faith in the ability of the police to control crime may in fact not be so irrational, for Ennis (1967) reports that only about 2 percent of victimizations result in successful prosecution, and Skogan (1977) finds that citizen perceptions that "nothing can be done" about various types of crimes are in line with actual FBI clearance rates for those crimes. If we use these outcome measures as estimates of what in fact can be accomplished by reporting crimes to the police, the lack of faith in police may not be so irrational. This perceived ineffectiveness of the official agents of control contributes to laymen's sense of helplessness with regard to crime, as seen in the following comments:

> [Question: Is there anything that could stop that kind of thing from happening again?] "No, I don't see what. . . . A while back, on our block, we were getting a whole lot of burglaries. The houses were being hit two,

three times. . . . The police arrested him one time, but he
was out right away again. You can't really get them unless
you catch them in the act."

"We've caught a couple of them (kids), but nothing
ever happens."

[So the cops don't do much around here?] "No, we
take care of them [offenders]. The cops lock guys up and
they're out the next day. People deal drugs on every corner,
and the cops don't do nothing."

Sometimes, the reluctance to call the police results from a
fear of retaliation or simply of becoming involved:

"I had my window busted with a BB gun." [Ques-
tion: What did you do?] "We even saw who did it. What
could we do? These days, we're scared to do anything . . . and even if we're not scared . . . it don't do no
good to do nothin' anyway."

"People are afraid to call the police."

Frustration is also expressed about the leniency of judges
after offenders are convicted.

"The judges let 'em off too easy. . . . There aren't
enough facilities for kids who break the law, so they let 'em
go."

"Makes you feel like you're not safe anywhere. Especially, when somebody you know should be locked up is
out. . . . The law is more for the criminal now. There are all
these loopholes that people can be let out on."

Ironically, there is a prevailing belief that insufficient law
enforcement is a cause of crime, but adding more police does not
always appear to be an effective solution, because "the cops lock
guys up and they're out the next day" or "more police won't do
nothing." These beliefs are not mutually exclusive; complaints
about insufficient law enforcement may refer not only to the police.
There may be weak links at any point in that system. If more police
apprehend more offenders, but judges let them off easy, the
police's efforts appear ineffective. To prevent crime by improving

law enforcement would require a foolproof system of apprehension, conviction, sentencing, and either imprisonment or rehabilitation. Loopholes anywhere in the system may make people feel "you're not safe anywhere," if they attempt to rely on that system as a last line of defense.

Individual Protection Measures. Strictly individualized protective measures, such as using special locks, guns, or dogs or marking valuable possessions, are efforts directed at the proximal causes of victimization. Such fortifications make only one person or household safe. We have evidence from both our field work and survey data that individualized protective measures are associated with fear and feelings of helplessness. Respondents in a survey conducted in Hartford in 1973 and 1974 (Fowler and Mangione, 1974) were asked whether they took any of a variety of personal precautions, including not walking out at night, using special locks, and engraving their valuables. Those who said they did none of these things were the least fearful, those who took such precautions were next less fearful, and those who took two, three, or four precautionary actions were most fearful (Kim, 1976). We cannot conclude that taking these precautions made people feel afraid; it is equally plausible that they felt afraid and therefore tried to protect themselves. The surveys do not give evidence that people felt less afraid after they engraved their valuables or bought locks or alarms, however. It is plausible that these defensive measures made crime more salient in their lives and constituted daily reminders that danger lurks outside.

The field work provides similar evidence. The following comes from a woman whose solution was to lock herself in as soon as she got home:

> My neighborhood's not safe, but I have to put up with it. My husband comes to pick me up after work. We go shopping . . . when I get home, I close the door and don't go out no more. [Question: Is there much difference in the day?] At least I can see who I'm dealing with. I been here thirty-three years, so I know the characters around here. I know who's doing the numbers. I recognize stolen articles on the block. I'm aware of the drug traffic. But I don't say

anything. I'm afraid to. I don't want my house all painted
up. If a guy doesn't come back on you, he'll get a friend to
do something. People know what's going on, but they don't
want to say.

There is further evidence that individual protective measures do not appear to solve the problem. Victims of home
burglaries said they became more cautious after the break-in, but
they actually did not use locks or take protective measures more
than nonvictims did (Miransky and Langer, 1978; Scarr and others,
1973). Perhaps, they reasoned that locks had not safeguarded them
in the first instance, and they had little hope that they would in the
future.

In contrast to the sense of helplessness that seems to characterize the descriptions of individual efforts to prevent victimization,
there is a sense of optimism and newly discovered efficacy that
accompanies the description of collective efforts to reduce victimization. We propose that this is so, because the collective efforts
seem to operate on the distal factors, making a locality safer.

Neighborhood Improvement Measures. Reliance on one's
neighbors takes many forms, ranging from formalized citizen patrols to the use of piercing whistles or horns to informal street and
house watching (Reed, 1979). Regardless of the actual crime-
prevention value of the efforts mentioned previously, we have
numerous testimonials about the good psychological value of programs sponsoring whistles and horns.

> "Before, I was concerned, but I didn't know what to
> do. Now I react to screams if I hear them . . . [because I
> have a whistle]. In the past, it would have just been apathy.
> It's not that people were unfeeling but a feeling of being
> inadequate."

In addition to enhancing a sense of personal efficacy, such
programs engender the feeling that the official agents of control
may become more reliable, too.

> "I like [this whistle program]. . . . It has good
> psychological value. The police where it is in effect have

> been very pleased with it and respond even faster than they would for a woman just calling 'help.'"

> "It [the whistle program] is effective, because the police know that the neighborhood is involved, and they'll react more quickly if they know they'll have support from the people."

Survey data again support the field work. Respondents in Hartford who described their neighbors as concerned about others, as willing to help the police, and as willing to watch neighboring homes were significantly less fearful than those who regarded their neighbors as unreliable in these matters (Kim, 1976). These data, and those reported by Cohn (1978) and Cohn, Kidder, and Harvey (1979) show that strictly individualized protective measures do not make people feel less fearful or more in control of crime. People who engage in actions that are collective and involve neighborly reliance and participation report feeling less afraid and more in control of their neighborhoods.

The real effectiveness of such citizen-alert techniques in reducing crime or victimization is unclear (Maltz, 1972; Weidman and others, 1975). For this reason, the leaders and participants in such programs often claim other forms of success and emphasize the psychological benefits derived from providing a means for responding and rekindling a sense of community (Knopf, 1970; Nash, 1968). In lieu of reporting actuarial data, the participants in such programs tell "success stories." These stories sometimes appear in local newspapers and are retold many times by the organizers and favorably impressed participants. The following story was told independently by two women and reported in the local newspaper of a community in Midwestown:

> A young girl with a knife tried to attack someone and steal the victim's groceries. The victim blew a whistle, and whistles started blowing all over the neighborhood. A passerby threw a book at the attacker and knocked her down. The police arrived before she could escape.

One of the most important features of such collective activities is their visibility. If one whistle blows, and fifty others start, these are signs that something will happen if a person acts. These programs do what Seligman (1975) recommends to ward off feelings of helplessness; they let people feel effective, if not in reducing crime, at least in producing a response in neighbors and police. By involving more than one person, they also act on what we have called *distal causes of victimization*—they make a locality or neighborhood seem safer, because the neighbors are involved in collective action (DuBow, McCabe, and Kaplan, 1977). Cohn (1978) compared the levels of fear and sense of control reported by two groups of residents in one urban community. The people who engaged in individualized protective measures (who avoided dangerous areas, relied on locks and alarms, and stayed home at night) reported feeling more fearful and less in control of their environment than did people who belonged to a community organization that tried to make an area safer.

Strictly individualized measures, which make one home secure but leave the locality and the larger world full of danger, seem to do little to promote a sense of security. They operate at the most proximal level, at the doorstep of the potential victim, and, if they fail, their possessor can fall prey to all that lurks outside. There are no guarantees that any locks, burglar alarms, dogs, or other measures will work. Each one is presumed to lower the probabilities that their possessor will become a victim, but none offers certainty. Moreover, by locking themselves behind closed doors and seldom venturing into the streets, people are in effect imprisoning themselves. There are some protests to this effect in the field work:

> I'm not going to be made a prisoner in my own house!

> I don't like people putting restrictions on me. I have a friend who . . . tells me I am going to get murdered one of these days. Well, that kind of pessimism I can do without . . . I don't like putting limits on my life.

Both our field work data and survey data indicate that efforts to work on the proximal causes of victimization are associated with fear rather than perceived efficacy. Efforts directed at distal causes of victimization, such as making a locality safer, at least have good psychological value, even if crime statistics or other data do not demonstrate their success. What about efforts directed at the distal causes of crime, such as poverty and unemployment? These are causes that survey respondents acknowledge are important but that crime-prevention programs ignore.

Social-Change Measures. Youth services and summer programs are among the few crime-prevention programs that address the social conditions we have labeled *distal causes* in the offender's chain. There are admittedly many social programs designed to reduce poverty and unemployment, but these are no longer portrayed as crime-prevention programs, as they were in the 1960s, perhaps because the hopes of affecting crime rates through job training or preschool Head Start programs have dimmed. The connection between such programs and crime rates seems less immediate than the connection between burglar alarms or police patrols and crime.

Social programs designed to change the distal causes of crime are also much more difficult to implement (Pressman and Wildavsky, 1973) than are programs to distribute whistles or organize citizen patrols. The community organizations and federal programs that work for social change show far fewer successes than the victimization programs. We also know that they have taken on difficult tasks: They have worked to change the policies of banks to provide loans to neighborhoods previously denied money; they have petitioned city agencies to enforce building codes and require landlords to repair buildings that contribute to a neighborhood's deterioration; they have tried to hasten the removal or sale of abandoned buildings, which may become centers of drug dealing. Such action-oriented programs settle for far fewer success stories. Both local efforts and federally sponsored programs to create a "Great Society" have encountered problems in implementation when they tried to accomplish significant social change.

Few crime-prevention programs studied in our field work included such social action as a major part of their crime-related agenda. Cohn's research (1978) did evaluate one such community-action program, however, and found the participants reported feeling less fear and greater control than nonparticipants. We also have evidence from the field work that people respond with fear to signs of poverty and community deterioration, such as abandoned housing (Baumer, 1977; DuBow, 1978; Hunter, 1977). They also think that places where young people congregate are dangerous (Kidder, 1977). This means that programs that succeed in removing abandoned housing and providing work or other activities for otherwise idle men and young people ought to give a sense of safety. Whether such programs would really reduce crime and whether they can be implemented are separate issues. According to laymen's theories about the causes of crime, however, these are the solutions.

Conclusions and Implications

Our observation that people talk about one set of factors as the causes of crime and act on another set when they choose to do something about crime is in accord with an observation made by Furstenberg (1971, 1972), when he analyzed national surveys. Furstenberg reports a discrepancy between people's concerns with crime as a *social problem* and their fears or perceptions of their *own risk*. He found that people living in areas with relatively low crime rates report a high concern with crime as a social problem but a low fear of personal victimization. People living in areas with high crime rates, however, report a low concern with crime as a social problem and a high fear of personal victimization. It may be that, when people talk about crime as a social problem, they attribute it to social conditions, such as poverty, unemployment, neglect of children, and other social factors that appear to be linked with high crime rates. However, when they choose to do something in response to their own *fears,* they act to reduce their personal risk of victimization. Consequently, their actions to prevent crime do not fit with their identification of the causes they attribute to crime.

We have argued that people *talk* about one thing and *do* something else. They talk about social conditions that cause crime, such as unemployment, poverty, drug addiction, and neglect of children; but, when they engage in crime-prevention efforts, they work closer to home and try to protect their own bodies, homes, or neighborhoods by staying in at night, installing locks, or joining neighborhood patrols. Conklin (1975) speaks of these actions as "avoidance" measures and "hardening the target." We have called them *victimization-prevention* instead of crime-prevention measures

(DuBow, McCabe, and Kaplan, 1977; McCabe and Kaplan, 1976). It is as though they operate with two sets of theories—one about the causes of crime and another about the prevention of victimization. Perhaps crime is not unique in this respect. If we looked at people's theories about the causes of mental illness, we might find they identify one set of conditions as causes but operate on another set when they look for solutions. The existence of social programs and institutions for handling such problems as mental illness, juvenile delinquency, and crime may shape people's responses to these problems by offering a more immediate solution that bears little relationship to the laymen's analysis of the causes. Andrew Gordon and his colleagues (1974, 1976) argue that some social service institutions often serve their own interests more than those of their clients. Programs for "problem children," for instance, locate the problem within the child and thereby create a large body of clients who need the agency's help. If the agency's diagnosis included other causes, such as the housing and employment conditions of the child's family, it would open another avenue of action, but one that the agency is not equipped to handle.

Crime prevention seems to operate the same way. The existing programs and prevailing beliefs concerning crime prevention focus on the more immediate factors within the potential victim's control. These efforts may seem more practical, because they are easier to implement. They do not, however, appear to promote a feeling that the world is now safer or that crime rates have been reduced, for they were not directed toward the conditions that people say cause crime. Nonetheless, in their search for a sense of control, people appear to be ready to accept what is offered—solutions that promise to reduce their risks of becoming victims.

The most striking feature of the variety of crime-prevention activities is that, with the exception of summer employment and recreation programs for young people, none of the programs or actions addresses the social conditions that people name as the primary causes of crime. Social programs do exist to reduce unemployment, to revive declining neighborhoods, and to redress the social conditions that constitute distal factors in the offender's chain, but these actions are not done in the name of crime prevention. Instead, people talk about these as the causes of crime, but they switch their emphasis when they *do* something about crime. According to some community organizers, most crime-prevention programs avoid the basic causes of crime, the problems with youth and unemployment, education, and so on. Why?

Both individual responses and crime-prevention programs may be guided by considerations of efficacy—not in actually reducing crime but in showing some measurable results. Without signs of success or efficacy, people give up trying; their efforts become extinguished, and they conclude they are helpless (Seligman, 1975; Wortman and Brehm, 1975). In addition to making individuals feel frustrated or helpless, failure to produce the desired effects actually threatens the survival of programs whose funds were granted on the basis of a promise of success. Therefore, program administrators often use measures that make their programs look successful (Cochran, Gordon, and Campbell, 1977). The collective wisdom among community organizers who have worked in the area of crime prevention and victimization prevention is that crime is not a good organizing issue, because it's a difficult issue on which to show obvious results. Consequently, program administrators often measure the number of blocks organized, numbers of horns or whistles distributed, numbers of engraving tools used to mark valuables, or numbers of Operation ID stickers passed out. These statistics are easy to collect and report. They also provide impressive numbers.

By contrast, the community-organization programs that focus on the distal part of the offender's chain report far fewer successes. These programs try to effect changes in unemployment rates, abandoned housing, or the delivery of city services. They regard themselves fortunate to complete two such actions in six months.

We can compare these two different approaches to two sports. The whistle-selling, valuables-marking approach produces scores, like a basketball game, with large numbers of successes. One organizer reported that approximately 100 blocks in his area were organized after six months of hard work. Another reported he was ordering freon horns in large quantities, because he felt he could distribute them easily. The action-oriented approach, on the other hand, produces low scores, like a hockey game, because a good action takes a long time to organize. It is not coincidental that action-oriented programs are often funded by charitable groups, community support, and local parishes. The high-scoring programs that promote devices for victimization prevention, however, are often funded by distant agencies, where funding decisions are made on the basis of easily tabulated and multiple successes.

Our attributional analysis of crime-prevention efforts raises several issues that have implications for social policy and social action. Were we to evaluate crime-prevention programs, we could assess them from several perspectives. We could ask the obvious question: Do they effectively prevent crimes from occurring to those persons or groups who participate in the programs or efforts? In addition, we could ask: Do they raise or lower the participants' fear of crime? If we found that the programs reduced victimization but increased fear, we would have to weigh the relative gains and losses in some formula that compared the quantity and quality of life that such programs produce. Some of our respondents in the field and other writers concerned with the quality of life have said that some acts of prevention may not be worth the sense of imprisonment they create (DuBow, 1978). Finally, we can ask: What is the theory of crime and victimization that any one crime-prevention program promotes? Is it a theory that locates the causes of crime in personal behaviors or in social conditions, in the loss of control by criminal justice agents or in the loss of community? We have argued that crime-prevention efforts do imply causal analysis, and they purport to identify critical links in a causal network—links that are practical points of entry. We think it important to ask what happens not only to victimization rates but also to community life and social attitudes when people adopt a crime-prevention measure and its theory. Some collective crime-prevention efforts reportedly rekindle a sense of community and promote greater trust, at least in the circle of people who cooperate to protect one another. Others may do the opposite. Studying successful crime-prevention programs in particular communities may be the next step in bridging the gap between people's perceptions of the causes of crime and their actions to prevent victimization.

Biases and Jury Decision Making

In our system of justice, a trial by jury represents the most comprehensive and formal means available for judging a matter in dispute. In addition to the already elaborate rules of evidence and procedure common in court trials, jury trials involve the complexity of selecting an impartial jury, providing jurors with instructions regarding the law, and conducting jury deliberations. Jurors are asked to judge the past actions of a defendant in light of relevant legal standards and to arrive at a verdict of guilt or innocence. This decision is typically the result of many separate judgments on the part of jurors. Jurors may need to ask themselves first whether the defendant actually committed the alleged offense and second whether the defendant *intended* the offense to occur. In short, jurors must conclude that the defendant was legally responsible for the offense. Individuals have many common-sense techniques for making such judgments, and legal theorists have long been interested in the common person's theories of causation, intentionality, and responsibility. The recent research by social psychologists

on attributional mechanisms has added systematic empirical data to
the existing storehouse of intuitions regarding how people judge
the behavior and characteristics of others.

This chapter provides a review of research on the attributional processes of jurors and suggests policy modifications to help
reduce potential juror biases. In considering the issues in this chapter, the continuity between juror decision making and jugmental
processes in everyday life should be kept in mind. Juries resolve
disputes through a highly formal technique, but individuals engage
in less formal approaches throughout their lives.

Recent Legal Issues Regarding Juries

The Sixth Amendment to the Constitution guarantees the
right to a trial by an impartial jury. In 1968, the Supreme Court
extended the guarantee of jury trials to the state courts. Specifically, the Court held in *Duncan* v. *Louisiana* that the Fourteenth
Amendment guarantees a right to a jury trial in all criminal cases in
state courts, if a comparable case would receive a jury trial in the
federal courts. The Fourteenth Amendment provides, in part, that
no state shall "deprive any person of life, liberty, or property, without due process of law." Due process is interpreted in *Duncan* v.
Louisiana to include the provision of trial by an impartial jury included in the Sixth Amendment but earlier considered to only be
applicable to the federal government.

Court decisions have established that the jury need not have
a fixed structure or decision rule. In 1970, in *Williams* v. *Florida* the
Supreme Court held that a twelve-person jury panel is not a necessary ingredient of "trial by jury" and allowed Florida to continue its
practice of providing six-person juries in certain cases. Justice
White noted in the Court's opinion on this case that, although it was
important to have the option of interposing "the common-sense
judgment of a group of laymen" between the "accused and his
accuser," the particular number *twelve* was a "historical accident"
and that different and smaller numbers of jurors could serve the
same purpose of insulating the defendant from possible injustice.
In 1972, in *Apodaca* v. *Oregon*, the need for unanimous verdicts on

the part of juries was judged by the Supreme Court not to be required by the Constitution, and Oregon's procedure of requiring only ten of twelve jurors to agree was allowed to continue. Presumably, states could reduce the requirement for a verdict to a simple majority of the jurors.

Many Supreme Court cases have dealt with issues relating to juror biases. The mere existence of a possible bias is not sufficient for a potential juror to be considered constitutionally unacceptable. Justice Clark noted in 1961 in the *Irvin* v. *Dowd* decision that, "To hold that the mere existence of any preconceived notion as to the guilt or innocence of an accused without more is sufficient to rebut the presumption of a prospective juror's impartiality would be to establish an impossible standard. It is sufficient if the juror can lay aside his impression or opinion and render a verdict based upon the evidence present in court." The case of *Reynolds* v. *United States* resulted in the decision that it is the burden of the individual accusing a juror of partiality to demonstrate that the prejudice is "manifest." The court is aware of the difficulty in determining the threshold of unacceptability and has noted in *Irvin* v. *Dowd* that "for the ascertainment of this mental attitude of appropriate indifference, the Constitution lays down no particular tests, and procedure is not chained to any ancient and artificial formula." In *Irvin* v. *Dowd,* the court found that the jury in the case was not sufficiently impartial and concluded that a change of venue might have been appropriate. The court opinion notes that, of 430 prospective jurors interviewed during the *voir dire* (jury selection) procedure, almost 90 percent "examined on the point . . . entertained some opinion as to guilt—ranging in intensity from mere suspicion to absolute certainty." Eight of the jurors finally comprising the twelve-person jury stated during *voir dire* that they thought the defendant was guilty. These jurors indicated that they could overcome their bias to provide the defendant with an impartial trial, but, given the overall prejudice in the jury pool, the Supreme Court felt that such impartiality was likely to be impossible.

A recent case, *Ham* v. *South Carolina* (1973), shed further light on how the court views biases in juror judgment. In that case, a young, bearded, black civil-rights activist was found guilty of possession of marijuana and sentenced to eighteen months in prison. The defense attorney in the case had requested the judge to ask potential jurors during the *voir dire* procedure a number of questions, including whether the potential jurors were prejudiced on the basis of race or against people with beards. The judge in the case asked the jurors very general questions regarding the defendant, such as "Are you conscious of any bias or prejudice for or against him?" but did not pose specific questions regarding race or beards. The Supreme Court held that the judge should have asked the prospective jurors specifically about their racial biases and overturned the conviction. This ruling was in keeping with a previous Supreme Court decision *(Aldridge* v. *United States)* and numerous state court rulings, and it was also argued that the decision was supported by the aim of the Fourteenth Amendment, which in part was passed to prohibit the states "from invidiously discriminating on the basis of race" *(Ham* v. *South Carolina)*. The court did not agree that the jurors had to be examined regarding their prejudices regarding beards. Justice Rehnquist stated in the court's opinion, "While we cannot say that prejudice against people with beards might not have been harbored by one or more of the potential jurors in this case, this is the beginning and not the end of the inquiry as to whether the Fourteenth Amendment required a trial judge to interrogate the prospective jurors about such possible prejudice. Given the traditionally broad discretion accorded to the trial judge in conducting *voir dire,* and our inability to constitutionally distinguish possible prejudice against beards from a host of other possible similar prejudices, we do not believe the petitioner's constitutional rights were violated when the trial judge refused to put this question." In a dissenting opinion, Justice Douglas argued that prejudices about such matters as hair length should be probed in *voir dire* examinations, if relevant. In regard to hair length, Justice Douglas stated, "Since hair growth is an outward manifestation by which many people determine whether to apply deeprooted prejudices to an individual, to deny a defendant the right to examine this aspect of a prospective juror's personality is to deny him his most effective means of *voir dire* examination."

Recently, the Supreme Court has elaborated somewhat on the topic of the impact of stereotyping by prohibiting the state to compel prisoners to appear in court in prison attire. In *Estelle* v. *Williams* (1976), the court noted that observations of prison clothes could potentially bias judgments and pointed out that "courts must do the best they can to evaluate the likely effects of a particular procedure, based on reason, principle, and common human experience." Lown (1977) has provided an interesting analysis of this Supreme Court decision and its implications for stereotyping based upon physical characteristics other than clothing.

Psycholegal Research on Juries and Jury Biases

Psychological research on legal issues has increased in recent years. Tapp (1976) has provided a review of psychology and law research in the *Annual Review of Psychology* and noted that, "Among psychologists concerned with social behavior perhaps the oldest, best known, and continuous work has been in jury research" (p. 188). Shaver, Gilbert, and Williams (1975) have also surveyed the general area of research on psychology and law and noted that, "Social psychology's current interest in the law and law enforcement may well have been kindled by the jury studies ... of Strodtbeck, James, and Hawkins, 1958, or by the pioneering work of Kalven and Zeisel, 1966, and jury research abounds" (p. 472). The degree to which psychological jury research "abounds" is highlighted by the many recent reviews of jury research, (Davis, Bray, and Holt, 1977; Kaplan, 1977; Kessler, 1975; Sales, 1977; and Stephan, 1975).

Research on juries has also been conducted by lawyers, sociologists, and others. The University of Chicago Law School Jury Project produced many valuable reports and served as a general stimulus to jury research. Kalven and Zeisel's (1966) classic, *The American Jury,* is particularly noteworthy. The study provides a panoramic view of the operation of criminal court juries. More recently, Rita Simon has edited a collection of articles by both lawyers and social scientists on the operations of juries titled *The Jury System in America: A Critical Overview* (1975). Articles in the book provide valuable information on the history of the use of juries in the United States, methods of jury selection, jury decision-making processes, and views regarding the value of the jury system.

Much of the jury research done by psychologists deals with the structural characteristics of juries. For example, numerous studies have been conducted regarding the functioning of juries made up of fewer than twelve jurors (Saks and Hastie, 1978). Research on methods of selecting jurors from jury pools has also been plentiful (Christie, 1972). Studies of simulated juries have varied many aspects of the trial: defendant characteristics (Landy and Aronson, 1969), victim characteristics (Hatton, Snortum, and Oscamp, 1971), juror characteristics (Vidmar, 1972), offense characteristics (Shaver, 1970), characteristics of the evidence (Hoiberg and Stires, 1973), and the judge's instructions (Sue, Smith, and Caldwell, 1973). The reviews cited previously provide valuable guidance to this extensive literature.

Research on Stereotyping Biases: Simple Attributional Judgments

A large portion of the psycholegal research literature attempts to assess the degree of stereotyping biases in juror judgments. Stereotyping involves the attribution of characteristics to an individual simply on the basis of the person's group membership. Stereotyping can be viewed as a very simple attributional mechanism in which the perceiver moves directly from knowledge of category membership to trait attributions without applying the more complex attributional calculations discussed later in this chapter. Research on stereotyping biases has focused on biases due to the sex, age, race, and socioeconomic status of defendants and has been conducted using both the decisions of actual juries and data from simulated juries made up of college students or individuals representative of the local jury pool.

Hagan (1974) has reviewed the literature on the influence of extralegal attributes on criminal sentencing and has cited research involving both jury trials and nonjury trials. He concludes, in regard to judges' decisions regarding sentences, that, "There is generally a small relationship between extralegal attributes of the offender and sentencing decisions" (p. 375). These significant relationships particularly occurred for racial and socioeconomic differences between defendants and were maintained in some studies after controls were introduced for offense type and prior record. Hagan stresses the importance of considering the magnitude of the relationship as well as its statistical significance and in general observes that the relationships are weak, although still statistically significant. Increasingly, the exceptions to this finding occur in studies that primarily or exclusively dealt with jury trials. For example, Wolfgang and Riedel (1973) observed a very large difference in sentences (execution versus imprisonment) given in eleven southern states for interracial versus intraracial rape cases. Similarly, Judson and others (1969) conducted a study using only jury trials and observed a highly significant difference in jury decisions as a function of the socioeconomic characteristics of defendants. These relationships stayed relatively constant following the use of controls for prior record and other confounding variables. Hagan (1974) concludes, regarding the jury trial studies in his sample, that, "such studies may, then, say more about the inadequacies of the jury system, particularly as it has been involved in the invocation of the death penalty, than about the general operations of the courts" (p. 378).

Stephan (1975) has similarly reviewed the jury stereotyping literature and reports that substantial inconsistencies occur among the various studies. For example, in the case of possible sex discrimination, experimental evidence from simulated juries suggests that jurors discriminate in favor of same-sex defendants, whereas studies of actual trials suggest no discrimination in some studies, discrimination in favor of females in others, and discrimination in favor of males in still others. Stephan (1975) reiterates the earlier cited finding that low socioeconomic status defendants appear to be discriminated against. For example, Reed (1965) conducted a study of Louisiana jurors and reports that the probability of convictions was significantly higher for low status defendants.

Stephan (1975) concludes that "a great number of variables have been shown to have influenced the jury verdict. However, with few exceptions, there are too little data employing these variables to draw firm conclusions about their effects" (p. 115). The lack of data poses a major problem, since the apparent inconsistencies between the various studies may be quite understandable, if other aspects of the cases are controlled. Females may be consistently discriminated against in certain types of cases, males in others, and, in still others, sex may not be relevant. A similar possibility exists for racial discrimination. Some studies report discrimination against blacks (Silverstein, 1965), others report blacks receiving lower sentences than whites (Bernstein, Kelly, and Doyle, 1977), and others fail to show differences in the treatment of whites and blacks (Green, 1961). One possibility is that blacks are discriminated against in cases perceived to be threatening to whites, such as those involving rape and burglary, but are not discriminated against in cases occurring among blacks, such as intraracial assaults. In these latter cases, whites may be quite tolerant of violations of the law, considering the offense to be more acceptable in another subculture, and might actually engage in reverse discrimination by recommending less harsh treatment to a black than a comparable white (Bernstein, Kelly, and Doyle, 1977).

Interpretation of the various studies of biases is complicated by methodological difficulties. Many studies of actual trials do not attempt to control adequately for such variables as type of offense, prior criminal record, and various demographic variables, such as age and social class. In the case of simulated trial studies, many problems occur in attempting to generalize these studies to actual trials. Subjects are often simply exposed to brief accounts of a criminal case, given a few minutes to read the case, and then asked to make judgments regarding the defendant (verdict, sentence, personal characteristics) without any deliberation with other simulated jurors. Subjects in such studies have not had the opportunity to see the defendant, listen to testimony, or consider the issues at hand for a substantial period of time. Although maximizing the experimenter's control over the stimuli to which the subject is exposed, this approach clearly limits the generality of the findings in regard to actual trial settings. The problem is exacerbated by the fact that many of the subjects in such trial simulations are college students. These students differ from the typical juror in many respects, including age, socioeconomic status, likely skepticism regarding research, and so forth, and the combined impact of the artificiality of experimental manipulations and the unrepresentativeness of the subjects makes extrapolation from these studies difficult.

In summary, little doubt exists that stereotyping biases occur in juror judgments, at least under some circumstances, resulting in jurors either favoring or disfavoring specific types of defendants on the basis of information other than the law and the evidence in the case. Racial and socioeconomic status biases have received particular attention in the research literature. Such biases are in direct opposition to the Anglo-American legal tradition that a defendant is to be considered innocent unless proven guilty, to Sixth Amendment provisions regarding the right to an impartial jury, and to Fourteenth Amendment rights to due process and equal protection of the laws. Defense attorneys and judges often enquire if potential jurors have such biases and if they can overcome such biases to provide the defendant with a fair and impartial trial.

The remainder of this chapter presents an analysis of attributional biases in juror judgment. Research literature is reviewed, and an empirical study of juror judgmental biases is presented. The study sheds light on the influence of social stereotypes in juror judgment. In addition, the implications of attributional research for court policies are explored, including policy issues relating to initial juror orientation, *voir dire* procedures, judges' instructions to jurors, and decisions of citizens engaged in other roles in the justice system (for example, mediators and arbitrators).

An Attributional Approach to Jury Biases

Attribution theories are well suited to provide the basis for an understanding of judgmental biases. These theories have incorporated the earlier social psychological research on social stereotyping (for example, see Brigham's 1971 review), which dealt primarily with the content of stereotypes. In addition, these theories have provided insights regarding how stereotypes are combined with information regarding specific target persons performing specific behaviors in specific settings. Jones and Davis' (1965) correspondent-inference theory explicitly deals with the ways stereotypical judgments regarding a target person's intentions and dispositions are modified in light of behavioral information.

Jones and McGillis (1976) have noted that a variety of

sources of stereotypical information exist. First, individuals may attribute characteristics to another based simply on the person's category membership (race, sex, age, and so on). Subtypes of category-based expectancies include *stereotypical expectancies* (traits attributed to a group member simply because of the person's membership in the group) and *normative expectancies* (expectancies that are supported by societal norms and are punished when violated). These expectancies tend to be attributed to virtually all members of a given subculture. Individuals may also attribute characteristics to another based on prior information regarding the specific target person. Subtypes of such target-based expectancies include *structural expectancies* (in which traits attributed to the target person are deduced from other traits believed to be possessed by the target person through the perceiver's implicit personality theory) and *replicative* and *conceptual-replicative expectancies* (based on previous observations of the specific target person). In the case of juror judgment, particular concern has arisen regarding stereotypical beliefs based on limited information regarding group membership (race, social class) and specific information regarding a defendant, such as pretrial publicity.

Clearly, either favorable or unfavorable stereotypical biases are in opposition to constitutional safeguards and legal traditions. The typical case of stereotypical judgment discussed earlier involves instances in which demographic information (race, socioeconomic status, and so on) is used to make invidious distinctions among defendants. Attributional theorizing suggests that traditional negative stereotypes can, under some circumstances, have reverse effects, potentially resulting in positive consequences rather than negative consequences for a defendant, depending on the type of defense presented by the defendant. The reason for this possible reversal in the impact of stereotypes on juror judgment is the occurrence of contrast effects (see Jones and McGillis, 1976; Jones and others, 1971). A contrast effect involves giving a person who has violated an expectation a more extreme rating of a characteristic in line with an action than that given an individual who has merely confirmed an expectation. For example, in the context of jury judgment, a defendant from a negatively stereotyped group would be predicted to be judged more favorably when acting for altruistic purposes than a defendant from a positively stereotyped group and less favorably than the positively stereotyped defendant when acting for apparently selfish reasons. The negative stereotype is simply reinforced in the selfish condition but is violated in the altruistic condition, resulting in the prediction of the contrast effect for the latter condition.

Contrast effects have been discussed at length in the psychophysical literature, and Campbell (1967) describes them as "a pervasive cognitive process noted in perception as the enhancement of contrast through homogenization of differences within gestalt boundaries and the exaggeration of differences across boundaries" (p. 824). Sherif and Hovland (1961) have drawn an analogy between the contrast effects observed in perception research and their findings in the area of social judgment theory. Jones and others (1971) have applied similar reasoning to that of the social judgment theorists in predicting that a comparable contrast effect would occur in the case of perceptions when confidently held expectancies were unequivocally disconfirmed. In Jones' research, the subject's expectancy is likened to the internal attitude anchor in the social judgment theory research, and further discussion of this analogy is provided by Jones and Gerard (1967). Jones and others (1971) investigated the attribution of attitudes related to marihuana legalization and observed that target persons violating expectancies were perceived as more extreme on the attitude issue than were target persons who confirmed the subject's expectancies. An analogous finding was reported by Mills and Jellison (1967), and additional studies providing suggestive support for the contrast phenomena include Jones and Harris (1967), Jones, Davis, and Gergen (1961), and Feldman (1972).

Ross (1977) carefully reviews the attributional literature and views the "fundamental attribution error" as the "general tendency to overestimate the importance of personal or dispositional factors relative to environmental influences" (p. 184). This error has been demonstrated repeatedly in social psychological research, including the forced-compliance dissonance research and research on the role-based nature of behavior (for example, Jones, Davis, and Gergen, 1961). In addition, Ross (1977) notes the tendency of individuals to engage in the false-consensus or egocentric-attribution bias. Egocentric-attribution biases involve deviations in the subjective probability estimates of laymen regarding the prevalence of specific traits and behavior. These biases are due in part to faulty sampling techniques of the perceiver as well as possible self-serving motivational biases.

The various biases discussed by Ross (1977) have profound implications for juror judgments. The tendency to overestimate the importance of personal over environmental factors as determinants of behavior can lead perceivers to attribute readily the characteristic of criminality to a defendant's behavior. The egocentric-attribution bias can result in biased judgments either due to the perceiver's lack of experience with the range of behaviors in question (for example, an upper-middle-class juror finding the aggressive behavior of a lower-class defendant highly unique and shocking, even though the behavior may be virtually normative in the lower-class community) or due to motivational factors (for example, racial biases causing a juror to readily assign negative traits to a defendant purely on the basis of the defendant's group membership). The Ross (1977) review provides numerous cogent examples of the impact of attributional biases on judgment. Miller and Ross (1975) provide numerous additional insights regarding the underlying mechanism of attributional biases.

A Study of Contrast Effects in Juror Judgments

Robert Morin (a graduate student at the University of Illinois, Urbana-Champaign) and I have conducted a project to assess the existence of contrast effects in juror judgment. As was noted earlier, these effects can result in paradoxical judgments, whereby defendants from negatively stereotyped groups might be treated better than defendants from positively stereotyped groups under certain conditions. Specifically, we hypothesized that a defendant from a group associated with criminality would be more favorably rated than a defendant not associated with criminality if both defendants were presented as having committed their crime for altruistic reasons, but the defendant from the criminal group would be less favorably rated than the defendant from the noncriminal group if no positive ulterior motive were presented for the defendants, leaving the subjects to assume greed as the motive.

The subjects for the research were 120 students at the State University of New York at Albany and 86 members of the jury pool of the Suffolk County (Boston) Superior Court. They were informed that their task would be to take the role of a juror and read a summary of a case presented to actual jurors at a trial. Subjects were given one of two forms of stereotyped information, indicating that the defendant was from a group that either had a high or low level of involvement in the crime charged. Subjects were informed in the prosecutor's opening statement that members of the defendant's profession (contractors) had a high or low level of investigations and arrests for the crime of fraud. Prior to constructing the questionnaires, a number of trial lawyers and one judge were asked whether such information would be likely to be ruled inadmissible in an actual trial, since it is potentially prejudicial. They felt that it would not be ruled inadmissable, because highlighting it to a jury would be viewed as more harmful than leaving it stand. Subjects were also told through testimony from a character witness that the defendant's potential motive for the crime was either altruistic or apparently selfish. In the latter condition, no motive for the crime was offered by the character witness, and selfish gain was thus the only plausible motivation. (A third variable, consistency of the criminal act, was included in the study. The defendant was alleged to have sent one bill to a company for services he had not in fact rendered in the low consistency condition and to have sent three separate bills totaling the same amount in the high consistency condition. This variable produced virtually no significant findings.)

Subjects were requested to indicate their judgment of the guilt or innocence of the defendant, to recommend a sentence from a list of options, to rate the defendant's traits and behavior, and to fill out manipulation checks indicating their recall of the independent-variable manipulations. Information was also requested regarding the demographic characteristics of subjects and their perceptions of the study.

The questionnaires were pretested to make it highly likely that subjects would perceive the defendant to be guilty. Eighty-nine percent (184 of the 206 subjects) judged the defendant to be guilty. Judgments of guilt were comparable for both the juror (81 of 86) and student (103 of 120) samples. Data analyses were conducted using the data from subjects who judged the defendant to be guilty, and judgments of guilt did not vary significantly by condition in either subject population.

Jury Pool. Subjects from the juror sample were very sensitive to the motive variable. The average sentence recommended for defendants in the altruistic-motive condition was 2.32 years, whereas the average sentence in the no-motive (selfish) condition was 3.93 years $(F\ (1, 80) = 7.36, p < 0.008)$. Similarly, subjects in the altruistic-motive condition perceived the defendant to be significantly more generous, helpful, likeable, trustworthy, and good. When asked to evaluate the defendant's behavior, subjects rated the altruistic defendant's act as more "excusable" and more for "good purposes" than the no-motive defendant. Irrelevant measures included in the trait list, such as "insecure" and "emotional," were not affected by the motive variable.

The motive variable and the stereotype variable interacted in the predicted direction on all the relevant variables, and the interaction was statistically significant for the helpful, trustworthy, good purposes, and excusable variables. In each case, the defendant from the high frequency of crime group was judged to be better than the defendant from the low frequency group in altruistic conditions and worse in no-motive (selfish) conditions. The sentence variable tended toward significance for the motive by stereotype interaction $(F = 1.69, df\ (1, 80), p < 0.19)$ but did not reach significance in the juror sample.

Students. Subjects from the student sample provided a somewhat different pattern of data than the juror subjects. The motive-variable main effect was significant for only two variables: generous $(F\ (1, 80) = 9.49, p < 0.002)$ and helpful $(F\ (1, 80) = 6.35, p < 0.01)$, with the altruistic defendant being viewed as more generous and helpful than the no-motive (selfish) defendant. These variables were the two most significant trait measures for the motive variable with juror subjects, and the student responses suggest that they were more conservative in making judgments based on the motive data than the juror subjects—students made only the safest judgments based on the data and did not generalize to broader traits such as "likeable" and "good."

The motive by stereotype interaction was not significant for any of the trait variables in the student sample. Interestingly, the interaction was significant for the sentence variable (F (1, 80) = 5.48 p <0.02). Table 1 presents a summary of the student data for the motive and stereotype variables and shows that defendants from the high-criminality-stereotyped group were given lower sentences in altruistic motive conditions than low-criminality-group defendants but higher sentences than low-criminality defendants in no-motive conditions. This observation mirrors the trend in the juror data, also shown in Table 1. The student sentencing data differ from the juror data, however, in that the motive main effect is not observed, and altruistic-condition low-frequency defendants actually receive higher sentences than no-motive defendants from the students, whereas they receive relatively lower sentences from jurors. The overall sentences also vary between students and jurors, with students providing an average sentence recommendation of 2.01 years and jurors recommending an average sentence of 3.12 years. Thus, the jury interaction between the motive and stereotype variables is in line with prediction but only tends toward significance, whereas the student interaction is significant but deviates somewhat from the prediction. The harsher sentence recommendation for altruistic low-criminality defendants than for no-motive low-criminality defendants was unexpected and seems to imply a rejection of the altruistic defense and a boomerang judgment of the defendants.

Table 1. Average Length of Sentence of Juror and Student Samples for Altruistic and Selfish Motives of Defendants Associated with High-Criminality and Low-Criminality Populations

| | | Juror Sample Motive | |
		Altruistic	No-Motive
Stereotype	High Crime	1.74 years	4.13 years
	Low Crime	2.90 years	3.74 years
		Student Sample Motive	
		Altruistic	No-Motive
Stereotype	High Crime	1.72 years	2.51 years
	Low Crime	2.37 years	1.45 years

The juror data in this study provide considerable support for the study's hypotheses. Subjects' perceptions of the defendants differ in line with the predictions regarding the motive and stereotype variables, and the sentence variable tends in the appropriate direction. The predicted contrast effect occurs for many trait variables. The student data are a very weak image of the juror data in most cases, and very few measures resulted in significant findings. The motive by stereotype interaction for the sentence variable was significant but not totally in line with expectations. The student data would seem in large part to reflect the greater conservatism of the students in making judgments of the defendants on the basis of the written testimony.

The appearance of the interaction and the lack of a main effect for the stereotype variable on the sentence measure suggests that studies reporting no significant differences in sentences between stereotyped defendants may actually mask significant variations in sentences due to the combined impact of strength of defense and stereotype. Stereotyping is perhaps still occurring, but sentences counterbalance one another, depending on the nature of the defendant's defense. Detailed data on the perceived strengths of defenses in a sample of cases are needed to test this hypothesis in actual jury trials. Multiple raters could presumably be used to assess the reliability of judgments of defense strength.

Implications of Attributional Research for Court Policies

The research on jury attributional biases reported in this chapter has potential policy implications for initial juror orientation, *voir dire* procedures, judge's instructions to jurors, and decisions of citizens engaged in other roles in the justice system.

Initial Juror Orientation. Jurors frequently receive an initial orientation from the court when they first appear to become jurors. These orientation sessions may involve a brief talk by the clerk of the court or a judge or the combination of a speech and a slide show or film discussing their obligations as jurors. These sessions provide an excellent opportunity for the courts to inform jurors of potential biases, and most courts are likely to stress the importance of making decisions only on the basis of the evidence presented at trial and the law as it is described by the judge. These presentations could be supplemented with insights from social science research on the prevalence of biases and the importance of minimizing such biases in judgment.

The findings of our study on jury decision making suggest that jurors need to be aware of very subtle biases in judgment. In our study, the mere knowledge of the criminal activities of the defendant's peer group markedly affected juror judgments. Jurors in many cases displayed an attributional contrast effect, which distorted their judgments and led them to treat otherwise comparable defendants differently. Jurors could be informed of such biases during their initial orientation sessions through the citation of examples of cases in which such an effect might occur. In these examples, the influence of differing types of defenses on the judgments of different types of defendants could be noted. Jurors could also be sensitized to the fact that many biases may involve reverse prejudice, with lenient rather than harsh judgments being the result.

It is not certain that the mere presentation of information to jurors regarding attributional biases will eliminate the occurrence of these biases in the courtroom. Research is needed on the degree to which jurors can be made aware of and made to minimize their tendencies to attributional biases in their judgments. This research could be conducted in cooperation with a court that was willing to implement different orientation programs for different groups of jurors. Particularly, if jurors could be assigned randomly to the orientation groups, research might indicate the value of informing jurors (and perhaps also judges) of their possible attributional biases.

Voir Dire Procedures. Supreme Court rulings regarding biases and *voir dire* procedures have been discussed earlier in this chapter. The *Ham* v. *South Carolina* case indicated the court's distinction between constitutionally relevant racial biases and less prominent biases, such as those against individuals with beards. Numerous studies have been conducted recently on methods for the conduct of *voir dire*. Fried, Kaplan, and Klein (1975) summarize many of these studies in a recent review. In general, the *voir dire* procedure provides an opportunity for the attorneys to determine the impartiality of jurors, and, with recent advances in research techniques on juror selection, many attorneys are attempting "scientifically" to select favorable rather than merely impartial juries.

At present, attorneys have the opportunity during *voir dire* to investigate prospective juror prejudices through questioning, and they often have available the juror's initial jury application form, with such information as the juror's age and occupation as a guide for their questioning. If attributional biases are consistently found to be significant in research studies, it may be possible also to include vignettes of cases on jury application forms for prospective jurors to judge. Responses to these vignettes may reveal the extent to which prospective jurors are likely to possess substantial attributional biases based on simple prejudice or more complex attributional mechanisms. Attorneys could then use such information in selecting jurors. The use of such a drastic technique would require far more data than are currently available, substantiating the reliable occurrence of such biases in real jurors serving on real trials. And, even if such data are available, legal issues relating to such an intrusion on jurors would need to be explored carefully before such a system was experimentally implemented.

Judges' Instructions to Jurors. Sales, Elwork, and Alfini (1977) have recently conducted a study on the impact of judges' instructions on jurors. As in the case of initial orientation sessions, the court is provided with an opportunity to sensitize jurors to their biases. These instructions typically include a recommendation to jurors that they decide the case only in light of the evidence and the law. The findings of social science research on biases could also be cited in these instructions to sensitize jurors further regarding the possibility of unconscious biases.

The freedom of judges to comment on a case during instructions varies among the states. Some states limit the judge to comments regarding the law, others allow the judge to summarize the evidence and comment regarding the law, and still others allow for additional comments regarding the weight of the evidence and the credibility of witnesses. Kalven and Zeisel (1966) indicate which states allow which types of procedures and comment on the implications of these rules for the cases in their study. These rules may limit the ability of a judge to comment on specific biases in his instructions in some states, which makes initial juror orientation a more appropriate point for educating jurors regarding their biases.

Decisions of Citizens Engaged in Other Roles in the Justice System. Jury trials in the United States account for approximately 80 percent of all jury trials in the world, according to Kalven and Zeisel (1966). Nevertheless, jury trials are employed in only a very small proportion of court cases and typically account for less than 10 percent of court cases in a jurisdiction. In some jurisdictions, as few as 1 percent of the cases proceed to jury trial. Guilty pleas, dismissals, and bench trials account for the bulk of case processing. Furthermore, jury trials are typically used only in more serious cases. Kalven and Zeisel (1966) noted "The result is that the law has withdrawn from the universe of jury trials a wide range of matters, which, although described as petty, may well involve the most frequent source of contact between the ordinary citizen and the law" (p. 17).

The recent effort by the Department of Justice to develop Neighborhood Justice Centers may reverse the current situation, and citizens may become involved in a wide range of minor criminal and civil cases. Neighborhood Justice Centers are facilities that provide mediation and arbitration for minor cases, and current projects are operated by prosecutors' offices, courts, and private agencies. The projects stress an understanding of the underlying problems between disputants, and they work toward compromises between the disputants—a goal difficult to reach in conventional adjudication with judges and jurors. Formal rules of evidence are not used, and the hearings stress informality and communication. Nevertheless, citizens are likely to bring their biases with them in processing disputes.

Mediators should receive much the same training as jurors to sensitize them to potential biases in their judgments. The American Arbitration Association and the Institute for Mediation and Conflict Resolution have provided training to citizens in some of the current projects and have stressed problems with judgmental biases. The Department of Justice has established a program to develop experimental Neighborhood Justice Centers in three cities, and legislation has been submitted to establish an office within the Department of Justice to fund experimental projects. If the effort is successful, citizens will soon assist the justice system both as jurors in serious cases and as mediators and arbitrators in minor cases. The research reviewed in this chapter is likely to be applicable to both jury decisions and mediation and arbitration activities. Further research will be needed to determine if significant differences in attributional biases occur between the formal juror decision-making process and the more informal mediation and arbitration processes at Neighborhood Justice Centers.

Chapter 12

John S. Carroll

Judgments Made by Parole Boards

An incarcerated criminal is usually subject to a set of parole procedures, which govern his time of release from prison and supervision in the community. These procedures begin when the judge sets bounds on the sentence (for example, two to six years) without specifying the exact time to serve. An administrative entity, the parole board, reviews the case periodically and decides exactly when to release the offender. A person paroled before the maximum sentence is on conditional release. He is supervised by the paroling authority and is subject to special rules (for example, must hold a job, must not use alcohol), to which he must adhere or face a revocation of parole and return to prison. Conditional release ends when the maximum sentence expires, and the parolee then becomes a free citizen.

Note: Support for this research was provided by National Science Foundation Grant #SOC75-18061 to the author and John W. Payne and by National Institute of Mental Health Grant #1R01MH31055 to the author. I am grateful for the continued cooperation of the Pennsylvania Board of Probation and Parole.

These parole procedures are generally directed at enabling the correctional authorities to tailor their rehabilitative programs to the individual offender and to ease the transition from prison to community through the supervision and treatment offered during conditional release. The legislative mandate of parole authorities is provided by individual state legislatures (or the U.S. Congress for the U.S. Board of Parole). Generally, legislatures mention that the parole decision involves considerations or goals, such as protecting the public through incapacitation and deterrence, punishing crime, treating the offender, and encouraging good behavior in the prisons. However, these goals are loosely specified, at best vague, and often conflicting (Gottfredson, 1975b; Wilson, 1975).

Research investigating the factors influencing parole decisions has revealed, not surprisingly, that different parole boards appear to value different goals (Stanley, 1976). Some boards focus on punishment by assigning prison terms according to crime seriousness, and others try to incapacitate "dangerous" offenders by denying parole when they judge the probability is high that the offender will commit a future crime. There are boards primarily concerned with institutional discipline and boards balancing combinations of goals, and boards that have displayed inconsistent patterns in their decisions.

The individual members of a single parole board may also exhibit diverse opinions about what goals are important in a case. To illustrate, consider the Pennsylvania Parole Board, observed during a meeting in which they evaluated the back time to be set for several convicted parole violators. When a parolee is convicted of a new offense while on parole, he or she has a revocation hearing, at which time the board considers whether or not to revoke parole. If parole is revoked, the parole violator is returned to prison to serve more time on the original sentence from which he or she was paroled. The board designates a future date at which the parolee may be considered for reparole. The time the parolee must serve in prison before consideration for reparole is analogous to a new minimum sentence and is called *back time*.

On one of the observed cases, the five board members took very different stances in regard to the goals of a particular amount of back time for this offender. One member expressed the feeling that jail was a waste of time for this man, and a mental health outpatient program should be provided in hope of rehabilitation (a Rehabilitation orientation). A second member said that retribution was an invalid rationale, that the offender should either get the maximum to protect society and "get his attention," or no time in jail at all (an Incapacitation and Special Deterrence viewpoint). A third member also mentioned protecting society but added that putting him on the street with no time would be rewarding him for crime (Incapacitation, Punishment, and Special Deterrence). The remaining board members both stressed the need to protect society from a potentially dangerous person (Incapacitation). Thus, the consensus of the board was incapacitation, but other values were expressed by individual members that were possibly related to the specifics of this case.

For whatever goals are salient to a decision maker on a given case, there is the additional question of how best to achieve them. For the goal of punishment, the board must agree on offense seriousness and the relationship between seriousness and time to be served. Research has shown the agreement on offense seriousness among parole decision makers to be high (Hoffman, Beck, and DeGostin, 1973); diverse populations of people also agree on offense ratings (Figlio, 1975; Rossi and others, 1974). However, there is little evidence that such a high level of agreement exists between seriousness and time in prison.

For the goal of incapacitation, parole boards must attempt to predict future criminal behavior. The basic model of indeterminate sentencing is that the offender is not released into society until he is treated or reformed (Miller, 1972)—that is, no longer "dangerous" (von Hirsch, 1972). The available evidence indicates that parole boards are not very good at predicting recidivism (Hakeem, 1961; Kastenmeier and Eglit, 1973). This has provided substantial impetus to the movement for statistical prediction devices to act as decision aids in evaluating this aspect of the parole decision. Such a decision aid is now formalized in the procedures of the U.S. Board of Parole (Gottfredson and others, 1975).

Furthermore, the effects of various correctional methods on offenders are largely unknown and are currently under debate, and decision makers rarely have access to information about the results of past parole decisions (Gottfredson, 1975a). Not only do parole boards operate on poor information, but they also are pressed by high volume and low funds to make judgments on a case in fifteen minutes or less, and parole boards often have no special training for this task (Stanley, 1976). It should not be at all surprising that tremendous variability exists in parole decisions (Kingsnorth, 1969; Wilkins and others, 1973).

Yet, this body is charged with making decisions to provide individual treatment to offenders (release at the optimal moment) and to confine dangerous offenders (Miller, 1972). Parole boards are generally entrusted with at least as much responsibility over their cases as are judges (Genego, Goldberger, and Jackson, 1975).

Thus, the parole decision maker is thrust into a situation in which vague imperatives are matched by ineffective alternatives, time pressure, and few resources. From a societal viewpoint, the parole board is at the center of a maelstrom of community outrage over crime and professional debate over policy. From a theoretical viewpoint, the parole decision maker structures this ill-defined yet important situation through the use of *discretion*. Discretion may be found elsewhere in the criminal justice system (Davis, 1971; Shaver, Gilbert, and Williams, 1975), but parole decisions are nearly unique from a methodological viewpoint. The parole decision is relatively accessible, lacking the legal restrictions placed on judges and juries. It is also controlled—brief, repetitive, localized, paper-and-pencil—in ways that make research more practical than street observation of police. In short, the parole decision is an excellent place to begin psychological research on the criminal justice system.

The basic premise of this chapter is that the discretionary judgments made by a parole decision maker combine his or her knowledge about the specific case and about other people (especially other offenders) into inferences about the nature of the offender, the etiology of his criminal behavior, the prospects for treatment, and predictions of future behavior. Further, we propose that important aspects of these inferences can be understood as causal attributions about the crime and the offender.

Attribution-Theory Approach

Consider the following example from Carroll and Payne (1977a), in which an expert parole decision maker from the

Pennsylvania system examined an actual case in order to prepare a summary and recommendation. The expert made his usual examination of the information and produced the actual summary but was instructed to "think out loud" while doing so. His remarks were tape recorded and analyzed for attributions. From the analysis of the recorded remarks, it became apparent that the board member was concerned not only with the crime description but also with the causes of the crime. In examining the evidence, he stated several potential causes for the crime. Some time later, he found that alcohol abuse was involved, and he then gradually built a picture of the parole applicant as a person who can usually control his alcohol use but was frustrated over losing his job. Such a causal attribution provides a consistent way of interpreting the crime, the criminal record, and institutional behavior and for preparing treatment plans.

Excerpts from a Parole Recommendation Protocol

AB1: All right, well, the first thing I usually do is see what he's here on.

AB2: Since it's a, you know, this guy's been convicted of burglary.

AB3: Plead guilty to it.

AB10: Now this is not too bad.

AB11: He broke a window and entered a food market.

AB12: He left a credit card box uh, left with the credit card box containing uh, 37, . . . oh, a cardboard box containing 37 cartons of associated cigarettes

AB13: totaling so much money.

AB14: So, he stole a bunch of cigarettes.

AB15: And, he did this with un . . . one other person.

AB16: So, that's really not too bad.

AB34: I really don't have to delve too much into . . .

AB35: into what he actually did.

AB36: But on more serious crimes,

AB37: I like to get a better picture of what he actually did in terms of uh.

AB38: That might indicate psychological motivations for the crimes.

AB55: So well, I wanna look at prior records.
AB56: To see if the present offense is along with other types of behavior.

AB106: But, both reports indicate that he hasn't been in trouble since '64 'til 75.
AB107: So then, I start reading social history on him.
AB108: I look for things like supports

AB114: Uh, . . . how skilled he is.
AB115: his intelligence level,
AB116: his potential, that way.
AB117: Uh . . . and the things goin' against him
AB118: Drug abuse
AB119: Alcohol abuse
AB120: Uh, psycho . . . extreme psychological problems
AB121: uh, family problems
AB122: interpersonal kin . . .
AB123: uh, behavior problems

AB149: Sometimes, uh . . . the parents are overprotective
AB150: and they've always covered him for everything he's ever done.
AB152: And if that's indicated here,
AB153: That would certainly be a, you know, somethin' that I would look at
AB154: as . . . as a reason for the way he is now
AB155: and also somethin' that would you know . . . add . . . detract from him bein' able to make it when he hits the street.
AB156: Nothing like that is indicated here.

AB299: He indicated he was intoxicated at the time of the crime.

AB302: Whether you know, it points out that he's been in and out of trouble without being convicted or arrested for a criminal act
AB303: which in my estimation, he was awful lucky that he didn't get caught,
AB304: or he was staying in to, . . . staying out of trouble
AB305: And uh . . . I think the staying out of trouble was probably closer to the case.

AB412: he . . . he also indicated to the counselor
AB413: That when he found himself out of work

    AB414:   That he started hitting the bottle.
    AB415:   Which is, you know, that's his, you know, reason
              for . . . for doin' it.
    AB416:   For goin' to the alcohol.
    AB417:   as to why . . . why there would be some alcohol
              abuse.

    AB1128:   Uh . . . The guy . . . the difficulties that the guy
              had in the past
    AB1129:   . . . The records would show that it was due to
              alcoholism you know.
    AB1130:   Uh . . . and since he's been here uh,
    AB1131:   he has been participating in the AA

    AB1210:   OK, you know, what he did was so . . . was done
              so impulsively, man.
    AB1211:   He was out . . .
    AB1212:   he had been drinking with this cat . . .
    AB1213:   and uh, . . . they were drunk . . .
    AB1214:   and they needed cigarettes.
    AB1215:   And he went into this place
    AB1216:   and he got the cigarettes,
    AB1217:   They didn't even go in it.

    AB1231:   you know, with superior intelligence . . .
    AB1232:   and he's not using it.
    AB1233:   And that's this man's case.
    AB1234:   So . . . I would seek . . . I would seek therapy
    AB1235:   also in the areas of trying to wh . . . get him to
              realize you know, his capabilities.

Carroll and Payne (1977a) collected eighteen protocols, including the previous example, from five expert decision makers. There were three protocols from each of six actual cases. A coding scheme was developed, which classified those statements going beyond the factual information already present in the case folders into seven categories: judgments about the severity of the crime, judgments about the risk of recidivism, institutional behavior evaluations, information-seeking requests, attributions, parole release recommendations, and supervision recommendations. Attributions were the single largest category of judgments, representing 22 percent of all coded statements. Thus, decision makers spend considerable time and effort in making attributions.

Attributions were further coded by type: internal and stable (45 percent of all attributions), internal and unstable (3 percent), internal and intentional (20 percent), external (16 percent), and external acting with internal (16 percent). Although internal attributions (the first three types) were twice as predominant as external attributions, the cases receiving favorable parole decisions consistently received the highest proportion of external attributions from expert decision makers, which provides some support for the importance of attributions. Internal-stable attributions, such as personality descriptions, accounted for nearly half of all attributions, again demonstrating the predominant perceptual tendency to organize events in terms of personal dispositions (Heider, 1958; Ross, 1977). With these findings in mind, we can examine in more detail the concepts of attribution theory most relevant to parole decisions and the results of empirical investigations in this area.

Attributional Dimensions. Carroll and Payne (1976) suggest that Weiner's (1974a) three-dimensional model of attributions in achievement situations could be considered as the key portion of a framework for studying parole decisions. Carroll and Payne observe that attribution researchers have found that internal attributions to an actor, particularly internal, intentional attributions, lead to more praise for good acts and more blame for bad acts than do external attributions. Piliavin, Rodin, and Piliavin (1969) found that people in trouble are helped more when their distress is perceived to be due to external causes than to internal causes. Sosis (1974) found that persons who characteristically consider actors as the sources of events (Internals on Rotter's (1966) Internal-External Locus of Control Scale) evaluated criminals as more responsible for crime and gave longer prison sentences than those who attribute causality to the environment (Externals). Reed and Reed (1973) found that persons who attribute criminality to dispositions state that they wish to avoid criminals in public or private. Shaw and Reitan (1969) found that police recommended more punishment for criminals who more clearly intended to commit the crime.

In Weiner's model, expectations for future behavior are separable from praise or blame considerations and relate directly to the stability dimension. Research has demonstrated that expectations for future behavior are based on past behavior, to the extent that the perceived cause is stable with time (Valle and Frieze, 1976; Weiner, Nierenberg, and Goldstein, 1976). When some act is attributed to a stable cause, people expect similar acts in the future; the same act attributed to an unstable cause generates a much more moderate expectation.

Carroll and Payne (1976) suggest that praise or blame and future expectations, which are directly and separately related to attributional dimensions, could be seen as defining the two most important factors in parole decisions—punishment for past crime and incapacitation for predicted future risk of crime. Let us consider four explanations for why a businessman might be engaged in illegal business (or political) activities and their judgmental consequences: (1) He lacks moral knowledge of right and wrong. This is an internal, unintentional, and stable cause, which should lead to high blame (hence, high punishment) and high risk predictions (hence, high incapacitation). Further, to the extent that an internal cause is perceived as intentional—that is, under the control of the person—blame would be even higher. (2) He was following typical business practice in the corporate community. This is an external and stable cause, which should lead to low blame but high risk predictions. (3) He made an usually bad decision during a period of mood depression. This is an internal, unintentional, and unstable cause, which should lead to moderately high blame (not as high as an internal, intentional cause) but low risk predictions. (4) He was under unusual pressure from business associates to go along. This is an external and unstable attribution, which should lead to low blame and low risk predictions. The precise response, such as a prison term or treatment plan, would depend on the relative importances of the punishment and incapacitation aspects of the decision. Figure 1 schematically represents this conceptualization of the parole decision.

In a major test of this attributional framework, Carroll and Payne (1977a, 1977b) presented each of sixty-four college student subjects and twenty-four expert parole decision makers working for the Pennsylvania Board of Probation and Parole with eight brief crime reports. Each crime report included one of eight crime descriptions, such as robbery, rape, and burglary, and one of eight pieces of background information designed to suggest a causal at-

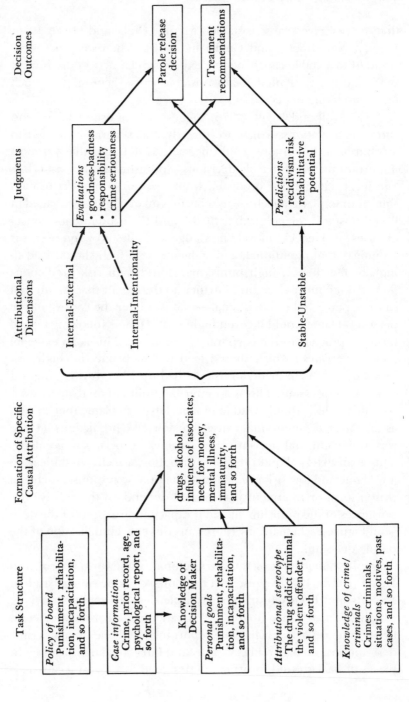

Figure 1. Attributional Analysis of Perceptions of Crime and Criminals.

tribution about the crime. Backgrounds were in a 2 × 2 × 2 design of internal versus external, stable versus unstable, and intentional versus unintentional causal attributions. Crime descriptions were paired with different background information for different subjects, such that each subject saw each crime and each background only once, in combinations and orders determined by a Latin Square design. After each crime report, subjects responded to a battery of questions regarding crime seriousness, suggested prison term, predictions about recidivism, and so forth. An example of one crime report from this study was the following:

> Mr. Green is a twenty-five-year-old male convicted of second-degree murder. He was in a bar having a drink and talking to the victim, when they began to argue, push, and punch each other. He pulled out a gun and shot the victim several times; the victim was pronounced dead on arrival at the hospital. Mr. Green surrendered himself to police, called by the bartender. He has no previous record of convictions. Interviews indicated that he could not find a good job, because his skill had been replaced by mechanization. The circumstances around the crime had been acting on him for some time.

The results provided several important insights. In the responses from college students, there was clear evidence that the background information suggesting causal attributions was used to evaluate crimes and offenders in ways predicted by attribution theory. Attributions to causes internal to the offender generally led to more punitive responses—lower ratings of liking and higher ratings of crime severity, responsibility for the crime, desire to punish, and longer recommended prison term. Attributions to stable, long-term causes led to higher expectations for recidivism, higher ratings of criminality, desire to incapacitate, longer prison term, and responsibility. Prison terms were assigned on the basis of both punishment and incapacitation factors and thus were an additive combination of internal-external judgments and stable-unstable judgments. For example, crimes with internal causes were given an average prison term of 7.8 years, but crimes with external causes were given an average prison term of 4.4 years.

The experts, in contrast, showed a clear tendency on nearly

all judgments to consider internal and stable causes as different from any other types of causes. These causes led to higher judgments of both crime seriousness and recidivism risk than any others. For example, the average recommended prison term was 5.9 years for internal-stable causes as compared with 3–4 years for other causes. Thus, although attributional information was important to both students and experts, only the students clearly showed the predicted separability of the internal-external and stable-unstable dimensions and the resultant punishment and incapacitation judgments. Further, the impact of the attributional information was clearly much greater for the students than for the experts.

The results regarding the role of intentionality as the third attributional dimension were only suggestive. The manipulation itself was not at all strong, and there was some contamination of intentionality differences in the other dimensional manipulations. Examination of the results from the analyses of variance and from a multiple-regression reanalysis using the manipulation checks to predict other judgments led to the following conclusions: For students, internal intentionality does influence the same judgments as does internality, and it is of particular importance in judging responsibility for the crime; for experts, the results are more confusing, in that effects for internality appear only as internal intentionality and are important for judgments of responsibility, criminality, and risk of recidivism.

Students and experts were high in agreement over crime seriousness but less in agreement on prison term and still less in agreement on risk of recidivism. For example, experts rated a murderer as least likely to commit another crime, whereas students saw him as third most likely. This is probably an instance of experts knowing that murderers are statistically good risks. The background describing the offender as aggressive in personality was reacted to much more unfavorably by experts, as was a background of recent divorce, which students treated leniently as an excuse, but experts perhaps saw as a pattern of social instability.

It was clear from comments made by the experts during and after the task that they felt uncomfortable making decisions based on so little information, although students liked the task, and studies of experts have shown that they *use* only a little information in a case (Wilkins and others, 1973). Thus, firm conclusions about expert parole decision makers should await a replication using more naturalistic materials.

However, strong evidence in support of the role of causal attributions in parole decisions is available from a nonexperimental study. Carroll (1978) had the five members of the Pennsylvania Board of Probation and Parole fill out a questionnaire immediately following parole release hearings. One of the five experts acted as hearing examiner for each of 272 hearings during October and November of 1977. The two-page posthearing questionnaire contained over seventy items and was designed to evaluate the implicit policy of the board and subsequently to assist in the development of decision guidelines (Carroll and Ruback, in press; Gottfredson and others, 1975). The addition of two open-ended assessments of causal attributions enabled the questionnaire to serve as a research instrument regarding attributions. These items were "Opinion on underlying cause for offense committed" and "Opinion on reason for criminal record/history."

The 557 total attribution statements were grouped into categories on the basis of similarity. Each category of cause was coded on three five-position scales for internality (1 = Internal, 5 = External), stability (1 = Stable, 5 = Unstable), and intentionality (1 = Intentional, 5 = Unintentional). The categories, category frequencies, and codes are shown in Table 1. Each case received three dimensional codes for cause of offense and three for cause of criminal history. In cases with multiple attributional statements, statements were combined to focus on underlying causes, when apparent, or simply averaged (noninteger scale values were used). All cases were coded by a single coder, and a randomly selected subset was coded by a second coder. The two coders agreed on 88 percent of the codes for causes of offense and 87 percent of the codes for causes of criminal history.

Parole release recommendations were examined in a multiple-regression analysis, using as independent variables: (1) four objective characteristics from each case—minimum sentence, crime type, number of prior convictions, and board member; (2) six attribution variables—attributions made about the offense and the criminal history, each coded for internality, stability, and

Table 1. Attributional Categories for Causes of Offense and Causes of Criminal History, with Attributional Dimensions

Category	Frequency (Percentage)			Attributional Coding		
	Offense	History	Total	Internality [a]	Stability [b]	Intentionality [c]
1. Drugs	15	23	19	I	S	M
2. Alcohol	12	19	16	I	S	M
3. Influence of associates	6	11	9	E⁻	M	M
4. Monetary gain	9	7	8	I	S	I
5. Get money	7	2	4	I	U	I
6. Lack of control	4	5	4	I	S	U
7. Immature	2	6	4	I	S⁻	U
8. Easily influenced	3	4	4	I	S	U
9. Victim precipitated	7	1	4	E	U	M
10. Mental problems	4	3	3	I	M	U
11. Drunk	7	0	3	I	M	I
12. Aimless	1	4	3	I	S	U
13. Domestic problems	4	1	3	M	M	U
14. Environment	2	2	2	E	M	U
15. No job	2	1	1	M	M	M
16. High on drugs	3	0	1	I	M	I
17. Acting "smart"	2	1	1	I	U	I
18. Passive	0	1	1	I	S	U
19. Family needs	2	2	1	E	U	U
20. Low IQ	1	0	1	I	S	U
21. Parental neglect	0	2	1	E	S	M
22. Poor attitude	1	1	1	I	S	I

23. Aggressive	0	1	1	I	S	U
24. Lack of social support	0	1	1	E	S	U
25. Language problem	0	1	0	I	S	U
Uncodable	7	1	4			
Total Responses	260	297	557			

[a]Coded on a five-point scale of I = Internal (1), I⁻ = Somewhat Internal (2), M = Mixed (3), E⁻ = Somewhat External (4), E = External (5).
[b]Coded as above with S = Stable, S⁻, M, U⁻, U = Unstable.
[c]Coded as above with I = Intentional, I⁻, M, U⁻, U = Unintentional.

intentionality; (3) twenty-six subjective variables, consisting of ratings of the importance of twenty-two decision considerations, ratings of the severity of the offense and the record, and ratings of the risk of a new offense and of a new dangerous offense; and (4) 144 bilinear interaction terms computed as the product of the objective and attributional variables in standardized form. Interaction terms were not computed for the subjective variables. Recommendations were on a five-point scale (definite no, no, mixed, yes, definite yes). We have found that Hearing Examiner recommendations become the final board decisions in over 95 percent of cases.

This analysis revealed that parole recommendations did *not* depend on sentences, crime type, or record. Recommendations did depend on the individual decision maker, the stability of the cause of the offense, and five subjective decision considerations: (1) need to get offender's attention; (2) risk of subsequent crime; (3) optimal time for community reentry; (4) need for psychiatric or psychological treatment; and (5) risk of subsequent dangerous crime. More stable attributions were associated with less favorable recommendations. Further analyses showed that stability affected recommendations by affecting predictions of the risk of subsequent crime. More stable attributions led to greater risk and less desire to parole.

These results provide strong support for half of the attributional analysis of parole decisions—stability affects risk and hence release decisions. The other half received little support. Internality was not shown to affect punishment or release decisions. Further analyses revealed a likely reason for these null results. Ratings of the importance of the twenty-two decision considerations, the severity of the offense and the record, and the risk of a new offense or of a new dangerous offense were factor analyzed. Six oblique factors emerged that could best be labeled: (1) Special Deterrence, (2) Rehabilitation, (3) Institutional Recommendations, (4) Punishment, (5) Seriousness, and (6) Risk. There was some tendency for Seriousness, Punishment, and Special Deterrence to cluster as one higher-order factor and for Rehabilitation and Risk to cluster as a second factor, which broadly corresponds to Carroll and Payne's praise or blame and future expectations factors. However, of central importance was the result that, although decision makers made seriousness and punishment judgments on the postdecision questionnaire, these judgments were not related to release recommendations. The five decision considerations that were predictive of recommendations came from the Risk, Rehabilitation, and Special Deterrence factors. It may be that the board believes the judge's sentence already represents the appropriate punishment. In fact, the judge's minimum sentence was strongly related to the rated offense severity, crime type, and severity of criminal record but was not at all related to the risk of subsequent offenses or the release recommendation. Thus, the board seems to take the viewpoint that *the judge* evaluates the criminal record and punishes the offender, whereas *the parole board* predicts the risks to the community and the benefits to the client.

These results are consistent with the experimental manipulations of attributions previously discussed (Carroll and Payne, 1977a,b), which demonstrated that expert parole decision makers do use stability information in evaluating risk of subsequent offenses. Differences between the experimental results and the posthearing questionnaire study seem adequately explained by the fact that the experts made recommendations about *parole release* in the latter study but about *prison sentence* (time to serve) in the former. In Pennsylvania, the parole board focuses on prediction when making release judgments, but the sentencing decision contains a punishment component. Interestingly, the same parole board is considerably more punishment oriented when making a different decision—parole revocation and back-time setting for convicted parole violators (Carroll and Ruback, in press). Clearly, then, the goal structure of the decision maker can change when the same decision maker confronts a different task.

Individual Differences Among Decision Makers. We have previously discussed how the possible goals of the parole decision—punishment, incapacitation, rehabilitation, deterrence—can be of varying importance to individual decision makers and how the perceived utility and availability of alternative means for achieving these goals can differ. Such factors could explain the variability found in parole decisions. For example, a person who employs a social-defense model (Miller, 1972) would weigh the risk element and incapacitation function of prison heavily; one who employs a treatment model would be more concerned with where a given person's rehabilitation could best be pursued. Hogarth (1971) found that judges' sentences were related to the perceived purposes of incarceration in the specific case, particularly incapacitation and punishment. Analyses based on how the individual judge perceived and understood the facts of the case were several times more predictive than analyses based on facts in the case files coded objectively by the researcher. He concluded that "One can explain more about sentencing by knowing a few things about the judge than by knowing a great deal about the facts of the case" (p. 350).

My own data from parole decision makers, some of which is discussed in Carroll (1978), also demonstrate substantial individual differences. Among the five Pennsylvania Board members, who work with each other on a close and continual basis, there were marked differences in recommendations and stated decision criteria. Multiple-regression analyses were performed for each board member, relating the rated decision criteria to release recommendations. The five board members seemed to base their recommendations on the following factors, in order of importance: Board Member A, Incapacitation, Rehabilitation; Board Member B, Rehabilitation; Board Member C, Rehabilitation, Incapacitation, Special Deterrence; Board Member D, Special Deterrence; Board Member E, Rehabilitation, Community Reaction to Release (related to punishment). Thus, the individual board members hold divergent views of the release decision, although overall the board is Rehabilitation oriented, with some attention to Incapacitation and Special Deterrence.

More generally, one can easily construe attributional biases as the bases for differences of opinion among political ideologies, scientific theories of crime, and correctional orientations. Political conservatives believe that people are responsible for their acts, whereas political liberals blame the society (Miller, 1973). Psychiatrists and psychologists focus on individual personality dynamics or biological irregularities in crime causation, whereas sociologists study subcultural norms, the opportunities for success in a person's life, or the social disorganization of areas of society (Schrag, 1971). Similarly, retribution, special deterrence, and incapacitation responses to criminal acts focus on the offender as the source of crime, whereas rehabilitation and reintegration (and, to some degree, general-deterrence) orientations focus on society's responsibility for crime (Schrag, 1971). Thus, people who make internal attributions about a crime (something about the offender) are likely to proffer retributive sentences (especially for intentional attributions), incapacitative sentences (if stable attributions are made), or therapeutic programs focusing on personal problems. People who make external attributions would avoid retribution and focus on system reform and rehabilitation (providing opportunities lacking in the previous environment), with lesser emphasis on incapacitation (stable environment) as necessary but somewhat unjust to the offender.

Studies of individual differences in responses to criminals have found that subjects who attribute criminality to factors internal to offenders judge the offenders more harshly (Sosis, 1974) and avoid contact with known criminals (Reed and Reed, 1973). Carroll and Payne (1976, 1977a) studied what information subjects sought about a case in order to make parole release recommendations. Simulated parole cases were presented, with each case consisting of twenty-four categories of information, such as age and offense. Subjects could see the information in a category by turning a 3 × 5 card (Carroll and Payne, 1976) or asking for the category information to be shown on a random-access slide projector (Carroll and Payne, 1977a). Results showed that Internals (on Rotter's scale) looked at information earlier that dealt with the crime (crime description, cooperation with police, time served, time left on sentence) and with the person (age, prior arrests, previous parole revocations, education level, susceptibility to influence). Externals, who view the environment as causally potent, looked earlier at information about the environment (release job plans, recent employment) and the prison (disciplinary problems, changes in attitude noted, prior convictions). Externals also looked at a base-rate prediction earlier. Thus, the attributional bias of the individual subject induced a *confirmatory set,* in which information to confirm the hypothesized cause of criminal behavior was looked at earlier than information about other possible causes. This biased information-seeking undoubtedly makes confirmation more likely (Snyder, Tanke, and Berscheid, 1977) and supports an attributional basis for individual differences in responses to crime. Insofar as the attributional bias makes hypothesized causes more salient, these more salient causes would be more likely to be implicated as the attributions for a crime (Taylor and Fiske, 1978).

Antecedents of Attributions. The research previously discussed in this chapter has dealt with how an attribution, once made, will produce particular evaluations and responses about a parole applicant. However, the framework presented in Figure 1 also considers how a person *forms* a causal attribution. Information in case histories and the knowledge of decision makers are combined to produce a causal attribution. Glaser (1964) poses the issue in stating that, "parole boards face the problem of how to integrate knowledge of characteristics of a particular prisoner with general knowledge about broad categories of offenders" (p. 289). We have proposed that an important aspect of this process is the formation of a causal attribution, and we have further examined how individual differences in beliefs about crime or causal biases can influence the attribution process. The lingering question, as yet unaddressed in parole research, is how the information in the case is used to form an attribution.

Attribution research in other areas has extensively investigated the information used to make an attribution. Such factors as the previous occurrences of similar behavior in the actor and in others, the presence of multiple causes of a discounting or facilitative nature, the availability of multiple observations from which to derive covariation information, the desirability of the consequences of the behavior for the actor and for the perceiver, and evidence of intent have all been considered important for the formation of a causal attribution (Jones and Davis, 1965; Kelley, 1973; Shaw and Sulzer, 1964; Weiner, 1974a).

As yet, little research has directly investigated the antecedents of attributions in the criminal justice system, and none has looked specifically at parole. Pepitone (1975) and Perlman (in press) analyze attributions in the criminal justice system and summarize research showing that: (1) victims are often blamed for crimes, especially when they are of bad character (Landy and Aronson 1969); (2) offenders are blamed more for crime when they are less likable or attractive (Landy and Aronson, 1969) or when they have a prior record (Lussier, Perlman, and Breen, 1977);

(3) offenders are blamed more if there are more serious consequences of their crimes (Rosen and Jerdee, 1974; Walster, 1966);
and (4) blame varies with the perceived intent of the offender
(Shaw and Reitan, 1969).

Evidence of what information is used in parole decisions
comes from regression studies attempting to predict decisions on
the basis of coded case information and from judgments by parole
experts of what they use in making decisions. The case factors that
emerge include: (1) the seriousness of the crime, (2) mitigating and
aggravating factors surrounding the crime, (3) the criminal record,
(4) assault and weapons present in the crime or in the criminal
history, (5) prior parole and probation performance, (6) drug and
alcohol use, (7) family situation, (8) social and economic stability
and status, (9) age, (10) institutional conduct and program participation, and (11) IQ score and education (Heinz and others, 1976;
Stanley, 1976; Wilkins and others, 1973).

Whereas we could provide plausible interpretations of this
case information in attributional terms (for example, past record is
consistency information, social status is distinctiveness information,
drug use is a possible cause), a proper analysis of the antecedents of
attributions requires careful research directed at that goal. In my
own work, I found surprisingly few relationships between attributions and crime type or prior record (Carroll, 1978). Longer prior
records were not reliably associated with more stable attributions.
Some crimes (such as drug offenses and burglaries) were attributed
to significantly more internal causes than were others (such as
murder). Specific case information may be used to infer specific
attributions; for example, psychological reports may reveal a drug
problem. Causal attributions may have a similar structure to
schemas (Abelson, 1976); in this example, case information triggers
a "drug habit" schema, which contains suppositions about past social history and criminal behavior, suggestions for treatment, and
predictions about future behavior.

Summary and Policy Implications

Research generated by the theoretical framework proposed
by Carroll and Payne (1976, 1977a,b) has demonstrated that judg-

ments about crime and criminals by college students do closely parallel the theory adapted from Weiner (1974a). Internal causes lead generally to more blame and punishment of the offender than do external causes; stable causes lead to predictions of more future crime and a desire to incapacitate the offender, when compared with unstable causes; intentionality seems to act along with internality, although the evidence is weaker.

Although the prevalence and importance of causal attributions in experts' judgments about offenders was demonstrated, their judgments did not fully conform to the theory. An experiment using brief simulated case descriptions did not reveal the predicted separability of blame and future expectations in punishment judgments and risk judgments, respectively. Experts treated internal, stable causes as more serious in all ways than other causes. Further, information about intentions seemed central to experts' inferences, yet such information was weakly specified in the theory and was difficult to manipulate. However, a correlational study of judgments about actual cases demonstrated that the stability of attributed causes was strongly associated with judgments of risk of future crime and subsequent recommendations for parole.

Finally, suggestive evidence was provided that individual student decision makers differ in the information they desire about parole applicants, corresponding to their general tendency to see persons or environments as causally potent (measured by Rotter's I-E Scale). This attributional bias probably produces confirmation of the hypothesized attribution through selective information-search and salience effects. Further, parole experts were shown to have individualized goals for the parole process—some consider rehabilitation and others consider incapacitation or special deterrence.

Implications for the Criminal Justice System. The development of an attributional analysis of the parole decision provides several potential opportunities for improving phases of the decision process. First, parole decision makers are faced with poorly defined and conflicting goals. These goals are based on assumptions of what causes and cures criminal behavior. Insofar as attribution theory can offer a single parsimonious description of the beliefs underlying different goals, policy makers should be better able to create an explicit and clear policy governing parole applicants. Thus, the attribution framework may help to represent and sharpen the issues, speeding up the process of creating a policy.

Second, the attribution approach can provide a means of evaluating the attributional biases of individual decision makers or of entire parole systems. The approach suggests how to characterize decision makers in terms of their underlying causal assumptions. Thus, differences among decision makers could be detected, as could differences between decision makers and legislated policy. This enhanced ability to examine current practices could be tied to attempts at changing policy, improving decisions, or training decision makers.

Third, the attributional framework suggests that a goal for training decision makers might be to make them aware of specific causal schemas or hypothesized causes for various criminal behaviors that have demonstrable validity. Attribution researchers have successfully used their insights in constructing training procedures in the classroom (Dweck, 1975); training programs for parole decision makers could be similarly specified. For example, research dealing with the causes of specific offenses can be used to influence parole decisions and treatment plans regarding specific cases.

Finally, the attributional approach suggests how decision aids might be created to improve parole decision making. It is well known that attributors are subject to various biases, which lead them to characteristically wrong attributions (Ross, 1977). Decision aids that allow decision makers to represent case information in a fashion that allows more factors to be considered, that encourages the use of information currently underutilized, and that otherwise corrects attributional biases could improve decisions. In short, the naive attributor could be assisted by bringing scientifically verified knowledge into his decision process in a way that encourages its use. For example, consider the well-known difficulty that people have in properly using consensus or base-rate information (Nisbett and others, 1976). The U.S. Board of Parole has incorporated a statistical-prediction device in its decisions, which has brought parole judgments more closely in line with established research on the antecedents of recidivism (Gottfredson and others, 1975).

Implications for the Legal System. The law bears an interesting relationship to attribution theory, in that it also codifies naive causal judgments. The questions of responsibility, causality, and intention are crucial legal questions with centuries of legal thought behind them (Hart and Honore, 1959; Marshall, 1968). Essentially, the law distinguishes accidents from intended acts: "An act does not make (the doer of it) guilty, unless the mind be guilty; that is, unless the intention be criminal" (Black, 1933, p. 48). The meaning of *intent*, however, differs from common usage: "A person who contemplates any result, as not unlikely to follow from a deliberate act of his own, may be said to intend that result, whether he desires it or not" (Black, 1933, p. 933). The more common meaning of *intent*, the deliberate desire for the resultant consequences of acts, is considered to be a deeper form of intent, called *motive* or *malice*. As stated by Oliver Wendell Holmes (1881), "Intent again will be found to resolve itself into two things; foresight that certain consequences will follow from an act, and the wish for these consequences working as a motive which induces the act" (p. 53). Further, legal scholars readily admit that *probable intent* is judged by social norms—what the "reasonable man" would have done or not done in such circumstances (Marshall, 1968).

The importance of an attributional analysis of intentionality is not that we have reproduced legal distinctions in our ideas of causality, foreseeability, and intentionality (Heider, 1958; Shaw and Sulzer, 1964). Rather, the attributional approach can serve to separate legal philosophy from normative or general knowledge and to specify the antecedent information leading people to infer particular levels of intentionality. Again, as with the criminal justice system, the ultimate goals would be a deepening of our understanding of judicial and juridic discretion and the ability to frame issues and alter practice in a rational manner. Although attribution research has only begun to approach these issues, there is the promise of valuable applications in the future.

Chapter 13

Mark R. Lepper
Janet L. Dafoe

Incentives, Constraints, and Motivation in the Classroom

Schools are ubiquitous and complex institutions. By the time the average child in our society is ready to enter high school, he or she will have spent nearly 10,000 hours attending school. Along the way, most of these students will have learned a great deal (although perhaps less than we would like) about reading, writing, arithmetic,

Note: Preparation of this chapter was supported in part by Research Grants MH-24134 from the National Institute of Mental Health and HD-MH-09814 from the National Institute of Child Health and Human

and the other subjects that comprise the formal academic curriculum of the school. The attainment of these academic accomplishments is the goal of our system of compulsory education, and these accomplishments provide the criteria by which the effectiveness of schools as educational institutions is typically evaluated.

Issues of motivation are central to any consideration of the ways in which schools achieve or might better achieve these academic goals. Learning is inherently an active process that requires attention, effort, and persistence on the part of the learner. Questions of how to instill motivation in children or how to match programs to children's motivational predispositions are as old as the history of formal education. Over the years, answers to these questions have ranged from the use of the rod and the dunce cap to the implementation of systematic incentive programs designed to promote children's interest and achievement in a more humane fashion.

In this chapter, we shall examine the relevance of attribution theory to understanding the ways in which children's performance and interests may be affected by the systems of evaluation and social control to which they are exposed in schools. Underlying this analysis is the assumption that a child's acquisition of academic skills and knowledge takes place in a complex social environment, the school, in which rewards and sanctions may play many roles. For a child to succeed in school, we will argue, requires mastery of both the formal academic curriculum and the norms and conventions that govern social interchanges and learning in the classroom environment. What the child learns in school, as a number of authors have suggested (Dreeben, 1968; Holt, 1964; Jackson, 1968; Silberman, 1970), consists of not only academic skills but also a variety of more general but less explicit lessons concerning deference to authority, delay of gratification, social comparison and evaluation, and adaptation to a system of social constraint and social control.

In a penetrating analysis of the ecology of classroom life,

Development to Mark R. Lepper. The authors wish to express their appreciation to David Greene, Charlotte Patterson, Gerald Sagotsky, and the editors for their thoughtful comments on an earlier draft of this chapter.

Philip Jackson (1968) has coined the term *hidden curriculum* to describe these social aspects of school life to which children are expected to adjust. In particular, Jackson focuses on three interrelated aspects of the classroom that significantly determine the context in which learning and progress through both the formal academic and the hidden social curriculums occur: crowds, praise, and power. The first of these presuppositions of classroom life is obvious; in school, both formal instruction and informal social interaction and exchange occur most frequently in the context of a large group of children confined to a reasonably small physical space. The pervasive impact of crowded conditions on the character of classrooms is perhaps less evident. The requisite "traffic management," systematization of routines, and inevitable delays occasioned by the demands of simultaneously dealing with (or at least keeping occupied) a large number of children provide the broader framework within which teachers, students, and instructional methods interact.

Of more immediate relevance to this chapter are the remaining two focal points of Jackson's analysis: praise and power. The focus on praise emphasizes the fact that schools are places where children are subjected to a continuous and unrelenting process of evaluation. The evaluations the child receives include frequent informal assessments concerning the content and form of his classroom performance, more palpable rewards and privileges inherent in the day-to-day operation of classes, and the formalized tests, grades, and reports that comprise the student's official transcript. The focus on power highlights the extent to which the operation of functional classrooms necessitates the use of social-control techniques and the exercise of power by teachers and other school personnel. Although educators may disagree concerning the extent to which a quiet or docile classroom environment is conducive to optimal achievement (O'Leary, 1972; Winett and Winkler, 1972), it remains a fundamental fact of life in schools that attendance and some modicum of decorum and compliance with institutional rules and expectations are indeed compulsory. Although individual schools and teachers differ widely in the manner and context of the application of techniques of social control, the use of incentives or sanctions designed to minimize deviant or inappropriate behavior is as much a part of the average classroom as blackboards and pencil sharpeners.

These several functions of incentives in the classroom—to motivate, evaluate, and control behavior—form the background for our attributional analysis. In particular, we shall contend that the effects of incentives, sanctions, and performance evaluations on the child's behavior depend not only on what they tell the child about the instrumental value of that behavior in the future but also on what attributions they lead the child to make about his behavior. These attributions are of two kinds: those concerning the *causes* of his success or failure and those concerning the *reasons* underlying his actions.

Historically, classrooms have provided fertile ground for theorists concerned with the processes by which individuals understand and explain their own behavior and that of others (Bar-Tal, 1978; Frieze, 1976a, 1976b; Heider, 1958; Kelley, 1967, 1973; Weiner, 1972a, 1972b, 1974a, 1974b). Much of this research has focused on attributions and inferences concerning students' abilities and dispositions as a function of the perceived causes of their successes or failures. This research is considered in detail in Chapter Fourteen and elsewhere (Bar-Tal, 1978, Frieze, Snyder, and Fontaine, 1977; Weiner, 1974a) and will be outlined only briefly here, so that parallels and comparisons with our own approach might be noted.

The second approach deals with students' attributions concerning their reasons for engaging in particular activities—the conditions that lead students to see themselves as intrinsically or extrinsically motivated and the consequences of those perceptions (Condry, 1977; Deci, 1975; Lepper and Greene, 1978a, 1978b)— and will form the central focus of this chapter. Hence, after touching briefly on issues concerning students' attributions about the causes of their success or failure, we shall consider in more detail the issues and experimental evidence concerning students' attributions about the reasons for their actions in school. We conclude by examining the implications of this literature and our arguments for understanding the potential costs and benefits of the use of incentive systems in classrooms.

Attributions Concerning the Causes of Performance Outcomes

In this section, we consider the school as a context of evaluation, in which the rewards and feedback children receive are frequently based on inferences concerning their abilities and motivation. The way in which students' performance and subsequent motivation are affected by their past academic successes and failures is the central issue to which this literature is addressed. In traditional mechanistic models (Weiner, 1972a), a child's motivation to engage in a task is seen as a general function of the proportion of successful to unsuccessful encounters he has had with that task in the past. An attributional account, by contrast, suggests that the effects of feedback concerning one's success or failure at an activity can only be understood in the context of the person's interpretations or attributions concerning the *causes* of his or her success or failure. Performance outcomes, this model suggests, typically evoke a set of inferences that explain the outcome. These inferences concern the abilities and dispositions of the actor, the characteristics of the task, and the setting in which it was presented. Successful and unsuccessful outcomes are then understood in terms of these attributions, and their effects on the individual will differ as a function of the causal inferences made.

Obviously, both teachers and students engage in such an inference process. Teachers must judge when praise is warranted for a particular performance or how difficult an assignment or test to present to a student. These judgments necessarily depend on the teacher's perceptions of the child's ability and motivation and the general difficulty of the tasks assigned. The student attempting to decide how much work a particular assignment will require or whether it is worth trying harder in a particular subject faces similar issues. Such decisions clearly depend on the student's judgments concerning his or her own abilities and limitations and the requirements posed by the task itself. The manner in which one's past successes and failures are interpreted can thus have important consequences for one's performance and subsequent motivation.

Classification of Performance Attributions. Students' causal attributions for success and failure have been studied extensively. Although we will not attempt a detailed review of this literature, several characteristics of this approach will be outlined, so that we may contrast it with our own. At the heart of this analysis lie fundamental distinctions among attributions, which specify causes of outcomes on two dimensions: locus of control and stability. Locus of control differentiates between causes external to the individual (task variables, chance factors, help or interference from others) and internal to the individual (the ability, effort, or personality of the actor). Stability differentiates between stable causes (ability, personality) and unstable causes (effort, chance factors). Research has focused on the consequences of different types of attributions concerning performance outcomes and on antecedents of these attributions.

Consequences of Performance Attributions. First, a person's attributions as to the causes of his success or failure at an achievement-related activity have been found to affect his subsequent reactions toward that activity. Generally, a person who attributes his success at a task to internal factors, such as high ability or effort, will be more likely to feel pride in this success and more likely to choose or initiate that activity again in the future. However, a person who does not take personal responsibility for his success but attributes it to external factors will be less likely to feel such positive affect and will thus be less likely to initiate the activity in the future (Weiner and others, 1972). Similarly, persistence at a task following prior failure appears to depend heavily on the attributions one has made concerning the causes of that failure. A person who attributes his failure to lack of effort—an unstable cause—has reason to expect that he might succeed with increased effort and may, therefore, continue striving. If, instead, one attributes failure to a lack of ability or to external factors beyond one's control, one has less hope for effecting a change in the future that would lead to eventual success. Persistence, as a result, becomes less probable (Dweck and Repucci, 1973; Weiner and others, 1972).

In addition to these effects on subsequent behavior, causal attributions may affect immediate task performance. A person who believes that performance outcomes vary as a function of his own effort would be expected to perform an achievement activity with greater intensity, for example, than a person who believes his effort does not affect the outcome. The former individual would expend greater effort, because he believes it will make a difference; the latter person does not believe this. Similarly, the level of the difficulty of achievement tasks a person prefers are affected by the kinds of attributions he makes. Persons who make ability and effort attributions in cases of success and effort attributions in cases of failure tend to choose tasks of intermediate difficulty, where their success or failure will provide information about their relative ability and effort; persons making external attributions in cases of success and ability attributions in cases of failure tend to choose either quite easy tasks (at which almost all persons succeed) or very difficult tasks (at which almost all persons fail), both of which provide little information concerning their abilities relative to others (Weiner and others, 1972).

Children in school receive a great deal of feedback concerning their success or failure at different tasks. Sometimes, performance feedback may be built into the structure of the tasks they attempt; more frequently, this feedback may come in the form of adult praise or criticism or more tangible rewards that are contingent on their performance. The effects of such procedures on students' subsequent motivation, the literature on achievement-related attributions suggests, will depend on the inferences the child draws concerning his or her ability and the consequences of sustained effort.

There is a considerable experimental literature suggesting that teachers consciously attempt to reward students for effort and, to a lesser extent, ability (Lanzetta and Hannah, 1969; Rest and others, 1973; Salili, Maehr, and Gillmore, 1976; Weiner and Kukla, 1970). Implicit in this attempt is the goal of leading children to expect a covariation between the effort they expend on a task and the rewards they receive as a result (Bar-Tal, 1978). Were this underlying goal realized, one would expect the use of contingent rewards to produce greater subsequent success, persistence, and approach to those tasks for which rewards had been previously offered.

Recent observational work by Dweck and her colleagues, however, indicates that this is only part of the story. In an elegant observational study of fourth- and fifth-grade classrooms, Dweck and others (1978) found that a strikingly high proportion of the evaluative feedback that students received was concerned more with the form of students' behavior and adherence to social conventions than the intellectual adequacy of their performance. Similar trends in the use of structured-incentive programs in classrooms have been documented by Winett and Winkler (1972). The additional issues raised by the fact that extrinsic rewards are used to control behavior as well as to signal success and reward effort lead to a consideration of other ways in which extrinsic rewards may affect subsequent motivation.

Attributions Concerning the Reasons for Actions

Complementing the literature on the effects of causal attributions concerning performance outcomes, a more recent attributional approach to issues of motivation has examined the consequences of attributions people make concerning the reasons for their actions (Lepper and Greene, 1978a). In this research, differences in the extent to which individuals view their actions as either voluntary or constrained have been shown to have an important influence on an individual's subsequent interest in and performance at activities previously undertaken in the presence or absence of explicit instrumental contingencies.

Such a focus on volition and constraint, of course, relates to the issues of power and social control in the classroom raised in our earlier discussion. Classroom incentives and sanctions, we have noted, are necessarily employed not only to reward successful achievement but also to maintain order, to motivate students to engage in particular activities at specific times, and to encourage students to respond to tasks with appropriate form as well as intellectual content. An analysis of the effects of classroom contingencies on students' attributions concerning their reasons for engaging in various activities is of particular significance, because it suggests that the *inappropriate* use of tangible rewards (and other highly visible techniques of social control) may have *detrimental* effects on performance and subsequent interest in the task. Superfluous or unnecessarily powerful incentives may produce immediate functional control over the child's behavior at the price of decreases in the child's intrinsic interest in the activity, when these contingencies are no longer in effect.

Intrinsic versus Extrinsic Attributions

Central to this second approach is a distinction between actions perceived as intrinsically motivated and those perceived as extrinsically motivated. Historically, this distinction derives from several sources. In an early account, deCharms (1968) suggested that a person may be said to be intrinsically motivated to engage in an activity when he perceives himself as having originated his behavior, and extrinsically motivated when he perceives himself to be an instrument of some external agent or influence. More recently, Deci (1971, 1975) has hypothesized that a person's attitudes and subsequent behavior toward an activity may be determined by his or her perceived motives for engaging in the activity.

Similarly, attribution theorists (Bem, 1967, 1972; Kelley, 1967, 1973; Kruglanski, 1975; Lepper, Greene, and Nisbett, 1973) have hypothesized that the inferences a person makes concerning his or her motives will, in part, determine the person's subsequent attitudes and behavior toward that activity. If a person engaged in an activity perceives his actions to be controlled by salient and powerful extrinsic contingencies, he will be likely to attribute his behavior to those extrinsic constraints. To the extent that such extrinsic constraints are not salient or are not sufficient to explain this engagement in the activity, the person will attribute his behavior to intrinsic factors.

This distinction can be contrasted with the distinction between factors internal and external to the individual employed in the analysis of the causes of one's success or failure. The relevant distinction in this analysis is between reasons for engaging in an activity that involve the inherent value of engaging in the activity as an end in itself versus reasons that involve the instrumentality of engagement in that activity as a means to some goal extrinsic to task engagement (Beck, 1975). In the former case, the individual makes an *endogenous* attribution, viewing his engagement in the activity as an end in itself; in the latter case, he makes an *exogenous* attribution, viewing his engagement in the activity as a means to some further end (Kruglanski, 1975, 1978a; Lepper and Greene, 1978b). The consequences of this difference in attributions concerning the reasons for one's actions—whether they are viewed as intrinsically or extrinsically motivated—form the focus of the following section.

Effects on Subsequent Motivation. One implication of this approach, initially christened the *overjustification hypothesis* (Bem, 1972; Lepper and others, 1973), is that, when powerful extrinsic contingencies are employed to induce a person to engage in an activity of high initial interest, the person will be likely to attribute his behavior to these salient extrinsic constraints rather than to his intrinsic interest in the activity itself. Engagement in an activity of initial interest under conditions that make salient its instrumental value as a means to some extrinsic goal, in this view, will decrease the perceived value of the activity and therefore result in less subsequent interest in the activity in settings where further extrinsic goals are not salient.

To test this hypothesis requires several conditions. First, an experimental activity of initial interest to subjects in the absence of extrinsic contingencies is needed. Second, this activity must be presented to some subjects under conditions that make salient its instrumentality to some extrinsic goal and to others under comparable conditions in which engagement in the activity will not be seen as instrumental. Finally, to permit inferences concerning subjects' subsequent *intrinsic* interest, later behavior must be observed in a setting in which the activity is not perceived as having continued instrumental value as a function of the previous contingency.

In a paradigmatic study meeting these conditions, Lepper, Greene, and Nisbett (1973) examined this overjustification hypothesis in ongoing preschool classrooms. In this study, pupils were selected as subjects on the basis of their demonstrated preexperimental interest in a target activity during free play periods in their classrooms. In this setting, children were free to choose among a variety of activities in the absence of external pressures and were not aware that their behavior was being observed. Next, in individual experimental sessions in a different setting, these children were asked to engage in the activity under one of three conditions. In the Expected Award condition, subjects were first shown an extrinsic reward, a Good Player certificate, and were asked if they wished to engage in the drawing activity in order to win this award. This procedure was designed to induce subjects to see their engagement in the activity as instrumental to an extrinsic goal. In the Unexpected Award condition, subjects were asked to engage in the activity without mention of any reward, but they unexpectedly received the same award and the same feedback after they had finished the activity. This procedure provided a control for task engagement and receipt of the reward, without providing the conditions likely to promote a perception of task engagement as instrumental to an ulterior goal. Finally, in the No Award control condition, subjects neither expected nor received a reward but otherwise duplicated the experience of subjects in the other conditions. Two weeks later, children's subsequent intrinsic interest in the activity was assessed. The target activity was again placed in the children's classrooms for several days, and postexperimental interest in the activity was observed unobtrusively, as during the baseline period, in the absence of any expectation of further extrinsic rewards.

From an attributional perspective, it was expected that children in the Expected Award condition would attribute their engagement in the task to the extrinsic incentive and would thus show less subsequent interest in the activity than children in the Unexpected Award or No Award conditions. The results strongly supported this prediction. Subjects who had agreed to engage in the activity in order to obtain the award subsequently spent significantly less time with the activity than did subjects in the other two conditions. Relative to uniform high levels of baseline interest, Expected Award subjects also showed a significant decrease in interest from baseline to postexperimental observations, whereas subjects in the No Award and Unexpected Award conditions showed no significant change in overall interest.

As predicted by an attributional analysis, these results suggest that extrinsic rewards will decrease subsequent intrinsic interest only when the reward is presented in a manner that leads the child to consider his or her engagement in .the activity as a means to the attainment of that reward. These basic findings have been replicated and extended in later research. Several additional studies, for example, have also compared expected and unexpected reward procedures and provide further evidence that detrimental effects on subsequent interest typically depend on the prior designation of the activity as a means of obtaining the proffered reward (Greene and Lepper, 1974; Lepper and Greene,

1975; Lepper, Sagotsky, and Greene, 1978a; Smith 1976).[1] Other investigations have demonstrated that expectation of a reward presented as contingent on the mere passage of time, while the subject is incidentally engaged in the target activity, does not produce the same decrement in subsequent interest as expected rewards presented as contingent on task engagement (Deci, 1972b; Ross, Karniol, and Rothstein, 1976; Swann and Pittman, 1977).

Similarly, since the perception of one's actions as extrinsically motivated should depend on the salience of the extrinsic reward offered, other experiments have addressed the prediction that extrinsic rewards will undermine intrinsic interest to the extent that the contingency between task engagement and the receipt of reward is made perceptually or ideationally salient. In two complementary studies, Ross (1975) explicitly varied the salience of instrumentality and found that detrimental effects were apparent only when the expected reward was salient. More indirectly, further studies have compared verbal approval—which represents, from an attributional perspective, a less visible and psychologically salient form of social control (Kelley, 1967; Kruglanski, 1978a; Lepper and Greene, 1978b)—with more tangible rewards. These studies suggest that detrimental effects observed as a consequence of the use of superfluous tangible rewards are less likely to occur when social approval alone is used (Anderson, Manoogian, and Resnick, 1976; Deci, 1971, 1972a).[2]

Additional recent experiments have attempted to provide a more direct test of the utility of our proposed means-ends analysis of this literature. Pittman, Cooper, and Smith (1977), for instance, have demonstrated that the detrimental effects of superfluous extrinsic rewards may be moderated by manipulations designed to induce expected-reward subjects to attribute their engagement in an activity to either intrinsic or extrinsic factors. In their experiment, subjects engaged in an activity of initial interest either with or without expectation of a monetary reward contingent on task performance. There were three expected-reward conditions. Subjects in two of these groups received false physiological feedback, ostensibly indicative of either their interest in the task itself (intrinsic attribution) or their interest in winning money by engaging in the task (extrinsic attribution); subjects in a third group received no feedback. Subsequent behavioral measures of intrinsic interest in the activity demonstrated a detrimental effect of expected rewards for no-feedback subjects relative to unpaid control subjects. As predicted by a means-ends analysis, however, this detrimental effect was significantly decreased when subjects had been provided with feedback suggesting an intrinsic attribution but was nonsignificantly increased when an extrinsic attribution had been made salient. Comparable support for a means-ends analysis was also obtained in a later investigation by Johnson, Greene, and Carroll (1978), which employed a related, though considerably more subtle, procedure. In their study, the manipulation designed to lead some expected-reward subjects to attribute their actions to either intrinsic or extrinsic factors was a single sentence emphasizing either subjects' own interest in the task or their receipt of payment as a reason for engaging in the activity. Making salient intrinsic reasons for engaging in the activity served to eliminate the detrimental effects of a standard expected-reward procedure, whereas making extrinsic reasons salient for subjects already expecting payment had little effect.

Although a majority of these experimental studies have been conducted with children and have frequently involved measures of subsequent behavior in ongoing classroom settings, one may still question the ecological relevance of these experimental results to more long-term reward programs of the sort common in public school classes. Two studies have examined this issue directly. In the first of these studies, Colvin (1972) exposed elementary school students in art classes to a four-week reinforcement program and observed their subsequent behavior after the rewards were removed. For experimental subjects, during the treatment phase, tangible rewards were contingent on the time children spent each day with their initially preferred art activities. Control subjects received equivalent but noncontingent tangible rewards. These rewards were then withdrawn, without efforts to maintain the changes in behavior that had occurred during the treatment phase. During this period, experimental subjects who had received superfluous contingent rewards spent significantly less time with their previously preferred art activities than control subjects, and they engaged in these activities significantly less than they had during the baseline period.

Using a more extensive design, Greene, Sternberg, and

Lepper (1976) compared three different experimental-reward programs with a nondifferentially rewarded control group. Four sets of instructional materials composing a mathematics laboratory were introduced into elementary school classrooms. Following baseline observations of children's choices among these activities in the absence of extrinsic rewards, a treatment phase was instituted. Experimental subjects were provided with tangible rewards contingent on their engagement in two of the four activities—either the two activities the child spent more time with during the baseline phase, the two activities the child spent less time with during baseline observations, or two activities selected by the child himself. Control subjects received rewards for engagement in any of the four activities. After several weeks, these extrinsic incentives were withdrawn, but the activities remained in the room. Subsequent intrinsic interest in the activities was assessed in the absence of any attempt to influence children's choices.

During the treatment phase, each of the three experimental-reward systems proved effective in producing significant increases in children's engagement in the rewarded activities. Withdrawal of the reward program, however, produced decrements in response below baseline levels, which were significant for two of these three groups. Children rewarded for engagement in the two activities of their choice and children rewarded for engagement in the two activities of lesser initial interest, in addition, showed significantly less interest during withdrawal than control subjects. Children rewarded for engagement in the two activities of more initial interest did not differ from control subjects during the withdrawal phase, although interpretation of these latter findings is hindered by gradual shifts in the response patterns of control subjects with time.

Taken together, these studies and others (Johnson, Bolstad, and Lobitz, 1976; Meichenbaum, Bowers, and Ross, 1968) provide instances of detrimental effects of demonstrably effective and relatively long-term reward programs in typical classroom settings. Two points about these findings, however, should be made clear. First, the relevance of the results of any long-term applied reinforcement program to our present concerns requires a demonstration that measures of subsequent behavior were obtained in settings where students did not expect further social or tangible rewards contingent on their behavior in accordance with previously imposed contingencies. In most applied reward programs, this has not been the case; yet, without such a demonstration, it is impossible to draw conclusions about students' intrinsic motivation (Lepper and Greene, 1978b; Lepper, Sagotsky, and Greene, 1978b). Second, the attributional processes we have discussed are only one of a number of factors that may determine subsequent behavior in any applied setting, as we shall discuss in more detail in the final section of this chapter. Whether the net effects of an incentive program will be positive or negative will, therefore, depend on the multiple effects of these different factors (Lepper and Greene, 1978b, 1978c).

Finally, although much of the relevant research has concentrated on the consequences of extrinsic attributions induced by the use of functionally superfluous tangible rewards, it should be clear that the theoretical model underlying these studies is not specifically concerned with the effects of rewards but deals more generally with any form of highly visible external control that may lead the student to view his behavior as extrinsically motivated. Hence, it is important to note that other forms of extrinsic constraint may produce conceptually parallel results. The imposition of salient adult surveillance (Lepper and Greene, 1975), superfluous temporal deadlines (Amabile, DeJong, and Lepper, 1976), and enforced-rehearsal procedures (Rosenhan, 1969) on an individual's engagement in an activity have all been shown to decrease the probability of subsequent engagement in the activity in the absence of extrinsic pressures. Thus, this literature addresses the consequences of salient extrinsic constraints rather than the consequences of specific rewards, surveillance, or deadlines.

Effects on Task Performance. The foregoing studies have concentrated primarily on the possible deleterious consequences of supplanting intrinsic attributions with extrinsic attributions on subsequent intrinsic interest in an activity. Other related investigations have explored potential adverse effects of similar procedures on measures of immediate task performance. Although these latter studies address questions conceptually parallel to those considered in the previous section, they raise somewhat more complex theoretical and methodological issues. This added complexity arises because the effects of extrinsic rewards on performance are necessarily measured in a context where both intrinsic and extrinsic motivation may affect one's behavior. Performance under conditions of extrinsic motivation will thus reflect both the student's own intrinsic interest in the activity and his or her perception of how best to perform the activity to obtain the extrinsic incentive.

From an attributional perspective, the primary effect of inducing an individual to see his or her engagement in an activity as a means to some extrinsic goal should be to focus the person's attention on those aspects of the activity that are perceived as relevant to the attainment of that goal (Condry and Chambers, 1978; Kruglanski, 1978a; Kruglanski, Friedman, and Zeevi, 1971; Lepper and Greene, 1978b). This instrumental orientation toward the activity should affect the student's manner of approaching the activity, the criteria that guide and determine his or her performance, and decisions about when to terminate engagement in the activity. Consequently, demonstrations of detrimental effects of extrinsic constraints on immediate performance should be expected to depend specifically on the nature of the activity and the nature of the particular performance measures obtained (for example, qualitative versus quantitative or central versus incidental performance). To the extent that extrinsic constraints supplant intrinsic motivation, aspects of performance with high instrumental value for achieving the extrinsic goal may be affected positively, whereas aspects of performance not relevant to the attainment of this goal may be affected adversely. In spite of these complications that make it difficult to assess the role of intrinsic interest with immediate performance measures, a number of studies have provided evidence consistent with the prediction that unnecessarily powerful extrinsic rewards and constraints may have negative effects on immediate task performance as well as subsequent intrinsic interest.

One line of relevant research has examined students' choices among tasks of different levels of difficulty as a function of the presence or absence of salient extrinsic contingencies. Harter (1978), for example, examined the choices of sixth-grade students presented with an anagrams task comprising a range of problems at different levels of difficulty. Some students were asked to under-take the activity for its own sake; others were led to expect that their performance on the task was to be graded. Students expecting to be graded chose significantly less difficult problems, which they also appeared (from observational data on their facial expressions) to enjoy less than students not exposed to this extrinsic con-tingency. Comparable data on the presence or absence of monetary rewards have been reported with adult subjects by Shapira (1976) and Condry and Chambers (1978).

If one assumes that less learning is likely to take place when students select only those problems they are certain they can solve easily, these data suggest that the imposition of inappropriate ex-trinsic contingencies may produce "superior" performance at the expense of children's avoidance of more educational but riskier alternatives. Indeed, evidence from a study by Blackwell (1974) suggests that children themselves may be aware of this distinction between learning and performance. In this study, elementary school children were offered tangible rewards for working on mathematics problems, either for learning the most they could from these problems or for achieving their best performance on the task. Relative to nonrewarded control subjects, students re-warded for learning did not display the marked preference for simpler and less challenging problems shown by students rewarded for performance.

A second, related line of research has examined the general proposition that focusing attention on instrumentally relevant parameters of task performance, under conditions of extrinsic motivation, may result in decrements in performance on aspects of the task not of immediate instrumental relevance. In an early study, for example, Kruglanski, Friedman, and Zeevi (1971) examined the effects of the offer of an extrinsic incentive on high school students' performance on several tasks of initial interest. Subjects offered an extrinsic reward showed less creativity and less adequate task recall. These subjects, in addition, exhibited a lessened tendency to recall differentially uncompleted as opposed to completed tasks (a less-ened Zeigarnik effect) and tended to report the tasks as less enjoy-able. Later investigations have produced similar results. In two studies (Greene and Lepper, 1974; Lepper and others, 1973) of the effects of rewards on subsequent interest, preschool subjects who were offered an expected reward for engagement in an art activity produced a greater number of pictures in a constant time period, with a resultant decrease in the average quality of these drawings.[3] Similarly, McGraw and McCullers (in press) found that subjects who were paid for their performance on a traditional functional-fixedness problem had more difficulty breaking set to discover a novel and more simple solution to the problem when it became available.

Perhaps more striking in this context are studies demonstrating that the provision of superfluous extrinsic rewards may sometimes produce detrimental effects even on central task performance. In an extensive review, McGraw (1978) concludes that such effects are likely to occur to the extent that the activity for which subjects are rewarded is initially attractive to the subject and requires heuristic (open-ended) rather than algorithmic solutions. The former requirement, of course, establishes the task as one of initial intrinsic interest to the subject, which makes the issue of intrinsic versus extrinsic attributions relevant. The latter constraint implies a set of conditions under which exclusive concentration on the most obvious instrumentally relevant parameters may impede rather than aid performance.

Two studies provide particularly illustrative examples. In the first, Condry and Chambers (1977, 1978) presented subjects with a series of concept-attainment tasks, with or without the promise of rewards for solution. Subjects who were offered payment for correct solutions attempted, not surprisingly, to short-circuit the learning process by trying to guess the correct answer much earlier than was warranted, and they generally made less efficient use of the information they obtained (see Holt, 1964). Even more impressively, when later given similar tasks with specific instructions not to answer until they could be certain that their answer was correct, previously rewarded subjects were more likely to offer solutions before they could logically have certified the correctness of their hypothesis. In the second study, Garbarino (1975) asked sixth-grade children to serve as tutors for first-grade children and compared the performance of tutors offered a tangible reward for success and those offered no reward. Generally, children who were paid for tutoring exhibited a more instrumental orientation toward their pupils. The interactions between tutor and pupil were characterized, in the reward condition, by more criticism, more demands, a less efficacious use of time, and a more negative emotional tone. Under these conditions, the tutees learned the task significantly less well and made more errors than those in the no-reward condition.

Effects of Individual Differences. A third class of issues raised by the study of attributions of intrinsic and extrinsic motivation concerns the possible development and consequences of more stable differences in students' general tendencies to view their behavior as intrinsically versus extrinsically motivated. Here, experimental evidence is relatively sparse, though several studies deserve brief mention. In two of these studies, deCharms (1972, 1976) provided elementary school teachers with training designed to aid them in enhancing their students' perceptions of themselves as origins rather than as pawns. Although the training programs in these studies were quite complex and susceptible to a number of interpretations, the results suggested that these training procedures enhanced not only students' perceptions of themselves as origins but also their academic motivation and achievement during the course of the study. In a related study, Blackwell (1974) assessed subjects' perceptions of themselves as origins versus pawns and found significant positive correlations between students' general perceptions of themselves as origins and their tendency to select problems of intermediate difficulty on an achievement-related task as well as their motivation to engage in this task in the absence of extrinsic constraints. Although further research is needed, the general parallels between these long-term results and the experimental data considered earlier are apparent.

Implications and Applications

Rewards may play many roles in the classroom. An attributional approach alerts us to the fact that the impact of rewards on performance and subsequent motivation is mediated by the ways in which students construe their meaning. In this chapter, we have touched briefly on the role of students' attributions concerning the causes of their success or failure and have examined in more detail the role of students' attributions concerning the reasons for their actions. Let us summarize the complementary results of these two approaches.

First, we considered classroom incentives as sources of performance feedback to the child concerning his ability and effort, and we considered the relationship between incentives and his success or failure at academic tasks. The attributions children make about the causes of their success or failure were shown to have important consequences for their immediate and subsequent approach to particular activities. Second, we considered classroom incentives as techniques of social control, and we examined the effects of superfluous extrinsic incentives on children's perceptions of their actions as intrinsically versus extrinsically motivated. The attributions children make about their reasons for engaging in particular tasks were shown to have significant effects on their performance and subsequent interest in these activities. In the former case, attributions of personal competence and the belief that one's outcomes depend on one's effort enhanced performance and subsequent interest, whereas attributions of low ability or a belief that outcomes and effort are uncorrelated had negative effects. In the latter case, attributions of subjective freedom and intrinsic motivation maintained or enhanced subsequent interest and performance, whereas attributions of constraint and extrinsic motivation had detrimental effects on subsequent interest and performance.

In most classroom applications, of course, rewards and sanctions may simultaneously carry many meanings. As Dweck and others (1978) have shown, formal academic and hidden social curricula are often intertwined. Feedback children receive, purportedly concerning their academic performance, often deals as much with adherence to social norms and conventions as it does with the quality of the students' work. Understanding the effects of rewards in classrooms will, therefore, require attention to the interaction of the different categories of information that rewards may convey.

In the foregoing sections, we have reviewed the attributional literature concerning the ways in which tangible rewards and other forms of social control can affect children's performance and subsequent interest in activities undertaken in school. These data suggest that salient incentive programs can have both beneficial and detrimental effects on performance and subsequent behavior, to the extent to which they affect children's attributions concerning the causes of their success and failure and their reasons for engaging in particular activities. These attributions, in turn, depend both on the initial skills and interests of the child and the manner and context in which the incentives are presented.

The Multiple Functions of Rewards. These findings have important implications for understanding how tangible rewards can be used more effectively in classrooms. Rather than providing a simple prescription for classroom practice, however, they emphasize the complexity of the issues involved in predicting the effects of a given incentive program. This approach suggests that we must attend to three primary functions that rewards serve in school: the incentive function, the evaluative function, and the social-control function.

First, rewards typically serve an *incentive function*. When students receive tangible rewards in school, it usually signals that comparable behaviors are likely to produce further extrinsic rewards or social approval in that setting. To the extent that the receipt of contingent extrinsic rewards leads the child to believe that the rewarded behavior will continue to have instrumental value, it should increase the child's motivation to engage in that behavior in subsequent settings perceived as functionally similar to that in which the rewards were obtained (Bandura, 1977; Estes, 1972; Lepper and Greene, 1978b, 1978c). To predict the student's response in other situations, where the behavior is not expected to have continued instrumental value, however, requires attention to other roles rewards may play in the classroom.

Rewards may also serve an *evaluative* or *feedback function*. They may signal success or failure or provide normative feedback on the quality of the student's performance relative to others. The effects of this feedback will depend on the attributions students make concerning the causes of their successes or failures. If the positive evaluation that rewards convey leads students to believe that their performance is contingent on their efforts and that they are capable of succeeding at the rewarded task in the future, the result should be an enhancement of performance and an increase in subsequent approach to that activity (Bar-Tal, 1978; Weiner, 1974).

Finally, rewards may serve a *social-control function*. They may focus students' attention on their reasons for engaging in the rewarded activity. To the extent that students are led to see their actions as extrinsically rather than intrinsically motivated, they will be likely to see the activity as one worth engaging in only when further extrinsic rewards are expected. When incentive and feedback functions of rewards are controlled, this process will lead to less subsequent intrinsic interest in the activity and to performance focused narrowly on those aspects of the activity likely to be of direct instrumental value to the child (Lepper and Greene, 1978a).

Although this analysis captures some of the complexity of the use of rewards in ongoing classrooms, it also poses several problems for predicting the consequences of any particular reward program in the school. First, these different primary functions of a reward system may prove to be in conflict. A single incentive system may, at the same time, have quite different effects on attributions of competence and constraint. Providing children with unnecessary but performance-contingent rewards for engaging in a task of high initial interest, for example, may simultaneously have *positive* effects on the child's perceptions of his ability at the task or his belief that his performance is contingent on the effort he exerts but *negative* effects on his perceptions of the inherent value of the task in the subsequent absence of extrinsic incentives. In practical terms, existing data provide reasonably clear predictions of the *relative* likelihood of these competing effects under different conditions but offer considerably less guidance to those interested in the pragmatic question of predicting the *absolute* effects of any particular procedure in a given classroom setting.

In two excellent comparative studies, Karniol and Ross (1977) and Boggiano and Ruble (1978) have shown that tangible rewards made contingent on successful performance are relatively less likely to produce decrements in interest than the same tangible rewards made contingent on mere task engagement. However, when one looks at the studies that compare the absolute effects of performance-contingent rewards with no-reward control conditions, it becomes clear that such performance-contingent reward procedures may result in either decrements, increments, or no change in subsequent intrinsic interest because of the competing effects they have on perceptions of competence and constraint (Boggiano and Ruble, 1978; Condry, 1977; Deci and Porac, 1978; Karniol and Ross, 1977; Lepper and Greene, 1978b; Ross, 1976).

Practical recommendations are further complicated by the need to consider the secondary consequences of the changes in students' behavior produced by the use of extrinsic incentive systems. In particular, prediction of the ultimate effects of long-term use of any system of incentives or sanctions that produces changes in the child's behavior requires attention to the specific consequences of those changes in behavior (Lepper and Greene, 1978b). An increase in the amount of academic work completed by the child—whether caused by the direct reinforcement of academic performance or more indirectly through the provision of reinforcement for decreases in behaviors that may interfere with sustained concentration on academic work (talking out of turn, leaving one's seat, socializing with other children)—may result in the child's acquisition of new skills and knowledge. These newly acquired skills can, in turn, affect the child's perceptions of his or her abilities or determine the extent to which the child is capable of deriving inherent satisfaction from complex activities previously beyond his or her grasp. Thus, an increase in mastery as the result of added exposure to an activity should enhance the value of that activity for the student.

A third and final constraint imposed on the practical prescriptions one might draw from this analysis derives from the crowded condition of the average classroom. If there is one conclusion that seems apparent from the evidence we have reviewed, it is that particular incentives and particular techniques will be differentially suited to different children (or to the same child in different contexts) as a function of variations in children's initial abilities and interests in the various tasks they are asked to undertake in school. Therefore, any system of incentives or controls applied uniformly to an entire class of children will have predictably different effects on different members of the class. Rigid deadlines or powerful contingencies during certain periods may be absolutely necessary for some children, who would not otherwise have anything to do with the subject, yet may be wholly superfluous for others, who enjoy the challenge imposed by the subject. Similarly, prizes for superior performance may enhance feelings of competence among superior students while providing students of less ability with further evidence of their incompetence. Any decision to implement a particular incentive program in a classroom, then, must come to grips with the formidable challenge posed by the teacher's task of dealing simultaneously with a large number of children of divergent interests and capabilities.

Systematic Reward Programs and Self-Reinforcement Procedures in the Classroom. Although these issues concerning the application of experimental research to ongoing classrooms are complex, they should not prove ultimately intractable. Nor are these concerns likely to lessen in the immediate future. Although our techniques of dealing with these problems have changed significantly, with rewards replacing punishment, the question of how best to motivate and encourage learning, interest, and curiosity remains a central concern of schools and teachers (Bruner, 1966; Cremin, 1961; Ravitch, 1974). Indeed, the growing use of explicit systems of tangible rewards in such programs as the token economy promises to keep these issues in sharp focus (Brophy, 1972; Good, 1972; Hodges, 1972; O'Leary, Poulos, and Devine, 1972).

Token economies are interventions involving the creation of an artificial economy, in which tangible rewards or privileges are made explicitly contingent on demonstrable increases in targeted behavior patterns. Their widespread use in classrooms is a relatively recent phenomenon, but one with an instructive history. Initially, these programs focused primarily on the demonstration of functional control—that is, the demonstration that the provision of sufficiently powerful and attractive rewards that were contingent on appropriate behavior would lead to the appropriate changes in behavior in the face of experimentally manipulated contingencies. In this respect, the history of token programs is a chronicle of striking success (Kazdin, 1975, 1977; Kazdin and Bootzin, 1972; O'Leary, in press; O'Leary and Drabman, 1971).

More recently, however, increasing attention has been directed toward issues of maintenance and generalization of these behavior changes in subsequent settings where the rewards are no longer available. Although the sorts of reward procedures typically employed in applied token-economy programs and those typically employed in the experimental investigations reported in this chapter differ on a number of possibly critical dimensions that make direct comparisons very difficult (see Lepper and Greene, 1978c, for a more thorough discussion of this question), these issues of maintenance and generalization fall considerably closer to the issues addressed in this chapter. Notably, the effectiveness of traditional reinforcement procedures in achieving these more remote goals of maintenance and generalization has been considerably less impressive (Kazdin, 1975, 1977; O'Leary, in press). Correspondingly, recent research in this area has shifted from a preoccupation with functional analysis to a consideration of the dynamics of self-reinforcement and self-regulatory processes and the manner in which these cognitive variables may affect and be affected by externally generated reward procedures (Kazdin, 1977; Mahoney, 1974; O'Leary, in press).

From our own perspective, this shift in emphasis is significant. The experimental study of self-regulatory processes and their relationship to the attributional processes outlined in this chapter provides an important avenue for examining the practical relevance of an attribution model in educational settings. To the extent that performance standards and contingencies are viewed as self-imposed rather than externally imposed, they should be less likely to lead the child to view his behavior as extrinsically motivated. Thus, permitting the child some measure of control over the contingencies that govern his life in school may provide an important antidote to the detrimental effects such contingencies might otherwise have on his or her subsequent behavior (Lepper and Greene, 1978c).

Lepper, Sagotsky, and Greene (1978b), for example, compared the effects of reward procedures, in which children determined for themselves whether their performance warranted a reward, or this determination was made by an adult experimenter. Relative to control conditions, externally determined rewards produced decrements in subsequent interest, whereas self-determined rewards did not. Similar findings appear in an elegant applied investigation by Brownell and others (1977). In this study, elemen-

tary school students were rewarded for solving mathematics problems according to a performance criterion either imposed on the
student by an adult experimenter or determined by the student
himself. Following the eventual withdrawal of this reward program, students' engagement in and performance on the mathematics problems were assessed. Decreases in performance and task
engagement that were evident during extinction among subjects
exposed to externally imposed standards were virtually eliminated
among subjects who had been given some voice in determining the
standards to be applied to their efforts. Coupled with other data
demonstrating the effectiveness of procedures that explicitly attempt to supplant externally imposed contingency systems with
self-imposed programs (Bandura, 1976; O'Leary, in press;
Sagotsky, Patterson, and Lepper, 1978; Turkewitz, O'Leary, and
Ironsmith, 1975), these results illustrate the educational benefits of
our suggested focus on self-management techniques in schools.

Beyond these specific questions, of course, loom the larger
issues with which we started, the role of the school as an agency of
socialization and the lessons it may teach children about society's
view of authority and obedience, effort and value, and work and
play. If for no other reason than the sheer amount of exposure
children have to the social structure of the school, it seems likely
that these potential by-products of the educational system will have
lasting impact on children's beliefs about their social environments.
As Jackson (1968, p. 31) put it:

> The distinction between work and play has far-
> reaching consequences for human affairs, and the classroom
> is the setting in which most people encounter this distinc-
> tion in a personally meaningful way. According to one of its
> many definitions, work entails becoming engaged in a pur-
> poseful activity that has been prescribed for us by somebody
> else; an activity in which we would not at the moment be
> engaged if it were not for some system of authority relation-
> ships. As preschoolers, the students may have played with
> the concept of work, but their fanciful enactments of adult
> work usually lack one essential ingredient, namely: the use
> of some kind of external authority system to tell them what
> to do and to keep them at their job. The teacher, with his

prescriptive dicta and his surveillance over the students'
attention, provides the missing ingredient that makes work
real.

The correlative hazard, to which the present analysis should alert
us, is that these prescriptive dicta and continuous surveillance may
also define activities once considered enjoyable in their own right as
work, to be undertaken only in the presence of appropriate extrinsic rewards, surveillance, or constraints.

Notes

[1] The obvious exception that "proves" this rule is the intriguing study by
Kruglanski, Alon, and Lewis (1972), which demonstrated a detrimental
effect of unexpected rewards on subsequent reported intrinsic interest in
the task. In this study, all students engaged a series of competitive games
without expectation of extrinsic reward. Subsequently, however, subjects in
one condition were led, erroneously, to attribute their engagement in these
games to a reward they received after completing the activities—through a
procedure in which they were falsely informed that the reward had initially been promised to them. With this explicitly deceptive procedure,
Kruglanski and colleagues found that subjects who received unanticipated
prizes, allegedly promised beforehand, reported less intrinsic interest than
subjects who did not receive prizes. Since the adverse effect of the extrinsic
reward was almost wholly accounted for by the responses of subjects who
(mistakenly) described themselves as having initially engaged in the games
in order to obtain the reward, these data provide further evidence consistent with an attributional analysis. Thus, although unexpected rewards
should not typically induce the individual to view his prior behavior as
having been directed toward the attainment of that reward, unexpected
reward procedures that do induce retrospective misattributions can
undermine subsequent interest.

[2] These comparisons of types of rewards have frequently confounded the
distinction between verbal and tangible rewards with the expectedness of
the reward and the informational value of the reward concerning one's
relative ability at the activity. Thus, unexpected verbal rewards that inform
the individual that his or her performance has been superior are often
compared with expected tangible rewards that have been shown to the
individual before the task is undertaken and do not convey comparable
information about one's relative competence. Further research is clearly
needed to distinguish which of these components are necessary and sufficient to account for the different effects these two procedures appear to
have on subsequent motivation (Kruglanski, 1978a; Lepper and Greene,
1978b; Smith, 1976). We should make clear, however, that it is not an easy
task to design verbal-reward procedures precisely comparable with the
expected tangible-reward procedures employed in most experimental

work. It seems quite natural, for example, to ask someone to contract explicitly to engage in an activity to earn money or to obtain some other valued tangible reward; it seems considerably less natural to ask someone to contract to engage in an activity to obtain particular positive verbal statements from another. Conceptually, this difference may be symptomatic of the different scripts and expectations most of us have developed concerning social versus tangible rewards and may contribute to the relative invisibility of social pressures postulated by the attribution model.

[3] The appearance of detrimental effects on immediate performance in these two studies suggests the possibility that decrements in subsequent interest may have been the result of these immediate performance effects. Hence, it is important to note that, in subsequent studies where more specific contingencies were employed, analogous decreases in subsequent intrinsic interest have been obtained in the absence of performance decrements (Lepper and Greene, 1975; Lepper and others, 1978a, 1978b). Although an extended review is not possible here, we believe that the existing literature is sufficient to establish that decrements in immediate performance are neither a necessary nor a sufficient condition for the production of decreases in subsequent intrinsic interest (Lepper and Greene, 1978b; Ross and others, 1976).

Interactions
of Teachers
and Pupils

For decades, the influence of psychology on education has been limited mainly to the study of the effects of pupils' cognitive skills on their scholastic achievements. However, in recent years, a recognition has been developing that social psychology can also be of great help in understanding educational outcomes and processes (see Bar-Tal and Saxe, 1978). Classrooms are social environments where social processes as well as learning take place. Individuals in the classroom—pupils and teachers—interact socially with each other. These interactions determine, to a great extent, the subjective perceptions, attitudes, and behaviors of pupils and teachers. Furthermore, it has been recently recognized that academic achievement is not solely determined by cognitive factors but is also determined by a variety of social variables of a personal and inter-

337

personal nature, and much research has recently been devoted to the study of these processes.

One specific model that attempts to explain achievement-related behavior on the basis of social cognition was proposed by Weiner (Weiner and others, 1972; Weiner, 1974a). He suggested that an individual's causal perceptions of success and failure mediate between the antecedent conditions and achievement-related behavior. Weiner presented his model as an attributional analysis of an individual's general achievement-related behavior. Since its publication, numerous studies have successfully supported predictions derived from the proposed model (for example, Ames, in press; Bar-Tal and Frieze, 1977; Dweck and Repucci, 1973; Frieze, 1976a, 1976b; Frieze and Bar-Tal, 1977; Frieze and Weiner, 1971; Kukla, 1972; McMahan, 1973; Ruble, Parsons, and Ross, 1976; Shaklee, 1976; Weiner and others, 1972; Weiner and Kukla, 1970; Weiner, Nierenberg, and Goldstein, 1976). Most of these studies were carried out in laboratories or in simulated situations and therefore are limited in their applicability to other settings. Achievement-related behavior takes place in many situations and places, but in few settings is it so characteristic as in the classroom. It is therefore not surprising that Weiner (1972b, 1977) pointed out the implications of his model for students' behaviors in educational settings.

This chapter will analyze the educational implications of Weiner's achievement-related behavior model. We will not review the details of the model or the empirical research that supports it (see extensive reviews in Weiner 1974a, 1978) but will focus on those elements of the model that have direct applications for the understanding of the perceptions and behaviors of pupils and teachers. Specifically, we will discuss (1) how pupils' causal perceptions of their successes and failures determine their achievement-related behavior; (2) how teachers' causal perceptions of their pupils' successes and failures determine their behavior toward pupils; (3) how teachers' behavior influences pupils' causal perceptions of successes and failures; and (4) how pupils' achievement-related behavior affects teachers' causal perceptions of pupils' successes and failures. The discussion of these issues will be carried out in three sections. First, the model of pupils' and teachers' perceptions and behaviors will be described. Second, empirical evidence to support the model will be presented. Finally, possible educational applications will be discussed.

Attribution Model of Pupils' and Teachers' Behavior

Pupils' causal perceptions of success and failure may be of major importance in understanding their achievement-related behavior. Pupils use a variety of causal perceptions, but our analysis of Weiner's model will be limited to four causes originally suggested by Weiner and others (1972). The four causes are ability, effort, task difficulty, and luck. These causal elements (and other causes) can be classified in two dimensions. One dimension differentiates causal elements in terms of their internality-externality (locus of control); the second dimension differentiates them in terms of their stability.

Weiner (1974b) suggested that the causal elements can also be classified on the intentionality dimension, but, since the implication of this dimension has not been thoroughly elaborated, it is omitted from the present analysis. Thus, ability and effort are considered to be internal, because they originate within the person, and task difficulty and luck are considered to be external, because they originate outside the person. Ability and task difficulty are considered to be stable, because they do not vary if the task is attempted again, and effort and luck are considered to be unstable, because they may vary with time.

The locus of control dimension influences affective reactions of pride and shame to success or failure. Weiner, Russell, and Lerman (in press) suggest that specific causal perceptions invoke specific emotional reactions—internal attributions intensify some affective reactions, and external attributions augment other affective reactions. In our analysis, we will consider only pride and shame as the emotional consequences of success and failure (see Atkinson, 1964).

In a failure situation, pupils feel maximum shame (self-dissatisfaction) when they attribute their outcome to either lack of ability or lack of effort—both internal causes. Attributions of failure to bad luck or the task difficulty produce considerably less shame, since no personal responsibility is taken. Success attributed to ability or effort results in pride (self-satisfaction), and success attributed to good luck or ease of task results in little pride. The stability dimension affects cognitive changes in expectancy of future outcomes following success or failure. Thus, when pupils perceive their success as caused by good luck, the resulting expectancy is that failure might occur in the future, since luck is believed to be an unstable cause. Corresponding expectations are found for attributions to bad luck in a situation of failure. Attribution to lack of effort (unstable cause) in a failure situation results in higher expectancy for future success, since it is believed that the pupil can exert more effort to improve the performance. Success attributed to ability results in high expectancy for future success, since pupils assume that ability is stable and therefore performance will not deteriorate. Also, because ability is a stable cause, failure attributed to lack of ability results in low expectancy for future success. According to the same reasoning, attribution of success to ease of task, a stable cause, results in high expectancy for success, whereas attribution of failure to task difficulty results in low expectancy for success (see Weiner, 1974b, 1977, for a review of the empirical evidence).

The types of causes pupils use to explain their successes or failures are important determinants of their achievement-related behavior. Thus, for example, approaching achievement-related activities is related to the pupil's satisfaction with successful achievement experience. Pupils who tend to attribute success to ability and effort (internal causes) experience pride for their successful performance and therefore intend to approach achievement tasks. Pupils who tend to attribute success to external causes experience less pride for their success and therefore tend to avoid achievement tasks. Also, pupils who tend to attribute their failure to stable causes, such as lack of ability, persist little in the face of failure, since they believe that ability is a stable, unmodifiable disposition that does not allow the possibility of changing the outcome in the future. However, pupils who tend to attribute their failure to unstable-internal causes, such as lack of effort, persist in the face of failure, since they believe that effort is changeable and leaves open the possibility of modifying the outcome in the future. Finally, pupils who believe that the outcome is greatly determined by effort perform tasks with greater intensity than those who believe that the outcome is determined by external causes. The belief in effort makes the pupils try harder, because effort is believed to be an unstable-internal cause (see Weiner, 1974b, 1977, for a review of the empirical evidence).

Weiner (1974b) also discusses the antecedents of causal perceptions of success and failure. Two main factors that affect the particular set of causes that pupils ascribe in explaining their successes and failures are information received in the situation and personal dispositions. Examples of information the pupils might receive in the achievement situation include the outcome itself, past outcomes on the same test, or outcomes of other pupils on the same test. Personal characteristics of pupils that have been found to be related to the use of specific patterns of causal perception include sex, need for achievement, locus of control, and self-esteem.

The attributional analysis of pupils' perceptions can also be extended to an understanding of teachers' perceptions and behaviors and the interrelationship between the perceptions and behaviors of pupils and teachers. Teachers also ascribe causes for their pupils' successes or failures, and their causal perceptions may not correspond to their pupils' perceptions. Teachers' causal perceptions may be of major importance in understanding teachers' behavior toward their pupils.

The causes that teachers use can also be classified on the same two dimensions, locus of control and stability. In the case of teachers, the stability dimension is of great importance, since it influences teachers' expectations regarding pupils' future successes. Attributions of success or failure to stable causes indicate that the same outcome is expected to be repeated, since people believe that stable causes do not change with time. Attributions of success or failure to unstable causes indicate that the outcome may not be repeated in the future, since people believe that unstable causes may change with time. Rosenthal and Jacobson (1968a, 1968b) and Dweck and Goetz (1978) found that teachers' expectations are related to their behavior toward their pupils. One reason teachers behave differently toward their pupils is the differing expectations they have regarding their pupils' future achievements. Furthermore, it is proposed that teachers' behavior toward pupils greatly affects pupils' causal perceptions of their own successes or failures, and pupils' achievement behaviors greatly affect their own academic outcomes as well as teachers' causal perceptions of pupils' successes or failures. In the former relationship, teachers verbally and nonverbally transmit to their pupils information that the pupils use when they ascribe causes for their academic performance (for example, a teacher may openly say to a pupil that the pupil has great ability, or a teacher may nonverbally communicate to a pupil that the teacher thinks the pupil lacks motivation). The latter relationship indicates that the achievement behaviors of the pupil function as one category of the antecedents of the teacher's causal perceptions of the pupil's success or failure. A pupil's persistence in case of failure or intensity of academic performance is important information for a teacher's attributions regarding the pupil's ability, effort, diligence, or interest.

The model of pupils' and teachers' perceptions and behaviors is illustrated in Figure 1. Figure 1 shows that the pupil and the teacher ascribe causes to the pupil's outcome (success or failure). This ascription is affected by numerous dispositional and informational antecedents. The pupil's causal perception is related to his or her achievement behavior (choice, persistence, and intensity) through the affective reactions and expectations regarding future success. The teacher's causal perception is related to his or her behavior toward the pupil through the expectations regarding the pupil's future outcomes. The behavior of the teacher greatly influences the pupil's causal perception of academic outcomes, whereas the pupil's achievement-related behaviors influence not only the outcome but probably also the teacher's causal perception of the outcome, although there is no evidence to support this latter contention. In the next section, empirical evidence will be reviewed that demonstrates the relationships between pupils' and teachers' perceptions and behaviors as depicted in the model. The review will especially emphasize naturalistic studies carried out in school settings in Israel. Thus, although the suggested model can be used in any culture, results may be different in another culture. Nevertheless, because urban Israeli society, like American society, values individual achievement, competitiveness, and individual rather than group goal attainment (see Solberg, 1977), no major

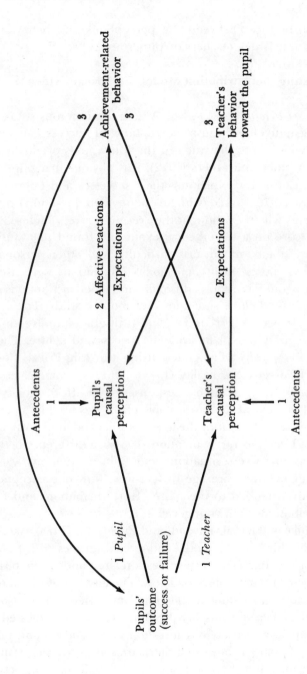

Figure 1. The Attribution Process of Pupils and Teachers.

cultural differences between the perceptions and behaviors of American and Israeli teachers or pupils are expected.

Testing the Attribution Model: Empirical Evidence

Causal Perceptions of Pupils. Although numerous studies investigating individuals' causal perceptions of success and failure limited themselves to the study of the four causes originally proposed by Weiner and others (1972), it is obvious that pupils use additional causes for explaining their successes and failures. Indeed, Frieze (1976a) asked (with an open-ended questionnaire) college students why they thought they received a very high score or very low score on a hypothetical exam and found that students used effort, ability, mood, task difficulty, and other personal attributions as causes. Effort and ability attributions were used in both success and failure; task difficulty and mood attributions were used mainly in failure situations. In another study, Frieze and Snyder (1978) asked first-, third-, and fifth-grade pupils to list the causes they used to explain academic success and failure. The answers of the pupils were coded using the Elig-Frieze Coding Scheme of Perceived Causality (1975). The results indicated that 65 percent of all the codable responses were effort. Ability was used in 14 percent of the cases, stable effort was used in 5 percent of the cases, and the rest of the answers were coded in a variety of categories. Luck was rarely mentioned. Also, a difference between attributions in success situations and failure situations was not found, and neither were age differences, with one exception— older children tended to use more effort attributions and fewer ability attributions than younger children.

Similarly Bar-Tal, Ravgad, and Zilberman (1978) asked 124 students of third, sixth, ninth, and twelfth grades to list all the possible factors that can cause success on a test and all the possible factors that can cause failure on a test. The answers of the students were classified according to the Elig and Frieze (1975) Coding Scheme of Perceived Causality (CSPC). The results indicated that the students use a variety of causes to explain success and failure (see Table 1). Table 1 shows that there are some differences among the age groups, but there are not distinctive differences between

Table 1. Percentage of Causal Explanations According to CSPC Categories in Third (N=33), Sixth (N=33), Ninth (N=33), and Twelfth (N=23) Grades

Category	Success				Failure			
	Third Grade	Sixth Grade	Ninth Grade	Twelfth Grade	Third Grade	Sixth Grade	Ninth Grade	Twelfth Grade
Ability	3.1	1.8	6.3	5.4	4.0	2.4	3.6	9.1
Effort	41.2	23.1	15.3	14.5	36.7	13.6	13.1	15.9
Stable effort	0.6	2.8	5.8	4.6	—	3.2	1.9	2.2
Mood	27.5	24.5	15.3	8.5	27.5	30.0	27.8	20.4
Intrinsic motives	4.3	9.4	11.7	6.2	6.3	5.2	11.4	5.3
Personality	0.6	3.7	2.2	2.3	1.1	6.8	4.2	2.2
Ability × task interaction	6.8	8.0	9.9	13.7	7.4	7.6	5.9	12.8
Task	5.6	7.5	6.7	7.0	5.1	6.0	3.6	4.5
Other's help or hurt	1.2	6.1	11.7	19.3	5.1	4.4	7.8	13.6
Luck	—	0.4	2.2	6.9	—	0.4	0.3	3.0
Other's motives	—	—	0.4	4.6	—	—	0.9	4.5
Personality interaction	—	0.9	—	1.5	—	2.8	0.3	3.0
Extrinsic motives	—	0.5	4.5	5.4	—	1.2	3.2	3.0
Other activities	0.6	8.4	5.4	—	0.5	14.8	13.7	—
Other's personality	—	—	1.3	—	—	—	1.3	—
Uncodable	8.5	2.9	1.3	0.1	6.3	1.6	1.0	0.5

Source: Bar-Tal, Ravgad, and Zilberman, 1978.

success and failure. Across age and outcome, students tend primarily, with few exceptions, to use causes in the categories of effort and mood (internal-unstable factors). Also, it was found that, in general, students tend to use more internal than external causes and more unstable than stable causes to explain success and failure. An additional result of this study indicates that, until grade nine, there is a linear increase in the average number of causes pupils use to explain success and failure. In grade twelve, there is a drop in this number. With increase of age, there is a linear decrease in the use of internal causes and a linear increase in the use of external causes to explain success and failure.

In another study, Bar-Tal and Darom (in press) used structured questionnaires with a limited number of causes to investigate pupils' causal perceptions of success and failure in naturalistic situations. Two hundred fifty fifth- and sixth-grade pupils were asked to evaluate the degree to which the cause influenced the grade received on a real classroom test. The list of causes used in the investigation was derived from a pilot study, in which sixty-three pupils of the fifth grade were asked on an open-ended questionnaire to list all the causes that contributed to the grade received on a real test. A cause that was mentioned by at least two pupils was used in the list of causes. The following eight causes were derived: ability in the subject matter, difficulty of subject material, effort exerted during the test, difficulty of the test, preparation for the test at home, quality of teacher's explanation of the material, interest in the subject matter, and conditions at home. Bar-Tal and Darom found that pupils tended to attribute success mainly to teacher's explanation, home conditions, easy subject material, easy test, and high interest. They attributed failure to insufficient preparation at home, low ability, insufficient effort, difficulty of the subject matter, and difficulty of the test. These results indicate that pupils tended to attribute success mainly to external causes and failure mainly to internal causes.

Of special interest for the model is a study by Bar-Tal and others (1978), which examined the consistency of pupils' causal perceptions of successes and failures across time and outcomes. In this study, pupils of sixth grade were asked to indicate their attributions regarding the same causes following tests in Mathematics,

Geography, and Bible during one trimester. There were two tests in a trimester for each subject matter, but not all the pupils participated in all the tests. Consistency scores between two questionnaires were calculated (the accepted range of consistency scores is between 0 and 1—(for details, see Bar-Tal and others, 1978). The results indicated that, in general, there was high consistency in attributions—that is, pupils' attributional patterns were more consistent across time than one would expect from random attributions. However, when the consistency for pupils who had gotten the same outcome on the two tests (success or failure) was compared with that of pupils who had gotten different outcomes, it was found that the former group had more consistent attributions than the latter.

The reviewed studies have demonstrated that pupils use a variety of causes to explain their academic successes and failures. Nevertheless, the first three described studies found that students tended to attribute the academic outcome mainly to effort, ability, mood, and task difficulty. These three studies used a similar technique (open-ended questionnaire) regarding a hypothetical situation, whereas Bar-Tal and Darom used a closed-ended questionnaire regarding a realistic situation. It is therefore not surprising that the results of the first three studies are somewhat similar, even though carried out with different age-group subjects. The first two studies were carried out in the United States; the other studies were carried out in Israel.

These results suggest that the predetermined use of causes may limit the understanding of the consequences of causal perceptions in the classroom. It is therefore necessary to determine the specific attributional patterns of the investigated population, as particular affective, cognitive, and behavioral reactions are related to these patterns (see Weiner, 1978; Weiner and others, 1978). Also, although Bar-Tal and others (1978) shows that pupils are consistent in their use of causes, future research should further investigate whether attributional patterns are consistent across time and situations.

The Effect of Pupils' Causal Perceptions on Their Achievement Behavior. Several studies have explored the relationship between children's causal perceptions of success and failure and achievement-related behavior. For example, Dweck and Repucci (1973) created a situation in which children were subjected to continued, noncontingent failure. The experimenters were interested in finding what distinguishes those children whose performance deteriorated from those who persisted in spite of the failure. The results of this study showed that children whose performance worsened in the face of noncontingent failure took less personal responsibility for outcomes, as measured by the Intellectual Achievement Responsibility Scale (Crandall, Katkovsky, and Crandall, 1965). These children assumed less credit for their success and less blame for their failure. In contrast, children who persisted in spite of the failure assumed greater personal responsibility for their performance. These latter children placed a much greater emphasis on the role of effort in determining outcomes, and they tended to attribute their failure to lack of effort. In another study (Diener and Dweck, 1978), the experimenters categorized children as helpless or mastery-oriented on the basis of their tendency to perceive or disregard effort as a determinant of failure. Then, all the children were trained to employ problem-solving strategies to solve discriminatory learning problems, and, upon reaching success, they were given insoluble test problems. The results showed that whereas the mastery-oriented children, who perceived effort-outcome covariation, persisted in the problem-solving strategy, helpless children showed a steady regression in a problem-solving strategy across the failure problems. Also, a correlational study by Weiner and others (1972) has shown that individuals' causal attributions are related to the persistence of their performance. These experimenters included consecutive failures on a task and asked high school students to ascribe attributions in terms of the four causal factors. The results showed that students who tended to attribute failure to bad luck or effort performed with greater persistence than students who tended to attribute failure to lack of ability or task difficulty. All these studies consistently indicate that pupils who attribute failure to unstable causes, mainly low effort, show more persistent achievement behavior than pupils who attribute failure to stable causes.

Thus, the empirical evidence demonstrates that pupils can clearly explain the causality of their successes and failures.

Moreover, the types of causes they use determine, to a great extent, their achievement-related behavior.

   Causal Perceptions by Teachers and Their Effect on Behavior Toward Pupils. A number of studies have attempted to investigate teachers' causal perceptions regarding pupils' academic performance (Ames, 1975; Beckman, 1970, 1973; Johnson, Feigenbaum, and Wiley, 1964). However, these studies were carried out in laboratory settings. Two recent separate investigations (Bar-Tal and Guttmann, 1978; Darom and Bar-Tal, 1977) examined teachers' causal perceptions regarding pupils causal perceptions regarding their success or failure in realistic classroom situations. In a study by Darom and Bar-Tal (1977), eight female teachers of fifth and sixth grades were asked to ascribe causes on a closed-ended rating scale for their pupils' performance following a test in the classroom (235 pupils). The results indicated that the teachers tended to attribute pupils' success mainly to home conditions, their own good explanation of material, and, to a lesser extent, the pupils' effort and interest. Failure was attributed by teachers to pupils' lack of preparation, low ability, and test difficulty (see Table 2).

   In another study (Bar-Tal and Guttmann, 1978), eight female teachers of mathematics of fourth and fifth grades were asked to attribute causes on a closed-ended rating scale for their pupils' trimester grades (sixty-nine pupils). The results indicated that they tended to attribute successful outcomes to pupils' diligence, effort, interest, and their own quality of explanations.

Table 2. Teachers' Mean Attribution of Causality

	Outcome	
Cause	*Success*	*Failure*
Ability	2.78	2.96
Difficulty of subject matter	2.80	2.78
Effort exerted on test	3.05	2.70
Test difficulty	2.77	2.93
Preparation for test	2.72	3.36
Teacher's explanation	3.18	2.31
Interest in studying	3.05	2.80
Home conditions	3.43	1.91

Note: Low mean indicates low ascription of causality. The range is from 1 to 4.
Source: Darom and Bar-Tal, 1977.

Teachers tended to attribute failure to pupils' lack of effort, difficulty of the material, and inappropriate home conditions. The results of both studies showed that teachers tended to share the credit for success with the pupils but tended to blame failure on causes other than themselves.

The relationship between teachers' causal perceptions and their behavior toward pupils can be explained through the mediating variable of teachers' expectations regarding pupils' future outcomes. First, it is proposed that teachers' causal perceptions of their pupils' success or failure influences teachers' expectations regarding pupils' future outcomes (see Bar-Tal, 1977). Second, it is proposed that teachers' expectations regarding pupils' future outcomes affect teachers' behavior toward pupils (see Dusek, 1975).

The first proposition is based on Weiner's original theorizing (Weiner and others, 1972), which suggested that the causes classified on the stability dimension affect individuals' expectations. That is, "ascriptions of an outcome to stable factors produce greater typical shifts in expectancy than do ascriptions to unstable factors. A *typical shift* is defined as an increment in the subjective expectancy of success following a success experience and a decrement in expectancy after a failure" (Weiner, 1974b, p. 21). This proposition was supported by numerous laboratory experiments (see Weiner, 1974a). However, our focus is specifically on the relationship between teachers' causal perceptions and expectations. Darom and Bar-Tal (1977), after receiving teachers' attributions regarding their pupils' outcomes, instructed the teachers also to indicate their expectations with respect to pupils' future success. A correlational analysis (see Table 3) between the attribution scores and expectations showed that only stable causes of pupils' successes were related positively to expectations of future success and only stable causes (except effort) of pupils' failures were related negatively to expectations of future success. That is, the more that success or failure was attributed to stable causes, such as ability, easy subject matter, or easy test, the more were future outcomes expected to be similar to the prior outcome.

Bar-Tal and Saxe (1979) also showed that teachers' expectations are affected by attributions. In this study, eighteen male teachers and twenty-five female teachers of elementary school were

Table 3. Correlations Between Teachers' Attributed Causes and Expectations

Perceived Outcome	Degrees of Freedom	Ability	Material	Effort	Test	Preparation	Teacher	Interest	Home Conditions
							Causes		
Success	163	0.80[b]	0.71[b]	0.03[a]	0.71[b]	0.13[a]	0.61[b]	0.63[b]	0.41[b]
Failure	68	−0.55[b]	−0.63[b]	−0.45[b]	−0.55[b]	−0.19[a]	−0.43[b]	−0.45[b]	−0.52[b]

[a] $p < 0.05$
[b] $p < 0.01$
Source: Darom and Bar-Tal, 1977.

asked to express their expectations about the future performance of a hypothetical pupil. Each teacher was asked to imagine that a pupil in his or her class took an examination under several different circumstances. The teachers were told for each situation how much ability the pupil had relative to other pupils on the particular examination, how much effort he or she exerted, how difficult the examination was, and how much luck the pupil had. The four possible factors were given at one of two levels in all possible combinations. Thus, each teacher expressed the expectations in sixteen situations (two levels for each of the four cues). A sample item is: "Imagine that a pupil in your class takes an exam in which he has low ability; he exerts high effort; the exam is difficult." The results indicated that teachers do form differential expectations on the basis of the causes. Specifically, it was found that pupils with high ability, high effort, and good luck were expected to do better than pupils with low ability, low effort, and bad luck. The magnitude of the ability effect was found to be the largest.

The second proposition is based on an extensive literature that has grown from the "pygmalion phenomenon" in school research (Rosenthal and Jacobson, 1968a). These studies have shown that teachers treat pupils differently in accordance with their differential expectations. The differential treatment takes the form of differential punishment, attention, praise, initiation of contact, smiling, and so forth. Since Braun (1976) and Dusek (1975) have reviewed the existing studies, which have demonstrated that teachers' expectations regarding future success greatly influence the behavior of teachers toward pupils, we will not do so here.

The studies we have reviewed in this section support the contention that teachers form expectations on the basis of the attributions they make regarding pupils' successes or failures. The stability dimension of the attributions determines to a great extent what kind of expectations the teacher forms concerning pupils' future outcomes. Furthermore, the expectations that the teacher forms affect his or her behavior toward the pupil.

The Relationship Between Teachers' Behavior and Pupils' Causal Perceptions. Several studies have investigated the effects of teachers' behavior on pupils' causal perceptions of success and failure. Blumenfeld and others (1977) suggested that teachers transmit to pupils three types of messages that affect pupils' causal perceptions. The three categories of messages are: (1) explicit attributional feedback, which refers to causes contributing to success or failure; (2) explanations for behavioral expectations and evaluative feedback; and (3) general statements referring to social or procedural expectations. They observed six classrooms for a period of two months and found that teachers, in their communications to pupils, provided feedback that emphasized the importance of ability and effort in achieving positive outcomes. Lack of ability was rarely mentioned. However, explanations given for engaging in scholastic activities were extrinsic in their nature, phrased in terms of authority, rules, or circumstances. Also, teachers more often utilized threats and punishments than rewards. Such practices encourage external attributions.

The relationship between teachers' behaviors and pupils' causal perceptions has been discussed by Dweck and her associates, who investigated sex differences in attribution (Dweck and Bush, 1976; Dweck and others, 1978). On the basis of empirical findings, Dweck and Goetz (1978) concluded that the different causal perceptions of boys and girls in the classroom are a result of teachers' differential behavior toward them. The differential behavior of teachers was found to be exhibited in the following instances: (1) teachers more often provide boys than girls with negative feedback regarding nonintellectual aspects of their work; (2) teachers more often provide boys than girls with feedback emphasizing effort in achievement situations; (3) teachers more often provide girls than boys with negative feedback regarding the intellectual quality of their work; (4) teachers more often provide boys than girls with positive feedback contingent on the intellectual quality of their work. This differential feedback of teachers helps determine boys' positive feedback noncontingent on the intellectual quality of their work. This differential feedback of teachers help determine boys' and girls' causal perceptions of success and failure; girls are less likely than boys to attribute failure to motivational factors and are more likely than boys to ascribe failure to lack of ability (see Dweck and Repucci, 1973). The negative feedback of teachers toward boys refers to intellectually irrelevant aspects of their performance and therefore is viewed by boys as reflecting teachers' attitudes toward them but not as an objective evaluation of their academic performance. At the same time, teachers frequently attribute boys' failures to lack of motivation. Thus, boys learn to attribute failures to lack of motivation and do not see failure as related to their abilities. Girls learn to attribute failures to lack of ability, since the teachers have, in general, positive attitudes toward them. Therefore, girls are less apt to see teachers' negative feedback as reflecting a negative attitude, since teachers' negative feedback is primarily directed toward girls' intellectual quality of work and does not emphasize lack of motivation.

A study by Cooper (1977) has also shown that teachers' behavior affects pupils' causal perceptions. In this study, it was found that pupils' perceptions of the covariation between effort and outcome was related to the amount of criticism (expressed anger as a result of incorrect academic performance or negative remarks regarding the pupil's ability or motivation) they received after initiating an academic interaction with the teacher. The more criticism the pupils received, the less they attributed the outcome to effort.

Thus, the evidence we have reviewed shows that teachers behave differentially toward pupils and that their behaviors influence pupils' attributions.

Conclusions: Implications and Applications

The attributional explanation of achievement-related behavior indicates that pupils differ in their causal perceptions of successes and failures and that these perceptions have direct implications for pupils' achievement behavior. For example, pupils who tend to perceive lack of ability as the cause of their failures expect to repeat failure as they attempt achievement tasks, because ability is believed to be a stable characteristic. With this orientation, they may avoid achievement activities and fail to reach their potential. The belief that their academic failure is due to their low ability could inhibit their motivation to try harder in the future. At the same time, the belief that success is due to external factors (such as luck) does not encourage one to make efforts to succeed and to believe in one's ability. An attributional pattern characterized by ascription of failure to internal-stable causes (such as ability) and success to external-unstable causes (such as luck) can be considered as maladaptive. An adaptive attributional pattern is characterized by ascription of failure to internal-unstable causes, especially effort, and ascription of success to internal causes.

The effect of causal attributions on academic performance has an important implication in the light of evidence that the pattern of forming causal attributions might differ in various social groups. The tendencies to form causal attributions are learned, and the evidence by Katz (1967) and Coleman and others (1966) suggests that the cognitive systems pertinent to achievement motivation may be learned differentially by various racial and social-class groupings. For example, Katz suggested that blacks do not develop the cognitive structures that support the efficacy of effort (that is, blacks do not appear to make effort attributions and do not perceive the covariation between effort and outcome that normally occurs in the world). A study by Friend and Neale (1972) directly compared the causal perceptions of success and failure of black and white fifth-grade children. The results showed that white children judged ability and effort as a more important cause for their performance outcome than task and luck, whereas the reverse tendency was true of black children. Raviv and others (1978) compared attributions of sixth-grade disadvantaged pupils of low socioeconomic class with attributions of advantaged pupils of middle-upper class. Pupils in both schools were asked to explain their perceived success or failure on a mathematics test. The disadvantaged children tended to attribute success to their own ability, interest in studying,. the high quality of teacher's explanation of material, and their effort during the test, and they tended to attribute failure to the low quality of teacher's explanation of material, their lack of interest, the difficulty of material, and lack of ability. The advantaged children tended to attribute success to high quality of teacher's explanation, interest in studying, and ability, and they tended to attribute failure to lack of effort during the test, low quality of teacher's explanation, and lack of preparation for the test at home. Thus, the main difference between the children appears to be in case of failure—the disadvantaged children tended to attribute failure mainly to internal-stable causes, such as ability and interest, whereas the advantaged children tended to attribute failure mainly to internal-unstable causes, such as effort. The latter children perceived the covariation between effort and outcome.

Also, attributional patterns of women appear to be an important factor that inhibits their achievement. Frieze and others (in press) have pointed out that, because people have low expectations for women and make detrimental causal attributions about their successes and failures, women internalize these beliefs and form maladaptive patterns. In a study by Nicholls (1975), it was found that fourth-grade white girls tended to attribute failure to low ability and did not tend to attribute success to high ability. The study also found that girls performed "relatively poorly when the task was presented as an important ability measure" (p. 388). This finding was explained as a consequence of the attributional pattern of girls who do not believe they have high ability. Perceiving a failure as caused by lack of ability causes a belief that effort cannot reverse the failure, whereas perceiving a success as caused by high ability causes a belief that a "succeeding trend could be maintained easily" (p. 388). These findings suggest that disadvantaged groups, such as blacks, low socioeconomic class females, and other individuals with certain causal perceptions, may perform below their abilities in the classroom because of their maladaptive patterns of attributions.

The attributional approach to an analysis of achievement behavior implies the necessity for reinforcing adaptive patterns of causal perceptions and modifying those that are maladaptive. A number of studies have demonstrated that it is possible to change pupils' maladaptive causal perceptions and, as a result, to improve their academic performance. In an experiment by Dweck (1975), children from elementary schools who were giving up on a task in the face of failure were chosen as subjects. These children tended to attribute failure to lack of ability and did not persist in their efforts. Dweck taught these children to attribute failure to lack of effort through verbal feedback in training sessions. The results revealed that these children started to improve their performance, and, at the same time, they started to attribute failure to insufficient effort. Dweck summarized this experiment by suggesting that the "results for the children receiving attribution retraining provide evidence for a change in behavior in that situation and for a greater emphasis on the role of motivation on determining failure in arithmetic" (p. 684). The results of Dweck (1975) were replicated by Chapin and Dyck (1976), who trained children experiencing reading difficulties. Their findings showed that children who received attribution retraining (were taught to attribute the success and failure to effort) developed more reading persistence than children who did not receive the retraining.

Similarly, Andrews and Debus (1978) found that sixth-grade children exhibited a high negative correlation between their persistence on a task and attributions of failure to lack of ability or task difficulty. Male subjects who least frequently attributed failure to lack of effort were then trained to make effort attributions. They were reinforced with social and token reinforcement techniques for making effort attributions in situations of success and failure. The results of the study showed that the trained subjects started to use effort attributions, and, moreover, their behavior changed in the direction of displaying more persistence. Thus, the evidence suggests that there is a possibility of maximizing achievement behavior by providing pupils with instructions and feedback that would encourage them to make internal attributions (ability, effort, interest) for success and internal-unstable attributions (effort) for failure.

Teachers in the classrooms can play an important function in maintaining pupils' adaptive causal perceptions and in modifying maladaptive ones. Teachers have great power over pupils in a classroom situation. They have the initiative to define the causes of pupils' successes and failures and to enforce these definitions on the pupils. Such influence might have positive consequences, if teachers transmit an adaptive pattern of attributions. But, special care has to be taken to avoid stereotypical causal perceptions based on such cues as pupils' sex, race, or social class (see Bar-Tal and Guttmann, 1977, for examples of such cases), which might help to maintain pupils' maladaptive attributional patterns. Therefore, teachers have to be aware of their influence during their interactions with pupils. A number of practices are recommended. When a student does well, the teacher's feedback should emphasize the student's ascription of causality for these internal factors, such as ability and effort. Similarly, the teacher needs to point out that failure is caused by lack of effort. In addition to suitable feedback, the teacher should also provide instructions prior to a task. Ideal instructions would emphasize the importance of effort in achieving a successful outcome. The teacher should directly reinforce pupils for positive beliefs in their abilities and should encourage use of effort as a crucial determinant of the outcome. An important element in the teacher's communication should be an emphasis that pupils are responsible for their outcomes, especially in the case of success.

An attribution of success to ability causes an increase in pride and high expectancy for future success, which, in turn, enhances the probability that the pupil will approach the next achievement task confidently. Attributions of success to high effort lead to a high level of satisfaction as well as to greater rewards from others, whereas attributions of failure to lack of effort, although associated with low satisfaction, induce greater effort in future attempts.

Such practices should not be designed to perpetuate unrealistic perceptions of pupils. Thus, for example, it is not desirable to change a pupil's belief that he is not able to do certain tasks when in reality he is incapable of doing them. The purpose of training programs or modifications of teacher practices should be to establish realistic perceptions of self-ability and to emphasize the importance of effort in achieving outcomes. One condition for establishing a realistic perception of self-ability is to provide tasks that are suitable to the pupil's own ability. On such tasks, a pupil may experience successful outcomes, and only through such experiences can a pupil raise confidence in his or her own ability.

Chapter 15

Marc W. Gold
Kathryn M. Ryan

Vocational Training for the Mentally Retarded

Intelligence is an important and desirable personal characteristic in modern society. Intelligence has been found to produce a generally positive impression in others (Solomon and Saxe, 1977) and to result in greater social acceptance (Dentler and Mackler, 1962). Conversely, lack of intelligence—especially extreme lack of intelligence, or mental retardation—is thought to be an undesirable characteristic that produces a generally negative impression in others. Mental retardation has been defined by the American Association on Mental Deficiency as "significantly subaverage general intellectual functioning existing concurrently with deficits in adaptive behavior, and manifested during the developmental period" (Begab, 1975, p. 5). This definition indicates the association between low levels of intellectual functioning and maladaptive behavioral functioning. It also implies two reasons for potential rejection of the mentally retarded: their lack of intelligence and their disruptive behavior.

Mental retardation is usually stereotyped by the general public in its most extreme form (Gottlieb, 1975; Mercer, 1973), and it is frequently confused with mental illness (Gottlieb, 1975; Latimer, 1970). Thus, the mentally retarded are considered to be, among other things, inadequate, helpless, and abnormal (Guskin, 1963). The mentally retarded are in reality, however, a very heterogenous population. The vast majority of persons labeled *retarded* score between 55 and 70 on intelligence tests. These individuals, referred to as *mildly retarded,* are thought to be most affected by the *mentally retarded* label, because, for the most part, their behavior and appearance are normal, so they would probably be accepted by others if they were not so labeled. The mildly retarded are usually labeled early in their school careers because of poor performance on intelligence tests, and they are generally segregated into special classes for the Educable Mentally Retarded (EMR) because of this label (Mercer, 1973). Thus, a deleterious consequence of the *mentally retarded* label is segregation (MacMillan, Jones, and Aloia, 1974). Later in their lives, the mildly retarded are frequently able to escape the *mental retardation* label and to lead fairly normal, useful lives (Baller, Charles, and Miller, 1967; Edgerton, 1967; Guskin and Spicker, 1968).

A much smaller group of individuals are labeled *moderately* or *severely retarded.* They score between 25 and 55 on standardized intelligence tests. School programs for this group are called *TMR classes* (for the Trainable Mentally Retarded). Persons scoring below 25 on intelligence tests are referred to as *profoundly mentally retarded.* Only recently have the public schools begun serving this population, and the label for such programs differs from place to place throughout the country. Persons labeled *moderately, severely,* and *profoundly retarded* generally behave and appear distinctively, so they are likely to be rejected, with or without the *mental retardation* label. Thus, they are thought to be less affected by the *mentally retarded* label than the mildly retarded. These individuals are, however, still quite affected by attributional and expectational implications of the *mentally retarded* label. This is apparent, for example, in the lack of adequate vocational training (and the consequent inability to find work) for most of these individuals due to the erroneous belief that they cannot learn.

Having remunerative employment is important in modern America for a variety of reasons: because self-worth is largely measured by occupation and wealth, because self-identification is largely through one's work role, and because of the Protestant ethic. The mentally retarded, especially the moderately, severely, and profoundly retarded, are excluded from remunerative employment for two basic reasons, their lack of competence (useful skills or ability) and their deviance (unusual and distinctive behavior and appearance). Both of these characteristics can be conceptualized as stable, internal, unintentional causes of maladaptive behavior. Thus, the individual's incompetence and deviance are thought to be stable characteristics that are caused by the retardation and are incapable of being changed or controlled. Farber (1968) believes, in the context of mental retardation, that incompetence refers to a personal problem and that deviance refers to a social problem. Further, Farber proposes that educational institutions focus on incompetence, whereas social agencies focus on deviance. It could be argued, however, that many mildly retarded children are first examined for mental retardation because they present behavior problems (Braginsky and Braginsky, 1971; MacMillan, Jones, and Aloia, 1974). Thus, assumed deviance is a central focus of much institutional treatment for the mentally retarded, in spite of the fact that intelligence tests are generally used to define mental retardation (Mercer, 1973), especially for the mildly retarded.

It is our contention that to focus on deviance and to expend a great amount of effort to terminate deviant behaviors leads one to neglect basic inadequacies resulting from the lack of adequate educational, social, and vocational training. This notion will be elaborated on later in the chapter. A second major contention deals with the deleterious attributional and expectational patterns that result from labeling an individual *mentally retarded*. In fact, mental retardation can be thought of as an attributional excuse for poor academic and social performance. This excuse may or may not be appropriately used, and it may or may not be a beneficial attribution for the retarded individual. Finally, this excuse can have different implications, depending on whether the excuse is invoked by the retarded individual or by persons dealing with this individual.

Attributional and Expectational Implications of the Mentally Retarded Label

Weiner and his colleagues (1972) proposed an attributional framework for achievement behavior that can be constructively applied to the mentally retarded. The Weiner framework included a two-dimensional categorization of the attributed causes of an individual's successful or failing performance. The two dimensions were the locus of the cause (whether the cause stemmed from within the individual or outside the individual) and the stability of the cause (whether the cause was something that was present for a long duration or something present for a short duration). Later, a third dimension, intentionality (whether the cause was something intended and controlled by the individual or whether it was unintended and uncontrolled by the individual), was added by Rosenbaum (1972). The first two dimensions, internality and stability, are related to affect and expectations, respectively. An internal cause (such as ability or effort) makes an individual feel more pride after his or her success and more shame after his or her failure than an external cause (such as task difficulty or luck), and a stable cause (such as ability or task difficulty) increases an individual's expectations after his or her success and decreases expectations after his or her failure more than an unstable cause (such as effort or luck). The last dimension, intentionality, is related to the individual's level of responsibility. An individual is held more responsible for a success or failure when the cause was intentional (such as effort) than when it was unintentional (such as ability).

Weiner's framework can be productively applied to mental retardation, because it illuminates an attribution-expectancy cycle that may well harm retarded individuals. Mental retardation, in accordance with popular stereotypes, leads to low expectations for the retarded person's competence and high expectations for his or her deviance. Many times, both of these expectations are inappropriately extreme (Gold, 1972) and may affect the individual's performance. For example, expectations concerning a retarded person's ability may be inappropriately low, and he or she will not be encouraged to perform to his or her potential. Present expectations can also affect future expectations, because different attributions are made for expected versus unexpected outcomes, and these attributions affect future expectations (Valle and Frieze, 1976; McMahan, 1973). Expected outcomes are attributed to stable factors, and unexpected outcomes are attributed to unstable factors. Thus, unexpected outcomes are discounted, whereas expected outcomes are inflated.

For retarded individuals, this means that poor performance and disruptive behavior will be attributed stably (to the retardation), and good performance and normative behavior will be attributed unstably (for example, to effort, the situation, or another person). In other words, a retarded person is thought to do poorly because of his or her retardation and to do well in spite of the retardation (because of external facilitating circumstances). So, a retarded individual generally feels very poorly about his or her failure, because failure is commonly attributed internally, and he or she rarely feels good about success, because success is commonly attributed externally. Also, the retarded person is expected to do poorly in the future, because stable attributions are made for his or her poor behavior, and unstable attributions are made for his or her good behavior. It is apparent that this is a harmful and unproductive attributional pattern, because it perpetuates low expectations and adversely affects performance. A possible cause of this attributional pattern may be a common belief that ability (and lack of ability) is a global, inclusive characteristic (Heider, 1958, p. 93). That is, it may be believed that, if someone fails at a task because of lack of ability, he or she will be unable to perform another task, even if it is unrelated to the first.

This attributional pattern may also be explained by using some of Kelley's (1967, 1973) notions concerning causal schemata. Kelley believes that individuals attribute causality according to a covariation principle. That is, individuals decipher the causal source of a behavior by analyzing the behavior for potential correlates. Potential correlates that are examined are: consensus (Do others behave the same way?), distinctiveness (Is this the only task that is affected?), and consistency (Does this happen all the time? Does this happen for all of the task-related behavior?). When a consistent correlate is found, the behavior is thought to be caused by that correlate. There may be a common belief that mental retardation is sufficiently low in consensus (most people do not have it), low in distinctiveness (it affects a large portion of tasks), and high in consistency (it affects most of the task-related behaviors a large portion of the time), so that mental retardation can be used as a brief and efficient causal explanation (or schema) for bad behavior. Mental retardation is a person-oriented schema because of its location on the consensus, distinctiveness, and consistency dimensions. Because mental retardation is person-oriented and high in consistency, the *mental retardation* attribution again leads to expectations for poor future performance. We shall separately review research concerning expectations, consequences of those expectations, and attributions for a retarded person's performance for observers and for the retarded.

Observers' Expectations for Retarded Individuals' Performance

Teachers' Expectations. Teachers have low expectations for their mildly retarded students, and they commonly attempt to segregate these students from normal students. The generally accepted rationale for segregating mentally retarded students is that, if these students are not segregated, they are likely to be unable to keep up with the rest of the class and so become frustrated and unwilling to learn. This rationale proposes that the purpose of segregation is to protect the retarded student. An equally important but often unstated rationale for segregation is that the retarded student often disrupts the class and requires a large portion of the teacher's time and effort, so adequate instruction of the rest of the class is often hindered by a retarded student's presence. This rationale proposes that the purpose of segregation is to protect the retarded student's nonretarded classmates and his or her teacher. Underlying both rationales is the assumption that retarded students cannot learn at the same speed as normal students and that they must be taught more slowly and meticulously because of this. It is also frequently assumed that retarded students cannot even learn the same types of things that normal students learn.

Once students are segregated, the assumptions concerning their low learning potential undoubtedly direct instructors to prepare lessons at a very low level. The assumptions may also affect teachers' expectations and behavior concerning the amount of learning to require from these students. Jones (1966) reviewed current research (including many unpublished studies) on special education teachers and special education teaching procedures. Guskin and Spicker (1968, p. 263) interpreted Jones' research review as suggesting that teacher orientation toward a mentally retarded student is more likely to be maternal than achievement oriented. Kurtz and others (1977) found that education students engaged in more nonverbal immediacy when reading to a child labeled *mentally retarded* than when reading to a child that was not so labeled. This result could be interpreted as further evidence of a maternal orientation. Beez (1968, as reported in Guskin and Spicker, 1968, p. 264) found that teachers working with a pupil who was expected to do poorly covered a mean of 5.66 words in instructing the student, whereas teachers working with a pupil who was expected to do well covered a mean of 10.43 words in instructing the student. Also, Sperry (1974) found that teachers planned higher-level instructional materials for students who were expected to do well than for those who were expected to do poorly. Thus, there is some evidence that expectancies can affect the amount and type of material a teacher attempts to cover. And, finally, Farina and others (1976) found that confederates labeled *mentally retarded* were shocked with less intensity and duration for failure at a learning task than confederates labeled *mentally ill* or *normal*. Farina and others interpreted this result to mean that individuals hold lower expectations for the performance of a mentally retarded individual. This research also supports the notion that the mentally retarded are less likely to be punished for failure than the nonretarded.

Much expectancy research has been done as a result of Rosenthal and Jacobson's (1968a, 1968b) famous study, in which falsely high teacher expectancies were said to lead to increased student performance in the lower grades (first and second grade) for all types of students. Most of the subsequent research that dealt with expectations for mentally retarded students (Babad, 1977; Gozali and Meyen, 1970; Schwartz and Cook, 1972; Soule, 1972) found no significant effect of teacher expectations on student performance. However, within these studies, there were two labeling effects operating—the student's initial label (EMR, TMR, mental retardate) and the experimental label (the manipulation of the student's potential for improvement). The initial label is, of course, a very potent factor that may have dominated and nullified any effects the experimental label may have had.

The effect of the initial label is also important, because a student's performance may be measured differently, depending on whether he or she is labeled *mentally retarded* or *normal*. That is, the frame of reference for retarded and nonretarded students is quite different, and this affects whether a given performance is perceived as good or bad. The frame of reference for a retarded student includes the performance of other retarded students or the performance of a stereotypical retarded student. The frame of reference for a normal student includes other normal students or the performance of a stereotypical normal student. Teachers' expectations for a retarded student's performance affect teacher-student interactions and the amount of material covered, probably because different frames of reference are held for normal and retarded students. These different frames of reference may also affect a teacher's attributions and his or her reward allocations to students. For example, a retarded student may be rewarded more than a normal student for a mediocre performance, because he or she is thought to be performing closer to his or her level of ability, putting forth greater effort, and working with a task that is more difficult for him or her to perform than a normal student.

Trainers' Expectations. Frequently, moderately and severely retarded persons are served in programs where the emphasis is on manual tasks. The rationale in these programs is usually to prepare the retarded for adequate social functioning. Teachers or trainers in such programs frequently hold very low expectations for the retarded person's ability. Changing these expectations is very important. It has been repeatedly demonstrated (Gold, 1975) that even severely retarded individuals are able to perform difficult tasks—for example, assembling bicycle brakes, electronic printed circuit boards, locking gas caps, spring-loaded hinges, and milking pumps. Most individuals working with the retarded, however, still do not believe that their clients are able to achieve success with these quite difficult tasks.

Gold (1972) engaged in an experiment in which four sheltered-workshop directors were asked if any of their clients would be able to assemble a fifteen- or twenty-four-piece bicycle brake. All directors said that their clients would not be able to learn these tasks, even if the clients were allowed to form an assembly line, in which each individual would only be required to assemble one or two pieces. Each director was then asked to select the sixteen most limited individuals in the agency, and these individuals were trained on a one-to-one basis. Half the subjects were trained using the form of the pieces as the only discriminant learning cue, and the other half were trained using the form and the color of the pieces as redundant learning cues. Every one of the subjects (N = 64) successfully learned to assemble the fifteen-piece bicycle brake. In addition, all but one subject successfully learned the 24-piece bicycle brake. Several follow-up tests indicated that performance capability continued for a very long time—one year and five years (Gold and Close, 1975). This experiment successfully demonstrated the tremendous discrepancy between directors' expectations and the actual performance ability of retarded individuals. This phenomenon, which has been repeatedly demonstrated by Gold's research, is thought to be one of the greatest deterrents of sufficient training for the retarded.

Consequences of Low Expectations. As a consequence of the expectation that the retarded have low ability and the belief that repeated failure frustrates them, teachers and trainers may spend too much time teaching the retarded easy tasks, they may overreward the retarded for easy successes, and they may not attempt to teach the retarded more difficult skills that may be useful in the future. These activities seem to be quite popular solutions to problems concerning the retarded, yet each of them may lead the retarded to learn harmful and unproductive attributional responses.

When retarded persons spend too much time learning easy

tasks, they do not learn the causal linkage between effort and ability, and they do not realize that effort must be expended to increase skills. Also, they do not learn that success at a worthwhile and challenging task demonstrates ability and achievement (Bailer, 1961).

It is possible that future unsuccessful experiences will be handled poorly by an individual who is inexperienced with failure. Also, overrewarding a student for success may undermine his or her intrinsic motivation to learn (Lee, Syrnyk, and Hallschmid, 1976; see also Chapter Ten), and it may lead the retarded student to believe that his or her teachers have very low standards. The most deleterious consequence of low expectations, however, is likely to be the lack of proper training in useful and essential vocational skills. This leads to future unemployment and all the personal and social problems associated with unemployment, such as lower self-concepts, higher dependency, and higher crime rates.

Observers' Attributions for the
Performance of the Retarded

Little direct research has been done on observers' attributions (rather than expectancies) for the successful and failing task performances of the retarded. One could expect, considering the arguments presented earlier, that observers would attribute retarded individuals' success to unstable, external causes (luck, effort) and their failure to the stable, internal cause of lack of ability. Severance and Gasstrom (1977) tested this hypothesis in a study in which attributions concerning the cause of a hypothetical individual's performance and expectations for his or her future performance were solicited. Results revealed that a retarded individual was attributed significantly greater lack of ability for failure than a nonretarded individual. However, a nonretarded individual was *not* attributed significantly greater ability for success than a retarded individual. It was also found that a retarded individual was attributed significantly more effort for success and significantly more task difficulty for failure than a nonretarded individual. Severance and Gasstrom concluded that observers of a retarded person's performance attribute failure to lack of ability and task difficulty and attribute success to effort.

The expectancy measure in Severance and Gasstrom's experiment revealed that a nonretarded individual's success led to high expectancies for the future, whereas a retarded individual's success led only to moderate future expectancies. This result is in agreement with the attributional results, because more unstable attributions (to effort) were made for the retarded individual's success than for the nonretarded individual's success. However, there was no significant difference found for expectancies for a nonretarded and a retarded individual's performance after failure. This is in spite of the fact that more attributions of lack of ability and task difficulty were made for a retarded individual's failure than for a nonretarded individual's failure. Perhaps this nonsignificant difference for expectancies after failure was because the individual, for whatever reason, was incapable of succeeding at the task. Thus, the individual was not expected to succeed in the future. In conclusion, the expectancy measure showed that expectations for a retarded individual's future performance are modifiable by observed success but that these modifications are not to the same degree as those for a nonretarded individual.

These general laboratory findings are supported by observations of people actually evaluating the performance of the retarded. It is Gold's experience that, with surprising frequency, when visitors observe individuals with severe retardation successfully performing a complex task, their comment is, "You are certainly excellent trainers." Thus, directly observed competence of the worker brings about attributions of ability, but not for the worker! Apparently, the biases found by Severance and Gasstrom are strong enough to require even more than direct observation of competence. Perhaps the direct observation of competence on a variety of complex tasks by numerous retarded individuals would alter attributions and replace the attribution-expectancy cycle, in which attributions lead to low expectations, and low expectations in turn lead to harmful and unproductive attributions.

This experience with observers suggests an attributional category, *training*, that is not frequently mentioned by attribution theorists. Training is a temporal interaction between the individual and another person, and it requires ability and effort on the part of both participants. The addition of training as a category of perceived causality requires closer inspection of the nature of ability. If ability is internal to the performer and stable, then it must be assumed, given Gold's research results, that even the most limited individuals may be capable of demonstrating considerable ability when powerful training procedures are available. The word *power* is used here to mean that the trainer must utilize ability and effort for the learner to acquire the task at hand. From our perspective, the difference between individuals is the amount of power (ability and effort) needed in the training process rather than any differences in *what* they can ultimately learn. The more difficult it is for someone to learn a task, the more power the trainer must utilize. Also, the more difficult the task is, the more effort the individual must exert to learn it. Thus, it is assumed that sufficient ability for the task is given, and training processes are seen as unstable and therefore modifiable.

Training plays an important role in the relationship between the difficulty of a task and the person's ability. The distinction between *can* and *try* made by Heider (1958) fails to acknowledge this. Weiner (1974, p. 6) acknowledges the difficulty of "explaining perceived improvement or learning [within the attribution theory perspective], inasmuch as both the determinants of "can" (ability and task difficulty) are conceptualized as fixed." The addition of the causal attribution of training requires no change in existing categories in the Weiner framework, but it allows for the recognition of a distinction between manifest and potential ability. Manifest ability is demonstrated, measurable performance, and potential ability is a testable hypothesis concerning an individual's capability of acquiring a new skill or behavior. It may be that focusing on the individual's potential rather than his or her manifest ability is what is needed to change the expectational and attributional biases of the observer of a retarded person's performance.

Retarded Individuals' Expectations
for Their Own Performance

Because most retarded individuals have had a past history of repeated failure, they are thought by many to have low expectancies for success and high expectancies for failure. Tymchuk (1972) concluded that previous research has shown this to be true. Mac-

Millan and his colleagues (Keogh, Cahill, and MacMillan, 1972; MacMillan, 1969; MacMillan and Keogh, 1971), for example, have found that retarded students are more likely than normal students to blame themselves for failure to complete a task. They found that this occurred, even when the task interruption was previously defined as a success, and they found that self-blame increased with increasing grade level. These results support the notion that retarded individuals have a higher expectancy for failure than normal individuals. The general acceptance of this belief, in fact, has led to the common practice of constructing tasks so that the retarded individual experiences only success, to reduce frustrations.

Other research, however, has shown that the retarded do not have a higher expectancy for failure than normals. Revi and Illyes (1976), for example, found that TMR children had higher expectancies for success than normal children. This, however, could have been caused by the type of task they used, a relatively easy motor task that may have been similar to other easy tasks the children had been given previously. MacMillan (1975) found no expectancy differences for EMR and normal children's initial success predictions and concluded that this result failed to support the "past history of failure" notion. In this study, experimentally induced success and failure were found to significantly affect expectancies for both groups of children. Success was found to increase performance expectancies, and failure was found to decrease performance expectancies. Schuster and Gruen (1971), in a similar study, found that mentally retarded children initially had higher expectancies for success than their same-age peers. In this study, it was also found that all the children raised their performance estimates after success and lowered them after failure.

Issues concerning expectancies of the retarded are more complicated than originally thought. For example, retarded individuals' expectancies may differ according to the type of task, the setting, the trainer, and the adequacy of the training procedure. Task characteristics would be especially important in determining expectancies, because past experience with similar tasks is used by an individual as evidence of his or her ability or inability to perform the present task. Thus, a retarded individual's expectancies for success or failure may widely vary according to the type of task.

Consequences of Low Expectations

An important issue concerns the effects a retarded individual's low expectations have on his or her performance. Cromwell (1963) proposed that retarded individuals' expectations for failure and normal individuals' expectations for success lead each group to adopt a different strategy in approaching a task. According to Cromwell, the retarded are "failure-avoiders," that is, they perform a task so as to minimize their chances of failing, whereas normal people are "success-strivers," that is, they perform a task so as to maximize their chances of succeeding. To support this notion, Cromwell cited a probability-task study (Shipe, 1960), which revealed that retarded subjects always guessed the predominant item in order to be correct on most of the trials (or fail the least number of trials), whereas normal subjects switched their guesses in order possibly to be correct on *all* the trials. Cromwell also noted that the assumption that the retarded are failure-avoiders led to research that presented evidence that retarded individuals enter situations with a performance level that is lower than what they are capable of, they are less affected by failure than normals (presumably because they are less surprised by failure), and they are less likely than normals to increase effort following failure. Also, retarded children have been found to attribute less negative affect to their teachers following failure than do normal children (Hayes and Prinz, 1976). These consequences may, in part, be due to harmful and unproductive attributions.

Retarded Individuals' Attributions
for Their Own Performance

It has been proposed that mentally retarded individuals do not learn the causal relationship between effort and success and lack of effort and failure, and thus they do not feel responsible for their own performance (Wooster, 1974). This would lead one to assume that retarded individuals would not attribute their performance to effort or to any other intentional causes. One could also assume that other harmful and unproductive attributions may be made by these individuals because of their tendency to blame themselves for failure. For example, one would expect retarded individuals to attribute their failure to their retardation, which would lead these individuals to feel very bad and to stop trying. Moreover, given the previous arguments, one would also expect retarded individuals to attribute their success to external, unstable causes.

However, research has shown that the mentally retarded make attributions for success and failure that are similar to those made by normals. For example, EMR junior high school students were found to make more external than internal attributions for failure situations (Panda and Lynch, 1974). Also, EMR adults have been found to make more effort and luck attributions for failure than for success and more ability attributions for success than for failure (Horai and Guarnaccia, 1975). However, Horai and Guarnaccia's findings are suspect. Because attributions were elicited verbally from the subjects, socially desirable responses may have been given. Also, because the success manipulation included the statement "You did better than any I have tested so far" and the failure manipulation included the statement "Most of the people I have tested so far did at least ten more than you" the manipulations included base-rate information. This may have activated social-comparison processes (Festinger, 1954), with other retarded individuals as the frame of reference, and affected the subjects' attributions. Finally, Horai and Guarnaccia did not analyze the attributions within the success and failure conditions. By examining the means, it appears that there were no differences between the attributions for success (on a scale between 0 and 3, Task-Difficulty mean = 1.7, Ability mean = 1.5, Luck mean = 1.4, and Effort mean = 1.35), whereas there were differences between the attributions for failure (on a scale between 0 and 3, Luck mean = 2.15, Effort mean = 1.85, Task-Difficulty mean = 1.3, and Ability mean = 0.70). In conclusion, it would seem that retarded individuals are able to attribute their failures favorably, but they have not been shown to attribute their successes favorably.

Another interesting question concerns the effects a retarded individual's attributions can have on his or her performance. Hoffman and Weiner (1978) examined the effects of manipulated attributions and outcomes on subsequent performance of TMR adults. The design was a 4 (ability, effort, task difficulty, or no attribution) × 2 (success or failure outcome) factorial. The independent variable was a success or failure experience combined with an appropriate attribution (or no attribution), and the dependent variable was subsequent performance on a second trial of the same coding task. Results revealed that an attribution of ability in the success condition enhanced the retardate's subsequent performance relative to the other attribution (and the no-attribution) conditions. No significant differences were found between the attribution conditions within the failure situation. Hoffman and Weiner interpreted these results as suggesting that retarded adults respond to attributions in a manner that is similar to normal adults and that their performances can be enhanced by proper attribution-outcome combinations.

Wooster (1974) was able to show that the retarded may be taught to attribute their performance optimally by having them repeatedly observe their responsibility for success and failure. So, it seems that a beneficial and productive attributional pattern can be learned by the retarded and that this attributional pattern is then used by them to enhance their performance. However, this attributional pattern is not habitually employed without such learning.

The Attribution-Expectancy Cycle: Conclusions

It has been demonstrated that the retarded and their instructors have low expectations for retarded individuals' ability. Consequently, they underestimate the kinds of tasks that can successfully be performed, and they do not give the retarded person deserved credit for success. Thus, successes are attributed to factors other than ability, which means that observations of a retarded person's manifest ability do not affect estimates of his or her potential ability. Failures are attributed to the retardation, so it is assumed that the retarded individual's inability to perform is both stable and unintentional. The latter factor implies lack of responsibility for failure, which may or may not be beneficial for the retarded individual. If the retarded individual does not have the potential ability to succeed at the task, the unintentional factor may be beneficial, because he or she is not punished for an inability that cannot be controlled. However, if the retarded individual does have the potential ability to succeed at the task, the unintentional factor may be harmful, because the individual will not be trained, and he or she will not try to succeed at something that can be done. Since it is impossible to assess the individual's potential, the appropriate strategy is to assume that the person is able and to place responsibility for nonattainment of criterion performance on the trainer.

We feel that the attributional process itself must become more conscious, so that implications of various attributions are recognized and a deliberate decision is made concerning the relative payoff of allowing individuals an excuse for failure versus allowing them hope for success. Training should become a key attributional precursor to ability for the retarded. This attribution could allow for greater fulfillment of each individual's goals for a full life.

The Relationship Between Competence and Deviance

Hollander's (1958, 1960) theory of idiosyncrasy-credits states a fundamental relationship between competence, conformity, and deviance in a group. Competence, according to Hollander, refers to an individual's ability, especially his or her ability to perform activities that reward the group. Deviance refers to an individual's eccentricities, which are negatively evaluated by the group. And conformity refers to an individual's conventionalities, which are positively evaluated by the group. Hollander theorized that an individual's perceived competence and his or her past conformity creates a "credit balance" within a group, called *idiosyncrasy-credits*. This credit balance allows the individual to deviate later without group censure. This is because the individual is of value to the group, and his or her value affects how his or her behavior is perceived and whether it will be punished. The perceptual component can be seen to fit the attributional framework discussed earlier. That is, behavior consistent with past behavior (present conformity and past conformity) is considered to be stably caused, and behavior inconsistent with past behavior (present deviance and past conformity) is considered to be unstably caused. Moreover, because the past behavior probably occurred at different times, in different contexts, and with different individuals, consistent behavior is likely to be perceived to be due to the individual, whereas inconsistent behavior is likely to be perceived as externally caused. So, consistent conformity is rewarded, consistent deviance is punished, and inconsistent behavior is treated intermediately. The punishment component is intuitively plausible, because one can readily see that other group members will not want to lose a potentially valuable group member.

Competence and Deviance of the Retarded

Hollander's theory of idiosyncrasy-credits can be restated as, "The more competence an individual has, the more deviance will be tolerated in that person by others" (Gold, 1975, p. 260). This hypothesis is readily applicable to the mentally retarded, because these individuals are likely to function concurrently as both incompetent and deviant. Thus, the retarded individual has two separate but related behavior problems.

It has already been shown that expectancies for a retarded individual's competence are low. Foster and Ysseldyke (1976) demonstrated that expectations for a retarded individual's deviance are high. In this study, teachers were assigned to one of four label groups, and the members of each group were asked to list the behavior they expected of a hypothetical normal, EMR, learning disabled, or emotionally disturbed child. Then, each teacher observed a videotape of the same normal boy, who was supposedly a representative of the labeled group. Results showed that the teachers held negative expectancies for children categorized with a deviant label and that they maintained these expectancies, even when confronted with normal behavior. In addition, it was found that the lowest expectancies were held for the EMR child.

Traditionally, trainers and teachers of the retarded have focused on their deviance. This may be because deviance is more apparent than incompetence, because modern tools (such as group teaching or behavior modification) are more applicable to deviance than to incompetence, or because it is believed that one must eliminate deviance to augment competence. The result of this focus is that the retarded individual's competencies are so low that any deviance can readily result in group sanctions. This is especially harmful, because a retarded individual's deviance may be more readily apparent than his or her competence, because there is a common discrepancy between a retarded individual's potential ability and his or her manifest ability, and because of the expectancy-attribution cycle previously mentioned.

We do not believe that a retarded person's deviance should be ignored; rather, his or her competence should be given more attention. Attending to the individual's competence, we believe, increases his or her employment potential, increases his or her self-confidence and self-worth, decreases his or her deviant behaviors, and breaks the deleterious attribution-expectancy cycle. It is self-evident that training the retarded will increase their job potential. Self-worth can also be increased by employment, because employment is an important goal for most retarded people (Edgerton, 1967) and for the society in which they live. Employment also increases buying power and the ability to enjoy the goods and activities available in this society. Also, because deviant behavior is sometimes incompatible with competent behavior, it can be assumed that increased competence may decrease deviance. In fact, Gold (1975) has found this to be the case for many of the retarded individuals in his training program. And, finally, it is felt that training the retarded individual will eventually lead to the elimination of the deleterious attribution-expectancy cycle described earlier.

Potential Solutions

Mainstreaming. A currently popular solution to the problems of retarded children in the public schools is to transfer retarded students from special classes back into regular classes. This solution derives from the belief that the *mentally retarded* label does more harm than good, especially because the label results in segregation. Budoff and Gottlieb (1976) found that mainstreamed EMR children were more internally controlled and had more positive attitudes toward school than their segregated peers. In addition, it was found that the more able EMR children benefitted more from mainstreaming than the less able EMR children. Most importantly, able EMR students were found to change their self-concept of ability and their beliefs concerning how competent others perceived them to be. Strang, Smith, and Rogers (in press) found that half-time mainstreaming (mainstreaming for half of the school day) optimally augmented EMR children's self-concepts. They felt that this was due to the fact that half-time mainstreamed students were able to compare themselves with students in special classes or regular classes, and, depending on the comparison item, they were able to enhance their egos with one or the other comparison. It appears that mainstreaming can allow EMR students to regain their self-concept of ability and can lead to beneficial attributions and expectancies. Thus, able EMR students that are mainstreamed are frequently able to show better performance.

The issue of mainstreaming more severely retarded students is more complicated because of the amount of time and effort needed to teach retarded students to form better attributions and expectancies and to perform to their fullest capacity. Regular classroom teachers do not have the time, and they may not have the skills to motivate and train retarded students properly.

Training. In Gold's instructional system (Gold and Pomerantz, 1978), it is believed that the severely and profoundly retarded can be trained to form healthier attributions through successful vocational experiences. It is also believed that this system may change trainers' attributions concerning their clients' abilities. In this system, the task is divided into teachable units, which are modified for each learner. This method results in high rates of acquisition for most learners, although there are differences in the rate of acquisition. Thus, each learner experiences much success from the beginning of the training process. This training procedure should not be misinterpreted to suggest that errorless learning is desired. On the contrary, errors and the reduction of errors are seen as important in developing a retarded person's ability to deal with errors (Dweck, 1975) and to recognize the importance of effort in the learning process.

It is common practice in most programs for the retarded to be reinforced for any and every little positive behavior. An unstated assumption is that these individuals have little if any ability, and so any positive actions must represent effort rather than ability. The present position is that reinforcement given for low levels of success results in support for the retarded individual's low self-concept. In other words, the individual believes that, if he or she is reinforced for very simple tasks, then others believe that he or she has very low ability. An alternative strategy is to provide little or no reinforcement for simple, positive behavior. Also, it is believed that silence can have reinforcing qualities, when the trainer is clearly paying attention to the learner. In this situation, when the trainer is not commenting, the learner learns that "no news is good news." Each time an error that has been made before is corrected, the trainer provides enough information to correct that error but less information (and frequently different information) than in the last correction. This approach combines many factors that will promote ability attributions for success and discourage lack of ability attributions for failure, and this type of training may lead the retarded to fulfill their substantial potential.

One final observation from Gold's program stems from anecdotal information collected during training sessions. It has been repeatedly observed that many of the clients who had been previously described as having severely deviant behavior displayed none of these behaviors during the training session. It could be that conventional extinction procedures were working throughout the session to extinguish these behaviors. However, it may also be that the clients were not deviant, because they were not *expected* to be deviant. This is felt to be a crucial component in adequate vocational training for the mentally retarded. The learner must be expected to perform the task competently, and he or she must not be expected to behave deviantly. Thus, trainers of the retarded must cease to form deleterious attributions and expectancies, and this will lead retarded individuals to form more beneficial attributions and expectations for themselves.

Conclusions

We believe that two basic problems currently inhibit efforts to provide adequate educational and vocational training of the retarded. These are a deleterious attribution-expectancy cycle and an almost exclusive focus on the retarded individual's deviance. Both of these problems are related to general expectations that the retarded individual should lack competence and be deviant. The attribution-expectancy cycle leads to the ascription of performance failure to the retardation and performance success to external, unstable factors. In this way, the cycle operates to perpetuate low expectations for the ability of the retarded. The focus on deviance leads to situations in which the retarded are fired from jobs or alienated from family and friends because of their limited ability to reward others. Retarded individuals today are taught so few skills that any deviance is punished quite severely. We believe that the focus of future training of the retarded must be on their competence. Also, there must be a concerted effort to change attributions and expectancies of those associated with the retarded and thus an effort to change attributions and expectancies of the retarded themselves. This may be done through a conscious effort to restructure attributions, or it may be done on a less conscious level by mainstreaming, at some level, all retarded individuals. By focusing on each retarded individual's potential ability through the teaching and training processes, retarded individuals can be allowed to fulfill their great social potential.

Chapter 16   *John S. Carroll*
Irene Hanson Frieze

Conclusion: Assessing the Application of Attribution Theory to Social Problems

Social psychologists of the 1930s and 1940s lived in a world where war, genocide, tyranny, racial discrimination, and public opinion were pressing in on their personal lives. Social problems were the crucible in which social psychology was born, and social psychologists felt the pain, the need to understand, and the need for change. When Lewin (1951) argued the practicality of social-psychological theories, he meant that the discipline could and should attack real problems with the knowledge and techniques then available and that a theoretical perspective was helpful in doing this. His concept of *action research* provided for both social usefulness and theoretical development as joint products of studying real people in real situations (Lewin, 1946).

Social psychology reached a kind of false maturity in the 1950s and 1960s. Driven by a desire for scientific rigor and the goal of identifying specific causal factors (developing theory) in social behavior, social psychologists sought to control social behavior in order to study it analytically (Weissberg, 1976). To achieve control, social psychology became the study of behavior in the laboratory. Theories were developed that explained laboratory phenomena but that typically were not or could not be applied to problems of people's daily lives. As social psychology attempted to gain scientific control and respectability through laboratory experiments, applications were slighted. Social psychologists who did applications did not publish in social-psychological journals; they got funding from different sources and called themselves *industrial psychologists, opinion pollsters, advertisers,* or *group-dynamics trainers.* These researchers were considered less respectable than "real" social psychologists.

Only in the past few years has major recognition grown within the field that the extreme emphasis on laboratory research may have been a mistake. Many now believe that the degree of control made possible in laboratory studies and the restrictions necessary to maintain that control have constricted the progress of social psychology. The Ring-McGuire exchange (1967) was the first modern outcry, and it rapidly became a part of graduate training in the late 1960s and 1970s. This reemergence of a social-problems orientation parallels the political awareness and activism of the late 1960s, following fifteen years of blissful disregard of sociopolitical events. Now, there is a willingness to seek a synthesis of the "ivory-tower scientists" and the "applied technicians," to trade some rigor for relevance, some control for complexity (Helmreich, 1975). Bickman (1976) argues that the development of new journals, new graduate programs, and new funding priorities illustrates this emerging synthesis.

Attribution theory followed this same course of events. The original work of Heider was oriented toward daily problems of living. The theory was broad and lacked specificity and control. As social psychologists became interested in attribution theory in the mid 1960s, the research gradually became more and more laboratory oriented. Precise, controlled studies were done with college students as subjects. We came to know more and more about the attributions of college students but little about what attributions were made in society and what effects they had on people's lives. However, with the emphasis on applications in social psychology, attribution theorists, too, have begun to work outside the laboratory.

This book represents one example of this new trend in social psychology. Theory and application are beginning to be reunited. Attribution researchers are finding that social problems outside the laboratory are an additional test of their theories and a good source for new ideas and approaches. The desire to serve and improve society has rekindled the desire to understand social behavior in social contexts, and the recognition is growing that science also may be served in this manner. For all these reasons, it is important to observe how attribution theory is being applied to social problems and what the results have been.

What Is an Application?

An *application,* according to the dictionary, is "a putting to use." Thus, an application of attribution theory to a social problem would be using attribution theory to solve this problem. However, this sets a very high standard for social psychologists: few of the chapters in this book actually report on the implementation of a program based on attribution theory that was intended to solve a social problem. Helmreich (1975) proposes that we should distinguish two goals for applied research: applicability, the potential for application; and utilization, the implementation of social change. He further argues that research is more appropriately concerned with applicability, whereas utilization involves a different role, that of social activist. Thus, a standard to which all the contributions in this book could aspire is the potential for application.

One way of assessing potential for application is to look at the importance of the social problem chosen for study. Some researchers study major social problems, whereas others are concerned with social problems that may not be as large in terms of the number of people affected or the cost (in financial and humanitarian terms) to society. Furthermore, once the overall problem is selected, the researcher must decide what aspect of that problem he or she wants to attack. Selecting a minor aspect of a major problem may have less potential impact than selecting a major aspect of a more narrowly defined problem. Thus, our first criterion for assessing the chapters in this book is:

• What is the potential social impact of the research?

Looking at the potential impact, or the applicability standard, one finds a serious attendant problem: How do we know that something is applicable unless we try it and see? In deriving indices of applicability, we can create additional criteria for discussing the chapters in this book:

• Does the research exhibit a high degree of external validity through the use of appropriate subject populations, stimuli, and settings?
• Can the research detect complex (longitudinal, multivariable) relationships? Does it allow for the simultaneous action of as many variables as would be true in any real setting?
• Are the constructs used by practitioners in the setting understood and encompassed by the analysis?
• Has the research been applied, and with what success?

In using these criteria to evaluate the chapters, we should avoid quick judgments that some chapters are good applications and others are poor. Certain problem areas have been studied for years, and applications of social-psychological theories have been tried before. Other areas are relatively new, both in theoretical analyses of the central variables and in application of scientific principles. In addition, some areas afford easy access and cooperation for researchers, and others do not. For these reasons, chapters that report actual applications or are more readily applicable because of contact with naturalistic settings, subjects, and situations often represent more *mature* rather than better research. Chapters that seem less applicable often reflect innovative approaches to social problems. In time, as research builds cumulatively, the applicability of such research will increase.

All these considerations reflect a desire to apply attribution theory in the sense of social activism or *control* over social problems. This is the dictionary definition of *application* and the typical way we think of an applied science. However, applied research may have value in ways other than directly demonstrating control or the possibility of control. First, applied research may increase our *understanding* of a social problem, suggest new approaches, and enable us to predict events without improving our control over them. This is the distinction Wells (1978) makes between causal variables that are potentially manipulable to bring change and those we can observe but not affect. Correlational studies often reveal powerful antecedents that would be impossible or improper to change. Such studies may help in developing new programs in the future, as our understanding of the problem grows. Second, applied research may affect the *development of theory.* By advancing science, it ultimately increases the possibility of an improved understanding and control. Thus, to the five criteria by which we will evaluate these chapters, we add two more:

- Does the research improve our understanding of or ability to predict events related to the social problem?
- Does the research advance theory that is relevant to the social problem?

The dictionary offers a final definition of *application* that suggests how to use our criteria. This definition is "relevance." An alternative to the laboratory-versus-field or theoretical-versus-applied dichotomies is one we have come to perceive while reviewing manuscripts for various journals and funding agencies. This alternative dichotomy is rigor versus relevance. As with the previous two dichotomies, there is no apparent reason why the poles of this dichotomy are mutually exclusive, but we get a strong inductive sense that they are. Early in our career as researchers and as reviewers, we tended to opt for rigor. Rigor was a must, relevance a plus. We now like relevance better. However, a goal we share with many of the authors of this book is to put as much rigor as possible into relevant research.

An Application of Attribution Theory

Rather than attempt an exhaustive analysis of each chapter in this book, we have chosen to analyze one chapter in some detail and then to give a general feeling for how the fourteen applications measure up against our criteria. In this way, we can avoid invidious distinctions while creating a model that can be applied to other relevant research. The chapter that we will discuss, Lepper and Dafoe's analysis of the classroom (Chapter Thirteen), was chosen because it illustrates most of the important issues and because we feel it is carefully conceived and well presented.

Lepper and Dafoe address the issue of students' motivations to engage in various activities in the classroom. In particular, they focus on how the provision of rewards by teachers may have the unintended effect of reducing motivation. The problem they address is of paramount importance. Virtually everyone in our society spends one-quarter of their waking hours for ten to fifteen formative years in school. The way we absorb the educational content and authority structure of school influences the rest of our lives.

The focus on the effects of rewards in the classroom is not only an important feature of classrooms but a central feature of our society. Rewards are an incentive and control mechanism in formal organizations, such as business and government, and in informal interpersonal relationships as well. For these reasons, the Lepper and Dafoe chapter has potential broad importance to society as well as specific importance for the problem of teachers' use of rewards in motivating students.

In considering the potential applicability of the conceptual analysis and research reported in the chapter, it is apparent that there is an impressive level of validity. A substantial portion of the research they report took place in actual classrooms using actual class materials and students. Subjects were unobtrusively observed, and the manipulations (for example, rewards offered contingent on task engagement) are typical of classrooms. Some of these studies took place over a period of several weeks, and time trends are often reported, although complex temporal models of behavior are neither envisioned nor attempted.

Analyses of the classroom by educators are reviewed, and their insights into issues and features of the classroom are integrated into the attributional analysis. One gets the strong sense that a teacher could read this chapter and recognize how the research affects his or her classroom. Teachers can recognize instances in their own classrooms where rewards may have decreased some students' motivations and can consider how to avoid this in the future.

The attribution theory of classroom incentives has been applied in this chapter, in the demonstrational sense of successful hypothesis-testing. Long-term policy changes as a result of this analysis are not reported (for example, a school altering its use of incentives because of this research). Perhaps the research is more useful as a warning of the dangers of incentives than as a proposal for promoting learning or other desired classroom behaviors in terms of incentives. Lepper and Dafoe admit that changing policy is a formidable task. However, the high level of validity in the research and the understanding of issues from the educator's viewpoint promotes confidence that applicability is high.

A major goal of the reported research has been the development of theory. Lepper and Defoe contrast their attributional analysis of reasons to more traditional attributional analyses of causes. Further, they contrast their ideas about incentives to the behaviorist viewpoint that rewarded activities will increase in frequency of occurrence. They find not only that theory can be developed through research in applied settings but also that problems of limiting conditions posed by demand characteristics and perceived freedom can best be addressed in natural settings. Natural settings thus pose problems that challenge theory and expand the relationship of one theory to other theories.

Attribution Theory Applied to Social Problems

This book did not begin as an enumeration of social problems, each of which would be addressed by attribution research. Instead, we sought contributions from anyone working in an applied attributional framework and then attempted to organize the applications we found. Thus, the distribution of chapters in this book represents, at least to some degree, the actual choices of attribution researchers of those areas in which they felt attribution theory could be best or most meaningfully applied. These chapters clearly demonstrate that the attributional perspective is an individual psychological perspective. The individual person's responses to his or her own illness, life-crisis, or the behavior of other people are the focus of the attributional analyses.

The majority of chapters address the areas of individual health, criminal justice, and education. It seems clear that each of these areas drew attribution researchers because of certain advantages each affords to this type of research. Health care is a primary contact point for psychologists doing applied work (other such contact points include personnel testing and selection, human factors engineering, advertising, and public opinion work). The importance of psychological factors in health and mental health in general has long been recognized, and there is a growing movement in behavioral medicine that makes such work even more topical and important.

Criminal justice might seem a strange place for an attribution researcher, but there are two strong linkages: law and mental health. Legal scholars have made formal analyses of such concepts as causality, intent, and responsibility, which makes criminal justice a natural place to examine the mutual relationship of legal concepts and naive attributional judgments. Crime and mental illness have strong parallels as social problems, and the line between the criminal-justice and mental-health systems is highly permeable. Finally, social psychologists know the classroom and educational system better than any other applied setting; we and our typical subjects live in it. As a result, access to issues, subjects, and settings is easy. Many universities have educational psychology as a formal speciality, either in the Education School or Department of Psychology. Psychologists are probably more accepted in educational settings than in any other applied setting, although theoretical psychologists still experience some difficulty if they are perceived as "too academic." For all these reasons, it makes sense that these would be the first social problems addressed by attribution researchers.

In the remainder of this chapter, we will discuss the contributions in this book using the criteria that were described and
applied to the Lepper and Dafoe chapter. We will be deliberately
general, in the hope that the impact of this book on applied work in
social psychology will not rest solely on individual chapters but on
the volume as a whole.

Potential Social Impact. There is no question that the chapters
in this book address important social problems. Large numbers of
people are affected by alcoholism, depression, medicinal drug use,
and crime. Consumerism, wife-battering, rape, loneliness, and insomnia are each substantial areas of concern. Are attribution-based
interventions capable of making substantial impact on these
problems?

In some of the chapters, social problems are confronted as a
whole (alcoholism, depression). Attributional analyses could increase our understanding and ability to alleviate these problems,
although these chapters are more directly aimed at understanding.
Chapters that are more focused on interventions are often tackling
a smaller segment of the larger social problem (training the retarded, making people feel safer about crime). Sometimes, the attributional analysis focuses on variables that are predictive but not
demonstrably controllable (a rape victim's self-presentation, a
juror's attributional biases). However, the evident progress and
success in the brief time that attribution theory has been applied to
these social problems suggests that continued research promises
real social benefits.

Validity. The degree of external validity of the attributional
applications concerns the generalizibility of the populations
studied, the research settings, and the types of experimental stimuli
used in research. On these criteria, our chapters do quite well. All
the chapters draw data from the actual target populations they are
attempting to understand. Often, these data are supplemented by
data from college students, but none attempts to understand a
social problem solely from studying college students. This use of
valid populations may be one of the most unique features of the
research in this book.

The record is not as good in the validity of research settings
or in the choice of experimental stimuli. Many of the chapters rely
on the typical types of questionnaires used in laboratory research.

Concepts derived from attribution theory are much in evidence. Less attention is given to using materials that approximate the stimuli someone would encounter if they were actually confronting the social problem at issue. In many cases, this lack is partially or completely due to the fact that written stimuli are not a part of the problem as it is usually experienced. Interview techniques, which are often believed to be more valid, are also artificial to some degree in these situations and are much more costly. Perhaps only the criminal justice and educational areas commonly use written stimuli. Strong behavioral validation of attributional analyses are most evident in chapters from these two areas.

Complex Relationships. Almost by definition, the more structured the research, the fewer are the opportunities for detecting the simultaneous actions of many variables. Research in a particular area often proceeds by first doing large-scale exploratory studies to see which of a great number of possible variables seem to be relevant for the predictions one wants to make. Once these variables are established, the research becomes more focused on a small number of key variables. Then, as these relationships are clearly understood, the researcher is again able to expand the scope of the analysis and to bring in other variables, doing complex multivariate analyses to determine their interactive effects. Further, applied researchers typically want to know what factors have the greatest effects, whereas theoretical research often ignores large effects but seeks to know whether a particular effect of theoretical importance exists.

Most, if not all, of the chapters in this book are at the stage of studying specific relationships between attributional variables and the chosen problem area. They are thus testing attributional concepts and often rely on separate studies to get the "big picture." None are at the stage of successfully studying the multiplicative effects of numerous variables. However, most are beyond the initial stage of exploratory studies. Thus, the chapters have not met the criterion of being able to study the relationship of many variables, but they are moving in this direction. We feel that these researchers have made significant strides to reach these levels of analysis, since controlled studies of specific variables are difficult in the laboratory and even more difficult in these applied settings.

Use of Constructs Relevant to Practitioners. An important criterion that affects the ease with which research results can be applied is whether the research relies on constructs used and readily understood by nonacademic practitioners now working in the area. This issue is again a difficult one for many of the studies here, because the basic constructs derived from attribution theory may not be readily understood by practitioners. This is most true, once again, in the clinical and everyday applications and less true in the criminal justice and educational areas. These studies suggest that one goal of applied research may be to educate practitioners about variables to which they should be more sensitive, if these have been shown to have a significant impact on events in their problem area.

Theoretical Development. Applied attribution research has of necessity expanded beyond the classic concern with when and how particular attributions are made. Applied research complements the interest in the antecedent of attributions with a focus on the consequences of attributions—we must know how causal attributions mediate *behavior.*

For this reason, many of the chapters are based on Weiner's framework as the most detailed and general discussion of the consequences of attributions. Yet, in attempting to use the Weiner framework, researchers have also made a number of theoretical advances. Several of the chapters based on the Weiner framework have found that they needed to expand the list of causal attributions relevant to their particular social setting. Many of the chapters go even farther and propose new classification systems for these causal attributions. As these researchers found, once one leaves the confines of the laboratory, the old neat systems no longer function as well. These new dimensions for analyzing causal attributions should now help in future laboratory research.

New theoretical advances within attribution theory have arisen, because natural settings are more stringent tests of theory than laboratories. The idea that we must examine attributions from a framework of reasons as well as causes arose in an applied setting. The idea that attributions act like hypotheses that are tested by active information-search arose from applied attribution research. Further, the integration of attributional insights with other judgments and behaviors can best be investigated in applied settings. Most of the chapters contribute to theoretical development in their applied area as well as to attribution theory per se (for example, Rehm and O'Hara's new theoretical model of depression). Thus, applied research seems to be a genuine spark for theoretical advances.

A Closing Word

Our analysis of the applications in this book has proceeded by establishing criteria against which the contributions are compared. This procedure can show that we are meeting the criteria or that we are falling short. Inevitably, then, there will be neutral comments and negative comments, stemming from the use of a reference point near the ideal. To redress this imbalance, the reader should recognize that the chapters in this book could also be compared to "average" social-psychology research. This comparison would reveal the chapters to be highly innovative, integrative, methodologically broad, and externally valid, with a high degree of interest and relevance. The chapters break new ground, suggest new directions, and provide a conceptual framework for those actually working with the social problems they address. Although actual programs based on attributional concepts are rarely implemented, the door is open for collaboration among academic researchers and nonacademic professionals and policy makers attempting to solve social problems. We hope this book will be one step in this direction.

References

Abelson, R. P. "Script Processing in Attitude Formation and Decision-Making." In J. S. Carroll and J. W. Payne (Eds.), *Cognition and Social Behavior.* Hillsdale, N.J.: Erlbaum, 1976.

Abramowitz, S. "Locus of Control and Self-Reported Depression Among College Students." *Psychological Reports,* 1969, *25,* 149–150.

Abrams, R. D., and Finesinger, J. E. "Guilt Reactions in Patients with Cancer." *Cancer,* 1953, *6*(3), 474–482.

Abramson, L. Y., Garber, J., Edwards, N. B., and Seligman, M E. P. "Expectancy Changes in Depression and Schizophrenia." *Journal of Abnormal Psychology,* 1978, *87,* 102–109.

Abramson, L. Y., and Sackeim, H. A. "A Paradox in Depression: Uncontrollability and Self-blame." *Psychological Bulletin,* 1977, *84,* 838–851.

Abramson, L. Y., Seligman, M. E. P., and Teasdale, J. D. "Learned Helplessness in Humans: Critique and Reformulation." *Journal of Abnormal Psychology,* 1978, *87,* 49–74.

Aderman, P., Brehm, B., and Katz, L. "Empathetic Observation of an Innocent Victim: The Just World Revisited." *Journal of Personality and Social Psychology,* 1974, *29,* 342–347.

Alcoholics Anonymous. *Twelve Steps and Twelve Traditions.* New York: Alcoholics Anonymous World Services, 1952.

Alcoholics Anonymous. *The Story of How Many Thousands of Men and Women Have Recovered from Alcoholism.* New York: Alcoholics Anonymous World Services, 1955.

Allen, C. H., and Straus, M. A. "Resources, Power and Husband-Wife Violence." Paper presented at the annual meeting of the National Council on Family Relations, 1975.

Amabile, T. M. "Effects of Extrinsic Constraint on Creativity." *Journal of Personality and Social Psychology,* in press.

Amabile, T. M., DeJong, W., and Lepper, M. R. "Effects of Externally-Imposed Deadlines on Subsequent Intrinsic Motivation." *Journal of Personality and Social Psychology,* 1976, *34,* 92–98.

Ames, C. "Children's Achievement Attributions and Self-Reinforcement: Effects of Self-Concept and Competitive Reward Structure." *Journal of Education Psychology,* in press.

Ames, R. "Teachers' Attributions of Responsibility: Some Unexpected Nondefensive Effects." *Journal of Educational Psychology,* 1975, *67,* 668–676.

Anderson, N. H. "Integration Theory and Attitude Change." *Psychological Review,* 1971, *78,* 171–206.

Anderson, R. E. "Consumer Dissatisfaction: The Effect of Disconfirmed Expectancy on Perceived Product Performance." *Journal of Marketing Research,* 1973, *10,* 38–44.

Anderson, R., Manoogian, S. T., and Resnick, J. S. "The Undermining and Enhancing of Intrinsic Motivation in Preschool Children." *Journal of Personality and Social Psychology,* 1976, *34,* 915–922.

Andrews, G. R., and Debus, R. L. "Persistence and the Causal Perception of Failure: Modifying Cognitive Attributions." *Journal of Educational Psychology,* 1978, *70,* 154–166.

Armor, D. J., Polich, J. M., and Stambul, H. B. *Alcoholism and Treatment.* Santa Monica, Calif.: Rand Corporation, 1976.

Atkinson, J. W. *An Introduction to Motivation.* New York: Van Nostrand, 1964.

Aubert, V., and Messinger, S. "The Criminal and the Sick." *Inquiry,* 1958, *1,* 137–160.

Babad, E. V. "Pygmalion in Reverse." *Journal of Special Education,* 1977, *11,* 81–90.

Bailer, I. "Conceptualization of Success and Failure in Mentally Retarded and Normal Children." *Journal of Personality,* 1961, *29,* 303–320.

Bailey, R. C., Helm, B., and Gladstone, R. "The Effects of Success and Failure in a Real-Life Setting: Performance, Attribution, Affect, and Expectancy." *Journal of Psychology,* 1975, *89,* 137–147.

Bakan, D. *Disease, Pain, and Sacrifice.* Chicago: University of Chicago Press, 1968.

Baker, W. Y., and Smith, L. H. "Facial Disfigurement and Personality." *Journal of the American Medical Association,* 1939, *112,* 303.

Bales, R. F. "Cultural Differences in Rates of Alcoholism." *Quarterly Journal of Studies on Alcohol,* 1946, *6,* 480–499.

Ball, P. G., and Wyman, E. "The Battered Wife Syndrome." *Viva,* May 1976.

Ball, P. G., and Wyman, E. "Battered Wives: Help for the Victim Next Door." *MS.,* August 1976.

Ball, P. G., and Wyman, E. "Battered Wives and Powerlessness: What Can Counselors Do?" *Victimology,* 1978, pp. 545–552.

Baller, W. R., Charles, D. C., and Miller, E. L. "Mid-Life Attainment of the Mentally Retarded: A Longitudinal Study." *Genetic Psychology Monographs,* 1967, *75,* 235–329.

Bandler, R. J., Madaras, G. R., and Bem, D. J. "Self-Observation as a Source of Pain Perception." *Journal of Personality and Social Psychology,* 1968, *9,* 205–209.

Bandura, A. *Principles of Behavior Modification.* New York: Holt, Rinehart and Winston, 1969.

Bandura, A. "Self-Reinforcement: Theoretical and Methodological Considerations." *Behaviorism,* 1976, *4,* 135–155.

Bandura, A. *Social Learning Theory.* Englewood Cliffs, N.J.: Prentice-Hall, 1977.

Barron, D. S. "Coping with the Stereotype of the Handicapped." *Journal of Rehabilitation,* 1967, *33,* 16–33.

Barry, H., III. "Psychological Factors in Alcoholism." In B. Kissin and H. Begleiter (Eds.), *The Biology of Alcoholism, Vol. 3, Clinical Pathology.* New York: Plenum, 1974, 53–108.

Bar-Tal, D. "The Formation of Teachers' Expectations: Attributional Analysis." Paper presented at the 85th annual meeting of the American Psychological Association, San Francisco, 1977.

Bar-Tal, D. "Attributional Analysis of Achievement Related Behavior." *Review of Educational Research,* 1978, *48,* 259–271.

Bar-Tal, D., and Darom, E. "Pupils' Attributions for Success and Failure." *Child Development,* in press.

Bar-Tal, D., and Frieze, I. "Attributions of Success and Failure for Actors and Observers." *Journal of Research in Personality,* 1976, *10,* 256–265.

Bar-Tal, D., and Frieze, I. "Achievement Motivation for Males and Females as a Determinant of Attributions for Success and Failure." *Sex Roles,* 1977, *3,* 301–313.

Bar-Tal, D., and Guttmann, J. "The Effect of Pupil's Sex and Origin on Teachers' Perceptions and Expectations." Unpublished manuscript, Tel-Aviv University, 1977.

Bar-Tal, D., and Guttmann, J. "A Comparison of Pupils', Teachers', and Parents' Attributions Regarding Pupils' Achievement." Unpublished manuscript, Tel-Aviv University, 1978.

Bar-Tal, D., Ravgad, N., and Zilberman, D. "Development of Causal Perception of Success and Failure." Unpublished manuscript, Tel-Aviv University, 1978.

Bar-Tal, D., Raviv, A., Raviv, A., and Bar-Tal, Y. "Consistency of Pupils' Attributions Regarding Success or Failure." Unpublished manuscript, Tel-Aviv University, 1978.

Bar-Tal, D., and Saxe, L. (Eds.) *Social Psychology of Education: Theory and Research.* New York: Halsted Press, 1978.

Bar-Tal D., and Saxe, L. "Teachers' Information Processing: The Effect of Information About Pupils on Teachers' Expectations and Affect." *Psychological Reports,* 1979, *44,* 599–602.

Baumer, T. "Dimensions of Fear: A Preliminary Investigation." Unpublished Report, Center for Urban Affairs, Northwestern University, 1977.

Beck, A. T. *Depression: Causes and Treatment.* Philadelphia: University of Pennsylvania Press, 1967a.

Beck, A. T. *Depression: Clinical, Experimental and Theoretical Aspects.* Philadelphia: University of Pennsylvania Press, 1967b.

Beck, A. T. "The Development of Depression: A Cognitive Model." In R. M. Friedman and M. M. Katz (Eds.), *The Psychology of Depression: Contemporary Theory and Research.* New York: Wiley, 1974.

Beck, A. T. *Cognitive Therapy and the Emotional Disorders.* New York: International Universities Press, 1976.

Beck, L. W. *The Actor and the Spectator.* New Haven, Conn.: Yale University Press, 1975.

Beckman, L. J. "Effects of Students' Performance on Teachers' and Observers' Attribution of Causality." *Journal of Educational Psychology*, 1970, *61*, 76–82.

Beckman, L. J. "Teachers' and Observers' Perceptions of Causality for Child's Performance." *Journal of Educational Psychology*, 1973, *65*, 198–204.

Beckman, L. J. "Self-Esteem of Women Alcoholics." *Journal of Studies on Alcohol*, 1978, *39*, 491–498.

Beckman, L. J. "Beliefs About the Causes of Alcohol-Related Problems Among Alcoholic and Non-Alcoholic Women." *Journal of Clinical Psychology*, in press.

Beckman, L. J., Day, T., Bardsley, P., and Seeman, A. Z. "The Personality Characteristics and Family Backgrounds of Women Alcoholics." *International Journal of the Addictions*, in press.

Beecher, H. K. "Pain, Placebos, and Physicians." *The Practitioner*, 1962, *189*(8), 141–155.

Beez, W. V. "Influence of Biased Psychological Reports on Teacher Behavior and Pupil Performance." Unpublished doctoral dissertation, Department of Educational Psychology; Indiana University, 1968.

Begab, M. J. "The Mentally Retarded and Society: Trends and Issues." In M. J. Begab and S. A. Richardson (Eds.), *The Mentally Retarded and Society: A Social Science Perspective.* Baltimore: University Park Press, 1975.

Bell, R. G. "Alcohol and Loneliness." *Journal of Social Therapy*, 1956, *2*, 171–181.

Bem, D. J. "Self-Perception: An Alternative Interpretation of Cognitive Dissonance Phenomena." *Psychological Review*, 1967, *74*, 183–200.

Bem, D. J. "Self-Perception Theory." In L. Berkowitz (Ed.), *Advances in Experimental Social Psychology*, Vol. 6. New York: Academic Press, 1972.

Benensohn, H. S., and Resnick, H. L. "A Jigger of Alcohol, a Dash of Depression and Bitters: A Suicidal Mix." *Annals of the New York Academy of Science,* 1974, *233,* 40–46.

Berger, P. L., and Luckmann, T. *The Social Construction of Reality: A Treatise in the Sociology of Knowledge.* New York: Doubleday, 1966.

Berke, B., and Peplau, L. A. "Loneliness in the University." Paper presented at the annual meeting of the Western Psychological Association, Los Angeles, April 1976.

Bernstein, I., Kelly, W., and Doyle, P. "Societal Reaction to Deviants: The Case of Criminal Defendants." *American Sociological Review,* 1977, *42,* 743–755.

Berry, R., Boland, J., Laxson, J., Hayler, D., Sillman, M., Fein, R., and Feldstein, P. "The Economic Costs of Alcohol Abuse and Alcoholism—1971." Unpublished report prepared for the National Institute on Alcohol Abuse and Alcoholism Under Contract No. HSM-42-73-114, Washington, D.C., March 1974.

Bettman, J. R. *An Information Processing Theory of Consumer Choice.* Reading, Mass.: Addison-Wesley, 1979.

Bickman, L. "Fulfilling the Promise: A Response to Helmreich." *Personality and Social Psychology Bulletin,* 1976, *2,* 131–133.

Biderman, A. D. *Report on a Pilot Study in the District of Columbia on Victimization Attitudes Toward Law Enforcement.* Washington, D.C.: U.S. Government Printing Office, 1967.

Black's Law Dictionary (3rd ed.). St. Paul, Minn.: West, 1933.

Blackwell, L. R. "Student Choice in Curriculum, Feelings of Control and Causality, and Academic Motivation and Performance." Unpublished doctoral dissertation, Department of Education, Stanford University, 1974.

Blumenfeld, P. C., Hamilton, L., Wessels, K., and Falkner, D. " 'You Can', 'You Should', and 'You'd Better': Teachers' Attributions Regarding Achievement and Social Behaviors." Paper presented at the 85th annual meeting of the American Psychological Association, San Francisco, 1977.

Boggiano, A. K., and Ruble, D. N. "Perception of Competence and the Over-Justification Effect: A Developmental Study." Unpublished manuscript, Princeton University, 1978.

Bootzin, R. R., Herman, C. P., and Nicassio, P. "The Power of Suggestion: Another Examination of Misattribution and Insomnia." *Journal of Personality and Social Psychology*, 1976, *34*, 673–679.

Bornstein, P. E., Clayton, P. J., Halikas, J. A., Maurice, W. L., and Robins, E. "The Depression of Widowhood After Thirteen Months." *British Journal of Psychiatry*, 1973, *122*, 561–566.

Boudouris, J. "Homicide and the Family." *Journal of Marriage and the Family*, 1971, *33*, 667–676.

Bovard, E. W. "The Effects of Social Stimuli on the Response to Stress." *Psychological Review*, 1959, *66*, 267–277.

Boyd, V. "Domestic Violence: Treatment Alternatives for the Male Batterer." Paper presented at the 86th annual meeting of the American Psychological Association, Toronto, 1978.

Bradburn, N. *The Structure of Psychological Well-Being.* Chicago: Aldine, 1969.

Bradley, G. W. "Self-Serving Biases in the Attribution Process: A Reexamination of the Fact or Fiction Question." *Journal of Personality and Social Psychology*, 1978, *36*, 56–71.

Bragg, M. "A Comparative Study of Loneliness and Depression." Unpublished doctoral dissertation, Department of Psychology, University of California, Los Angeles, 1978.

Braginsky, D. D., and Braginsky, B. M. *Hansels and Gretels: Studies of Children in Institutions.* New York: Holt, Rinehart and Winston, 1971.

Braun, C. "Teachers Expectation: Sociopsychological Dynamics." *Review of Educational Research*, 1976, *46*, 185–214.

Brickman, P., Ryan, K., and Wortman, C. B. "Causal Chains: Attribution of Responsibility as a Function of Immediate and Prior Causes." *Journal of Personality and Social Psychology*, 1975, *32*(6), 1060–1067.

Brigham, J. "Ethnic Stereotypes." *Psychological Bulletin*, 1971, *76*, 15–38.

Brophy, J. E. "The Role of Rewards and Reinforcements in Early Education Programs: II. Fostering Intrinsic Motivation to Learn." *Journal of School Psychology*, 1972, *10*, 242–251.

Broverman, I. K., Vogel, S. R., Broverman, D. M., Clarkson, F. E., and Rosenbrantz, P. "Sex-Role Stereotypes: A Current Appraisal." *Journal of Social Issues*, 1972, *28*(2), 59–78.

Brown, G., Bhrolchain, M., and Harris, T. "Social Class and

Psychiatric Disturbance Among Women in an Urban Population." *Sociology,* 1975, *9,* 225–254.

Brownell, K., Colletti, G., Ersner-Hershfield, R., Hershfield, S. M., and Awilson, G. T. "Self-Control in School Children: Stringency and Leniency in Self-Determined and Externally-Imposed Performance Standards." *Behavior Therapy,* 1977, *8,* 442–455.

Bruner, J. S. *Toward a Theory of Instruction.* Cambridge, Mass.: Harvard University Press, 1966.

Budoff, M., and Gottlieb, J. "Special Class EMR Children Mainstreamed: A Study of Aptitude (Learning Potential) X Treatment Interaction." *American Journal of Mental Deficiency,* 1976, *81,* 1–11.

Bulman, R. J. "Self-Blame in Rape Victims: A Control-Maintenance Strategy." Paper presented at the 86th annual meeting of the American Psychological Association, Toronto, 1978.

Bulman, R. J., and Wortman, C. B. "Attributions of Blame and Coping in the 'Real World': Severe Accident Victims React to Their Lot." *Journal of Personality and Social Psychology,* 1977, *35,* 351–363.

Burgess, A. W., and Holmstrom, L. *Rape: Victims of Crisis.* Bowie, Md: Brady, 1974.

Burgess, A. W., and Holmstrom, L. "Four- to Six-Year Follow-Up of Rape Victims." Address by Ann Wolbert Burgess, University of Illinois at Chicago Circle, May 15, 1978.

Burnkrant, R. E. "Attribution Theory in Marketing Research: Problems and Prospects." In M. J. Schinger (Ed.), *Advances in Consumer Research,* Vol. 2. Chicago: Association for Consumer Research, 1974.

Burnside, I. M. "Loneliness in Old Age." *Mental Hygiene,* 1971, *55,* 391–397.

Bursten, B., and D'Esopo, R. "The Obligation to Remain Sick." *Archives of General Psychiatry,* 1965, *12,* 402–407.

Busfield, B., Schneller, P., and Capra, D. "Depressive Symptom or Side Effect? A Comparative Study of Symptoms During Pre-Treatment and Treatment of Patients on Three Antidepressant Medications." *Journal of Nervous and Mental Disease,* 1962, *134,* 339–345.

Caddy, G. R., Goldman, R. D., and Huebner, R. "Relationships Among Different Domains of Attitudes Towards Alcoholism: Model Cost and Treatment." *Addictive Behavior,* 1976, *1*(2), 159–167.

Cahalan, D., Cisin, I. H., and Crossley, H. M. *American Drinking Practices: A National Survey of Behaviors and Attitudes.* Monograph 6. New Brunswick, N.J.: Rutgers Center of Alcohol Studies, 1969.

Cahalan, D., and Room, R. *Problem Drinking Among American Men.* New Brunswick, N.J.: Rutgers Center of Alcohol Studies, 1974.

Calhoun, L. G., Cheney, T., and Dawes, A. S. "Locus of Control, Self-Reported Depression and Perceived Causes of Depression." *Journal of Consulting and Clinical Psychology,* 1974, *42,* 736.

Calhoun, L. G., Johnson, R. E., and Boardman, W. K. "Attribution of Depression to Internal-External and Stable-Unstable Causes: Preliminary Investigation." *Psychological Reports,* 1975, *36,* 463–466.

Calhoun, L. G., Selby, J. W., Cann, A., and Kelly, G. T. "The Effects of Victim Physical Attractiveness and Sex of Respondent on Social Reactions to Victims of Rape." *The British Journal of Social and Clinical Psychology,* in press.

Calhoun, L. G., Selby, J. W., and Warring, L. J. "Social Perception of the Victim's Causal Role in Rape: An Exploratory Examination of Four Factors." *Human Relations,* 1976, *29,* 517–526.

Calvert, R. "Criminal and Civil Liability in Husband-Wife Assaults." In S. Steinmetz and M. Straus (Eds.), *Violence in the Family.* New York: Dodd, Mead, 1974.

Campbell, D. T. "Social Attitudes and Other Acquired Behavioral Dispositions." In S. Koch (Ed.), *Psychology: A Study of a Science,* Vol. 6. New York: Holt, Rinehart and Winston, 1966.

Campbell, D. T. "Stereotypes and the Perception of Group Differences." *American Psychologist,* 1967, *31,* 817–829.

Cann, A., Calhoun, L. G., and Selby, J. W. "Sexual Experience as a Factor in Reactions to Rape Victims." Paper presented at the 85th annual meeting of the American Psychological Association, San Francisco, 1977.

Caplan, N., and Nelson, S. D. "Who's to Blame?" *Psychology Today,* 1974, 99–102.

Cardozo, R. N. "An Experimental Study of Consumer Effort, Expectation, and Satisfaction." *Journal of Marketing Research*, 1965, *2*, 244–249.

Carey, R. C. "Emotional Adjustment in Terminal Patients: A Quantitative Approach." *Journal of Counseling Psychology*, 1974, *21*, 433–439.

Carling, F. *And Yet We Are Human.* London: Chatto and Windus, 1962.

Carroll, J. S. "Causal Attributions in Expert Parole Decisions." *Journal of Personality and Social Psychology*, 1978, *12*, 1501–1511.

Carroll, J. S., and Payne, J. W. "The Psychology of the Parole Decision Process: A Joint Application of Attribution Theory and Information Processing Psychology." In J. S. Carroll and J. W., Payne (Eds.), *Cognition and Social Behavior.* Hillsdale, N.J.: Erlbaum, 1976.

Carroll, J. S., and Payne, J. W. "Crime Seriousness, Recidivism Risk, and Causal Attributions in Judgments of Prison Term by Students and Experts." *Journal of Applied Psychology*, 1977a, *62*, 595–602.

Carroll, J. S., and Payne, J. W. "Judgments About Crime and the Criminal: A Model and a Method for Investigating Parole Decisions." In B. Sales (Ed.), *Perspectives in Law and Psychology*, Vol. 1, *Criminal Justice System.* New York: Plenum, 1977b.

Carroll, J. S., Payne, J. W., Frieze, I. H., and Girard, D. L. "Attribution Theory: An Information Processing Approach." Unpublished manuscript, Carnegie-Mellon University, 1976.

Carroll, J. S., and Ruback, R. B. "Sentencing by Parole Board: The Parole Revocation Decision." In B. D. Sales (Ed.), *Perspectives in Law and Psychology.* Vol. 2: *The Jury, Trial, and Judicial Processes.* New York: Plenum, in press.

Chaikin, A. L., and Darley, J. M. "Victim or Perpetrator? Defensive Attribution of Responsibility and the Need for Order and Justice." *Journal of Personality and Social Psychology*, 1973, *25*, 268–275.

Chapin, M., and Dyck, D. G. "Persistence of Children's Reading Behavior as a Function of N Length and Attribution Retraining." *Journal of Abnormal Psychology*, 1976, *85*, 511–515.

Chodoff, P., Friedman, S. B., and Hamburg, D. A. "Stress Defenses and Coping Behavior: Observations in Parents of Children with Malignant Disease." *American Journal of Psychiatry,* 1964, *120,* 743–749.

Chodorkoff, B. "Alcoholism Education in a Psychiatric Institute, I. Medical Students: Relationship of Personal Characteristics, Attitudes Toward Alcoholism, and Achievement." *Quarterly Journal of Studies on Alcohol,* 1967, *28,* 723–730.

Choi, J. W. *Out-Of-Pocket Cost and Acquisition of Prescribed Medicines.* HRA 77–1542. Washington, D.C.: U.S. Department of Health, Education, and Welfare, 1977.

Christie, R. "Some Reflections on Social Science and the Law: The Harrisburg Conspiracy Trial as an Example." *Division Eight Newsletter, American Psychological Association,* 1972, *12,* 1–3.

Clayton, P. J., Halikas, J. A., and Maurice, W. L. "The Depression of Widowhood." *British Journal of Psychiatry,* 1972, *120,* 71–77.

Clore, G. L., and Jeffrey, J. M. "Emotional Role Playing, Attitude Change, and Attraction Toward a Disabled Person." *Journal of Personality and Social Psychology,* 1972, *23,* 105–111.

Coates, D., and Wortman, C. B. "Depression Maintenance and Interpersonal Control." In A. Baum, J. Singer, and Y. Epstein (Eds.), *Advances in Environmental Psychology.* Vol. 2. Hillsdale, N.J.: Erlbaum, in press.

Cobb, S. "Social Support as a Moderator of Life Stress." *Psychosomatic Medicine,* 1976, *38,* 300–314.

Cochran, N., Gordon, A., and Campbell, D. T. "Numbers in Bureaucracies: Reflections on the Positivist Stampede." Unpublished manuscript, Northwestern University, 1977.

Cohen, S., Rothbart, M., and Phillips, S. "Locus of Control and the Generality of Learned Helplessness in Humans." *Journal of Personality and Social Psychology,* 1976, *34,* 1049–1056.

Cohn, E. S. "Fear of Crime and Control: The Effect of Age and Family Composition." Unpublished doctoral dissertation, Department of Psychology, Temple University, 1978.

Cohn, E. S., Kidder, L. H., and Brickman, P. "The Relative Virtues of Restitution, Rehabilitation, and Retribution." Paper presented at the annual meeting of the Eastern Psychological Association, Washington, D.C., 1978.

Cohn, E. S., Kidder, L. H., and Harvey, J. "Crime Prevention Versus Victimization Prevention: The Psychology of Two Different Reactions." *Victimology,* Winter 1979, in press.

Coleman, J. *Abnormal Psychology and Modern Life.* (4th ed.) Glenview, Ill.: Scott, Foresman, 1972.

Coleman, J. S., Campbell, E. O., Hobson, C. J., McPartland, J., Mood, A. M., Weinfeld, F. D., and York, R. L. *Equality of Educational Opportunity.* Washington, D.C.: U.S. Department of Health, Education, and Welfare, 1966.

Colvin, R. H. "Imposed Extrinsic Reward in an Elementary School Setting: Effects on Free-Operant Rates and Choices." *Dissertation Abstracts International,* 1972, *32,* 5034-A.

Condry, J. "The Enemies of Exploration." *Journal of Personality and Social Psychology,* 1977, *35,* 459–477.

Condry, J., and Chambers, J. C. "How Rewards Change the Problem Solving Process." Unpublished manuscript, Cornell University, 1977.

Condry, J., and Chambers, J. C. "Intrinsic Motivation and the Process of Learning." In M. R. Lepper and D. Greene (Eds.), *The Hidden Costs of Reward.* Hillsdale, N.J.: Erlbaum, 1978.

Conklin, J. E. *The Impact of Crime.* New York: Macmillan, 1975.

Cooper, H. M. "Controlling Personal Rewards: Professional Teachers' Differential Use of Feedback and the Effects of Feedback on the Student's Motivation to Perform." *Journal of Educational Psychology,* 1977, *69,* 419–427.

Costello, R., and Mandus, K. "Locus of Control and Alcoholism." *British Journal of the Addictions,* 1974, *69,* 11–17.

Cotton, J. L., Baron, R. S., and Borkovec, T. D. "Caffeine Ingestion, Misattribution Therapy, and Speech Anxiety." Paper presented at the annual meeting of the Midwestern Psychological Association, Chicago, May 1977.

Cottrell, N. B., and Epley, S. W. "Affiliation, Social Comparison, and Stress Reduction." In J. M. Suls and R. L. Miller (Eds.), *Social Comparison Processes.* New York: Wiley, 1977.

Coyne, J. C. "Toward an Interactional Description of Depression." *Psychiatry,* 1976, *39,* 28–40.

Crandall, V. D., Katkovsky, W., and Crandall, V. J. "Children's Belief in Their Own Control of Reinforcement in Intellectual-

Academic Achievement Situations." *Child Development,* 1965, *36,* 91–109.

Creative Sociomedics Corporation. *Develop Improved Estimates of the Current Incidence and Prevalence of Alcohol Abuse.* Final report prepared for the National Institute on Alcohol Abuse and Alcoholism. New York: Creative Sociomedics Corporation, 1977.

Cremin, L. A. *The Transformation of the school.* New York: Vintage Books, 1961.

Cromwell, R. L. "A Social Learning Approach to Mental Retardation." In N. R. Ellis (Ed.), *Handbook of Mental Deficiency.* New York: McGraw-Hill, 1963.

Csikszentmihalyi, M. *Beyond Boredom and Anxiety: The Experience of Play in Work and Games.* San Francisco: Jossey-Bass, 1975.

Curlee, J. "Alcoholism and the Empty Nest." *Bulletin of the Menninger Clinic,* 1969, *33*(3), 165–171.

Darom, E., and Bar-Tal, D. "Causal Perceptions of Pupils' Success or Failure by Teachers and Pupils: A Comparison." Unpublished manuscript, Tel-Aviv University, 1977.

Davidson, T. "Wifebeating: A Recurring Phenomenon Throughout History." In M. Roy (Ed.), *Battered Women: A Psychosociological Study of Domestic Violence.* New York: Van Nostrand Reinhold, 1977.

Davidson, T. *Conjugal Crime: Understanding and Changing the Wifebeating Pattern.* New York: Hawthorn Books, 1978.

Davis, F. "Deviance Disavowal: The Management of Strained Interaction by the Visibly Handicapped." *Social Problems,* 1961, *9,* 120–132.

Davis, J. M. "Central Biogenic Amines and Theories of Depression and Mania." In W. E. Frann and others (Eds.), *Phenomonology and Treatment of Depression.* New York: Spectrum, 1977.

Davis, J., Bray, R., and Holt, R. "The Empirical Study of Social Decision Processes in Justice." In J. L. Tapp and F. Levine (Eds.), *Law, Justice, and the Individual in Society.* New York: Holt, Rinehart and Winston, 1977.

Davis, K. C. *Discretionary Justice: A Preliminary Inquiry.* Urbana: University of Illinois Press, 1971.

Davison, G. C., Tsujimoto, R. M., and Glaros, A. G. "Attribution and the Maintenance of Behavior Change in Falling Asleep." *Journal of Abnormal Psychology,* 1973, *82,* 124–133.

Davison, G. C., and Valins, S. "Maintenance of Self-Attributed and Drug Attributed Behavior Change." *Journal of Personality and Social Psychology,* 1969, *11,* 25–33.

Day, R. L., and Bodur, M. "A Comprehensive Study of Satisfaction with Consumer Services." In R. L. Day (Ed.), *Consumer Satisfaction, Dissatisfaction and Complaining Behavior.* Bloomington: Division of Business Research, Indiana University, 1977.

Day, R. L., and Landon, L. "Collecting Comprehensive Consumer Complaint Data by Survey Research." In B. B. Anderson (Ed.), *Advances in Consumer Research,* Vol. 3. Cincinnati: Association for Consumer Research, 1976.

Dean, J. P., Eichorn, R. L., and Dean, L. R. "Limitations and Advantages of Unstructured Methods." In J. T. Doby (Ed.), *An Introduction to Social Research.* (2nd ed.) New York: Irvington, 1967.

Dearaujo, G., Van Arsdel, P. P., Holmes, T. H., and Dudley, D. L. "Life Change, Coping Ability and Chronic Intrinsic Asthma." *Journal of Psychosomatic Research,* 1973, *17,* 359–363.

deCharms, R. *Personal Causation.* New York: Academic Press, 1968.

deCharms, R. "Personal Causation Training in the Schools." *Journal of Applied Social Psychology,* 1972, *2,* 95–113.

deCharms, R. *Enhancing Motivation in the Classroom.* New York: Irvington, 1976.

Deci, E. L. "Effects of Externally Mediated Rewards on Intrinsic Motivation." *Journal of Personality and Social Psychology,* 1971, *18,* 105–115.

Deci, E. L. "The Effects of Contingent and Non-Contingent Rewards and Controls on Intrinsic Motivation." *Organizational Behavior and Human Performance,* 1972a, *8,* 217–229.

Deci, E. L. "Intrinsic Motivation, Extrinsic Reinforcement, and Inequity." *Journal of Personality and Social Psychology,* 1972b, *22,* 113–120.

Deci, E. L. *Intrinsic Motivation.* New York: Plenum, 1975.

Deci, E. L., and Porac, J. "Cognitive Evaluation Theory and the Study of Human Motivation." In M. R. Lepper and D. Greene (Eds.), *The Hidden Costs of Reward.* Hillsdale, N.J.: Erlbaum, 1978.

Dentler, R. A., and Mackler, B. "Ability and Sociometric Status Among Normal and Retarded Children: A Review of the Literature." *Psychological Bulletin,* 1962, *59,* 273–283.

DeSimone, E., Peterson, C. F., and Carlstedt, B. C. "Pharmacist-Patient Interaction and Patient Expectations." *Journal of Pharmacy Education,* 1977, *41,* 167–171.

Deutsch, H. "The Significance of Masochism in the Mental Life of Women." *International Journal of Psychoanalysis,* 1939, *1,* 220.

Diener, C. I., and Dweck, C. S. "An Analysis of Learned Helplessness: Continuous Changes in Performance, Strategy, and Achievement Cognitions Following Failure." *Journal of Personality and Social Psychology,* 1978, *36,* 451–462.

Distefano, M. K., Jr., Pryer, M. W., and Garrison, J. L. "Internal-External Control Among Alcoholics." *Journal of Clinical Psychology,* 1972, *28,* 36–37.

Dobash, R. E., and Dobash, R. P. "Wives: The 'Appropriate' Victims of Marital Violence." *Victimology,* 1978, 426–442.

Dollard, J., and Miller, N. E. *Personality and Psychotherapy.* New York: McGraw-Hill, 1950.

Douglas, D., and Anisman, H., "Helplessness or Expectation Incongruity: Effects of Aversive Stimulation on Subsequent Performance." *Journal of Experimental Psychology: Human Perception and Performance,* 1975, *1,* 411–417.

Drabeck, T., and Quarantelli, E. L. "Scapegoats, Villains, and Disasters." *Trans-Action,* 1967, *4,* 12–17.

Dreeben, R. *On What Is Learned in School.* Reading, Mass.: Addison-Wesley, 1968.

DuBow, F. "Reactions to Crime: A Critical Review of the Literature." Pts. 2 and 3. Unpublished paper, Center for Urban Affairs, Northwestern University, 1978.

DuBow, F., McCabe, E., and Kaplan, G. "Reactions to Crime: A Critical Review of the Literature." Chicago: Center for Urban Affairs, Northwestern University, 1977.

Dunnell, K., and Cartwright, A. *Medicine Takers, Prescribers and Hoarders.* Boston: Routledge & Kegan Paul, 1972.

Dusek, J. B. "Do Teachers Bias Children's Learning?" *Review of Educational Research,* 1975, *45,* 661–684.

Dweck, C. S. "The Role of Expectations and Attributions in the Alleviation of Learned Helplessness." *Journal of Personality and Social Psychology,* 1975, *31,* 674–685.

Dweck, C. S., and Bush, E. S. "Sex Differences in Learned Helplessness: (I) Differential Debilitation with Peer and Adult Evaluators." *Developmental Psychology,* 1976, *12,* 147–156.

Dweck, C. S., Davidson, W., Nelson, S., and Enna, B. "Sex Differences in Learned Helplessness: (II) The Contingencies of Evaluative Feedback in the Classroom; (III) An Experimental Analysis." *Developmental Psychology,* 1978, *14,* 268–276.

Dweck, C. S., and Goetz, T. E. "Attributions and Learned Helplessness." In J. H. Harvey, W. J. Ickes, and R. F. Kidd (Eds.), *New Directions in Attribution Research.* Vol. 2. Hillsdale, N.J.: Erlbaum, 1978.

Dweck, C. S., and Repucci, N. D. "Learned Helplessness and Reinforcement Responsibility in Children." *Journal of Personality and Social Psychology,* 1973, *25,* 109–116.

Dyer, B. M. "Loneliness—There's No Way To Escape It." *Alpha Gamma Delta Quarterly,* Spring 1974, pp. 2–5.

Eastman, C. "Behavioral Formulations of Depression." *Psychological Review,* 1976, *83,* 277–291.

Eddy, P. D. "Loneliness: A Discrepancy with the Phenomenological Self." Unpublished doctoral dissertation, Adelphi College, 1961.

Edgerton, R. B. *The Cloak of Competence: Stigma in the Lives of the Mentally Retarded.* Berkeley: University of California Press, 1967.

Elig, T., and Frieze, I. H. "A Multi-Dimensional Scheme for Coding and Interpreting Perceived Causality for Success and Failure Events: The Coding Scheme of Perceived Causality (CSPC)." *JSAS: Catalog of Selected Documents in Psychology,* 1975, *5,* 313.

Elig, T., and Frieze, I. H. "Measuring Causal Attributions for Success and Failure." *Journal of Personality and Social Psychology,* 1979, *37,* 621–634.

Ellison, G. D. "Animal Models of Psychopathology: The Low-Norepinephrine and Low Scrotonin Rat." *American Psychologist,* 1977, *32,* 1036–1045.

Emmelkamp, P. M. G., and Cohen-Kettenis, P. T. "Relationship of Locus of Control to Phobic Anxiety and Depression." *Psychological Reports,* 1975, *36,* 390.

Engel, J., Kollat, D. T., and Blackwell, R. D. *Consumer Behavior.* (2nd ed.) New York: Holt, Rinehart and Winston, 1973.

Ennis, P. H. *Criminal Victimization in the United States: A Report of a National Survey.* Washington, D.C.: U.S. Government Printing Office, 1967.

Epley, S. W. "Reducation of the Behavioral Effects of Aversive Stimulation by the Presense of Companions." *Psychological Bulletin,* 1974, *81,* 271–283.

Erskine, H. "The Polls: Fear of Violence and Crime." *Public Opinion Quarterly,* 1974, *38,* (1), 131–145.

Estes, W. K. "Reinforcement in Human Behavior." *American Scientist,* 1972, *60,* 723–729.

Farber, B. *Mental Retardation: Its Social Context and Social Consequences.* Boston: Houghton Mifflin, 1968.

Farina, A., Allen, J., and Saul, B. "The Role of the Stigmatized Person in Affecting Social Relationships." *Journal of Personality,* 1968, *36,* 169–182.

Farina, A., Gliha, D., Boudreau, L. A., Allen, J. G., and Sherman, M. "Mental Illness and the Impact of Believing Others Know About It." *Journal of Abnormal Psychology,* 1971, *77,* 1–5.

Farina, A., Thaw, J., Felner, R. D., and Hust, B. E. "Some Interpersonal Consequences of Being Mentally Ill or Mentally Retarded." *American Journal of Mental Deficiency,* 1976, *80,* 414–422.

Feather, N. T. "Valence of Outcome and Expectation of Success in Relation to Task Difficulty and Perceived Locus of Control." *Journal of Personality and Social Psychology,* 1967, *7,* 372–386.

Feather, N. T. "Attribution of Responsibility and Valence of Success and Failure in Relation to Initial Confidence and Task Performance." *Journal of Personality and Social Psychology,* 1969, *13,* 120–144.

Feather, N. T., and Simon, J. G. "Attribution of Responsibility and Valence of Outcome in Relation to Initial Confidence and Success and Failure of Self and Other." *Journal of Personality and Social Psychology,* 1971a, *18,* 173–188.

Feather, N. T., and Simon J. G. "Causal Attribution for Success and Failure in Relation to Expectations of Success." *Journal of Personality,* 1971b, *39,* 527–541.

Feldman, J. "Stimulus Characteristics and Subject Prejudice as Determinants of Stereotype Attribution." *Journal of Personality and Social Psychology,* 1972, *21,* 333–340.

Feldman-Summers, S., and Lindner, K. "Perceptions of Victims and Defendents in Criminal Assault Cases." *Criminal Justice and Behavior,* 1976, *3,* 135–150.

Ferneau, E. "What Student Nurses Think About Alcoholic Patients and Alcoholism." *Nursing Outlook,* 1967, *15,* 40–41.

Ferneau, E. and Gertler, R. "Attitudes Regarding Alcoholism: Effect of the First Year of the Psychiatry Residency." *British Journal of Addiction,* 1971, *66,* 257–260.

Ferneau, E., and Mueller, S. "Attitudes Among a Group of College Students Toward Drug Abuse and the Drug Abuser." *Journal of Drug Education,* 1973, *3,* 175–182.

Ferneau, E., and Paine, H. J. "Attitudes Regarding Alcoholism: The Volunteer Alcoholism Clinic Counsellor." *British Journal of Addictions,* 1972, *67,* 235–238.

Festinger, L. "A Theory of Social Comparison Processes." *Human Relations,* 1954, *7,* 117–140.

Figlio, R. M. "The Seriousness of Offenses: An Evaluation by Offenders and Nonoffenders." *Journal of Criminal Law and Criminology,* 1975, *66,* 189–200.

Fischhoff, B. "Attribution Theory and Judgment Under Uncertainty." In J. Harvey, W. Ickes, and R. Kidd (Eds.), *New Directions in Attribution Research.* Vol. 1. Hillsdale, H.J.: Erlbaum, 1976.

Fishbein, N. "An Investigation of the Relationship Between the Beliefs About an Object and the Attitude Toward that Object." *Human Relations,* 1963, *16,* 233–240.

Fishbein, N. "Extending the Extended Model: Some Comments." In B. B. Andersen (Ed.), *Advances in Consumer Research.* Vol. 3. Cincinnati: Association for Consumer Research, 1976.

Fitch, G. "Effects of Self-Esteem, Perceived Performance and Choice on Causal Attributions." *Journal of Personality and Social Psychology,* 1970, *16,* 311–315.

Forrest, M. S., and Hokanson, J. E. "Depression and Autonomic Arousal Reduction Accompanying Self-Punitive Behavior." *Journal of Abnormal Psychology,* 1975, *84,* 346–357.

Foster, G., and Ysseldyke, J. "Expectancy and Halo Effects as a

Result of Artificially Induced Teacher Bias." *Contemporary Educational Psychology,* 1976, *1,* 37–45.

Fowler, F. J., and Mangione, T. W. *The Nature of Fear.* Unpublished paper; Survey Research Program, University of Massachusetts and the Joint Center for Urban Studies of M.I.T. and Harvard University, 1974.

Fox, S. S., and Scherl, D. T. "Crisis Intervention with Rape Victims." *Social Work,* 1972, *17* (1), 232–241.

Frankl, V. E. *The Will To Meaning: Foundations and Applications of Logotherapy.* Cleveland: World, 1969.

Freed, E. "Opinions of Psychiatric Hospital Personnel and College Students Towards Alcoholism, Mental Illness, and Physical Disability: An Exploratory Study." *Psychological Reports,* 1964, *15,* 615–618.

Freeman, H. E., and Simmons, O. G. "Mental Patients in the Community: Family Settings and Performance Levels." *American Sociological Review,* 1958, *23,* 147–154.

Freud, S. *The Standard Edition of the Complete Psychological Works of Sigmund Freud.* (I. Strachey, Ed.) London: Hogarth Press, 1955.

Fried, M., Kaplan, K., and Klein, K. "Juror Selection: An Analysis of Voir Dire." In S. Simon and R. J. Simon (Eds.), *The Jury System in America: A Critical Overview.* Vol. 4. Beverly Hills, Calif.: Sage, 1975.

Friedman, R., and Katz, M. (Eds.). *The Psychology of Depression: Contemporary Theory and Research.* New York: Wiley, 1974.

Friedson, E. "Disability as Social Deviance." In M. B. Sussman (Ed.), *Sociology and Rehabilitation.* Washington, D.C.: American Sociological Association, 1966.

Friend, R. M., and Neale, J. M. "Children's Perceptions of Success and Failure: An Attributional Analysis of the Effects of Race and Social Class." *Developmental Psychology,* 1972, *7,* 124–128.

Frieze, I. H. "Causal Attributions and Information Seeking to Explain Success and Failure." *Journal of Research in Personality,* 1976a, *10,* 293–305.

Frieze, I. H. "The Role of Information Processing in Making Causal Attributions for Success and Failure." In J. S. Carroll and J. W. Payne (Eds.), *Cognition and Social Behavior.* Hillsdale, N.J.: Erlbaum, 1976b.

Frieze, I. H. "Self Perceptions of Battered Women." Paper presented at the annual meeting of the Association for Women in Psychology, Pittsburgh, March 1978.

Frieze, I. H. "Women's Beliefs About the Causes of Alcoholism in Other Women." Unpublished paper, University of Pittsburgh, 1979.

Frieze, I. H., and Bar-Tal, D. "Developmental Trends on Cue Utilization for Attributional Judgments." Unpublished paper, University of Pittsburgh, 1977.

Frieze, I. H., Fisher, J., Hanusa, B., McHugh, M. C., and Valle, V. A. "Attributions of the Causes of Success and Failure as Internal and External Barriers to Achievement in Women." In J. Sherman and F. Denmark (Eds.), *Psychology of Women: Future Directions of Research*. New York: Psychological Dimensions, in press.

Frieze, I. H., and McHugh, M. C. "Debilitating Attributions of the Woman Alcoholic Undergoing Treatment." Paper presented at the 85th annual meeting of the American Psychological Association, San Francisco, 1977.

Frieze, I. H., and Snyder, H. N."Children's Beliefs about the Causes of Success and Failure in School Settings." Unpublished paper, Learning Research and Development Center, University of Pittsburgh, 1978.

Frieze, I. H., Snyder, H. N., and Fontaine, C. M. "Student Attributions and the Attribution Model During an Actual Examination." Paper presented at the 85th annual meeting of the American Psychological Association, San Francisco, 1977.

Frieze, I. H., and Washburn, C. "Battered Woman's Responses to Battering." Paper presented at the annual research conference of the Assocation for Women in Psychology, Dallas, 1979.

Frieze, I. H., and Weiner, B. "Cue Utilization and Attributional Judgments for Success and Failure." *Journal of Personality*, 1971, *39*, 591–606.

Fromm-Reichman, F. "Loneliness." *Psychiatry*, 1959, *22*, 1–15.

Fuchs, C. Z., and Rehm, L. P. "A Self-Control Behavior Therapy Program for Depression." *Journal of Consulting and Clinical Psychology*, 1977, *45*, 206–215.

Fulda, T. R. *Prescription Drug Data Summary, 1974*. SSA 76–11928.

Washington, D.C.: Department of Health, Education, and Welfare, 1976.

Furstenberg, F. F., Jr. "Public Reaction to Crime in the Streets." *The American Scholar,* 1971, *40,* 601–610.

Furstenberg, F. F., Jr. "Fear of Crime and Its Effect on Citizen Behavior." Paper presented at symposium on Studies of Public Experience, Knowledge, and Opinion of Crime and Justice, Washington, D.C., March 1972.

Gager, N., and Schurr, C. *Sexual Assault: Confronting Rape in America.* New York: Grosset & Dunlap, 1976.

Garbarino, J. "The Impact of Anticipated Rewards on Cross-Age Tutoring." *Journal of Personality and Social Psychology,* 1975, *32,* 421–428.

Garfinkel, H. *Studies in Ethnomethodology.* Englewood Cliffs, N.J.: Prentice-Hall, 1967.

Garland, H., Hardy, A., and Stephanson, L. "Information Search as Affected by Attribution Type and Response Category." *Personality and Social Psychology Bulletin,* 1976, *1,* 612–615.

Gatchel, R. J., McKinney, M. E., and Koebernick, L. F. "Learned Helplessness, Depression, and Physiological Responding." *Psychophysiology,* 1977, *14,* 25–31.

Gatchel, R. J., Paulus, P. R., and Maples, C. W. "Learned Helplessness and Self-Reported Helplessness." *Journal of Abnormal Psychology,* 1975, *84,* 732–734.

Gatchel, R. J., and Proctor, J. D. "Physiological Correlates of Learned Helplessness in Man." *Journal of Abnormal Psychology,* 1976, *85,* 27–34.

Geller, J. A., and Walsh, J. C. "A Treatment Model for the Abused Spouse." *Victimology,* 1978, 627–631.

Gelles, R. J. *The Violent Home: A Study of Physical Aggression Between Husbands and Wives.* Beverly Hills, Calif.: Sage, 1972.

Gelles, R., and Straus, M. "Determinants of Violence in the Family: Toward a Theoretical Integration." In W. Burr and others, (Eds.), *Contemporary Theories About the Family.* New York: Free Press, 1979.

Genego, W. J., Goldberger, P. D., and Jackson, V. C. "Parole Release Decision-Making and the Sentencing Process." *Yale Law Journal,* 1975, *84*(4), 810–902.

Gergen, K., and Wishnov, B. "Others' Self-Evaluations and Interaction Anticipations as Determinants of Self-Presentation." *Journal of Personality and Social Psychology,* 1965, *2,* 348–358.

Glaser, B. G., and Strauss, A. L. *The Discovery of Grounded Theory: Strategies for Qualitative Research.* Chicago: Aldine, 1967.

Glaser, D. *The Effectiveness of a Prison and Parole System.* New York: Bobbs-Merrill, 1964.

Glaser, E., and Whittow, G. "Experimental Errors in Clinical Trials." *Clinical Science,* 1954, *13,* 199–210.

Glick, I. O., Weiss, R. S., and Parkes, C. M. *The First Years of Bereavement.* New York: Wiley, 1974.

Glock, C. Y. "Images of Man and Public Opinion." *Public Opinion Quarterly,* 1964, *28,* 539–546.

Godfrey, B. W., and Lowe, C. A. "Devaluation of Innocent Victims: An Attribution Analysis Within the Just World Paradigm." *Journal of Personality and Social Psychology,* 1975, *31,* 944–951.

Goffman, E. *Stigma: Notes on the Management of Spoiled Identity.* Englewood Cliffs, N.J.: Prentice-Hall, 1963.

Gold, M. W. "Stimulus Factors in Skill Training of the Retarded on a Complex Assembly Task: Acquisition, Transfer, and Retention." *American Journal of Mental Deficiency,* 1972, *76,* 517–526.

Gold, M. W. "Vocational Skill Functioning of the Severely Retarded." Presented at the 83rd annual meeting of the American Psychological Association, Chicago, 1975a.

Gold, M. W. "Vocational Training." In J. Wortis (Ed.), *Mental Retardation and Developmental Disabilities; An Annual Review.* Vol. 7. New York: Bruner/Mazel, 1975b.

Gold, M. W., and Close, D. W. "Five Year Retention of an Assembly Task By the Severely Retarded." Unpublished paper, University of Illinois at Urbana-Champaign, 1975.

Gold, M. W., and Pomerantz, D. J. "Issues in Prevocational Training." In M. Snell (Ed.), Teaching the Moderately, Severely, and Profoundly Retarded. Columbus, Ohio: Merrill, 1978.

Goldstein, C. S. "The Dilemma of the Rape Victim: A Descriptive Analysis." *Criminal Justice Monograph,* 1976, *7* (2).

Gomberg, E. S. "Women and Alcoholism." In V. Franks and V. Burtle (Eds.), *Women in Therapy: New Psychotherapies for a Changing Society.* New York: Brunner/Mazel, 1974.

Good, T. L. "The Role of Rewards and Reinforcements in Early Education Programs: (III). The Use of Concrete Rewards." *Journal of School Psychology*, 1972, *10*, 252–261.

Goodwin, D. W., and Guze, S. B. "Heredity and Alcoholism." In B. Kissin and H. Begleiter (Eds.), *The Biology of Alcoholism*. Vol. 3: *Clinical Pathology*. New York: Plenum, 1974.

Gordon, A., Bush, M., Gordon, M. T., and Lebailly, R. "Beyond Need: Examples in Dependency and Neglect." Paper presented to the Sociology and Social Welfare Division, American Sociological Association, New York, August, 1976.

Gordon, A., Bush, M., McKnight, J., and others. *Beyond Need: Toward a Serviced Society*. Cuernevaca, Mexico: Centro Intercultural de Documentacion, 1974.

Gordon, M. T., and Riger, S. "Opinions of Women and Men in Three Cities About Rape Prevention Strategies." Paper presented at the 73rd annual meeting of the American Sociological Association, San Francisco, September, 1978.

Gordon, S. *Lonely in America*. New York: Simon & Schuster, 1976.

Goss, A., and Morosko, T. E. "Relationship Between a Dimension of Internal-External Control and the MMPI with an Alcoholic Population." *Journal of Consulting and Clinical Psychology*, 1970, *34*, 189–192.

Gottfredson, D. M. (Ed.). *Decision-Making in the Criminal Justice System: Reviews and Essays*. Rockville, Md.: National Institute of Mental Health, 1975a.

Gottfredson, D. M. "Some Research Needs." In D. M. Gottfredson (Ed.), *Decision-Making in the Criminal Justice System: Reviews and Essays*. Rockville, Md.: National Institute of Mental Health, 1975b.

Gottfredson, D. M., Hoffman, P. B., Sigler, M. H., and Wilkins, L. T. "Making Paroling Policy Explicit." *Crime and Delinquency*, 1975, *21*, 34–44.

Gottlieb, J. "Public, Peer, and Professional Attitudes Toward Mentally Retarded Persons." In J. J. Begab and S. A. Richardson (Eds.), *The Mentally Retarded and Society: A Social Sciences Perspective*. Baltimore: University Park Press, 1975.

Gove, W. "Societal Reaction as an Explanation of Mental Illness: An Evaluation." *American Sociological Review*, 1970, *35*, 873–884.

Gozali, J., and Meyen, E. L. "The Influence of the Teacher Expectancy Phenomenon on the Academic Performances of Educable Mentally Retarded Pupils in Special Classes." *Journal of Special Education,* 1970, *4,* 417–424.

Gozali, J., and Sloan, J. "Control Orientation as Personality Dimension Among Alcoholics." *Quarterly Journal of Studies on Alcohol,* 1971, *32,* 159–161.

Green, E. *Judicial Attitudes in Sentencing.* London: Macmillan, 1961.

Greene, D., and Lepper, M. R. "Effects of Extrinsic Rewards on Children's Subsequent Intrinsic Interest." *Child Development,* 1974, *45,* 1141–1145.

Greene, D., Sternberg, B., and Lepper, M. R. "Overjustification in a Token Economy." *Journal of Personality and Social Psychology,* 1976, *34,* 1219–1234.

Greenwald, S. G., Carter, J. S., and Stein, E. M. "Differences Between the Background, Attitude, Functioning and Mood of Drug Addicts, Alcoholics, and Orthopedic Patients." *International Journal of the Addictions,* 1973, *8,* 865–874.

Gross, M. "The Relation of the Pituitary Gland to Some Symptoms of Alcohol Intoxication and Chronic Alcoholism." *Quarterly Journal of Studies on Alcohol,* 1945, *6,* 25–35.

Gulliver, P. H. "Negotiations as a Mode of Dispute Settlement: Toward a General Model." *Law and Society Review,* 1973, *7,* 667.

Guskin, S. L. "Social Psychologies of Mental Deficiencies." In N. R. Ellis (Ed.), *Handbook of Mental Deficiency.* New York: McGraw-Hill, 1963.

Guskin, S. L., and Spicker, H. H. "Educational Research in Mental Retardation." In N. R. Ellis (Ed.), *International Review of Research in Mental Retardation.* Vol. 3. New York: Academic Press, 1968.

Haberman, P. W., and Sheinberg, J. "Public Attitudes Toward Alcoholism as an Illness." *American Journal of Public Health,* 1969, *59,* 1209–1216.

Hagan, J. "Extra-Legal Attributes and Criminal Sentencing: An Assessment of a Sociological Viewpoint." *Law and Society Review,* 1974, *8,* 357–384.

Hakeem, M. "Prediction of Parole Outcomes from Summaries of Case Histories." *Journal of Criminology, Criminal Law, and Police Science,* 1961, *52,* 145–150.

Halleck, S. L. "The Physician's Role in Management of Victims of

Sex Offenders." *Journal of the American Medical Association,* 1962, *180,* 273–278.

Handy, C. R. "Implications of the Index of Consumer Satisfaction for Public Policy Pertaining to Market Performance." In M. Venkatesan (Ed.), *Proceedings of the Third Annual Conference of the Association for Consumer Research.* Chicago: Association for Consumer Research, 1972.

Hanusa, B. A., and Schulz, R. "Attributional Mediators of Learned Helplessness." *Journal of Personality and Social Psychology,* 1977, *35,* 602–611.

Harper, W. E. "From Combat to Contract: A Behavioral-Systemic Approach to Marital Violence." Paper presented at the 86th annual meeting of the American Psychological Association, Toronto, 1978.

Harris, L. *The Public and High Blood Pressure: A Survey.* NIH 75–356. Washington, D.C.: Department of Health, Education, and Welfare, 1975.

Harrow, M., and Ferrante, A. "Locus of Control in Psychiatric Patients." *Journal of Consulting and Clinical Psychology,* 1969, *33,* 582–589.

Hart, H. L. A., and Honore, A. M. *Causation in the Law.* London: Oxford University Press, 1959.

Harter, S. "Pleasure Derived From Optimal Challenge and the Effects of Extrinsic Rewards on Children's Difficulty Level Choices." *Child Development,* 1978, *49,* 788–799.

Harvey, J. H., Harris, B., and Barnes, R. D. "Actor-Observer Differences in the Perceptions of Responsibility and Freedom." *Journal of Personality and Social Psychology,* 1975, *32,* 22–28.

Harvey, J. H., Ickes, W. J., and Kidd, R. F. (Eds.). *New Directions in Attribution Research,* Vol. 1. Hillsdale, N.J.: Erlbaum, 1976.

Harvey, J. H., Ickes, W. J., and Kidd, R. F. (Eds.). *New Directions in Attribution Research.* Vol. 2. Hillsdale, N.J.: Erlbaum, 1978.

Harvey, J. H., Wells, G. L., and Alvarez, M. D. "Attribution in the Context of Conflict and Separation in Close Relationship." In J. H. Harvey, W. J. Ickes, and R. F. Kidd (Eds.), *New Directions in Attribution Research,* Vol. 2. Hillsdale, N.J.: Erlbaum, 1978.

Hastorf, A. H., Schneider, D. J., and Polefka, J. *Person Perception.* Reading, Mass.: Addison-Wesley, 1970.

Hatton, D., Snortum, J. R., and Oscamp, S. "The Effects of Biasing

Information and Dogmatism upon Witness Testimony." *Psychonomic Science*, 1971, *23*, 425–427.

Hayes, C. S., and Prinz, R. J. "Affective Reactions of Retarded and Nonretarded Children to Success and Failure." *American Journal of Mental Deficiency*, 1976, *81*, 100–102.

Hayman, M. "Current Attitudes to Alcoholism of Psychiatrists in Southern California." *American Journal of Psychiatry*, 1956, *112*, 488–493.

Haynes, R. B., Sackett, D. L., Taylor, D. W., Gibson, E. S., and Johnson, A. L. "Increased Absenteeism from Work After Detection and Labeling of Hypertensive Patients." *New England Journal of Medicine*, 1978, *299*, 741–744.

Haynes, S. N., Follingstad, D. R., and McGowan, W. T. "Insomnia: Sleep Patterns and Anxiety Level." *Journal of Psychosomatic Research*, 1974, *18*, 69–74.

Heider, F. "Social Perception and Phenomenal Causality." *Psychological Review*, 1944, *51*, 358–374.

Heider, F. *The Psychology of Interpersonal Relations*. New York: Wiley, 1958.

Heinz, A. M., Heinz, J. P., Senderowitz, S. J., and Vance, M. A. "Sentencing by Parole Board: An Evaluation." *Journal of Criminal Law and Criminology*, 1976, *67*, 1–31.

Helmreich, R. "Applied Social Psychology: The Unfulfilled Promise." *Personality and Social Psychology Bulletin*, 1975, *1*, 548–560.

Hilberman, E., and Munson, K. "Sixty Battered Women." *Victimology*, 1978, *2*, 460–471.

Hill, C. T., Rubin, Z., and Peplau, L. A. "Breakups Before Marriage: The End of 103 Affairs." *Journal of Social Issues*, 1976, *32* (1), 147–168.

Hinchliffe, M. K., Hooper, D., and Roberts, J. F. *The Melancholy Marriage: Depression in Marriage and Psychosocial Approaches to Therapy*. New York: Wiley, 1978.

Hindelang, M. J. "Public Opinion Regarding Crime, Criminal Justice, and Related Topics." *Journal of Research in Crime and Delinquency*, 1974, *10*, 101–116.

Hiroto, D. S. "Locus of Control and Learned Helplessness." *Journal of Experimental Psychology*, 1974, *102*, 187–193.

Hiroto, D. S., and Seligman, M. E. P. "Generality of Learned

Helplessness in Man." *Journal of Personality and Social Psychology,* 1975, *31,* 311–327.

Hodges, W. L. "The Role of Rewards and Reinforcements in Early Education Programs: (I) External Reinforcement in Early Education." *Journal of School Psychology,* 1972, *10,* 233–241.

Hoffman, J., and Weiner, B. "Effects of Attributions for Success and Failure on the Performance of Retarded Adults." *American Journal of Mental Deficiency,* 1978, *82,* 449–452.

Hoffman, P. B., Beck, J. L., and DeGostin, L. K. *The Practical Application of a Severity Scale.* (Supplemental Report 13.) Davis, Calif.: National Council on Crime and Delinquency Research Center, 1973.

Hogarth, J. *Sentencing as a Human Process.* Toronto: University of Toronto Press, 1971.

Hoiberg, B., and Stires, L. "The Affect of Several Types of Pretrial Publicity on the Guilt Attributions of Simulated Jurors." *Journal of Applied Social Psychology,* 1973, *3,* 267–275.

Hokanson, J. E., Degood, D. E., Forrest, M. S., and Brittain, T. M. "Availability of Avoidance Behaviors in Modulating Vascular Stress Response." *Journal of Personality and Social Psychology,* 1971, *19,* 60–68.

Hollander, E. P. "Conformity, Status, and Idiosyncracy Credit." *Psychological Review,* 1958, *65,* 117–127.

Hollander, E. P. "Competence and Conformity in the Acceptance of Influence." *Journal of Abnormal and Social Psychology,* 1960, *61,* 365–369.

Hollon, S. D., Rush, A. J., Beck, A. T., and Kovacs, M. "Cognitive Therapy of Depression: An Outcome Study with Six-Month Follow-Up." Paper presented at the Society for Psychotherapy Research, Madsion, Wis., 1977.

Holmes, O. W., Jr. *The Common Law.* Boston: Little, Brown, 1881.

Holt, J. *How Children Fail.* New York: Dell, 1964.

Horai, J., and Guarnaccia, V. J. "Performance and Attributions to Ability, Effort, Task, and Luck of Retarded Adults After Success or Failure Feedback." *American Journal of Mental Deficiency,* 1975, *79,* 690–694.

Horn, J. "Regriefing: A Way to End Pathological Mourning." *Psychology Today,* 1974, 184.

Horton, D. "The Functions of Alcohol in Primitive Societies: A Cross-Cultural Study." *Quarterly Journal of Studies on Alcohol,* 1965, *26,* 449–459.

House, W. C., and Perney, V. "Valence of Expected and Unexpected Outcomes as a Function of Locus of Goal and Type of Expectancy." *Journal of Personality and Social Psychology,* 1974, *29,* 454–463.

Huggins, M. D., and Straus, M. A. "Violence and the Social Structure as Reflected in Children's Books from 1850 to 1970." Paper presented at the annual meeting of the Eastern Sociological Society, 1975.

Hulka, B. S., Kupper, L. L., Cassell, J. C., and Efird, R. L. "Medication Use and Misuse: Physician-Patient Discrepancies." *Journal of Chronic Diseases,* 1975, *28,* 7–21.

Hunter, A. "Symbols of Incivility: Crime and the Urban Community." Paper presented at the Center for Urban Affairs, Northwestern University, 1977.

Ickes, W., and Harvey, J. H. "Fritz Heider: A Biographical Sketch." *Journal of Psychology,* 1978, *98,* 159–170.

Ickes, W., and Layden, M. A. "Attributional Styles." In J. H. Harvey, W. J. Ickes, and R. F. Kidd (Eds.), *New Directions in Attribution Research,* Vol. 2. Hillsdale, N.J.: Erlbaum, 1978.

Irwin, T. "Attacking Alcohol as a Disease." *Today's Health,* 1968, *46,* 21–74.

Isbell, H., and Chrusciel, T. L. *Dependence Liability of "Non-Narcotic" Drugs.* Geneva, Switzerland: World Health Organization, 1970.

Jackson, P. *Life in Classrooms.* New York: Holt, Rinehart and Winston, 1968.

Jacobs, J. *Adolescent Suicide.* New York: Wiley, 1971.

Jamison, K. R., Wellisch, D. K., and Pasnau, R. O. "Psychosocial Aspects of Mastectomy: (I) The Woman's Perspective." *American Journal of Psychiatry,* 1978, *135,* 432–436.

Janoff-Bulman, R. "Self-Blame in Rape Victims: Control-Maintenance Strategy." Paper presented at the 86th annual meeting of the American Psychological Association, Toronto, 1978.

Janoff-Bulman, R. "The Two Sides of Self Blame: Inquiries into Depression and Rape." *Journal of Personality and Social Psychology,* in press.

Jellinek, E. M. *The Disease Concept of Alcoholism.* Highland Park, N.J.: Hillhouse Press, 1960.

Jessor, R., Carman, R. S., and Grossman, P. H. "Expectations of Need Satisfaction and Drinking Patterns of College Students." *Quarterly Journal of Studies on Alcohol,* 1968, *29,* 101–116.

Johnson, E. J., Greene, D., and Carroll, J. S. "Overjustification and Reasons: A Test of the Means-Ends Hypothesis." Unpublished paper, Carnegie-Mellon University, 1978.

Johnson, E. J., and Russo, J. E. "What Is Remembered After a Purchase Decision?" Unpublished paper, Carnegie-Mellon University, 1978.

Johnson, R. E., Calhoun, L. G., and Boardman, W. K. "The Effects of Severity, Consistency, and Typicalness Information on Clinician's Causal Attributions." *Journal of Clinical Psychology,* 1975, *31,* 600–604.

Johnson, R. N. *Aggression in Man and Animals.* Philadelphia: Saunders, 1972.

Johnson, S. M., Bolstad, O. D., and Lobitz, G. K. "Generalization and Contrast Phenomena in Behavior Modification with Children." In E. J. Marsh, L. C. Handy, and L. A. Hamerlynch (Eds.), *Behavior Modification and Families.* New York: Brunner/Mazel, 1976.

Johnson, T. J., Feigenbaum, R., and Wiley, M. "Some Determinants and Consequences of Teacher's Perception of Causation." *Journal of Educational Psychology,* 1964, *55,* 237–246.

Jones, C., and Aronson, E. "Attribution of Fault to a Rape Victim as a Function of Respectability of the Victim." *Journal of Personality and Social Psychology,* 1973, *26,* 415–419.

Jones, E. E., and Berglas, A. "Control of Attributions About the Self Through Self-Handicapping Strategies: The Appeal of Alcohol and the Role of Underachievement." *Personality and Social Psychology Bulletin,* 1978, *4,* 200–206.

Jones, E. E., and Davis, K. E. "From Acts to Dispositions: The Attribution Process in Person Perception." In L. Berkowitz (Ed.), *Advances in Experimental Social Psychology.* Vol. 2. New York: Academic Press, 1965.

Jones, E. E., Davis, K. E., and Gergen, K. "Role Playing Variations and Their Informational Value for Person Perception." *Journal of Abnormal and Social Psychology,* 1961, *63,* 302–310.

Jones, E. E., and Gerard, H. *Foundations of Social Psychology.* New York: Wiley, 1967.

Jones, E. E., and Harris, V. "The Attribution of Attitudes." *Journal of Experimental Social Psychology,* 1967, *3,* 1–24.

Jones, E. E., Kanouse, D. I., Kelley, H. H., Nisbett, R. E., Valins, S., and Weiner, B. (Eds.). *Attribution: Perceiving the Causes of Behavior.* Morristown, N.J.: General Learning Press, 1972.

Jones, E. E., and McGillis, D. "Correpondent Inferences and the Attribution Cube: A Comparative Reappraisal." In J. Harvey, W. Ickes, and R. Kidd, (Eds.), *New Directions in Attribution Research.* Vol. 1. Hillsdale, N.J.: Erlbaum, 1976.

Jones, E. E., and Nisbett, R. E. "The Actor and Observer: Divergent Perceptions of the Causes of Behavior." In E. E. Jones and others (Eds.), *Attribution: Perceiving the Causes of Behavior.* Morristown, N.J.: General Learning Press, 1972.

Jones, E. E., Worchel, S., Goethals, G., and Grumet, J. "Prior Expectancy and Behavioral Extremity as Determinants of Attitude Attribution." *Journal of Experimental Social Psychology,* 1971, *7,* 59–80.

Jones, E. E., and Wortman, C. B. *Ingratiation: An Attributional Approach.* Morristown, N.J.: General Learning Press, 1973.

Jones, R. L. "Research on the Special Education Teacher and Special Education Teaching." *Exceptional Children,* 1966, *33,* 251–257.

Jones, S. L., Nation, J. R., and Massad, P. "Immunization Against Learned Helplessness in Man." *Journal of Abnormal Psychology,* 1977, *86,* 75–83.

Jones, W. H., Freemon, J. E., and Goswick, R. A. "The Persistence of Loneliness: Self and Other Rejection?" Unpublished paper, University of Tulsa, 1978.

Joseph, F. R. "Task Force Recommendations." In I. Drapkin and E. Viano (Eds.), *Victimology.* Lexington, Mass.: Health, 1974.

Judson, C., Pandell, J., Owens, J., McIntosh, D., and Matschullat, D. "A Study of the California Penalty Jury in First Degree Murder Cases." *Stanford Law Review,* 1969, *21,* 1297.

Kales, A., and Kales, J. "Recent Advances on the Diagnosis and Treatment of Sleep Disorders." In G. Usdin (Ed.), *Sleep Research and Clinical Practice.* New York: Brunner/Mazel, 1973.

Kalven, H. Jr., and Zeisel, H. *The American Jury.* Boston: Little, Brown, 1966.

Kanfer, F. H. "Self-Regulation: Research, Issues, and Speculations." In C. Neuringer and J. L. Michael (Eds.), *Behavior Modification in Clinical Psychology.* New York: Appleton-Century-Crofts, 1970.

Kanfer, F. H. "The Maintenance of Behavior by Self-Generated Stimuli and Reinforcement." In A. Jacobs and L. B. Sachs (Eds.), *The Psychology of Private Events: Perspectives on Covert Response Systems.* New York: Academic Press, 1971.

Kanouse, D. E. "Language, Labeling, and Attribution." In E. E. Jones and others (Eds.), *Attribution: Perceiving the Causes of Behavior.* Morristown, N.J.: General Learning Press, 1972.

Kaplan, M. "Judgment by Juries." In M. Kaplan and S. Schwartz (Eds.), *Human Judgment and Decision-Making in Applied Settings.* New York: Academic Press, 1977.

Karniol, R., and Ross, M. "The Effects of Performance-Relevant and Performance-Irrelevant Rewards on Children's Intrinsic Motivation." *Child Development,* 1977, *48,* 282–287.

Kast, E. C., and Loesch, J. "Influence of the Doctor-Patient Relationship on Drug Action." *Illinois Medical Journal,* 1961, *119,* 390–393.

Kastenmeier, R., and Eglit, H. "Parole Release Decision-Making: Rehabilition, Expertise, and the Demise of Mythology." *American University Law Review,* 1973, *22,* 477–525.

Katz, I. "The Socialization of Academic Achievement in Minority Group Children." In D. Levine (Ed.), *Nebraska Symposium on Motivation.* Vol. 15. Lincoln: University of Nebraska Press, 1967.

Kaufman, I. C. "Mother-Infant Separation in Monkeys: An Experimental Model." In J. P. Scott and E. C. Senay (Eds.), *Separation and Depression: Clinical and Research Aspects.* Washington, D.C.: American Association for the Advancement of Science, 1973.

Kazdin, A. E. "Recent Advances in Token Economy Research." In M. Hersen, R. M. Eisler, and P. M. Miller (Eds.), *Progress in Behavior Modification.* Vol. 1. New York: Academic Press, 1975.

Kazdin, A. E. *The Token Economy: A Review and Evaluation.* New York: Plenum, 1977.

Kazdin, A. E., and Bootzin, R. R. "The Token Economy Review: An Evaluative Review." *Journal of Applied Behavior Analysis,* 1972, *5,* 343–372.

Keller, M. "The Disease Concept of Alcoholism Revisited." *Journal of Studies on Alcohol,* 1976, *11,* 1701.

Kelley, H. H. "Attribution Theory in Social Psychology." In D. Levine (Ed.), *Nebraska Symposium on Motivation.* Vol. 15. Lincoln: University of Nebraska Press, 1967.

Kelley, H. H. "Causal Schemata and the Attribution Process." In E. E. Jones and others (Eds.), *Attribution: Perceiving the Causes of Behavior.* Morristown, N.J.: General Learning Press, 1972.

Kelley, H. H. "Attribution and Social Interaction." In E. E. Jones and others (Eds.), *Attribution: Perceiving the Causes of Behavior.* Morristown, N.J.: General Learning Press, 1972.

Kelley, H. H. "The Processes of Causal Attribution." *American Psychologist,* 1973, *23,* 107–128.

Kelley, H. H., and Michela, J. "Attribution Research in Social Psychology." In M. R. Rosenzweig and L. W. Porter (Eds.), *Annual Review of Psychology.* Vol. 31. Palo Alto, Calif.: in press.

Kelling, G., Pate, T., Dieckman, D., and Brown, C. *The Kansas City Preventive Patrol Experiment: A Technical Report.* Washington, D.C.: Police Foundation, 1974.

Kellogg, R., and Baron, S. "Attribution Theory, Insomnia and Reverse Placebo Effect: A Reversal of Storms and Nisbett's Findings." *Journal of Personality and Social Psychology,* 1975, *32,* 231–236.

Kelman, H. A., Lowenthal, M., and Muller, J. M. "Community Status of Discharged Rehabilitation Patients: Results of a Longitudinal Study." *Archives of Physical Medicine and Rehabilitation,* 1966, *47,* 670–675.

Kennedy, R. L., and Associates. *A Survey of Public Attitudes Toward the Criminal Justice System in Multnomah County, Oregon.* Salem: Richard L. Kennedy and Associates, 1973.

Keogh, B. K., Cahill, C. W., and MacMillan, D. L. "Perception of Interruption by Educationally Handicapped Children." *American Journal of Mental Deficiency,* 1972, *77,* 107–108.

Kessler, J. "The Social Psychology of Jury Deliberations." In R. J. Simon (Ed.), *The Jury System in America: A Critical Overview.* Beverly Hills, Calif.: Sage, 1975.

Kidder, L. H. "What's the Trouble with Kids?" Unpublished paper. Center for Urban Affairs, Northwestern University, 1977.

Kidder, R. "Courts and Conflict in an Indian City." *Journal of Commonwealth Political Studies*, 1973, *11*(2), 121–139.

Kiesler, C., and Munson, P. A. "Attitudes and Opinions." In M. R. Rosenzweig and L. W. Porter (Eds.), *Annual Review of Psychology*. Vol. 26. Palo Alto, Calif.: Annual Reviews, 1975.

Kilty, K. M. "Attitudes Toward Alcohol and Alcoholism Among Professionals and Non-Professionals " *Journal of Studies on Alcohol*, 1975, *36*(3), 327–347.

Kim, Y. A. "The Social Correlates of Perceptions of Neighborhood Crime Problems and Fear of Victimization." Unpublished paper, Center for Urban Affairs, Northwestern University, 1976.

Kingsnorth, R. "Decision-Making in a Parole Bureaucracy." *Journal of Research in Crime and Delinquency*, 1969, *6*, 210–218.

Kissin, B. "Theory and Practice in the Treatment of Alcoholism." In B. Kissin and H. Begleiter (Eds.), *The Biology of Alcoholism*. Vol. 5: *Treatment and Rehabilitation of the Chronic Alcoholic*. New York: Plenum, 1977.

Kleck, R. "Physical Stigma and Nonverbal Cues Emitted in Face-To-Face Interaction." *Human Relations*, 1968, *21*, 19–28.

Kleck, R., Buck, P. L., Goller, W. L., London, R. S., Pfeiffer, J. R., and Vulcevic, D. P. "Effects of Stigmatizing Conditions on the Use of Personal Space." *Psychological Reports*, 1968, *23*, 111–118.

Kleck, R., Ono, H., and Hastorf, A. H. "The Effects of Physical Deviance upon Face-To-Face Interaction." *Human Relations*, 1966, *19*, 425–436.

Klein, D. C., Fencil-Morse, E., and Seligman, M. E. P. "Learned Helplessness, Depression, and the Attribution of Failure." *Journal of Personality and Social Psychology*, 1976, *33*, 508–516.

Klein, D. C., and Seligman, M. E. P. "Reversal of Performance Deficits and Perceptual Deficits in Learned Helplessness and Depression." *Journal of Abnormal Psychology*, 1976, *85*, 11–26.

Klerman, G. L. "Drugs and Social Values." *International Journal of Addictions*, 1970, *5*, 312–319.

Klingbeil, K. "A Treatment Program for Male Batterers." Paper presented at the 86th annual meeting of the American Psychological Association, Toronto, 1978.

Knapp, D. E., Oeltjen, P. D., and Knapp, D. A. "Anatomy of an

Illness (as Perceived by Consumers in a Longitudinal Study)." *Medical Marketing and Media,* 1974, *9,* 26–28.

Knoble, J., and Frieze, I. "General Beliefs About Violence Towards Women." Paper presented at the annual meeting of the Association for Women in Psychology, Dallas, 1979.

Knopf, T. A. "Youth Patrols: An Experiment in Community Participation." *Civil Rights Digest,* 1970, *3* (2), 1–7.

Komarovsky, M. *Blue Collar Marriage.* New York: Vintage Books, 1964.

Krantz, D. S., Glass, D. C., and Snyder, M. C. "Helplessness and Coronary Prone Behavior Pattern." *Journal of Experimental Social Psychology,* 1974, *10,* 284–300.

Kruglanski, A. W. "The Endogenous-Exogenous Partition in Attribution Theory." *Psychological Review,* 1975, *82,* 387–406.

Kruglanski, A. W. "Endogenous Attribution and Intrinsic Motivation." In M. R. Lepper and D. Greene (Eds.), *The Hidden Costs of Reward.* Hillsdale, N.J.: Erlbaum, 1978a.

Kruglanski, A. W. "Lay Epistemo-Logic, Its Content, and Process: Another Look at Attribution Theory." Unpublished paper, Tel-Aviv University, 1978b.

Kruglanski, A. W., Alon, S., and Lewis, T. "Retrospective Misattribution and Task Enjoyment." *Journal of Experimental Social Psychology,* 1972, *8,* 493–501.

Kruglanski, A. W., and Bar-Tal, D. "Emerging Conceptions of Attribution: An Integrative Review." Unpublished paper, Tel-Aviv University, 1978.

Kruglanski, A. W., Friedman, I., and Zeevi, G. "The Effects of Extrinsic Incentives on Some Qualitative Aspects of Task Performance." *Journal of Personality,* 1971, *39,* 606–617.

Kruglanski, A. W., Hamel, I. Z., Maides, S. A., and Schwartz, J. M. "Attribution Theory as a Special Case of Lay Epistemology." In J. H. Harvey, W. Ickes, and R. F. Kidd (Eds.), *New Directions in Attribution Research.* Vol. 2. Hillsdale, N.J.: Erlbaum, 1978.

Krulewitz, J. E., Nash, J., and Payne, E. "Sex Differences in Attributions About Rape, Rapists, and Rape Victims." Paper presented at the 85th annual meeting of the American Psychological Association, San Francisco, 1977.

Kukla, A. "Attributional Determinants of Achievement-Related

Behavior." *Journal of Personality and Social Psychology,* 1972, *21,* 166-174.

Kun, A., and Weiner, B. "Necessary Versus Sufficient Causal Schemata for Success and Failure." *Journal of Research in Personality,* 1973, *7,* 197–207.

Kurtz, P. D., Harrison, M., Neisworth, J. T., and Jones, R. T. "Influence of 'Mentally Retarded' Label on Teachers' Nonverbal Behavior Toward Preschool Children." *American Journal of Mental Deficiency,* 1977, *82,* 204–206.

Lamont, J. "Depression, Locus of Control, and Mood Response Set." *Journal of Clinical Psychology,* 1972a, *28,* 342–345.

Lamont, J. "Item Mood-Level as a Determinant of the I-E Test Response." *Journal of Clinical Psychology,* 1972b, *28,* 190.

Lana, R. E. *Assumptions of Social Psychology.* New York: Appleton-Century-Crofts, 1969.

Landon, E. L. "A Model of Consumer Complaint Behavior." In R. L. Day (Ed.), *Consumer Satisfaction, Dissatisfaction, and Complaining Behavior.* Bloomington: Division of Business Research, Indiana University, 1977.

Landy, D., and Aronson, E. "The Influence of the Character of the Criminal and His Victim on the Decisions of Simulated Jurors." *Journal of Experimental Social Psychology,* 1969, *5,* 141–152.

Langer, E. J. "The Illusion of Control." *Journal of Personality and Social Psychology,* 1975, *32*(2), 311–328.

Langer, E. J. "Rethinking the Role of Thought in Social Interaction." In J. H. Harvey, W. J. Ickes, and R. E. Kidd (eds.), *New Directions in Attribution Research.* Vol. 2. Hillsdale, N.J.: Erlbaum, 1978.

Langer, E. J., and Rodin, J. "The Effects of Choice and Enhanced Personal Responsibility for the Aged: A Field Experiment in an Institutional Setting." *Journal of Personality and Social Psychology,* 1976, *34,* 191–198.

Lanzetta, J. T., and Hannah, T. E. "Reinforcing Behavior of 'Naive' Trainers." *Journal of Personality and Social Psychology,* 1969, *11,* 245–252.

Latimer, R. "Current Attitudes Toward Mental Retardation." *Mental Retardation,* 1970, *8,* 30–32.

Lee, D. V., Syrnyk, R., and Hallschmid, C. "Self-Perception of Intrinsic and Extrinsic Motivation: Effects on Institutionalized Mentally Retarded Adolescents." *American Journal of Mental Deficiency,* 1976, *81,* 331–337.

Lefcourt, H. M. "The Function of the Illusions of Control and Freedom." *American Psychologist,* 1973, *28*(5), 417–425.

Leiderman, P. H. "Loneliness: A Psychodynamic Interpretation." In E. S. Shneidman and M. J. Ortega (Eds.), *Aspects of Depression.* Boston: Little, Brown,1969.

Lemert, E. M. "Paranoia and the Dynamics of Exclusion." *Sociometry,* 1962, *25,* 2–20.

Lepper, M. R., and Dafoe, J. L. "Incentives, Constraints, and Motivation in the Classroom." In I. H. Frieze, D. Bar-Tal, and J. S. Carroll (Eds.), *New Approaches to Social Problems: Applications of Attribution Theory.* San Francisco: Jossey-Bass, 1979.

Lepper, M. R., and Greene, D. "Turning Play into Work: Effects of Adult Surveillance and Extrinsic Rewards on Children's Intrinsic Motivation." *Journal of Personality and Social Psychology,* 1975, 31, 479–486.

Lepper, M. R., and Greene, D. "Divergent Approaches to the Study of Rewards." In M. R. Lepper and D. Greene (Eds.), *The Hidden Costs of Reward.* Hillsdale, N.J.: Erlbaum, 1978a.

Lepper, M. R., and Greene, D. "Overjustification Research and Beyond: Toward a Means-Ends Analysis of Intrinsic and Extrinsic Motivation." In M. R. Lepper and D. Greene (Eds.), *The Hidden Costs of Reward.* Hillsdale, N.J.: Erlbaum, 1978b.

Lepper, M. R., and Greene, D. (Eds.), *The Hidden Costs of Reward.* Hillsdale, N.J.: Erlbaum, 1978c.

Lepper, M. R., Greene, D., and Nisbett, R. E. "Undermining Children's Intrinsic Interest with Extrinsic Rewards: A Test of the 'Overjustification' Hypothesis." *Journal of Personality and Social Psychology,* 1973, *28,* 129–137.

Lepper, M. R., Sagotsky, G., and Greene, D. "Effects of Choice and Self-Imposed vs. Externally-Imposed Contingencies on Children's Subsequent Intrinsic Motivation." Unpublished paper, Stanford University, 1978a.

Lepper, M. R., Sagotsky, G., and Greene, D. "Overjustification Effects Following Multiple-Trial Reinforcement Procedures: Experimental Evidence Concerning the Assessment of Intrinsic Interest." Unpublished paper, Stanford University, 1978b.

Lerner, M. J. "The Desire for Justice and Reactions to Victims." In J. Macauley and L. Berkowitz (Eds.), *Altruism and Helping Behavior.* New York: Academic Press, 1970.

Lerner, M. J. *Deserving Versus Justice: A Contemporary Dilemma.* Report No. 24. Waterloo: University of Waterloo, 1971.

Lerner, M. J., and Miller, D. T. "Just World Research and the Attribution Process: Looking Back and Ahead." *Psychological Bulletin,* 1978, *85* (5), 1030–1051.

Lerner, M. J., Miller, D. T., and Holmes, J. "Deserving and the Emergence of Forms of Justice." In L. Berkowitz and E. Walster (Eds.), *Advances in Experimental Social Psychology.* Vol. 9. New York: Academic Press, 1976.

Lerner, M. J., and Simmons, C. H. "Observer's Reactions to the 'Innocent' Victim: Compassion or Rejection." *Journal of Personality and Social Psychology,* 1966, *4,* 203–210.

Levinger, G. "Physical Abuse Among Applicants for Divorce." In S. Steinmetz and M. Straus (Eds.), *Violence in the Family.* New York: Dodd, Mead, 1974.

Levitt, E. E., and Lubin, B. *Depression: Concepts, Controversies and Some New Facts.* New York: Springer, 1975.

Lewin, K. "Action Research and Minority Problems." *Journal of Social Issues,* 1946, *2,* 34–46.

Lewin, K. *Field Theory in Social Science.* New York: Harper & Row, 1951.

Lewinsohn, P. M. "Clinical and Theoretical Aspects of Depression." In K. S. Calhoun, H. E. Adams, and K. M. Mitchell (Eds.), *Innovative Treatment Methods in Psychopathology.* New York: Wiley, 1974.

Lewinsohn, P. M. "Review of *Helplessness* by M. E. P. Seligman." *Behavior Therapy,* 1975, *6,* 735–737.

Lewinsohn, P. M., Biglan, A., and Zeiss, A. M. "Behavioral Treatment of Depression." In P. O. Davidson (Ed.), *The Behavioral Management of Anxiety, Depression, and Pain.* New York: Brunner/Mazel, 1976.

Lewinsohn, P. M., Lobitz, W. C., and Wilson, S. "Sensitivity of Depressed Individuals to Aversive Stimuli." *Journal of Abnormal Psychology,* 1973, *81,* 259–263.

Linsky, A. S. "Theories of Behavior and the Social Control of Alcoholism." *Social Psychiatry,* 1972, *7,* 47-52.

Linton, H. B., and Langs, R. J. "Placebo Reactions in a Study of LSD (LSD 25)." *Archives of General Psychiatry,* 1962, *6,* 364–383.

Lion, J. "Clinical Aspects of Wifebattering." In M. Roy (Ed.), *Battered Women: A Psychosociological Study of Domestic Violence.* New York: Van Nostrand Reinhold, 1977.

Lipman, R., Park, L. C., and Rickels, K. "Paradoxical Influence of a Therapeutic Side Effect Interpretation." *Archives of General Psychiatry,* 1966, *15,* 462–474.

Lisansky, E. S. "The Etiology of Alcoholism: The Role of Psychological Predisposition." *Quarterly Journal of Studies on Alcohol,* 1960, *21,* 314–343.

Litman, T. J. "The Influence of Self-Conception and Life Orientation Factors in the Rehabilitation of the Orthopedically Disabled." *Journal of Health and Human Behavior,* 1962, *3,* 249–256.

Lopata, H. Z. "Loneliness: Forms and Components." *Social Problems,* 1969, *17,* 248–261.

Lowenthal, M. F. "Social Isolation and Mental Illness in Old Age." *American Sociological Review,* 1964, *29,* 54–70.

Lowery, C. R., Denney, D. R., and Storms, M. D. "The Treatment of Insomnia: Pill Attributions and Nonpejorative Self-Attributions." *Cognitive Therapy and Research,* 1979, *3,* 161–164.

Lown, C. "Legal Approaches to Juror Stereotyping by Physical Characteristics." *Law and Human Behavior,* 1977, *1,* 87–100.

Lussier, R. J., Perlman, D., and Breen, L. J. "Causal Attributions, Attitude Similarity, and the Punishment of Drug Offenders." *British Journal of Addiction,* 1977, *72,* 353–364.

Lutz, R. J., and Bettman, J. R. "Multi-Attribute Models in Marketing: A Bicentennial Review." In A. G. Woodside, J. N. Sheth, and P. D. Bennett (Eds.), *Consumer and Industrial Buying Behavior.* New York: Elsevier North-Holland, 1977.

Lyerly, S., Ross, S., Krugman, A., and Clyde, D. "Drugs and Placebos: The Effects of Instruments upon Performance and Mood Under Amphetamine Sulfate and Chloral Hydrate." *Jour-*

nal of Abnormal Social Psychology, 1964, *68*(3), 321–327.

Lynch, J. J. *The Broken Heart: The Medical Consequences of Loneliness in America.* New York: Basic Books, 1976.

McArthur, L. "The How and What of Why: Some Determinants and Consequences of Causal Attribution." *Journal of Personality and Social Psychology,* 1972, *22,* 171–193.

McCabe, D. J., and Kaplan, G. "A Review of the Literature on Reactions to Crime." Unpublished paper, Center for Urban Affairs, Northwestern University, 1976.

McClelland, D. C., Atkinson, J. W., Clark, R. W., and Lowell, E. L. *The Achievement Motive.* New York: Appleton-Century-Crofts, 1953.

McClelland, D. C., Davis, W. N., Kalin, R., and Wanner, E. *The Drinking Man.* New York: Free Press, 1972.

McCord, W., McCord, J., and Gudeman, J. *Origins of Alcoholism.* Stanford: Stanford University Press, 1960.

McGraw, K. O. "The Detrimental Effects of Reward on Performance: A Literature Review and a Prediction Model." In M. R. Lepper and D. Greene (Eds.), *The Hidden Costs of Reward.* Hillsdale, N.J.: Erlbaum, 1978.

McGraw, K. O., and McCullers, J. C. "Some Detrimental Effects of Reward on Laboratory Task Performance." Paper presented at the 83rd annual meeting of the American Psychological Association, Chicago, September 1975.

McGraw, K. O., and McCullers, J. C. "Extrinsic Incentives for Water-Jar Task Performance: Evidence of a Detrimental Effect of Incentives on Problem Solving." *Journal of Experimental Social Psychology,* in press.

McGuire, W. J. "Some Impending Reorientations in Social Psychology: Some Thoughts Provoked by Kenneth Ring." *Journal of Experimental Social Psychology,* 1967, *3,* 124–139.

McHugh, M. C. "Causal Explanations of Male and Female Alcoholics." Paper presented at the annual meeting of the Midwestern Psychological Association, 1977.

McHugh, M. C. "Causal Explanations of Alcoholics, Nonalcoholics, and College Students for Male and Female Alcoholism." Unpublished master's thesis, Department of Psychology, University of

Pittsburgh, 1979.

McHugh, M. C., and Frieze, I. H. "Self Attributions of Alcoholics and Nonalcoholics for Hypothetical Achievement and Interpersonal Outcomes." Unpublished paper, University of Pittsburgh, 1979.

MacKay, J. R. "Clinical Observations of Adolescent Problem Drinkers." *Quarterly Journal of Studies on Alcohol,* 1961, *22,* 124–134.

McLean, P. "Therapeutic Decision-Making in the Behavioral Treatment of Depression." In P. O. Davidson (Ed.), *The Behavioral Management of Anxiety, Depression, and Pain.* New York: Brunner/Mazel, 1976.

McLean, P. D., Ogston, K., and Grauer, L. "A Behavior Approach to the Treatment of Depression." *Journal of Behavior Therapy and Experimental Psychiatry,* 1973, *4,* 323–330.

McMahan, I. D. "Relationships Between Causal Attributions and Expectancy of Success." *Journal of Personality and Social Psychology,* 1973, *28,* 108–114.

MacMillan, D. L. "Motivational Differences: Cultural-Familial Retardates Versus Normal Subjects on Expectancy for Failure." *American Journal of Mental Deficiency,* 1969, *74,* 254–258.

MacMillan, D. L. "Effect of Experimental Success and Failure on the Situational Expectancy of EMR and Nonretarded Children." *American Journal of Mental Deficiency,* 1975, *80,* 90–95.

MacMillan, D. L., Jones, R. L., and Aloia, G. F. "The Mentally Retarded Label: A Theoretical Analysis and Review of the Research." *American Journal of Mental Deficiency,* 1974, *79,* 241–261.

MacMillan, D. L., and Keogh, B. K. "Normal and Retarded Children's Expectancy for Failure." *Developmental Psychology,* 1971, *4,* 343–348.

Mahoney, M. J. *Cognition and Behavior Modification.* Cambridge, Mass.: Ballinger, 1974.

Maisel, R. "Report on the Continuing Audit of Public Attitudes and Concerns." Cambridge: Laboratory of Community Psychiatry, Harvard Medical School, 1969.

Maltz, M. D. *Evaluation of Crime Control Programs.* Washington, D.C.: National Institute of Law Enforcement and Criminal

Justice, 1972.

Market Opinion Research Company. *The Michigan Public Speaks Out On Crime: 1973, 1974, 1975.* Detroit: Market Opinion Research Co., 1975.

Marris, P. *Widows and Their Families.* London: Routledge & Kegan Paul, 1958.

Marshall, J. *Intention in Law and Society.* New York: Funk & Wagnalls, 1968.

Martin, D. *Battered Wives.* San Francisco: Glide, 1976.

Maslach, C. "Burned-Out." *Human Behavior,* 1976, *5,* 16–22.

Medea, A., and Thompson, K. *Against Rape.* New York; Farrar, Straus, & Giroux, 1974.

Meichenbaum, D. H., Bowers, K. S., and Ross, R. R. "Modification of Classroom Behavior of Institutionalized Female Adolescent Offenders." *Behavior Research and Therapy,* 1968, *6,* 343–353.

Meir, A. Z. "General Systems Theory: Developments and Perspectives for Medicine and Psychiatry." *Archives of General Psychiatry,* 1969, *21,* 302–310.

Mendels, J. *Concepts of Depression.* New York: Wiley, 1970.

Mendelson, J. H., Wexler, D., Kubzansky, P. E., Harrison, R., Leiderman, G., and Solomon, P. "Physician's Attitudes Toward Alcoholic Patients." *Archives of General Psychiatry,* 1964, *11,* 392–399.

Mercer, J. R. *Labelling the Mentally Retarded.* Berkeley: University of California Press, 1973.

Michela, J., Peplau, L. A., and Weeks, D. "Perceived Dimensions and Consequences of Attributions for Loneliness." Unpublished paper, University of California, Los Angeles, 1979.

Miller, D., and Ross, M. "Self-Serving Biases in the Attribution of Causality: Fact or Fiction?" *Psychological Bulletin,* 1975, *82,* 213–225.

Miller, M. "The Indeterminate Sentence Paradigm: Resocialization or Social Control?" *Issues in Criminology,* 1972, *7,* 101–121.

Miller, W. "Ideology and Criminal Justice Policy: Some Current Issues." *Journal of Criminal Law and Criminology,* 1973, *64,* 141–162.

Miller, W. R., and Seligman, M. E. P. "Depression and the Perception of Reinforcement." *Journal of Abnormal Psychology,* 1973, *82,* 62–73.

Miller, W. R., and Seligman, M. E. P. "Depression and Learned Helplessness in Man." *Journal of Abnormal Psychology,* 1975, *84,* 228–238.

Miller, W. R., and Seligman, M. E. P. "Learned Helplessness, Depression, and the Perception of Reinforcement." *Journal of Behavior Research and Therapy,* 1976, *14,* 7–17.

Miller, W. R., Seligman, M. E. P., and Kurlander, H. M. "Learned Helplessness, Depression, and Anxiety." *Journal of Nervous and Mental Disease,* 1975, *161,* 345–356.

Mills, J., and Jellison, J. "Effect on Opinion Change of How Desirable the Communication Is to the Audience the Communicator Addressed." *Journal of Personality and Social Psychology,* 1967, *6,* 98–101.

Miranasky, J., and Langer, E. J. "Burglary (Non) Prevention: An Instance of Relinquishing Control." *Personality and Social Psychology Bulletin,* 1978, *4,* 399–405.

Mitler, M. M., Guilleminault, C., Orem, J., Zarcone, V. P., and Dement, W. C. "Sleeplessness, Sleep Attacks, and Things That Go Wrong in the Night." *Psychology Today,* 1975, *12,* 45–50.

Monroe, L. J. "Psychological and Physiological Differences Between Good and Poor Sleepers." *Journal of Abnormal Psychology,* 1967, *72,* 255–264.

Monson, T. C., and Snyder, M. "Actors, Observers, and the Attribution Process: Toward a Reconceptualization." *Journal of Experimental Social Psychology,* 1977, *13,* 89–111.

Moody, P. M. "Attitudes of Nurses and Nursing Students Toward Alcoholism Treatment." *Quarterly Journal of Studies on Alcohol,* 1971, *32,* 172–175.

Moore, J. A., and Sermat, V. "Relationship Between Self-Actualization and Self-Reported Loneliness." *Canadian Counsellor,* 1974, *8* (3), 194–196.

Morrell, D. C., and Wale, C. J. "Symptoms Perceived and Recorded by Patients." *Journal of the Royal College of General Practitioners,* 1976, *26,* 398–403.

Morris, L. A., and O'Neal, E. C. "Drug Name Familiarity and the Placebo Effect." *Journal of Clinical Psychology,* 1974, *7,* 280–282.

Morris, L. A., and O'Neal, E. C. "Judgments About a Drug's Effectiveness: The Role of Expectations and Outcomes." *Drugs in Health Care*, 1975, *2*, 179–186.

Mulford, H. A., and Miller, D. E. "Public Definitions of the Alcoholic." *Quarterly Journal of Studies on Alcohol*, 1961, *29*, 172–175.

Mulford, H. A., and Miller, D. E. "Measuring Public Acceptance of the Alcoholic as a Sick Person." *Quarterly Journal of Studies of Alcohol*, 1964, *25*, 314–323.

Murray, D. C. "Suicidal and Depressive Feelings Among College Students." *Psychological Reports*, 1973, *33*, 175–181.

Murray, S. R., and Mednick, M. T. S. "Perceiving the Causes of Success and Failure in Achievement: Sex, Race, and Motivational Comparisons." *Journal of Consulting and Clinical Psychology*, 1975, *43*, 881–885.

Mussen, P., and Barker, R. "Attitudes Toward Cripples." *Journal of Abnormal and Social Psychology*, 1944, *39*, 351–355.

Naditch, M. D., Gargan, M. A., and Michael, M. B. "Denial, Anxiety, Locus of Control, and the Discrepancy Between Aspirations and Achievements as Components of Depression." *Journal of Abnormal Psychology*, 1975, *84*, 1–9.

Nash, G. "The Community Patrol Corps: A Descriptive Evaluation of the One Week Experiment." Unpublished paper, Bureau of Applied Social Research, Columbia University, 1968.

Nash, J. E. "Attributions About Rape Victim Resistance." Paper presented at the 85th annual meeting of the American Psychological Association, San Francisco, 1977.

National Association of Blue Shield Plans. *The Alcoholic American.* New York: National Association of Blue Shield Plans, 1973.

National Commission on Marihuana and Drug Abuse. *Drug Use in America: Problems in Perspective.* (Second Report.) Washington, D.C.: U.S. Government Printing Office, 1973.

National Institute on Alcohol Abuse and Alcoholism. *Alcohol and Health.* (Second special report to the United States Congress.) Washington, D.C.: U.S. Government Printing Office, 1974.

Newtson, D. "The On-going Perception of Behavior: The Basis of Attribution." In J. Harvey, W. Ickes, and R. Kidd (Eds.), *New Directions in Attribution Research.* Vol. 1. Hillsdale, N.J.: Erlbaum, 1976.

Nicholls, J. G. "Causal Attributions and Other Achievement-

Related Cognitions: Effects of Task Outcomes, Attainment Value, and Sex." *Journal of Personality and Social Psychology,* 1975, *31,* 379–389.

Nisbett, R. E., Borgida, E., Crandall, R., and Reed, H. "Popular Induction: Information is Not Necessarily Informative." In J. S. Carroll and J. W. Payne (Eds.), *Cognition and Social Behavior.* Hillsdale, N.J.: Erlbaum, 1976.

Nisbett, R. E., Captuto, C., Legant, P., and Maracek, J. "Behavior as Seen by the Actor and Seen by the Observer." *Journal of Personality and Social Psychology,* 1973, *27,* 154–165.

Nisbett, R. E., and Schachter, S. "Cognitive Manipulation of Pain." *Journal of Experimental Social Psychology,* 1966, *2,* 227–236.

Nisbett, R. E., and Valins, R. *Perceiving the Cause of One's Own Behavior.* Morristown, N.J.: General Learning Press, 1971.

Nisbett, R. E., and Wilson, T. D. "Telling More Than We Can Know: Verbal Reports on Mental Processes." *Psychological Review,* 1977, *84,* 231–259.

Nuckolls, K. B., Cassell, J., and Kaplan, B. H. "Psychosocial Assets, Life Crisis, and the Prognosis of Pregnancy." *American Journal of Epidemiology,* 1972, *95,* 431–441.

O'Brien, J. E. "Violence in Divorce Prone Families." *Journal of Marriage and the Family,* 1971, *33,* 692–698.

O'Leary, K. D. "Behavior Modification in the Classroom: A Rejoinder to Winnett and Winkler." *Journal of Applied Behavior Analysis,* 1972, *5,* 505–510.

O'Leary, K. D. "Token Reinforcement Programs in the Classroom." In T. Brigham and C. Catania (Eds.), *The Analysis of Behavior: Social and Educational Processes.* New York: Irvington-Naiburg/Wiley, in press.

O'Leary, K. D., and Drabman, R. "Token Reinforcement Programs in the Classroom: A Review." *Psychological Bulletin,* 1971, *75,* 379–398.

O'Leary, K. D., Poulos, R. W., and Devine, V. T. "Tangible Reinforcers: Bonuses or Bribes? *Journal of Consulting and Clinical Psychology,* 1972, *38,* 1–8.

O'Leary, M., Donovan, D., Cysewski, B., and Chaney, E. "Perceived Locus of Control, Experienced Control, and Depression: A Trait Description of the Learned Helplessness Model of Depression." *Journal of Clinical Psychology,* 1977, *33,* 164–168.

Oliver, R. L. "A Theoretical Reinterpretation of Expectation and Disconfirmation Effects on Post-Exposure Product Evaluation: Experience in the Field." In R. I. Day (Ed.), *Consumer Satisfaction, Dissatisfaction, and Complaining Behavior.* Bloomington: Division of Business Research, Indiana University, 1977.

Olshavrsky, R. W., and Miller, J. A. "Consumer Expectations, Product Performance, and Perceived Product Quality." *Journal of Marketing Research,* 1972, *9,* 19–21.

Olson, J. C., and Dover, P. "Effects of Expectation Creation and Disconfirmation of Belief Elements of Cognitive Structure." In B. B. Andersen, (Ed.), *Advances in Consumer Research,* Vol. 3. Cincinnati: Association for Consumer Research, 1976.

O'Neill, M. J. "Calling the Cops: Responses of Witnesses to Criminal Incidents." Unpublished doctoral dissertation, Department of Sociology, Northwestern University, 1977.

Orcutt, J. D. "Ideological Variations in the Structure of Deviant Types: A Multivariate Comparison of Alcoholism and Heroin Addiction." *Social Forces,* 1976, *55*(2), 419–437.

Ortega, M. J. "Depression, Loneliness, and Unhappiness." In E. S. Shneidman and M. J. Ortega (Eds.), *Aspects of Depression.* Boston: Little, Brown, 1969.

Orvis, B. R., Cunningham, J. D., and Kelley, H. H. "A Closer Examination of Causal Inference: The Role of Consensus, Distinctiveness and Consistency Information." *Journal of Personality and Social Psychology,* 1975, *32,* 605–616.

Owens, D. M., and Straus, M. A. "The Social Structure of Violence in Childhood and Approval of Violence as an Adult." *Aggressive Behavior,* 1975, *1*(2), 193–211.

Pagelow, M. D. "Preliminary Report on Battered Women." Paper presented at the 2nd International Symposium on Victimology, Boston, September 1976.

Pagelow, M. D. "Secondary Battering: Breaking the Cycle of Domestic Violence." Paper presented at the annual meeting of the Sociologists for Women in Society Section of the American Sociological Association, September 1977.

Panda, K. C., and Lynch, W. W. "Effects of Race and Sex on Attribution of Intellectual Achievement: Responsibility for Success and Failure Situations Among Educable Mentally Retarded Children." *Indian Journal of Mental Retardation,* 1974, *7,* 72–80.

Parsons, T. "The Sick Role and the Role of the Physician Reconsidered." *Milbank Memorial Fund Quarterly*, 1975, *53*, 257–278.

Pepitone, A. "Social Psychological Perspectives on Crime and Punishment." *Journal of Social Issues*, 1975, *31*, 197–216.

Peplau, L. A., and Caldwell, M. A. "Loneliness: A Cognitive Analysis." *Essence*, 1978, *2*, 207–220.

Peplau, L. A., and Perlman, D. "Blueprint for a Social Psychological Theory of Loneliness." In M. Cook and G. Wilson (Eds.), *Love and Attraction*. Oxford, England: Pergamon Press, 1979.

Peplau, L. A., Russell, D., and Heim, M. "Impact of Duration on Perceived Causes of Loneliness." Unpublished paper, University of California, Los Angeles, 1977.

Peplau, L. A., Russell, D., and Heim, M. "Loneliness: A Bibliography of Research and Theory." *JSAS Catalog of Selected Documents in Psychology*, 1978, *8*, 38.

Perkins, R. *Perkins on Criminal Law*. Brooklyn, N.Y.: Foundation Press, 1957.

Perlman, D. "Attributions in the Criminal Justice Process." In P. D. Lipsett and B. D. Sales (Eds.), *New Directions in Psychological Research*. New York: Van Nostrand Reinhold, in press.

Phillips, D. L. "Rejection: A Possible Consequence of Seeking Help for Mental Disorders." *American Sociological Review*, 1963, *28*, 963–972.

Piliavin, I., Rodin, J., and Piliavin, J. "Good Samaritanism: An Underground Phenomenon?" *Journal of Personality and Social Psychology*, 1969, *13*, 289–299.

Pittman, D. J., and Handy, W. "Patterns in Criminal Aggravated Assault." *Journal of Criminal Law, Criminology and Police Science*, 1964, *55*(4), 462–470.

Pittman, T. S., Cooper, E. E., and Smith, T. W. "Attribution of Causality and the Overjustification Effect." *Personality and Social Psychology Bulletin*, 1977, *3*, 280–283.

Pizzey, E. *Scream Quietly or the Neighbors Will Hear*. London: If Books, 1974.

Plaut, F. A. *Alcohol Problems: A Report to the Nation by the Cooperative Commission on the Study of Alcoholism*. New York: Oxford University Press, 1967.

Pleck, J. H. "The Male Sex Role: Definitions, Problems, and Sources of Change." *Journal of Social Issues*, 1976, *32*(3), 155–164.

Pogge, R. "The Toxic Placebo." *Medical Times*, 1963, *91*, 773–778.

Prescott, S., and Letko, C. "Battered Women: A Social Psychological Perspective." Unpublished paper, Governors State University, 1977.

Pressman, J. L., and Wildavsky, A. *Implementation*. Berkeley: University of California Press, 1973.

Prociuk, T. J., Breen, L. J., and Lussier, R. J. "Hopelessness, Internal-External Locus of Control, and Depression." *Journal of Clinical Psychology*, 1976, *32*, 299–300.

Raphael, B. "Preventive Intervention with the Recently Bereaved." *Archives of General Psychiatry*, 1977, *34*, 1450–1454.

Rappaport, E. A. "Survivor Guilt." *Midstream*, August/September 1971, pp. 41–47.

Rausch, H. L., Barry, W. A., Hertel, R. K., and Swain, M. A. *Communication, Conflict and Marriage: Explorations in the Theory and Study of Intimate Relationships*. San Francisco: Jossey-Bass, 1974.

Ravitch, D. *The Great School Years*. New York: Basic Books, 1974.

Raviv, A., Bar-Tal, D., Raviv, A., and Bar-Tal, Y. "Causal Perceptions of Success and Failure by Advantaged, Integrated and Disadvantaged Pupils." Unpublished paper, Tel-Aviv University, 1978.

Reed, D., "Whistlestop: A Community Alternative for Crime Prevention." Unpublished doctoral dissertation, Department of Sociology, Northwestern University, 1979.

Reed, J. "Jury Deliberations, Voting, and Verdict Trends." *Southwestern Social Science Quarterly*, 1965, *65*, 361–374.

Reed, J. and Reed, R. "Status, Images, and Consequence: Once a Criminal, Always a Criminal." *Sociology and Social Research*, 1973, *57*, 460–471.

Regan, D. T., and Totten, T. "Empathy and Attribution: Turning Observers into Actors." *Journal of Personality and Social Psychology*, 1975, *32*, 850–856.

Rehm, L. P. "A Self-Control Model of Depression." *Behavior Therapy*, 1977a, *8*, 787–804.

Rehm, L. P. "Self-Control Therapy Manual IV—10 Session Manual." Unpublished paper, University of Pittsburgh, 1977b.

Rehm, L. P., Fuchs, C. Z., Roth, D., Kornblith, S. J., and Romano, J. "A Comparison of Self-Control and Assertion Skills Treatment of Depression." *Behavior Therapy*, in press.

Rehm, L. P., Roth, D., and Farmartino, R. Unpublished data, University of Pittsburgh, 1976.

Reidenberg, M., and Lowenthal, D. "Adverse Nondrug Reactions." *New England Journal of Medicine*, 1968, *279*, 678–679.

Rest, S., Nierenberg, R., Weiner, B., and Heckhausen, H. "Further Evidence Concerning the Effects of Perceptions of Effort and Ability on Achievement Evaluation." *Journal of Personality and Social Psychology*, 1973, *28*, 187–191.

Revi, J., and Illyes, S. "Success Expectancy and Achievement Expectancy in Trainable Mentally Retarded and in Nonretarded Children." *Studia Psychologica*, 1976, *18*, 222–228.

Ribordy, S., and Denney, D. R. "The Behavioral Treatment of Insomnia: An Alternative to Drug Therapy." *Behaviour Research and Therapy*, 1977, *15*, 39–50.

Rickels, K., Baum, M. C., Raab, E., Taylor, W., and Moore, E. "A Psychopharmacological Evaluation of Chlordiazexpoxide, LA-1, and Placebo Carried Out with Anxious, Neurotic Medical Clinic Patients." *Medical Times*, 1965, *93*, 238–245.

Rickels, K., Lipman, R., and Rabb, E. "Previous Medication, Duration of Illness and Placebo Response." *Journal of Nervous and Mental Diseases*, 1966, *142*, 548–554.

Richter, C. P. "On the Sudden Death in Animals and Man." *Psychomatic Medicine*, 1957, *19*, 191–198.

Ridington, J. "The Transition Process: A Feminist Environment as Reconstructive Milieu." *Victimology*, 1978, 563–575.

Ries, J. K. "Public Acceptance of the Disease Concept of Alcoholism." *Journal of Health and Social Behavior*, 1977, *18*, 338–344.

Riesman, D. "Foreword." In R. S. Weiss, *Loneliness: The Experience of Emotional and Social Isolation*. Cambridge, Mass.: M.I.T. Press, 1973.

Riesman, D., Glazer, N., and Denney, R. *The Lonely Crowd: A Study of the Changing American Character*. New Haven, Conn.: Yale University Press, 1961.

Ring, K. "Experimental Social Psychology: Some Sober Questions About Frivolous Values." *Journal of Experimental Social Psychology*, 1967, *3*, 113–123.

Rizley, R. "Depression and Distortion in the Attribution of Causality." *Journal of Abnormal Psychology*, 1978, *87*(1), 32–48.

Robinson, D. *From Drinking to Alcoholism: A Sociological Commentary.* New York: Wiley, 1976.

Robinson, J. C., and Lewinsohn, P. M. "Behavior Modification of Speed Characteristics in a Chronically Depressed Man." *Behavior Therapy,* 1973, *4,* 150–152.

Rosen, B., and Jerdee, J. H. "Factors Influencing Disciplinary Judgments." *Journal of Applied Psychology,* 1974, *59,* 327–331.

Rosenbaum, M., and Raz, D. "Denial, Locus of Control and Depression Among Physically Disabled and Nondisabled Men." *Journal of Clinical Psychology,* 1977, *33,* 672–676.

Rosenbaum, R. M. "A Dimensional Analysis of the Perceived Causes of Success and Failure." Unpublished doctoral dissertation, Department of Psychology, University of California, Los Angeles, 1972.

Rosenhan, D. "Some Origins of Concern for Others." In P. A. Mussen, J. Langer, and M. Covington (Eds.), *Trends and Issues in Developmental Psychology.* New York: Holt, Rinehart and Winston, 1969.

Rosenthal, R., and Jacobson, L. F. *Pygmalion in the Classroom: Teacher Expectations and Pupils' Intellectual Development.* New York: Holt, Rinehart and Winston, 1968a.

Rosenthal, R., and Jacobson, L. F. "Teacher Expectations for the Disadvantaged." *Scientific American,* 1968b, *218,* 19–23.

Ross, L. "The Intuitive Psychologist and His Shortcomings: Distortions in the Attribution Process." In L. Berkowitz (Ed.), *Advances in Social Psychology.* New York: Academic Press, 1977.

Ross, L., Rodin, J., and Zimbardo, P. G. "Toward an Attribution Therapy: The Reduction of Fear Through Induced Cognitive-Emotional Misattribution." *Journal of Personality and Social Psychology,* 1969, *12,* 279–288.

Ross, M. "Salience of Reward and Intrinsic Motivation." *Journal of Personality and Social Psychology,* 1975, *32,* 245–254.

Ross, M. "The Self-Perception of Intrinsic Motivation." In J. H. Harvey, W. J. Ickes, and R. F. Kidd (Eds.), *New Directions in Attribution Research.* Vol. I. Hillsdale, N.J.: Erlbaum, 1976.

Ross, M., and Ditecco, D. "An Attributional Analysis of Moral Judgments." *Journal of Social Issues,* 1975, *31,* 91–109.

Ross, M., Karniol R., and Rothstein, M. "Reward Contingency and Intrinsic Motivation in Children: A Test of the Delay of Gratification Hypothesis." *Journal of Personality and Social Psychology*, 1976, *33*, 442–447.

Rossi, P. H., Waite, E., Bose, C. E., and Berk, R. E. "The Seriousness of Crimes: Normative Structure and Individual Differences." *American Sociological Review*, 1974, *39*, 224–237.

Roth, S., and Kubal, L. "The Effects of Noncontingent Reinforcement on Tasks of Differing Importance: Facilitation and Learned Helplessness Effects." *Journal of Personality and Social Psychology*, 1975, *32*, 680–691.

Rotter, J. B. "Generalized Expectancies for Internal Versus External Control of Reinforcement." *Psychological Monographs*, 1966, *80*(1).

Rotter, J. B. "Some Problems and Misconceptions Related to the Construct of Internal Versus External Control of Reinforcement." *Journal of Consulting and Clinical Psychology*, 1975, *43*, 56–67.

Roy, M. "A Current Survey of 150 Cases." In M. Roy (Ed.), *Battered Women: a Psychosociological Study of Domestic Violence*. New York: Van Nostrand Reinhold, 1977.

Ruble, D. N., Parsons, J. E., and Ross, J. "Self-Evaluative Responses of Children in an Achievement Setting." *Child Development*, 1976, *47*, 990–997.

Ruesch, J. *Disturbed Communication*. New York: Norton, 1957.

Rush, A. J., Beck, A. T., Kovacs, M., and Hollon, S. "Comparative Efficacy of Cognitive Therapy and Pharmacotherapy in the Treatment of Depressed Outpatients." *Cognitive Therapy and Research*, 1977, *1*, 17–37.

Russell, D., Peplau, L. A., and Ferguson, M. L. "Developing a Measure of Loneliness." *Journal of Personality Assessment*, 1978, *42*(3), 290–294.

Ryan, W. *Blaming the Victim*. New York: Pantheon Books, 1971.

Sackett, D. "The Magnitude of Compliance and Noncompliance." In D. Sackett and B. Haynes (Eds.), *Compliance with Therapeutic Regimens*. Baltimore: Johns Hopkins University Press, 1976.

Sagotsky, G., Patterson, C. J., and Lepper, M. R. "Training Children's Self-Control: A Field Experiment in Self-Monitoring and Goal Setting in the Classroom. *Journal of Experimental Child Psychology*, 1978, *25*, 242–253.

Saks, M., and Hastie, R. *Social Psychology in Court.* New York: D. Van Nostrand, 1978.

Sales, B. (Ed.) *Perspectives in Law and Psychology.* Vol. 1: *The Criminal Justice System.* New York: Plenum, 1977.

Sales, B., Elwork, A., and Alfini, J. "Improving Comprehension for Jury Instructions." In B. Sales (Ed.), *Perspectives in Law and Psychology.* Vol. 1: *The Criminal Justice System.* New York: Plenum, 1977.

Salili, F., Maehr, M. L., and Gillmore, G. "Achievement and Morality: A Cross-Cultural Analysis of Causal Attribution and Evaluation." *Journal of Personality and Social Psychology,* 1976, *33,* 327–337.

Scarr, H. A., and others. *Patterns of Burglary.* (2nd ed.) Washington, D.C.: National Institute of Law Enforcement and Criminal Justice, 1973.

Schachter, S. *The Psychology of Affiliation.* Stanford, Calif.: Stanford University Press, 1959.

Schachter, S., and Singer, J. E. "Cognitive, Social, and Physiological Determinants of Emotional State." *Psychological Review,* 1962, *62,* 379–399.

Scheff, T. J. *Being Mentally Ill: A Sociological Theory.* Chicago: Aldine, 1966.

Scheff, T. J. "The Labelling Theory of Mental Illness." *American Sociological Review,* 1974, *34,* 444–452.

Schrader, S. L., Craighead, E. W., and Schrader, R. M. "Reinforcement Patterns in Depression." *Behavior Therapy,* 1978, *9,* 1–14.

Schrag, C. *Crime and Justice: American Style.* Rockville, Md.: National Institute of Mental Health, 1971.

Schultz, G. D. *How Many More Victims? Society and the Sex Criminal.* Philadelphia: Lippincott, 1965.

Schulz, R. "Effects of Control and Predictability on the Physical and Psychological Well-Being of the Institutionalized Aged." *Journal of Personality and Social Psychology,* 1976, *33,* 563–573.

Schuster, S. O., and Gruen, G. E. "Success and Failure as Determinants of the Performance Predictions of Mentally Retarded and Nonretarded Children." *American Journal of Mental Deficiency,* 1971, *76,* 190–196.

Schutz, A. *The Problem of Social Reality.* The Hague, Netherlands: Martinus Nijhatt, 1967.

Schwartz, R. H., and Cook, J. J. "Teacher Expectancy as it Relates to the Academic Achievement of EMR Students." *Journal of Educational Research,* 1972, *65,* 393–396.

Scott, C. A., and Yalch, R. F. "A Test of Self-Perception Explanation of the Effects of Rewards on Intrinsic Interest." *Journal of Experimental Social Psychology,* 1978, *14,* 180–192.

Scott, J. P., and Senay, E. C. *Separation and Depression: Clinical and Research Aspects.* Washington, D.C.: American Association for the Advancement of Science, 1973.

Scott, P. D. "Battered Wives." *British Journal of Psychiatry,* 1974, *125,* 433–441.

Secunda, S. K. "Special Report, 1973: The Depressive Disorders." Washington, D.C.: National Institute of Mental Health, 1973.

Selby, J. W., Calhoun, L. C., and Brock, T. A. "Sex Differences in the Social Perception of Rape Victims." *Personality and Social Psychology Bulletin,* 1977, *3,* 412–415.

Seligman, C., Brickman, J., and Kowak, D. "Rape and Physical Attractiveness: Assigning Responsibility to Victims." *Journal of Personality,* 1977, *45*(4), 554–563.

Seligman, M. E. P. "Chronic Fear Produced by Unpredictable Shock." *Journal of Comparative and Physiological Psychology,* 1968, *66,* 402–411.

Seligman, M. E. P. *Helplessness: On Depression, Development, and Death.* San Francisco: Freeman, 1975.

Seligman, M. E. P., Klein, D. C., and Miller, W. R. "Depression." In H. Leitenberg (Ed.), *Handbook of Behavior Modification and Behavior Therapy.* Englewood Cliffs, N.J.: Prentice-Hall, 1976.

Seligman, M. E. P., and Maier, S. F. "Failure to Escape Traumatic Shock." *Journal of Experimental Psychology,* 1967, *74,* 1–9.

Seligman, M. E. P., Rosellini, R. A., and Kozak, M. J. "Learned Helplessness in the Rat: Time Course, Immunization and Reversibility." *Journal of Comparative and Physiological Psychology,* 1975, *88,* 542–547.

Settle, R. B., and Golden, L. L. "Attribution Theory and Advertiser Credibility." *Journal of Marketing Research,* 1974, *11,* 181–185.

Severance, L. J., and Gasstrom, L. L. "Effects of the Label 'Mentally Retarded' on Causal Explanation for Success and Failure Outcomes." *American Journal of Mental Deficiency*, 1977, *81*, 547–555.

Shaklee, H. "Development in Inferences of Ability and Task Difficulty." *Child Development*, 1976, *47*, 1051–1057.

Shapira, Z. "Expectancy Determinants of Intrinsically Motivated Behavior." *Journal of Personality and Social Psychology*, 1976, *34*, 1235–1244.

Shapiro, A., Chassen, J., Morris, L., and Frick, R. "Placebo Induced Side Effects." *Journal of Operational Psychiatry*, 1974, *6*, 43–46.

Shapiro, A., Mike, V., Barton, H., and Shapiro, E. "Study of the Placebo Effect with a Self-Administered Test." *Comprehensive Psychiatry*, 1973, *14* (6), 535–548.

Shapiro, A., and Morris, L. "The Placebo Effect in Medical and Psychological Therapies." In A. Bergin and S. Garfield (Eds.), *Handbook of Psychotherapy and Behavior Change: An Empirical Analysis.* New York: Wiley, 1978.

Sharpe, T., and Mikeal, R. L. "Patient Compliance with Antibiotic Regimens." *American Journal of Hospital Pharmacy*, 1974, *31*, 479–484.

Shaver, K. G. "Defensive Attribution: Effects of Severity and Relevance on the Responsibility Assigned for an Accident." *Journal of Personality and Social Psychology*, 1970, *14*, 101–113.

Shaver, K. G. *An Introduction to Attribution Process.* Cambridge, Mass.: Winthrop, 1975.

Shaver, K. G., Gilbert, M. A., and Williams, M. C. "Social Psychology, Criminal Justice, and the Principle of Discretion: A Selective Review." *Personality and Social Psychology Bulletin*, 1975, *1*, 471–484.

Shaw, J. I., and Skolnick, P. "Attribution of Responsibility for a Happy Accident." *Journal of Personality and Social Psychology*, 1971, *18* (3), 380–383.

Shaw, M. E., and Reitan, H. T. "Attribution of Responsibility as a Basis for Sanctioning Behavior." *British Journal of Social and Clinical Psychology*, 1969, *8*, 217–226.

Shaw, M. E., and Sulzer, J. L. "An Empirical Test of Heider's Levels in Attribution of Responsibility." *Journal of Abnormal and Social Psychology,* 1964, *69,* 39–46.

Sherif, M., and Hovland, C. *Social Judgment: Assimilation and Contrast Effect in Communication and Attitude Change.* New Haven, Conn.: Yale University Press, 1961.

Shipe, D. "The Relationship Among Locus of Control and Some Measures of Persistence in Mentally Retarded and Normal Subjects." *Abstracts of Peabody Studies in Mental Retardation,* 1960, *1,* 58.

Shipley, C. R., and Fazio, A. F. "Pilot Study of a Treatment for Psychological Depression." *Journal of Abnormal Psychology,* 1973, *82,* 372–376.

Silberman, C. *Crisis in the Classroom.* New York: Random House, 1970.

Silverstein, L. *Defense of the Poor in Criminal Cases in American State Courts.* Chicago: American Bar Foundation, 1965.

Simon, R. J. *The Jury System in America: A Critical Overview.* Beverly Hills, Calif.: Sage, 1975.

Simons, C., and Piliavin, J. "The Effect of Deception on Reactions to a Victim." *Journal of Personality and Social Psychology,* 1972, *21,* 56–60.

Singerman, K. J., Borkovec, T. D., and Baron, R. S. "Failure of 'Misattribution Therapy' Manipulation with a Clinically Relevant Target Behavior." *Behavior Therapy,* 1976, *1,* 306–313.

Skogan, W. G. "Public Policy and the Fear of Crime in Large American Cities." In J. Gardner (Ed.), *Public Law and Public Policy.* New York: Praeger, 1977.

Slater, P. *The Pursuit of Loneliness: American Culture at the Breaking Point.* Boston: Beacon Press, 1970.

Smith, R. E., Keating, J. P., Hester, R. K., and Mitchell, H. E. "Role and Justice Considerations in the Attribution of Responsibility to a Rape Victim." *Journal of Research in Personality,* 1976, *10,* 346–357.

Smith, R. E., and Hunt, S. D. "Attributional Processes and Effects in Promotional Situations." *Journal of Consumer Research,* 1978, *5,* 149–158.

Smith, T. W., and Pittman, T. S. "Reward, Distraction, and the

Overjustification Effect." *Journal of Personality and Social Psychology,* 1978, *36,* 565–571.

Smith, W. E. "The Effects of Social and Monetary Rewards on Intrinsic Motivation." Unpublished doctoral dissertation, Department of Human Development and Family Studies; Cornell University, 1976.

Smits, S. J. "Variables Related to Success in a Medical Rehabilitation Setting." *Archives of Physical Medicine and Rehabilitation,* 1974, *55,* 449–454.

Snyder, M. "Attribution and Behavior: Social Perception and Social Causation." In J. H. Harvey, W. J. Ickes, and R. F. Kidd (Eds.), *New Directions in Attribution Research.* Vol. 1. New York: Wiley, 1976.

Snyder, M., Tanke, E. D., and Berscheid, E. "Social Perception and Interpersonal Behavior: On the Self-Fulfilling Nature of Social Stereotypes." *Journal of Personality and Social Psychology,* 1977, *35,* 656–666.

Snyder, M. L., Stephan, W. G., and Rosenfield, D. "Attributional Egotism." In J. H. Harvey, W. J. Ickes, and R. F. Kidd (Eds.), *New Directions in Attribution Research.* Vol. 2. Hillsdale, N.J.: Erlbaum, 1978.

Solberg, S. "The Perception of Values Among Adolescents with Different Cultural Background." Paper presented at the annual meeting of the Israeli Psychological Association, Jerusalem, Israel, 1977.

Solomon, S., and Saxe, L. "What Is Intelligent, as Well as Attractive, Is Good." *Personality and Social Psychology Bulletin,* 1977, *3,* 670–673.

Sorrentino, R. M., and Boutilier, R. G. "Evaluation of a Victim as a Function of Fate Similarity/Dissimilarity." *Journal of Experimental Social Psychology,* 1974, *10,* 84–93.

Sosis, R. "Internal-External Control and the Perception of Responsibility of Another for an Accident." *Journal of Personality and Social Psychology,* 1974 *30,* 393–399.

Soule, D. "Teacher Bias Effects with Severely Retarded Children." *American Journal of Mental Deficiency,* 1972, *77,* 208–211.

Sperry, L. "Effects of Expectation, Social Class, and Experience on

In-Service Teacher Behavior in Small Groups." *Journal of Applied Psychology,* 1974, *59,* 244–246.

Stanley, D. T. *Prisoners Among Us: The Problem of Parole.* Washington, D.C.: Brookings Institution, 1976.

Stark, R., and McEvoy, J. "Middle Class Violence." *Psychology Today,* 1970, *4,* 52–65.

Steiner, I. D. "Perceived Freedom." In L. Berkowitz (Eds.), *Advances in Experimental Social Psychology.* Vol. 5. New York: Academic Press, 1970.

Steiner, I. D. "Whatever Happened to the Group in Social Psychology?" *Journal of Experimental Social Psychology,* 1975, *32,* 125–135.

Steinmark, S. W., and Borkovec, T. D. "Active and Placebo Treatment Effects on Moderate Insomnia Under Counterdemand and Positive Demand Instructions." *Journal of Abnormal Psychology,* 1974, *82,* 157–163.

Stephan, C. "Selective Characteristics of Jurors and Litigants: Their Influences on Juries' Verdicts." In S. Simon and R. J. Simon (Eds.), *The Jury System in America: A Critical Overview.* Vol. 4. Beverly Hills, Calif.: Sage, 1975.

Stevenson, C. L. *Facts and Values: Studies in Ethical Analysis.* New Haven, Conn.: Yale University Press, 1963.

Stoll, C. S. "Images of Man and Social Control." *Social Forces,* 1968, *47,* 119–127.

Storms, M. D. "Videotape and the Attribution Process: Reversing the Actors' and Observers' Points of View." *Journal of Personality and Social Psychology,* 1973, *27,* 165–175.

Storms, M. D., and McCaul, K. D. "Attribution Processes and Emotional Exacerbation of Dysfunctional Behavior." In J. H. Harvey, W. J. Ickes, and R. F. Kidd (Eds.), *New Directions in Attribution Research.* Vol. 2. Hillsdale, N.J.: Erlbaum, 1978.

Storms, M. D., and Nisbett, R. E. "Insomnia and the Attribution Process." *Journal of Personality and Social Psychology,* 1970, *16,* 319–328.

Strang, L., Smith, M. D., and Rogers, C. M. "Social Comparison, Multiple Reference Groups, and the Self-Concepts of Academically Handicapped Children Before and After Mainstreaming." *Journal of Educational Psychology,* in press.

Straus, M. A. "Sexual Inequality, Cultural Norms and Wife-Beating." In E. Viano (Ed.), *Victims, Criminals and Society.* Leyden, Netherlands: Sijthoff, 1976.

Straus, M. A. "A Sociological Perspective on the Prevention and Treatment of Wifebeating." In M. Roy (Ed.), *Battered Women: a Psychosociological Study of Domestic Violence.* New York: Van Nostrand Reinhold, 1977a.

Straus, M. A. "Wife-Beating: How Common, and Why?" Paper presented at the conference "Battered Wives: Defining the Issues," Center for Research on Women, Stanford University, May 20, 1977b.

Straus, M. A. "Wife Beating: How Common and Why?" *Victimology,* 1978, *2,* 443–459.

Straus, M. A., Gelles, R. J., and Steinmetz, S. K. "Violence in the Family: An Assessment of Knowledge and Research Needs." Paper Presented at the American Association for the Advancement of Science session "Crime: What We Know and What We Need to Know," 1976.

Straus, R. "Alcohol and Society." *Psychiatric Annals,* 1973, *3* (entire issue).

Strodtbeck, F., James R., and Hawkins, C. "Social Status in Jury Deliberations." In E. Maccoby, T. Newcomb, and E. Hartley (Eds.), *Readings in Social Psychology.* New York: Holt, Rinehart and Winston, 1958.

Sue, S., Smith, R., and Caldwell, C. "Effects of Inadmissible Evidence on the Decisions of Simulated Jurors: A Moral Dilemma." *Journal of Applied Social Psychology,* 1973, *3,* 345–353.

Sullivan, H. S. *The Interpersonal Theory of Psychiatry.* New York: Norton, 1953.

Swann, W. B., and Pittman, T. S. "Initiating Play Activity of Children: The Moderating Influence of Verbal Cues on Intrinsic Motivation." *Child Development,* 1977, *48,* 1125–1132.

Symonds, M. "Victims of Violence: Psychological Effects and Aftereffects." *The American Journal of Psychoanalysis,* 1975, *35,* 19–26.

Tapp, J. L. "Psychology and the Law: An Overture." *Annual Review of Psychology,* 1976, *27,* 359–404.

Taylor, S. E. and Fiske, S. T. "Point of View and Perceptions of Causality." *Journal of Personality and Social Psychology*, 1975, *32*, 439–445.

Taylor, S., and Fiske, S. "Salience, Attention, and Attribution: Top of the Head Phenomena." In L. Berkowitz (Ed.), *Advances in Experimental Social Psychology*. New York: Academic Press, 1978.

Teasdale, J. D. "Effects of Real and Recalled Success on Learned Helplessness and Depression." *Journal of Abnormal Psychology*, 1978, *87*, 155–164.

Tennen, H., and Eller, S. "Attributional Components of Learned Helplessness and Facilitation." *Journal of Personality and Social Psychology*, 1977, *35*, 265–271.

Thibaut, J. W., and Riecken, H. R. "Some Determinants and Consequences of the Perception of Social Causality." *Journal of Personality*, 1955, *24*, 113–133.

Tiffany, D. "Mental Health: A Function of Experienced Control." *Journal of Clinical Psychology*, 1967, *23*, 311–315.

Tolor, A., and Tamerin, J. S. "The Attitudes Towards Alcoholism Instrument: A Measure of Attitudes Towards Alcoholics and the Nature and Causes of Alcoholism." *British Journal of Addictions*, 1975, *70*, 223–231.

Tomes, N. "A 'Torrent of Abuse': Crimes of Violence Between Working-Class Men and Women in London, 1840–1875." *Journal of Social History*, 1978, *11*, 328–345.

Tunstall, J. *Old and Alone*. New York: Humanities Press, 1967.

Turkewitz, H., O'Leary, K. D., and Ironsmith, M. "Generalization and Maintenance of Appropriate Behavior Through Self-Control." *Journal of Consulting and Clinical Psychology*, 1975, *43*, 577–583.

Tymchuk, A. J. "Personality and Sociocultural Retardation." *Exceptional Children*, 1972, *38*, 721–728.

Uhlenhuth, E. H., Canter, A., Neustadt, J. O., and Payson, H. E. "The Symptomatic Relief of Anxiety with Meprobamate, Phenobarbital, and Placebo." *American Journal of Psychiatry*, 1959, *115*, 905–910.

U.S. Department of Justice, Criminal Justice Research Center.

Sourcebook of Criminal Justice Statistics, 1974. Washington, D.C.: U.S. Government Printing Office, 1975.

U.S. Department of Transportation. "Alcohol and Highway Safety." Report to the Congress from the Secretary of Transportation. Washington, D.C.: U.S. Department of Transportation, 1968.

Valins, S., Adelson, R., Goldstein, J., and Weiner, M. "The Negative Placebo Effect—Consequences of Overselling a Treatment." Paper presented at the International Association of Dental Research, 1971.

Valins, S., and Nisbett, R. E. "Attribution Processes in the Development and Treatment of Emotional Disorders." In E. E. Jones and others (Eds.), *Attribution: Perceiving the Causes of Behavior.* Morristown, N.J.: General Learning Press, 1972.

Valins, S., and Ray, A. A. "Effects of Cognitive Desensitization on Avoidance Behavior." *Journal of Personality and Social Psychology,* 1967, *7,* 345–350.

Valle, V. A., and Frieze, I. H. "The Stability of Causal Attributions as a Mediator in Changing Expectations for Success." *Journal of Personality and Social Psychology,* 1976, *33,* 579–587.

Valle, V. A., and Koeske, R. "Elderly Consumer Problems: Actions, Sources of Information and Attribution of Blame." Paper presented at the 85th annual meeting of the American Psychological Association, San Francisco, 1977.

Valle, V. A., and Wallendorf, M. "Consumers' Attributions of the Causes of Their Product Satisfaction and Dissatisfaction." In R. L. Day (Ed.), *Consumer Satisfaction, Dissatisfaction, and Complaining Behavior.* Bloomington: Division of Business Research, Indiana University, 1977.

Veroff, J., and Melnick, H. "Personal, Situational, and Interpersonal Attributions of Causes of Critical Life Problems." Paper presented at the 85th annual meeting of the American Psychological Association, San Francisco, 1977.

Vidmar, N. "Effects of Decision Alternatives on the Verdicts and Social Perceptions of Simulated Jurors." *Journal of Personality and Social Psychology,* 1972, *22,* 211–218.

von Hirsch, A. "Predictions of Criminal Conduct and Preventive

Confinement of Convicted Persons." *Buffalo Law Review,* 1972, *21,* 717–758.

Voorhis, J. "The Consumer Movement and the Hope of Human Survival." *The Journal of Consumer Affairs,* 1977, *11,* 1–16.

Waites, E. A. "Female Masochism and the Enforced Restruction of Choice." *Victimology,* 1978, 535–544.

Walker, L. E. "Battered Women and Learned Helplessness." *Victimology,* 1978, 525–534.

Walker, L. E. *The Battered Woman.* New York: Harper & Row, 1979.

Walker, M. J., and Brodsky, S. L. *Sexual Assault: The Victim and the Rapist.* Lexington, Mass.: Lexington Books, 1976.

Walster, E. "Assignment of Responsibility for an Accident." *Journal of Personality and Social Psychology,* 1966, *3,* 73–79.

Warland, R. H., Hermann, R. O., and Willits, J. "Dissatisfied Consumers: Who Gets Upset and Who Takes What Action." *Journal of Consumer Affairs,* 1975, *9,* 148–163.

Washburn, C., Frieze, I. H., and Knoble, J. "Some Subtle Biases of Therapists Towards Women and Violence." Paper presented at the annual research conference of the Association for Women in Psychology, Dallas, 1979.

Weidman, D. R., and others. "Intensive Evaluation for Criminal Justice Planning Agencies." Unpublished paper, National Institute of Law Enforcement and Criminal Justice, Washington, D.C., 1975.

Weiner, B. *Theories of Motivation: From Mechanism to Cognition.* Chicago, Ill.: Markham, 1972a.

Weiner, B. "Attribution Theory, Achievement Motivation, and the Educational Process." *Review of Educational Research,* 1972b, *42,* 203–215.

Weiner, B. (Ed.), *Achievement Motivation and Attribution Theory.* Morristown, N.J.: General Learning Press, 1974a.

Weiner, B. "Achievement Motivation as Conceptualized by an Attribution Theorist." In B. Weiner (Ed.), *Achievement Motivation and Attribution Theory.* Morristown, N.J.: General Learning Press, 1974b.

Weiner, B. "An Attributional Approach for Educational Psychology." In L. Shulman (Ed.), *Review of Research in Education.* Itasca, Ill.: F. E. Peacock, 1977.

Weiner, B. "An Attributionally Based Theory of Motivation and Emotion: Focus, Range and Issues." Unpublished paper, University of California, Los Angeles, 1978.

Weiner, B., Frieze, I., Kukla, A., Reed, L., Rest, S., and Rosenbaum, R. M. "Perceiving the Causes of Success and Failure." In E. E. Jones and others (Eds.), *Attribution: Perceiving the Causes of Behavior.* Morristown, N.J.: General Learning Press, 1972.

Weiner, B., Heckhausen, H., Meyer, W., and Cook, R. E. "Causal Ascriptions and Achievement Behavior." *Journal of Personality and Social Psychology,* 1972, *21,* 239–248.

Weiner, B., and Kukla, A. "An Attributional Analysis of Achievement Motivation." *Journal of Personality and Social Psychology,* 1970, *15,* 1–20.

Weiner, B., and Litman-Adizes, T. "An Attributional, Expectancy-Value Analysis of Learned Helplessness and Depression." In J. Garber and M. E. P. Seligman (Eds.), *Human Helplessness: Theory and Applications.* New York: Academic Press, in press.

Weiner, B., Nierenberg, R., and Goldstein, M. "Social Learning (Locus of Control) Versus Attributional (Causal Stability) Interpretations of Expectancy of Success." *Journal of Personality,* 1976, *44,* 52–68.

Weiner, B., Russell, D., and Lerman, D. "Affective Consequences of Causal Ascriptions." In J. H. Harvey, W. J. Ickes, and R. F. Kidd (Eds.), *New Directions in Attribution Research.* Vol. 2. Hillsdale, N.J.: Erlbaum, 1978.

Weisman, A. D., and Worden, J. W. "Psychological Analysis of Cancer Deaths." *Omega,* 1975, *6*(1), 61–75.

Weisman, A. D., and Worden, J. W. "The Existential Plight in Cancer: Significance of the First 100 Days." *International Journal of Psychiatry in Medicine,* 1976, *7,* 1–15.

Weiss, R. S. *Loneliness: The Experience of Emotional and Social Isolation.* Cambridge, Mass.: M.I.T. Press, 1973.

Weiss, R. S. "The Provisions of Social Relationships." In Z. Rubin (Ed.), *Doing unto Others.* Englewood Cliffs, N.J.: Prentice-Hall, 1974.

Weiss, R. S. *Marital Separation.* New York: Basic Books, 1975.

Weissberg, N. C. "Methodology or Substance? A Response to

Helmreich." *Personality and Social Psychology Bulletin*, 1976, *2*, 119–121.

Weissman, M. M., Klerman, G. L., Prusoff, B. A., Hanson, B., and Paykel, E. "The Efficacy of Psychotherapy in Depression: Symptom Remission and Response to Treatment." In R. L. Spitzer and D. F. Klein (Eds.), *Evaluation of Psychological Therapies.* Baltimore: Johns Hopkins University Press, 1976.

Wells, G. L. "Applied Eyewitness-Testimony Research: System Variables and Estimator Variables." *Journal of Personality and Social Psychology*, 1978, *36*, 1546–1557.

Wenz, F. V. "Seasonal Suicide Attempts and Forms of Loneliness." *Psychological Reports*, 1977, *40*, 807–810.

Whatley, C. D. "Social Attitudes Toward Discharged Mental Patients." *Social Problems*, 1959, *6*, 313–320.

Wilkins, L. T., Gottfredson, D. M., Robinson, J. O., and Sadowsky, A. "Information Selection and Use in Parole Decision-Making." Supplemental Report Five. National Council on Crime and Delinquency Research Center, Davis, CA, 1973.

Williams, R. J. *Alcoholism: The Nutritional Approach.* Austin: University of Texas Press, 1969.

Wilsnack, S. C. "Sex Role Identity and Female Alcoholism." *Journal of Abnormal Psychology*, 1973, *82*, 253–261.

Wilson, J. Q. *Thinking About Crime.* New York: Basic Books, 1975.

Wimer, S. and Peplau, L. A. "Determinants of Reactions to Lonely Others." Paper presented at the annual meeting of the Western Psychological Association, San Francisco, 1978.

Winett, R. A., and Winkler, R. D. "Current Behavior Modification in the Classroom: Be Still, Be Quiet, Be Docile." *Journal of Applied Behavior Analysis*, 1972, *5*, 499–504.

Wolfgang, M., and Riedel, M. "Race, Judicial Discretion, and the Death Penalty." *The Annals of the American Academy of Political and Social Science*, 1973, *407*, 119–134.

Wood, H. P., and Duffey, E. L. "Psychological Factors in Alcoholic Women." *American Journal of Psychiatry*, 1966, *123*, 341–345.

Wooster, A. D. "Acceptance of Responsibility for School Work by Educationally Subnormal Boys." *British Journal of Mental Subnormality*, 1974, *20*, 23–27.

Wortman, C. B. "Causal Attributions and Personal Control." In

J. H. Harvey, W. I. Ickes, and R. F. Kidd (Eds.), *New Directions in Attribution Research.* Vol. 1. Hillsdale, N.J.: Erlbaum, 1976.

Wortman, C. B., and Brehm, J. W. "Response to Uncontrollable Outcomes: An Integration of Reactance Theory and the Learned Helplessness Model." In L. Berkowitz (Ed.), *Advances in Experimental Social Psychology,* 1975, *8,* 277–336.

Wortman, C. B., and Dintzer, L. "Is an Attributional Analysis of the Learned Helplessness Phenomenon Viable?: A Critique of the Abramson-Seligman-Teasdale Reformulation." *Journal of Abnormal Psychology,* 1978, *87* (1), 75–90.

Wortman, C. B., and Dunkel-Schetter, C. "Interpersonal Relationships and Cancer: A Theoretical Analysis." *Journal of Social Issues,* in press.

Wortman, C. B., and Silver, R. "Coping with Undesirable Life Events." In M. E. P. Seligman and J. Garber (Eds.), *Human Helplessness: Theory and Applications.* New York: Academic Press, in press.

Wyer, R. S., Henninger, M., and Hinkle, R. "An Informational Analysis of Actors' and Observers' Belief Attributions in a Role-Playing Situation." *Journal of Experimental Social Psychology,* 1977, *13,* 199–217.

Zimbardo, P. *The Cognitive Control of Motivation.* Glenview, Ill.: Scott, Foresman, 1969.

Zuckerman, M., Lubin, B., and Robins, S. "Validation of Multiple Affect Adjective Checklist." *Journal of Consulting Psychology,* 1965, *29,* 594.

Zung, W. "A Self-Rating Depression Scale." *Archives of General Psychiatry,* 1965, *12,* 63–70.

Name Index

Subject Index